D0898001

Presented to the

Ironside Memorial Library

by

Publisher

PRINTED IN U.S.A.

THE WAY OF THE CROSS
IN HUMAN RELATIONS

✝

THE

WAY OF THE CROSS

IN

HUMAN RELATIONS

By Guy Franklin Hershberger

HERALD PRESS
SCOTTDALE · PENNSYLVANIA

Copyright © 1958 by Herald Press, Scottdale, Pennsylvania
Library of Congress Catalogue Card Number: 58-10992
Printed in the United States of America

First Printing, 1958
Second Printing, 1964

This volume is an expansion of the Conrad Grebel Lectures
delivered in 1954

TO HAROLD AND ELIZABETH

30458

INTRODUCTION

When Jesus commissioned the disciples to live the good life in an evil world, He gave them a task which He frankly informed them would not be easy. Even as Jesus went to the cross, so must the disciple take up his cross and follow the Master. The way of the cross is not easy. The Christian is called to endure hardness as a good soldier of Jesus Christ.

The social message of the Gospel has many implications, its ramifications reaching far and wide. As a result some Christians, preferring an easy religion of cheap grace, preach a gospel without a social message. Others, taking the social message seriously and recognizing the intricacy of its implications, take the complex social order with its ambiguities as their frame of reference to the neglect of the Gospel message itself. Overemphasis on the difficulties encountered in applying the New Testament ethic in a complex situation, however, means an underevaluation of the redemptive power of Christ. This in turn leads to a confusion of one's own making: we "raise a dust and then complain we cannot see."[1] True, the apostle says we see through a glass darkly; but there is no good reason why we should add to the darkness with dust of our own stirring.

The present volume assumes the divine imperative as the beginning point, and the redemptive work of Christ as the frame of reference, which must give direction to the disciple of Christ who would follow the light through the darkness of this present world. It assumes the life and work and the death and resurrection of Christ, with all that these involve, as a full and sufficient power for the redemption of

---

1 The words are those of Bishop Berkeley spoken in regard to another matter. Cf. Georgia Harkness, *Christian Ethics* (New York, 1957) 52.

man. It assumes that He who redeems man will also endow him with enabling power, under the lordship of Jesus Christ and the ministration of the Holy Spirit, to live redemptively in this present world, walking the way of the cross. It assumes that they who enter into the redemptive experience with Christ become laborers together with Him; that in so doing they constitute the light of the world whose mission it is to dissipate the darkness created by the dust of mere human reason.

A treatment of the social expression of Christianity requires an examination of some representative varieties of that expression. If the author at the same time lays serious claim to Christian discipleship, with a bias toward his own variety of expression, he assumes responsibility for a true report and a fair treatment of each expression so examined. Moreover, his own variety must be subjected to the same critical analysis as others are, the failures of its adherents coming into the picture as well as the successes. Although the author has been conscious of all this in the preparation of the volume, he cannot claim to have succeeded in the discharge of his responsibility. To the extent that he has failed, however, it is his hope that critics will be merciful enough to place the blame upon his head and not his heart.

While accepting Anabaptism as a high expression of Christian social ethics, and recognizing how inadequately the heirs of this tradition have succeeded in representing their own faith, the author has endeavored to treat both the faith and the shortcomings in an understanding manner which he trusts may inspire resolution for a higher level of performance as well as enabling many Christians to be challenged by the principles here set forth. Failure in this endeavor also, it is hoped, need not be charged to the author's heart.

If the length of the section on economic life seems out of proportion, the excuse is a twofold one: (1) Whereas the

2 Scottdale, 1944; revised, 1953.

Introduction

Christian's relation to the state has been previously treated, particularly in the author's *War, Peace, and Nonresistance,*[2] the economic life of the Christian has not received such extended treatment at his hand. (2) This phase of the Christian social ethic seems in special need of treatment since here the issues are not always as clear as in the area of politics, thus making the economic life of the disciple in many ways the most vulnerable point in his social ethic. This lack of clarity and the ever-changing economic situation, on the other hand, increase the difficulty of the writer in dealing satisfactorily with this phase of the Christian ethic. No doubt some conclusions here set forth are dated so as to require revision with the passing of time. Waiting until all issues are crystal clear, however, every answer firm and sure, would mean that publication could never take place. Therefore if this treatment can serve to stimulate Christians to think deeply, to search their own hearts, and to create a vision for ethical renewal in the economic sphere, it will have fulfilled its intended mission, however far some details may have missed the mark.

If their view of justice and social responsibility makes it difficult for some Christians to find the way of the cross, it is also true that the limitations of social responsibility assumed by others, if not soundly conceived, can lead to a distorted type of nonconformity making for personal relations equally far from the way of the cross. For this reason, if for no other, it seemed necessary to include a chapter on the way of the cross in personal relations.

Finally, he who would walk the way of the cross with confident assurance must not only begin with the divine imperative and the redemptive work of Christ. Perspective for the fulfillment of his mission is not complete without a view of the kingdom of God and its consummation, the goal toward which redemption moves. A Christian social ethic is impossible without a Christian eschatology. The work of the Christian is not man's work; it is God's work. The way of the cross is not man's way; it is Christ's way. The Christian's call is to follow the steps of the Master in this way; to be a laborer together with God. The goal toward which he moves is the goal of his Lord which is to be achieved in God's own time and in God's own way. May he ever keep that goal in view as he walks the way of the cross, pressing toward it with assurance which cannot be shaken.

The author owes a debt of gratitude, more than he can pay, to many friends who knowingly or unknowingly have contributed to whatever may be of value in what here appears in print. The Conrad Grebel Lectureship deserves special mention for making possible the present work which is an extension of lectures delivered under its sponsorship, first at Eastern Mennonite College in 1954 and later at Hesston and Goshen Colleges, and at Scottdale, Pennsylvania; and in briefer form before a number of local churches. All quotations of Scripture texts, unless otherwise indicated, are from the *Revised Standard Version.*

Guy F. Hershberger

Goshen College
May 22, 1958

CONTENTS

xi

FOUNDATIONS

1. THE DIVINE ORDER

It is obvious to nearly everyone that ours is a confused world, although not all are agreed on the cause or nature of the confusion. Many spiritually sensitive souls are convinced, however, that much of the confusion consists of mixing a small portion of Christian idealism with large portions of materialism, or of paganism in whatever form, often without being aware of the incongruity. Some forty-five years ago Methodist Bishop McConnell, following a visit in the Orient, suggested that Christian missionaries and American marines going to China be not sent on the same boat because "it confuses the Chinese."[1]

Although a generation later a new China had arisen to add to the confusion, the incongruous ways of the West continued unabated. In 1953 a *New York Times* correspondent, reporting his voyage to the Orient aboard the freighter *Maren Maersk,* described the ship's cargo as follows:

"For the Philippines: shotguns, rifles, and shells . . . medical supplies . . . replacement parts for American machines . . . twelve cartons of chewing gum . . . and vast quantities of Coca-Cola. . . .

"For Formosa: partial equipment for three new American power transformers . . .; 5,080 cases of fancy groceries costing $33,776.85, whose consignee turned out to be an American cloak-and-dagger outfit 'visiting' in the area; the inevitable shipment of jeep parts; and from the Mennonite Central Committee of Akron, Pa., to the Mennonite Central Committee, 94 North Chungsan Road, Taipei, an almost perfectly balanced shipment—eighty-three cartons of canned meat, four bales of new bedding, thirteen cases of soap, five cartons of Christmas cards, and one case of toys and dolls.

1 Editorial, "The Bishop," *The Christian Century* (Sept. 2, 1953) 70:984.

"For French Indo-China: more warlike cargo—aircraft ground maintenance equipment. . . ."[2]

The *Times* correspondent was seemingly unaware of the intended spiritual significance of the Mennonite Central Committee's shipment of food and clothing. He spoke freely of America's engagement "in one of the noblest enterprises in our history . . . with our power and our optimism—leading, bribing, goading, shaming, and occasionally threatening a whole catalogue of countries into strengthening their societies and defending their freedom."[3] From this point of view the incongruity of rifles, shells, and other warlike cargo *in the name of Uncle Sam,* shipped on the same boat with food *in the name of Christ,*[4] apparently did not occur to the correspondent.

The subversive efforts of communist propaganda are effective enough without the contribution of explosive materials by the supposedly Christian world itself. A recent communist cartoon showed the American secretary of state in clerical collar with a Bible under one arm and a hydrogen-headed missile under the other. This one piece of propaganda alone should cause no end of embarrassment to Christian people, not merely because of its effective impact on the non-Christian world, but because it symbolizes so effectively the transparent veneer of Christianity with which the nominal Christian world so often attempts to cover its deeds which are anything but Christian.[4a] No doubt the MCC is happy that it was the sympathetic *Times* reporter and not the communist cartoonist who discovered its shipment of food and clothing on the same boat with the rifles, the shells, and the aircraft. What a field day the cartoonist would have had, had

2 James Reston, "America in Asia: Time and a Little Hope," *The New York Times Magazine* (Aug. 30, 1953) 48.

3 *Ibid.,* 9.

4 Each piece of relief goods shipped by the Mennonite Central Committee bears the label, *In the Name of Christ.*

4a There is no attempt at this point to evaluate the quality of America's role in the game of power politics when judged as such. It is simply to say that power diplomacy must be recognized for what it is, without attempting to call it Christian, which it is not.

he discovered it! This is not to suggest that the MCC should have declined to ship the contribution of its nonresistant constituency on its mission of mercy and peace aboard the *Maren Maersk.* There was probably no other alternative; and the purpose of the MCC shipment was clear. The story is a dramatic illustration, however, of the confusion of values prevailing in our world, and of the enormity of the Christian's task as he goes forth to proclaim the Gospel in word and in deed to a needy and sin-sick world.

Unfortunately, the realism of many people is insufficient for the acceptance either of the term "sin-sick" itself or of the cure for man's ills which the New Testament prescribes. Even though the events of the past generation have done much to dispel the old illusion of inevitable human progress, many people, as Elton Trueblood tells us, still seem to think that economic and technical reconstruction will provide the cure; and that spiritual needs, if indeed there are any, will somehow take care of themselves. An illustration of this point of view is found in a recent book entitled, *Within Our Power.* This is a kind of sermon based on the "American creed" setting forth proposals for "beginning the world again." We must overcome fear; we must not be afraid of change; our understanding of human behavior and social relations must become more nearly equal to our scientific achievement. The author frankly admits that his own generation got off the track. But where and how he is not sure. "Surely we did not plan it this way .... We entered the twentieth century imbued with the hopeful philosophy of Herbert Spencer...."[5] Then came the bewilderments of 1914 and 1929 and 1939, and we began to realize that society has been less humanized than we thought. But why?

The author does not seem to realize that the past generation probably made its greatest mistake when it accepted the humanistic philosophy of Herbert Spencer; and it is disappointing to find him proposing nothing better than the same

5 Raymond B. Fosdick, *Within Our Powers: Perspective for a Time of Peril* (New York, 1952) 100, 101.

humanism with which to remake the world. His text is the words of Thomas Paine: "We have it within our power to begin the world over again." His hope for the future is found in the fact that medicine has wiped out malaria in one generation; that science has added so much to our understanding of man. This is our age searching for truth. It represents man at his best: "It is impossible to believe that this strange and undeflectable being is now going down in defeat before forces which he has himself created. Rather, we catch a glimpse of him as a heaven-storming creature, the purposeful architect of his own fortunes. . . . This is the faith we live by."[6]

The philosophy of this book seems so outdated that one would be tempted to dismiss it without further attention were it not for the fact that it evidently represents even in 1958 the thinking of a large section of the American people. Like the *Times* correspondent's story it illustrates their confusion as well; for it contains one prize illustration of a world made over again, an illustration which belies the thesis of the book itself. Saint Jerome, upon learning that the Goths had sacked Rome in A.D. 410, cried out: "What is left if Rome perishes?" Not despairing, however, he returned to his monastery cell and produced the *Vulgate,* thus proclaiming the power of God and the Christian faith which eventually dispelled the barbarian blight, even in the environment of a decadent, sensate civilization.

Had the author used this theme as his text and developed it, his conclusion would have been different. The power by which Jerome's world was remade did not rise from below to storm the gates of heaven. It flowed down from the gates of heaven. Our own world, likewise, can be made over again only as these same gates are reopened, and as power comes down from above with which to lift man upward and onward. A generation of neo-orthodox theology, though underrating (so it seems to this writer) heaven's power to change the human heart and to direct the ways of man into the path

6 *Ibid.,* 113, 114.

of Christian discipleship, has nevertheless rendered the superficial, optimistic philosophy of the American creed out-of-date, so that it is no longer taken seriously, even in former strongholds of theological liberalism. As one contemporary theologian sees it: since the Middle Ages a worldly, materialistic spirit has steadily drawn our western civilization away from God until today it "is disintegrating because it does not correspond to the divine . . . order of things."[7] It is to this divine order that we must turn if we would gain perspective for our time of peril, and power to cure its ills.

The humanistic individualism which underlies the American creed is man-centered. Its love is directed inwardly, a self-love whose fruit is the human disorder of our time. The divine order for man, on the other hand, is God-centered. Its love flows outwardly. It is love for God and love for the brother and neighbor. This divine order was set forth in the Decalogue and became fully manifest in Jesus Christ, the incarnate God, who not only demonstrated the way of love and the cross, but who makes that way effective in the lives of men today.

THE STEADFAST LOVE OF GOD

This love relationship stems from the nature of God Himself, "for God is love."[8] The psalmist expressed it in these words:

> But the steadfast love of the Lord is from everlasting
> to everlasting
> upon those who fear him,
> and his righteousness to children's children,
> to those who keep his covenant
> and remember to do his commandments.[9]

The steadfast love of God is a theme which runs throughout the Scriptures. The Decalogue itself is introduced with the words: "I am the Lord your God, who brought you . . .

---

7 H. R. Niebuhr, W. Pauck, and F. P. Miller, *The Church Against the World* (Chicago, 1935) 24.

8 I John 4:8.

9 Psalm 103:17, 18.

out of the house of bondage . . . , showing steadfast love to . . . those who love me and keep my commandments."[10] In the days of Judah's distress, Jeremiah speaks of God's everlasting love and of His continual faithfulness to man.[11] In the Psalms the steadfast love of God is a continuously recurring theme: "How precious is thy steadfast love, O God";[12] "Have mercy on me, O God, according to thy steadfast love; according to thy abundant mercy blot out my transgressions";[13] "Let me hear in the morning of thy steadfast love, for in thee I put my trust."[14]

The New Testament continues the theme: "For God so loved the world that he gave his only Son"[15]; "We love, because he first loved us"[16]; "If God so loved us, we also ought to love one another."[17]

MAN'S RESPONSE: LOVE AND OBEDIENCE

In the Scriptures God's relationship with man assumes the form of a covenant. God the Creator, whose nature is steadfast love, is holy and righteous. Man, the creature, responds with love toward God, walking in holiness and righteousness, obedient to the commands of God: "You shall be holy; for I the Lord your God am holy."[18] Righteousness and love toward God in turn mean love for brother and neighbor: "You shall love the Lord your God with all your heart, and with all your soul, and with all your mind. This is the great and first commandment. And a second is like it, You shall love your neighbor as yourself. On these two commandments depend all the law and the prophets."[19]

This is God's design as expressed in the covenant relationship. To violate the command of love is to walk in rebellion against God; to bring disorder and confusion into human relationships. To obey the command of love is to

10 Ex. 20:2, 6.
11 Jer. 31:3.
12 Psalm 36:7.
13 Psalm 51:1.
14 Psalm 143:8.

15 John 3:16.
16 I John 4:19.
17 I John 4:11.
18 Lev. 19:2.
19 Matt. 22:37-40.

identify one's self and to synchronize one's life with the divine order in all of man's affairs. The words, "you shall," are not the words of a tyrant. They are the words of a loving Father seeking the eternal welfare of His children. It is not a command of caprice. It is a command of love. Throughout the Scriptures love and obedience are associated in the most intimate manner. They are integral parts of the same experience. In the divine order of things there can be no love without obedience, nor obedience without love. "If you keep my commandments, you will abide in my love, just as I have kept my Father's commandments and abide in his love."[20] The commandment of love is an integral part of God's eternal order, the very essence of the divine law. "This is the message which you have heard from the beginning, that we should love one another. . . ."[21] "He who loves his neighbor has fulfilled the law."[22]

JUSTICE:[23] A FRUIT OF LOVE AND OBEDIENCE

Doing no wrong means obedient love which will not be party to injustice to the brother or neighbor. The Christian denies to no man that which is his due. Christian love, indeed, goes beyond mere justice; for even the non-Christian frequently gives his neighbor that which rightfully belongs to him. For this reason Paul says that the professing Christian who is so unjust to the members of his family as not to provide for their material needs "has disowned the faith and is worse than an unbeliever."[24] The point here, however, is that the divine order in human relations includes justice, giving

20 John 15:10.
21 I John 3:11.
22 Rom. 13:8-10.
23 The word "justice" is used here in the ordinary sense of *suum cuique* (to each his own). Closely related to this is the Scriptural use of the word to signify the good and the just (the righteous), who are doers of justice in the sense of *suum cuique*. The term is also used in the retributive sense of judgment upon sin; or closely related to it, the correction or the undoing of injustice, especially by coercive means. It is the writer's view that retributive justice is the prerogative of God alone; that men who follow the way of the cross are good and just; that they do justice, but do not serve as agents of God's wrath for the retribution of injustice. This view is developed further below, pp. 17-21.
24 I Tim. 5:8.

to each man his due. This is a recurring theme in the Old
Testament: The Lord loves righteousness and justice[25]; He
"executes justice for the fatherless and the widow, and loves
the sojourner."[26] Righteousness and justice are more acceptable to Him than sacrifice.[27]

The prophets persistently condemn oppression and injustice: "Enough, O princes of Israel! Put away violence and
oppression . . . cease your evictions of my people . . . . You
shall have just balances, a just ephah, and a just bath."[28] Woe
to those who "join house to house, who add field to field,
until there is no more room"[29]; who "sell the righteous for
silver, and the needy for a pair of shoes . . . [who] trample
the head of the poor into the dust."[30] Offerings, feasts,
and ritualistic worship are unacceptable unless justice first
rolls "down like waters, and righteousness like an ever
flowing stream."[31] "He has showed you, O man, what is
good; and what does the Lord require of you but to do justice, and to love kindness, and to walk humbly with your
God?"[32]

THE EVERLASTING COVENANT

The covenant relationship between God and man is
described as an eternal relationship, an everlasting covenant,
which God will never break. So long as man continues in
love, obedience, and justice, the steadfast love and mercy of
God will go on unendingly. "He is mindful of his covenant
for ever, of the word that he commanded, for a thousand
generations, the covenant which he made with Abraham, his
sworn promise to Isaac, which he confirmed to Jacob as a
statute, to Israel as an everlasting covenant . . . ."[33]

The endurance of the covenant, however, was always
dependent upon the faithfulness and the obedience of God's
people. Disobedience and the transgression of God's law

---

25 Psalm 33:5.
26 Deut. 10:18, 19.
27 Prov. 21:3.
28 Ezek. 45:9, 10.
29 Isa. 5:8.

30 Amos 2:6, 7.
31 Amos 5:21-24.
32 Mic. 6:8.
33 Psalm 105:8-10.

would surely bring its penalty: "The earth mourns and withers," said the Prophet, "for they have transgressed the laws, violated the statutes, broken the everlasting covenant. Therefore a curse devours the earth, and its inhabitants suffer for their guilt."[34]

Repentance and confession, however, always restored the broken covenant. It was for His people's sake that the covenant was made, and its purpose was ever a redemptive one: "He sent redemption to his people; he has commanded his covenant for ever."[35] "For a brief moment I forsook you, but with great compassion I will gather you. . . . With everlasting love I will have compassion on you, says the Lord, your Redeemer."[36] The weeping prophet looked forward to the day when the redemptive work of God would bring forth a new covenant, "not like the covenant . . . which they broke," but a new covenant in which God's law would reside within men themselves, written "upon their hearts."[37] Years afterward the writer of the book of Hebrews declared that the new covenant was now in operation through the redemptive work of Jesus Christ, making it a better covenant, enacted on better promises, giving men a new heart, their conscience cleansed "from dead works to serve the living God."[38]

THE ORDER OF CREATION

There is a sense in which the divine covenant is analogous to civil laws or contracts. The Biblical concept of covenant goes deeper than this, however. Since it is established upon the order of God's creation it has the character of a basic law, a charter, or a divine constitution, which is prior to all law. It plays a fundamental role like that sought by the philosophers in the idea of the social contract.[39] In Rousseau's social contract, sovereignty resides in the people.

---

34 Isa. 24:4-6.
35 Psalm 111:9.
36 Isa. 54:7, 8.
37 Jer. 31:31-33.
38 Heb. 8:6-10; 9:11-22; 10:15-17.
39 E.g., Rousseau, *The Social Contract;* Thomas Hobbs, *Leviathan;* John Locke, *Of Civil Government.*

In that of Thomas Hobbs sovereignty over the people comes into existence simultaneously with their formation of society. In that of John Locke the people establish a government to rule over them. Long before the eighteenth century, however, God had revealed to Israel the fundamental law for which the philosophers from the ancient Greeks to those of our own time have more or less vainly sought. The covenant is an expression of the eternal nature of God Himself. God is perfect love, holiness, righteousness, and justice. By His very nature, and by the very nature of His creation, God alone is sovereign. For its own welfare therefore and for its own harmonious and healthful operation, all nature, both physical and human, must be obedient to the order of creation and to the divine covenant which proceeds from it.

This is not the kind of covenant reached by two parties through a process of bargaining. It is a covenant which derives from the very nature of God and His universe; all of its requirements in themselves constitute an order of creation. The covenant extends to all creation. The covenant with Israel is an order of creation as much as are the laws of the physical universe. "If you can break my covenant with the day and my covenant with the night, so that day and night will not come at their appointed time, then also my covenant with David my servant may be broken . . . and my covenant with the Levitical priests my ministers."[40] God's covenant with the physical world and His covenant with man are orders of creation by which all things hold together[41]; and if it is unthinkable that the physical laws governing the heavens and the earth and the planetary universe can be broken, it is even more unthinkable that the spiritual laws governing the affairs of men can be broken.

The God of the covenant is not a constitutional monarch. As Paul Ramsey says: "What he promulgated was legal and righteous altogether; there was no law external to himself or whose source was the people's voice in accord with which

40 Jer. 33:20, 21.
41 Col. 1:17.

he must rule in order to remain truly a lord."[42] "Rousseau constructs a sovereign while Israel recognizes one."[43] When King David committed his sin against Uriah, the prophet Nathan rebuked the king, not for violating the constitution or the legislation of Israel, but for having "despised the word of the Lord, to do what is evil in his sight." Following the rebuke David confessed, "I have sinned against the Lord"[44]; and Ramsey says that in committing the sin "he had broken the only covenant binding upon him," the covenant of the sovereign God.[45]

The sovereignty of God alone is emphasized by Emil Brunner: "Sovereignty is a concept which cannot with impunity be transferred from God, to whom alone it belongs, to men or human beings. . . . The theory of sovereignty, even when it is not so intended, is the beginning of political atheism with its double potentiality, individualistic anarchy or the collectivistic totalitarian state. If we seriously believe in the sovereignty of the people, then, as Rousseau, the most eloquent advocate of this fallacy, noted, we proclaim thereby the *révolution permanente*. There is no limit to the caprice of a people which feels itself sovereign. And if we speak seriously of the sovereignty of the state, as modern legal positivism does, then, as recent times have shown, the totalitarian state already exists. Neither state nor people is sovereign. Both stand under a law which is binding upon them, which sets limits to their rights. Sovereignty belongs to God alone."[46] Or to put it in the words of the apostles, "We must obey God rather than men."[47]

The Genesis story tells us that man was created in the image of God. This is sometimes interpreted as meaning that he was created with powers of reason, of will, of imagination, and artistic creativity. These indeed are the qualities which distinguish man from animals; which make it possible for

42 Paul Ramsey, *Basic Christian Ethics* (New York, 1950) 377.
43 *Ibid.*, 378.
44 II Sam. 12:9, 13.
45 Ramsey, *op. cit.*, 380.
46 Emil Brunner, *Justice and the Social Order* (New York, 1945) 74, 75.
47 Acts 5:29.

him to know God, and to worship Him, or to reject Him.
These qualities, however, do not constitute the image of God.
God is love, holiness, righteousness, and justice. Man in his
original nature was like a mirror reflecting God's holiness
and love in a relationship of responsive obedience. This, I
believe, is what is meant when we are told that man was
created in the image of God. He was created in a relationship
of loving obedience. Man's reason, on the other hand, instead of constituting the image of God, is actually associated
with the fall of man. Not that rationality in itself is evil.
Reason is indeed an essential part of man's dignity as a creature of God. Human reason is rebellious and sinful, however,
unless it finds its proper place in responsive obedience to the
Creator.

It is when man loses this spiritual orientation, when he is
concerned only with the increase of his understanding, that
he interprets history in terms of economic determinism; that
the social and cultural milieu alone is said to explain human
behavior; that morals and ethics as derived from God's moral
law and the order of creation are degraded to the status of
mere mores and folkways of a given culture; or that religion
and the idea of God itself are explained away as the end
product of dreams and frustrations arising from the stimulation of man's sensory organs. Man's reason in an orientation such as this is far from the image of God. Rational man
is like God only as he takes his place in humble obedience,
reflecting as in a mirror the love, the holiness, the righteousness, and the justice of God. When he rejects this position
and pursues his own course, he reflects his own will and may,
if he pursues this course far enough, lose the image of God
entirely. This is the essence of sin. It is the opposite of response to the steadfast love of God which goes out to all men.
Ramsey says it is "any falling short of disinterested love for
neighbor for his own sake . . ., any falling short of the strenuous teachings of Jesus, any falling short of the full definition
of obligation contained in I Corinthians 13."[48] Sin as here

48 Ramsey, *op. cit.,* 290.

defined is universal in its scope, and total in its devastating effect upon those who have lost the image of God. The sovereignty of God is renounced. Love and compassion are gone. Selfish egoism controls the life and action of man. Righteousness is overthrown, and injustice prevails in human relations.

Social injustice follows the loss of the divine image as a matter of course, because justice is an integral part of the divine order of things. Justice is like truth. What is just, is so beyond argument, because it resides in the order of creation itself. As Brunner says: "The law of justice . . . not only expresses what ought to be; it expresses what *is*. [By the order of creation every creature is allotted] its sphere, its scope, its freedom, and its limitation. To every creature . . . the Creator gives the law of its being. . . . By the act of creation, he determines what is due to it. . . . Every creature *must* be what God created it to be. . . *must* respect the order of creation established by the Creator . . . *must* respect every other creature as a thing created, willed by God."[49]

Thus in the sense that all men and women are created in the image of God, all men and women as human beings are equal before God, and the dignity of every man and woman as a human being must be respected by every other man and woman. That is, the equality of men and women as founded in creation is the source of the inalienable rights which belong to every man and woman alike. To respect these inalienable rights which are equal to all is justice; to violate them is injustice.

At the same time the Creator has endowed every creature with a particular mode of being. A woman has certain rights which belong to her as a woman, and a man has certain rights which belong to him as a man. In this sense men and women are unlike and unequal. What is due to both as human beings is equal. At the same time, that which is due the man as a man is not the same as that which is due the woman as a woman. To respect these particular rights of

49 Brunner, *Justice and the Social Order*, 48, 49.

the man and the woman is just and natural; that is, in accord with the order of creation. Likewise, the child and the adult, as persons, are equal before God. As child and adult, however, they are not equal, and each has certain rights with which the order of creation has endowed it. The child has a natural right to be treated as a child. This is why a social system which fastens a cruel system of adult labor upon the child is unnatural and unjust. The adult, on the other hand, has a right to be treated as an adult. Therefore a social system which denies the adult the right to do the work for which God has created him is unnatural and unjust. It is contrary to God's order of creation. "The order of creation is the protection of the rights of the creature against the wantonness of men. The protection is sacred; it is the divine law of justice."[50]

When God created His creatures He also created the laws which govern their being and their relation to other created beings. The Apostle Paul recognized that even among men who do not have the benefit of divine revelation this order of creation is in operation to achieve the purposes of God: "When Gentiles who have not the law do by nature what the law requires . . . they show that what the law requires is written on their hearts . . . ."[51] That is, even the "natural man" has some sense of right and wrong, of what is just and unjust. Even as the planets move in accordance with the Creator's designs, so man from the time of his birth is directed by the order of his creation; and when he is able to reflect upon his experience he develops some awareness of the divine power which gives him his sense of justice and right. The ancient Greeks, the Stoics in particular, experienced this awareness, and expressed it in their "law of nature." To be sure, the Stoic philosophy is a form of pantheism whose god is identical with nature. But that the cosmic force of the universe directed the affairs of men they did not doubt.

50 *Ibid.*, 51.
51 Rom. 2:12-16.

Paul was perfectly aware that Stoic pantheism was far removed from the worship of Jehovah and of the risen Christ. This did not prevent him, however, from recognizing the truth which the pagan world had grasped in part. Then, having recognized this fact, he boldly proclaims the God who is the author of nature: "Ever since the creation of the world his invisible nature, namely, his eternal power and deity, has been clearly perceived in the things that have been made."[52] This is not pantheism. Much less is it modern naturalism. It is Christian theism which proclaims God as the Creator who gave to the creature the law of its being.

The term "natural law" has been used in a variety of ways in the history of western thought. While it has meant everything from pantheism to modern determinism and naturalism, it has also had, and still has, a Christian meaning. Even in Greek philosophy it generally meant an ideal of justice "rooted in the nature of man or of things and discoverable either with divine aid or by the human reason alone . . . ."[53] In the Bible, nature as created by God is not represented as evil but as good. Redemption is merely the instrument for restoring fallen human nature which has ceased to be natural in the true sense.

In the first chapter of Romans Paul describes the acts of evil men who no longer do that which is natural.[54] That is, they have departed from the order of creation in their sex and marriage relationships. When Jesus was questioned concerning marriage and divorce His answer was that marriage is grounded in the creation. "He who made them from the beginning made them male and female"; and "for this reason," because of this order of creation, it is natural and right that a man and a woman should be joined in wedlock.[55] In discussing the sabbath, Jesus said it was "made for man."[56]

---

52 Rom. 1:20.
53 James Luther Adams, "The Law of Nature: some general considerations," *The Journal of Religion* (April 1945) 25:88.
54 Rom. 1:26, 27.
55 Matt. 19:4, 5.
56 Mark 2:27.

That is, man's nature as given him by the Creator required a day of rest and worship as provided in the Decalogue.

The idea that the Decalogue is founded on the order of creation was basic in the thinking of the Protestant Reformers. Luther says: "The Decalog is lodged [*haeret*] in the conscience. If God had never given the Law by Moses, yet the mind of man naturally has this knowledge that God is to be worshipped and our neighbor to be loved."[57] Calvin takes the same view: "The internal law, which has . . . been . . . engraven on the hearts of all men, suggests to us in some measure the same things which are to be learned from the two tables." Man's sinfulness has so corrupted his nature, however, that he is unable to follow the order of creation without the aid of the written law: "Since it was necessary, therefore, both for our dullness and obstinacy, the Lord gave us a written law; to declare with greater certainty what in the law of nature was too obscure, and by arousing our indolence, to make a deeper impression on our understanding and memory."[58]

Luther places the Golden Rule as given by Jesus into the same relationship as he does the Decalogue. He refers to Matthew 7:12 and Luke 6:31 as "the natural law which Christ announces." Again, he says the Golden Rule expresses "the law which goes through all the world, well known to all men, written in all men's hearts."[59] Calvin says: "Equity [or justice], being natural, is the same to all mankind; and consequently all laws, on every subject, ought to have the same equity for their end. . . ."[60] In commenting on this emphasis, John T. McNeill says: "Calvin has a profound sense of the 'order of nature' and often invokes this idea to enforce a moral judgment, e.g., on such matters as obedience

57 Luther, *Die erste Disputation gegen die Antinomer* (1537), *Werke* (Weimar Ausgabe) 39, Part I, 374; quoted in J. T. McNeill, "Natural Law in the Teaching of the Reformers," *The Journal of Religion* (July 1946) 26:168.

58 John Calvin, *Institutes of the Christian Religion* (Seventh American Edition, Phila., 1936) 1:397.

59 Quoted in McNeill, *loc. cit.*, 26:170.

60 Calvin, *Institutes*, 2:789.

to parents; injustice to the poor; vanity and simplicity in dress; theft, war, drunkenness, marriage."[61]

Pilgram Marpeck, the sixteenth-century Anabaptist, had the same view. A fox has only one nature, he says. A baby fox reaching adulthood must have a fox nature and nothing else. Man, however, has two natures: The good nature with which God endowed him at the creation; and the bad nature which comes as a result of sin, and which ever strives against the good. When God created man, He breathed into him the breath of life,[62] and gave him moral understanding.[63] Marpeck cites the sermon before the Epicureans and the Stoics on the Areopagus, in which Paul proclaims the "unknown God" whom even the pagan poets had recognized as the one in whom "we live and move and have our being."[64] Then he quotes Paul's striking passage in which he declares that the "Gentiles who have not the law do by nature what the law requires," showing that "what the law requires is written on their hearts."[65] It is this higher nature, the "natural light" which man receives as an order of creation, that accounts for such noble characters, such "natural, pious, God-fearing men," as Cornelius the centurion.[66] Reference to Romans 2:14, 15 and the law written in the hearts of men is also made by Cornelis Ris in two articles of his Mennonite Confession of Faith compiled in the eighteenth century.[67]

THE CORRECTION OF INJUSTICE: THE NATURAL ORDER

Inherent within the order of creation is the universal conviction among men, even in a corrupt and sinful society, that when the moral law has been transgressed the wrong

---

61 McNeill, *loc. cit.*, 26:182.
62 Gen. 2:7.
63 Job 32:8.
64 Acts 17:22-31.
65 Rom. 2:14, 15.
66 Acts 10:1-33. J. Loserth, *Quellen und Forschungen zur Geschichte der oberdeutschen Taufgesinnten im 16. Jahrhundert: Pilgram Marpecks Antwort auf Kaspar Schwenckfelds Beurteilung des Buches der Bundesbezeugung von 1542.* (Vienna and Leipzig, 1929) 218, 219.
67 See Articles I and VII of Cornelis Ris, *Mennonite Articles of Faith* (Berne, Ind., 1925) 2, 7.

must in some manner be corrected. Man cannot continue suffering injustice indefinitely. Man's nature has been corrupted and the image of God has been marred; but it is not completely destroyed. What remains cannot make for holy living; but it can do something for the maintenance of order and justice in society. As God's order of creation determines what is just and right, so it also provides for the correction of injustice and unrighteousness in human society.

The manner and means for the correction of injustice, however, is dependent upon the degree to which the members of society have retained the image of God. When men have a true covenant relationship with God they practice the Golden Rule; they do unto others as they would have others do unto them. When the holy covenant is broken, however, and the law of love is inoperative among them, men will do unto others as others have done unto them. This procedure may maintain a kind of law and order; but it does not maintain a relationship of steadfast love and brotherhood among men, as was the intent of the moral law. It is rather a manifestation of the wrath of God in operation among evil men. It is the only way the moral law can work in a sinful society. It is the way of wrath, not the way of love.

The Scriptural record makes frequent reference to the wrath of God and its operation within a society of sinful men. Man is admonished to follow the way of love; and he is warned that if he fails to do so the very order of creation provides due consequences. "Whoever sheds the blood of man, by man shall his blood be shed,"[68] says the writer of Genesis. "They did not wait for his counsel," says the psalmist; "they had a wanton craving . . . and put God to the test . . . ; he gave them what they asked, but sent a wasting disease among them."[69] The prophets continuously warned Israel and Judah of the consequences which would follow a failure to heed the counsel of the Lord, whether the sin was in the form of military alliances and militarism, or of economic injustice and

68 Gen. 9:6.
69 Psalm 106:13-15.

materialism. "Woe to those," says Isaiah, "who go down to Egypt for help and rely on horses . . . and in horsemen . . . . When the Lord stretches out his hand, the helper will stumble, and he who is helped will fall, and they will all perish together."[70] "Woe to those," he says again, "who join house to house, who add field to field, until there is no more room, and you are made to dwell alone in the midst of the land. . . . Surely many houses shall be desolate, large and beautiful houses, without inhabitant."[71] "For three transgressions of Israel, and for four," says Amos, "I will not revoke the punishment; because they sell the righteous for silver, and the needy for a pair of shoes—they that trample the head of the poor into the dust of the earth, and turn aside the way of the afflicted."[72] The prophets' solemn warnings were not confined to Israel and Judah, however. Their responsibility reached to a warning of the pagan nations as well. "For three transgressions of Tyre, and for four," says the Lord's spokesman, "I will not revoke the punishment; because they delivered up a whole people to Edom, and did not remember the covenant of brotherhood."[73] And Jeremiah warns that "if any nation will not listen, then I will utterly pluck it up and destroy it, says the Lord."[74]

The theological basis for this prophetic responsibility is stated by Paul in the epistle to the Romans, as follows:

"For the wrath of God is revealed from heaven against all ungodliness and wickedness of men who by their wickedness suppress the truth. . . . And since they did not see fit to acknowledge God, God gave them up to a base mind and to improper conduct. They were filled with all manner of wickedness, evil, covetousness, malice. Full of envy . . . heartless, ruthless. . . . We know that the judgment of God rightly falls upon those who do such things. . . . Do you not know that God's kindness is meant to lead you to repentance? But by your hard and impenitent heart you are storing up wrath for

---

70 Isa. 31:1-3.   73 Amos 1:9.
71 Isa. 5:8, 9.   74 Jer. 12:17.
72 Amos 2:6, 7.

yourself on the day of wrath when God's righteous judgment will be revealed.''[75]

The wrath of God as set forth in the first two chapters of Romans is revealed both in a last judgment, and in the operation of the natural law by the order of creation, in human society continuously. An important manifestation of this continuous operation is found in the police power of the state which is described in Romans 13 as having been instituted by God "to execute his wrath on the wrongdoer," and to which the Christian must be subject.[76] Thus the apostle assumes the responsibility of warning a sinful world concerning the wrath of God; and at the same time he asserts the responsibility of the Christian to respect the place of the police power of the state, under the order of creation, for the restraint of evil.

THE CORRECTION OF INJUSTICE: THE SUPERNATURAL ORDER

It is important to note, however, that the Christian's responsibility with respect to the wrath of God ends at this point. He must sound a warning concerning the operation of the divine law; he must respect the police power of the state as an agency of God's wrath in an evil society; but he is not responsible to serve as an agency of the divine wrath. His calling is a higher one. It is to promote and implement the correction of injustice through the supernatural order, the way of love, of suffering, and of the cross, which alone can restore sinful men to the way of loving obedience. His responsibility is that of calling sinful men to repentance, and of leading them to the way of the cross, bringing them reconciliation with God and their fellow men. The Christian does not exercise vengeance in order *to obtain justice*. He suffers, even lays down his life if need be, in order that he might *do justice* and bring reconciliation among men.

The Christian does not mete out vengeance. Instead, he shares the spirit of the Suffering Servant who was oppressed

75 Rom. 1:18, 28-31; 2:2-5.
76 Rom. 13:1-7.

and afflicted, and who like a lamb led to the slaughter, opened not His mouth.[77] Like the tender husband in the prophecy of Hosea, whose heart goes out in loving forgiveness to his unfaithful wife, he pleads with the unjust and unfaithful neighbor, be he an industrial capitalist or a nation state, to "return . . . to the Lord your God, for you have stumbled because of your iniquity"; and he assures penitent sinners that God "will heal their faithlessness," and "love them freely, for . . . [his] anger has turned from them."[78]

In these days when so much is being said of the Christian's supposed responsibility for supporting the collective security program of the western nations it is important to remember that the plumb line of Amos found all of the nations guilty, and that his woes "for three transgressions . . . and for four" were pronounced, not only upon Damascus and Tyre, Edom and Moab, but upon Israel and Judah as well. The situation is not different today. It is not the responsibility of Christians to rally support for collective security programs directed by "Christian" nations against the "pagan" ones. God's plumb line has found all of them guilty; and who knows but that even now the so-called pagan nations may be the "rod of . . . [his] anger, the staff of . . . [his] fury"[79] for the chastisement of the "Christian" world? Thus it behooves Christians not to assume the responsibility for wielding the staff of God's fury; but rather the responsibility to lead a backsliding people steeped in nationalism and the spirit of militarism back to the God of peace; that they may be gathered "from the farthest parts of the earth . . . with weeping . . . and with consolations"; that they may bow down before the Lord, enabling Him to make a new covenant with them; that He may put His law "within them, and . . . write it upon their hearts"; that He may be their God, and that they may be His people.[80]

---

77 Isa. 53:7.
78 Hos. 14:1, 4.

79 Isa. 10:5.
80 Jer. 31:8, 9, 31, 33.

2. THE WAY OF THE CROSS

The heart of the New Testament message is the restoration of man's covenant relationship with God. Restoration comes through the new creation. For those who are in Christ, "the old has passed away, behold, the new has come." This great truth is most vividly stated in the second epistle to the Corinthians: "All this is from God, who through Christ reconciled us to himself and gave us the ministry of reconciliation; that is, God was in Christ reconciling the world to himself, not counting their trespasses against them, and entrusting to us the message of reconciliation. So we are ambassadors for Christ, God making his appeal through us."[1]

This great passage takes us to the heart of the Christian Gospel. Jesus Christ was God incarnate, living and dying among men in order that He might reconcile them to God. Christendom has had much to say about the death of Christ, and has offered many interpretations as to its meaning. Too often, however, the cross has been merely a beautiful symbol of an ignominious death which is supposed somehow to give men salvation, without adequate reference to the entire redemptive life and work of Christ; or to the character of that discipleship which is the fruit of men's redemption. Peter says Christ "bore our sins in his body on the tree, that we might die to sin and live to righteousness."[2] Certainly righteousness is meant for eternity also; but this passage appears in a context of righteous living in the present world. Those who have been redeemed through the reconciling work of Christ live righteously, taking the example of Christ, following His steps, here and now.

Such righteous living becomes possible through the cross of Christ as found in His life and death. Christ did not only

1 II Cor. 5:18-20.
2 I Peter 2:24.

die a cross death. He lived a cross life. Although He was the divine Son of God, with the powers of heaven at His command, these powers were used only sparingly, and then only in ministering to the needs of others. They never were used to satisfy His own hunger or to contribute to His own comfort. When Christ assumed human form He emptied Himself of His heavenly prerogatives. He became fully human, taking the form of a servant, becoming subject to every human limitation, restriction, and temptation. He hungered, He suffered, and He lived as other men, even the lowliest of the lowly. This was the cross life of Christ. Even though without sin, He identified Himself with sinners. He accepted a sinner's baptism. He worked with sinners and ate with them. He sympathized with sinners and comforted them. When they reviled Him He reviled not again. He lived the perfect life of love among them, never using the divine power at His command to save Himself or to withstand His opponents. When sinners abused Him He pleaded with them, and for them. Eventually He even allowed them to put Him to death.

This was the cross life of Christ, of which the cross death was the logical sequence and crowning achievement. The good life brought the opposition of evil men; but the way of love and nonresistance left no room for retaliation. By His assumed human limitations He declined to escape from the wrath of evil men. Thus the Son of God gave His life on the cross. By this act He endured the wrath of God and redeemed sinful men, reconciling them unto God. Christ came to redeem sinners and He did it by way of the cross: the cross life of love and nonresistance, and the cross death on Calvary. This in turn becomes the way for the Christian who has been redeemed and reconciled to God.

To the Greeks the cross was foolishness, and to the Jews it was a stumbling block. This statement is commonly understood to mean that these people were unable to comprehend the idea of redemption through the death of Christ. The cross life of Christ was foolishness to them, however, as much as was His cross death; while the early Christians accepted both the cross life and the cross death of their Master. Unfortunately, however, since the time of Constantine it has become the fashion for Christians to identify Christendom and the general social order. In our own day some would even equate Christianity with "the American way." To such professing Christians the cross life is as objectionable as it was to the ancient Greeks and Jews. To some it is foolishness. Others have called it cowardice. The commonly accepted term of disapprobation today is irresponsibility. Paul says to Christians, however: "Have this mind among yourselves, which you have in Christ Jesus, who . . . emptied himself, taking the form of a servant, . . . and . . . humbled himself and became obedient unto death, even death on a cross."[3] And Jesus Himself said: "He who loses his life for my sake will find it."[4]

The redemptive, reconciling work of Christ can be understood only as we realize how far the human race has gone wrong; how completely mankind is at enmity with God. Sin is not a mere transgression or a series of transgressions which men commit. It is rather a state or a condition in which all men are involved. The original meaning of the word is "missing the mark," going astray. Something has gone wrong with man. C. H. Dodd puts it this way:

"There is a racial, a corporate, a social wrongness of which we are made in some sense partakers by the mere fact of our being born into human society. That is the meaning of 'original sin.' . . . The problem of evil in man is more than the problem of a series of sinful acts, which of his own free will he can stop if he makes up his mind to it . . . the trouble lies deeper. There is a deep-grained wrongness about human life as it is."[5]

Sin is universal in its scope and devastating in its effect. The sovereignty of God is renounced. Love and compassion are gone. Selfish egoism controls the life and actions of man. Righteousness is overthrown, and injustice prevails in human relations. Man's nature is corrupted so that he no longer is

3 Phil. 2:5-8.
4 Matt. 10:39.
5 C. H. Dodd, *The Meaning of Paul for Today* (London, 1920) 60, 61.

capable of the covenant relationship, with the result that the wrath of God comes in to do its corrective work.

The wrath of God is not the capricious act of an angry despot. It is God, through the order of creation, permitting sinful human nature to suffer the natural consequences of its own willful course. Moreover, since man is a social being, man in society has a solidarity. He is a corporation in which every member affects the life of the entire body which he represents. When one member suffers, the whole body suffers with him. When one member does wrong, the entire race is affected; and when one member does that which is right, it has a wholesome effect upon the entire race. As Achan's sin disgraced all Israel; as a murderous representative of the clan brings upon his entire clan the wrath of the injured clan; so Adam the representative of corporate humanity involves the entire race.

If this is true, however, the obverse is also true. If the corporate body can be betrayed by its representative, it can also be redeemed by its representative. "Thus a blow struck at sin by any human being who partakes of the 'flesh' is struck in behalf of all."[6] Moreover, since the human race had missed the mark, had gone astray, through the act and volition of its own representative, so the redemption and restoration of humanity could be accomplished only through the act and volition of its own representative. This explains the need and the occasion for the incarnation of Christ. Since "only a real man of flesh and blood could strike the blow for all men," as C. H. Dodd says, "Jesus was made the representative of sinful man, and so before the law was responsible for sin."[7] Inasmuch as He lived without sin, however, the life of Christ was one of complete reconciliation with God. The covenant relationship of love and obedience to the Father, and of love to all mankind, was maintained unto perfection. Thus Christ as the representative of corporate humanity includes us in His perfection. His work of redemption and reconciliation

6 *Ibid.*, 95.
7 *Ibid.*, 96.

is available to all men "in proportion as they accept its implications, and make them the guiding principles of their own
lives."[8]

In the work of reconciliation the love of God is seen in
all its fullness. In the cross life and the cross death of Christ
God is both the reconciler and the reconciled. It is the divine
love itself that makes the redemption, that "has taken the
initiative, broken through the order of justice and merit, triumphed over the powers of evil, and created a new relation
between the world and God."[9] "He died for all, that those
who live might live no longer for themselves but for him who
for their sake died and was raised."[10]

This great truth then makes it clear what it means to be
a Christian. To be a Christian means to enter into the same
experience with Christ, presenting our bodies, our *entire
personality* that is, as a living sacrifice for the cause for which
Christ died.[11] During the first World War an editorial in a
religious periodical stated the meaning of the cross life for
that day in these words: "We are not what we ought to be
unless we share the love which prompted our heavenly Father
to send His Son into the world to save the lost. We cannot
take the place of Christ in the work of redemption, but we
can take our place as His followers and share in the love
which prompted Him to lay down His life for His enemies."[12]
As followers of Christ, the Christian shares in Christ's suffering, loving even his enemies, and bringing comfort to his
fellow men. Paul said to the Corinthians: "As we share
abundantly in Christ's sufferings, so through Christ we share
abundantly in comfort too. If we are afflicted, it is for your
comfort and salvation; and if we are comforted, it is for your
comfort, which you experience when you patiently endure
the same sufferings that we suffer."[13] When God was in Christ
reconciling the world to Himself, His victory over sin and

8 *Ibid.*, 97.
9 Gustaf Aulén, *Christus Victor* (London, 1931) 96.
10 II Cor. 5:15.
11 Rom. 12:1.
12 Daniel Kauffman, in *Gospel Herald* (April 12, 1917) 10:26.
13 II Cor. 1:5-7.

death was a moral achievement which has entered into the spiritual history of the race. To be a Christian is to enter into this historic stream, "to fling oneself without reserve into the stream of forces issuing from Christ's supreme moral achievement."[14]

The triumphant feature of Christ's work is His resurrection from the dead. Regardless of how much suffering the individual Christian or the church may experience, the fact that Christ is living today gives a confident assurance that for the correction of evil the supernatural order of love and obedience is supreme over the natural order; that the way of the cross and its ethical requirements are an integral part of the very stream of history; and that the resurrection of Christ is a promise of the triumph and the consummation which will eventually be experienced by those who follow the way of redemption and reconciliation.

It is this glorious assurance which enables the Christian in faith to appropriate the righteousness of God as his own. Surrendering himself in utter abandon to the will of God, he is able to say with Paul that he lives by the righteousness of the representative of the human race who died and rose again: "I have been crucified with Christ; it is no longer I who live, but Christ who lives in me; and the life I now live in the flesh I live by faith in the Son of God, who loved me and gave himself for me."[15] The new life, lived by this faith, is a life of ethical power. "If then you have been raised with Christ . . . set your minds on things that are above . . . . And above all . . . put on love, which binds everything together in perfect harmony. And let the peace of Christ rule in your hearts."[16]

It is this stream of moral energy flowing from the cross and the empty tomb which explains the power of the early Christian community following Pentecost. The spirit of power had possessed these early Christians to such a degree that the redemptive way of life was realized among them in an

14 Dodd, *op. cit.*, 104.
15 Gal. 2:20.
16 Col. 3:1-15.

amazing way. They were ready to lose their lives; they did lose them. They laid their worldly goods at the foot of the cross. They said their property was not their own; they shared it. Runaway slaves returned to their masters; and masters changed the status of slaves to that of brethren. The entire body of disciples followed the way of the cross. Selfhood was swallowed up in a community of Christian brotherhood. It was this way of the cross that baffled the Roman world, causing men to marvel and say: Behold, how they love one another. This was a major cause of the remarkable growth of the church in the early centuries.

C. H. Dodd has summarized the situation of the early church as follows:

"The moral demand of letting Christ's spirit rule you in everything is far more searching than the demand of any code, and at the same time it carries with it the promise of indefinite growth and development. . . .

"The indwelling of Christ's Spirit means not only moral discernment, but moral power. . . . Indeed, we may say that the thing above all which distinguished the early Christian community from its environment was the moral competence of its members. In order to maintain this we need not idealize unduly the early Christians. There were sins and scandals at Corinth and Ephesus, but it is impossible to miss the note of genuine power of renewal and recuperation—the power of the simple person progressively to approximate to his moral ideals in spite of failures. . . . So fully convinced is he [Paul] of the new and miraculous nature of this moral power that he can regard the Christian as a 'new creation.' This is not the old person at all: it is a 'new man,' 'created in Christ Jesus for good deeds.' "[17]

THE LAW OF CHRIST

The moral potency of the indwelling Christ brings the Christian into a new relationship with the law. In Chapter I frequent reference is made to the law of nature as well as to

17 Dodd, *op. cit.*, 134, 135.

the written law, both given by God for the direction of man's
affairs. Paul, however, speaks of having "died to the law"; of
being "discharged from the law"; and of Christ being the
"end of the law."[18] He asks the Galatians the rhetorical question: "Did you receive the Spirit by works of the law, or by
hearing with faith?" Then he says: "Christ redeemed us from
the curse of the law";[19] and in general he speaks disparagingly
of the "works of the law." On the other hand, Jesus says He
came not to abolish the law, but to fulfill it;[20] and even Paul
speaks of "the law of Christ" which the Christian is required
to fulfill.[21] Superficially, these statements might seem to con-
tradict each other. Actually, however, they simply announce
a new and higher relationship with God's unchanging moral
law. True, the ceremonial law of the old covenant has passed
away;[22] while the civil law of the Old Testament and the
interpretations of the lawyers and scribes have been superseded.[23] Through the Christian's new relationship with the
indwelling Christ, however, the moral law is to be fulfilled
as it never had been fulfilled under the old covenant.

The epistle to the Galatians[24] calls the law a custodian,
or guardian, who shows us what we ought to do and what we
ought to be. The custodian prods us unceasingly because of
our failure to meet up with his demands, so that our relationship with him is not a happy one. Finally, however, he brings
us to Christ the Redeemer who reconciles us with the author
of the law. Now the guardian ceases to be a tormentor, and
we obtain inward peace and victory. This would seem to be
the meaning of Romans 7 and 8. Jesus had made it clear that
the fulfillment of the law requires more than outward acts.
It is the inner attitude that must be right.[25] Paul recognizes
this truth when he speaks of the sin of covetousness in Romans 7. Covetousness is an inner attitude and when Paul
measured himself by the requirements of the law he saw how
far he had missed the mark.

---

18 Rom. 7:4, 6; 10:4.
19 Gal. 3:2, 13.
20 Matt. 5:17.
21 I Cor. 9:21; Gal. 6:2.

22 Col. 2:16, 17.
23 Matt. 5:20-48.
24 Gal. 3:24-26.
25 Matt. 5.

Romans 7 first describes a stage of relative innocence in which the distinction between right and wrong is dimly seen. Then comes a knowledge of the law when Paul realizes how far he had missed the mark. Here is where the struggle begins. As long as Paul had disregarded the law or was ignorant of its real meaning, he seemed good enough. When he really examined it, however, he realized how miserable a sinner he was: "If it had not been for the law, I should not have known sin. . . . The very commandment which promised life proved to be death to me."[26] This is the experience of every person who honestly examines his own inner life under the searchlight of God's moral law. As the law comes in, trespasses increase.[27] It is not that the number of sinful acts increases; but that many acts, and especially inner attitudes, which formerly seemed good enough are now recognized as sin. This is what made Paul throw up his hands and ask if there was any hope for such a sinner as he. The law had shown him how bad he actually was.

Happily, however, Paul met Jesus Christ face to face on that memorable day on the Damascus road. Here he discovered the representative of the human race in whom God dwelt, and through whom the world was being reconciled unto Himself. This experience made Paul a new man; for the life which he lived henceforth was one of faith in the Son of God. He no longer threw up his hands in despair, for now he was confident that "the law of the Spirit of life in Christ Jesus" had set him "free from the law of sin and death."[28] The man in Christ does not despair at the strenuous character of the moral law. He knows that God is for him; who then can be against him? Realizing that this was the great day toward which all history had been moving, Paul confidently invites all men to follow his steps within that historic stream of reconciliation, of redemption, and of salvation: For "the whole creation has been groaning in travail together until

26 Rom. 7:7-10.
27 Rom. 5:20.
28 Rom. 8:2.

now; and . . . we ourselves, who have the first fruits of the Spirit, groan inwardly as we wait for adoption as sons, the redemption of our bodies."[29]

Here Paul sees eye to eye with Jesus in the Sermon on the Mount. The case against Judaism was not its love for the law; but rather its arrogant adherence to a mere code of outward regulations which was blind to the real meaning of the law. Both Jesus and Paul urge the need for the fulfillment of the moral law in its true meaning in the life of the Christian disciple. Jesus states this as the purpose of His coming,[30] and after explaining the implications of this fulfillment He says: "You, therefore, must be perfect, as your heavenly Father is perfect."[31] Paul, after taking the reader through the experience of Romans 7 and 8, finally comes to the twelfth chapter where he appeals to the disciples to present their bodies, their whole personalities, "as a living sacrifice, holy and acceptable to God," being "transformed by the renewal of your mind, that you may prove what is the will of God, what is good and acceptable and perfect."[32]

If the disciple is not to fall into the same pit as that into which the Pharisees fell, however, let him not presume in his own strength or through his own righteousness to fulfill the law. This great task is to be achieved only through the sacrificial work of our Great Representative who lived the cross life and died the cross death. Having been crucified with Him, however, He lives in us and we follow His steps. Time and again, it is true, the disciple of Christ may get out of step; but when he does so he does not rationalize his action as a preferential ethic of protection, nor as a tragic necessity. Instead, he humbly confesses his sin and appeals to his Advocate to bring him back into the way of perfection. "I am writing this to you so that you may not sin," says the apostle; "but if any one does sin, we have an advocate with the Father, Jesus Christ the righteous."[33]

29 Rom. 8:22, 23.
30 Matt. 5:17.
31 Matt. 5:48.

32 Rom. 12:1, 2.
33 I John 2:1.

As Dietrich Bonhoeffer so aptly says, the difference between the Pharisee and the Christian is not that the latter has a better law, but that he has a better righteousness. This better righteousness, moreover, is possible only because Christ stands between the disciple and the law.

"There is no fulfillment of the law apart from communion with God, and no communion with God apart from the fulfillment of the law. . . . Jesus, the Son of God, who alone lives in perfect communion with Him, vindicates the law of the Old Covenant by coming to fulfill it. . . . Jesus Christ and He alone fulfills the law, because He alone enjoys perfect communion with God. It is Jesus Himself who comes between the disciples and the law, not the law which comes between Jesus and the disciples. They find their way to the law through the cross of Christ. Thus by pointing His disciples to the law which He alone fulfills, He forges a further bond between Himself and them. . . . But if Jesus comes between the disciples and the law, He does so not to release them from the duties it imposes, but to validate His demand that they should fulfill it. Just because they are bound to Him, they must obey the law as He does. The fact that Jesus has fulfilled the law down to the very last letter . . . it is precisely this which makes it properly valid for the first time. . . . Between the disciples and the law stands One who has perfectly fulfilled it, One with whom they live in communion. . . . He *is* the righteousness of the disciples. By calling them He has admitted them to partnership with Himself, and made them partakers of His righteousness in its fullness. . . . Of course the righteousness of the disciples can never be a personal achievement; it is always a gift, which they received when they were called to follow Him. In fact their righteousness consists precisely in their following Him, and in the beatitudes the reward of the kingdom of heaven has been promised to it. It is a righteousness under the cross; it belongs only to the poor, the tempted, the hungry, the peacemakers, the persecuted—who endure their lot for the sake of Jesus; it is the visible righteousness of those who for the sake of Jesus are the light of the world and the city set on the hill."[34]

THE CROSS LIFE OF THE DISCIPLE

Despite the fact that both the cross life and cross death of Christ are foolishness and a stumbling block to many people, the way of the cross, the strong suffering for the weak, is a principle which within certain limits is recognized by all. As James S. Stewart says, the principle can be seen at work in a limited way "in the patriot suffering for his country, in the research doctor sacrificing his own health for the victims of disease, in the philanthropist wearing himself out to ransom the downtrodden and oppressed, in the captain of a sinking vessel getting the women and children to safety and then going down with his ship."[35]

This limited application of the way of the cross is easily understood by most people. It is the broader application, going beyond love for the individual's family, his group, or his nation, which is so difficult to grasp. When the headmaster of a British school gathers his pupils into the air-raid shelter and then returns to make sure that none has been left behind only to be struck by a falling bomb, he is hailed as a hero who sacrificed his life for those in his care. When a family of non-resistant Christians on the American frontier, out of love for its enemies, however, leaves the hunting rifle on the rafters and allows its own members to be carried away by a band of warring Indians who imprison the father and murder the mother and babe in arms, it is less easily understood. Many would regard the father in this case as derelict in his obligation to protect and care for his own. If it is expedient, however, "that one man should die for the people, and that the whole nation should not perish,"[36] is it not equally expedient that a family, a group, or even a nation should die, that the entire human race should not perish?

This is a costly Christian grace, however, and as Bon-

34 Dietrich Bonhoeffer, *The Cost of Discipleship* (New York, 1949) 106-9.
35 James S. Stewart, *A Faith to Proclaim* (London, 1953) 92.
36 John 11:50.

hoeffer says, "Cheap grace is the deadly enemy of our church."[37] The cheap grace which so many seek is "a cheap covering" for men's sins. "No contrition is required, still less any real desire to be delivered from sin. Cheap grace therefore amounts to a denial of the living word of God, in fact, a denial of the Incarnation of the Son of God."[38] Costly grace, on the other hand, is the treasure hidden in the field; for which the Lord gave all that He had in order that He might purchase it.

"Such grace is *costly* because it calls us to follow, and it is *grace* because it calls us to follow *Jesus Christ*. It is costly because it costs a man his life, and it is grace because it gives a man the only true life. It is costly because it condemns sin, and grace because it justifies the sinner. Above all, it is *costly* because it cost God the life of His Son. 'Ye were bought at a price,' and what has cost God much cannot be cheap for us. Above all, it is *grace* because God did not reckon His Son too dear a price to pay for our life, but delivered Him up for us. Costly grace is the Incarnation of God. . . . Grace is costly because it compels a man to submit to the yoke of Christ and follow Him; it is grace because Jesus says: 'My yoke is easy and my burden is light.' "[39]

Costly grace is not asceticism, for even this can have a cheap, selfish motivation in its striving for the performance of meritorious work.

"Asceticism means voluntary suffering: it is *passio activa* rather than *passiva,* and it is just there that the danger lies. There is always a danger that in our asceticism we shall be tempted to imitate the sufferings of Christ. This is a pious but godless ambition, for beneath it there always lurks the notion that it is possible for us to step into Christ's shoes and suffer as He did. We are then presuming to undertake that bitter work of eternal redemption which Christ Himself wrought for us. . . . Our whole motive now becomes a desire for ostentation. We want other people to see our achieve-

37 Bonhoeffer, *op. cit.,* 37.
38 *Ibid.,* 37, 38.
39 *Ibid.,* 39.

ments and to be put to shame. Our asceticism has now become the way of salvation. Such publicity gives it the reward it seeks."[40]

When Jesus says, "If a man would come after me, let him deny himself and take up his cross and follow me," He is asking for something more than asceticism. He is calling for a discipleship which, forgetful of self, follows Christ completely. This discipleship is so oblivious of self that suffering and persecution, if they fall in the path of duty, will be taken as a matter of course. "To endure the cross is not a tragedy; it is the suffering which is the fruit of an exclusive allegiance to Jesus Christ."[41] Our bourgeois "respectability" has reduced the cross to a beautiful symbol with which to adorn our church edifices, or to be worn on the person as a badge of religion. The cross of the Gospel means suffering with Christ, however, and suffering itself is the badge of the true Christian.[42]

"Blessed are they that mourn," says the Master, "for they shall be comforted." The disciples do not make merry with the world, in conformity with its ways. They mourn for its follies. They bear its sorrows. They are the meek who when treated unjustly bear it with patience. They do not engage in retaliation, but like their crucified Saviour they renounce every personal right. Evil is to be requited, not by compensation in kind, but by the way of forbearance and nonresistance. The disciples are not overcome of evil; they overcome evil with good. This is the only way in which evil can be conquered. Resistance only serves to create further evil, to add fuel to the flames. It is only when resistance is completely rooted out and the disciple in utter abandon to the way of love lays down his life and his soul for his brother, his neighbor, or his enemy, that evil is conquered. For then nothing remains against which it can strike, and thus the furtherance of evil is stopped. This way of love is not a strategy or a technique. It is complete abandon to the way of the cross, and in

40 *Ibid.*, 147, 148.
41 *Ibid.*, 72.
42 *Ibid.*, 72, 73.

fellowship with the crucified. The disciple does not love his enemy in order to obtain relief from his persecution. Even in spite of his love the evil and the persecution may continue.

"But not even that can hurt or overcome us, so long as we pray for them. For if we pray for them, we are taking their distress and poverty, their guilt and perdition upon ourselves, and pleading to God for them. We are doing vicariously for them what they cannot do for themselves. Every insult they utter only serves to bind us more closely with God and with them. Their persecution of us only serves to bring them nearer to reconciliation with God and to further the triumphs of love. . . . The more we are driven along this road, the more certain is the victory of love over the enemy's hatred. For then it is not the disciple's own love but the love of Jesus Christ alone, who for the sake of His enemies went to the cross and prayed for them as He hung there."[43]

The utter abandon of self, which is the way of the cross, produces a sincerity, a humility, and a simplicity of life which leads the disciple to forget himself and to strive to serve only his God and his fellow men in all that he does. Here we are confronted by a striking paradox. If the disciple really follows the way of the cross the result will be good works seen of men, for they will not be hidden under a bushel. On the other hand, if they are really good works they will not be done in order that men may see them.[44] Good works are those which are done out of sheer love for God and neighbor, and he who does them is so absorbed with his concern for the object of his love that he is unaware that he is doing good works, much less concerned with displaying them to the gaze of men. He is concerned with his obligation to God and neighbor, not with his personal prestige. The good works are hidden, not from others, but from him who does them.

This explains why Saul, the proud young Pharisee who once had gloried in his own righteousness, was able after his conversion experience to speak of being "crucified with

43 *Ibid.*, 129.
44 Matt. 5:15, 16; 6:1.

Christ,"[45] counting all his righteousness as refuse that he might know Christ, sharing in His sufferings, becoming like Him in His death.[46] The greater his progress on the pilgrim road, the farther his pursuit of the way of the cross, and the richer his experience as a laborer with God, the more insignificant did his own achievements appear; so that near the close of his glorious career as the apostle to the Gentiles he was able to refer to himself as the chief of sinners whom God in His mercy was pleased to save. When compared with the mercy of God, Paul's own good works, though seen of men and a blessing to many souls, were so small that they were all but hidden from the author himself.

Such utter abandon to the way of the cross is the one and only cure for the economic materialism which is the curse of western Christendom today. The same apostle who spoke of being crucified with Christ and of pressing "toward the goal for the prize of the upward call of God in Christ Jesus,"[47] also tells us that

"There is great gain in godliness with contentment; for we brought nothing into the world, and we cannot take anything out of the world; but if we have food and clothing, with these we shall be content. But those who desire to be rich fall into temptation, into a snare, into many senseless and hurtful desires that plunge men into ruin and destruction. For the love of money is the root of all evils; it is through this craving that some have wandered away from the faith and pierced their hearts with many pangs."[48]

Material goods, food, raiment, and shelter, are intended as means to higher ends. When they become ends in themselves they are a snare and a delusion. Where to draw the line between legitimate use and unlawful accumulation may not always be easy. One thing is certain, however, we cannot serve God and mammon. He who follows the way of the cross is not anxious about his needed supply of this world's goods. He may give some thought, and he may exercise rea-

---

45 Gal. 2:20.　　　　　47 Phil. 3:14.
46 Phil. 3:7-11.　　　　48 I Tim. 6:6-10.

sonable care to provide for his own, but he is not anxious concerning his daily bread and his security for the morrow. His complete abandon to the way of the cross enlists him first and foremost in his search for the kingdom of God so that economic questions have a rating of secondary importance.

To the disciple of Christ the only comforter worthy the name is the Holy Spirit, even in a materialistic age which has degraded the concept of comfort to such a low level that this once noble word is now applied almost exclusively to a soft and downy bed cover. Knowing that even the birds of the air and the lilies of the field are cared for if only they are content to play the role which God has given them, the disciple who is crucified with Christ follows the way of the cross performing the task which God has given him, confident that the secondary things of life will be provided for without anxiety on his part. "Where your treasure is," says Jesus, "there will your heart be also."[49] And as Bonhoeffer so aptly says, if we would draw the line between legitimate use of earthly goods and unlawful accumulation we need but reverse the words of Jesus and say: "Where thy heart is, there shall thy treasure be also."[50] The disciple's heart is in the work of the kingdom. This, not economic wealth, is his treasure.

The utter abandon of self to the way of the cross means that love has taken the place of legalistic adherence to a code of regulations. "All things are lawful, but not all things build up," says Paul to the Corinthians. "Let no one seek his own good, but the good of his neighbor."[51] When you were dead in trespasses and sins, he says to the Colossians, you were constantly at war with the law in an effort to keep it through the observance of a code of rules. Since you have been raised with Christ, however, His love has taken possession of you so that out of love for your God and your neighbor you do those things which the law requires.[52] The way to keep the law is to forget it and to take up your cross and fol-

---

49 Matt. 6:21.   51 I Cor. 10:23, 24.
50 Bonhoeffer, *op. cit.*, 151.   52 Col. 2 and 3.

low Christ. Then you will no longer be tormented by legal requirements which you dislike. Paul Ramsey says you will "love and do as you *then* please."[53] This is quite the opposite of following one's own selfish will, and doing as one pleases. The Christian disciple has submerged his own will into the will of Christ. The love of Christ has taken possession of him so that now he is pleased only by doing that which responds to the will of God and which serves his neighbor's needs. Henceforth he walks not as unto himself, but with obedient "faith working through love."

The disciple of Christ has had a personal encounter with Him who is "perfect God and perfect manhood." He has personally confronted "Jesus Christ as the Lord of Life and the Sermon on the Mount as the perfect will of God." Being committed to this way, says Ramsey, the disciple of Christ undergoes the simultaneous experience of "increasing humility and increasing achievement."[54] The longer he looks into the face of his Master, the more he realizes that of himself he is only a sinner. The humility thus provoked, however, instead of pulling him down, lifts him up in gratitude to greater effort and greater achievement, without pride, since he glories only in the Lord. Thus lifted up he knows that all evil, of which war is the most typical symbol and the outstanding representative, must be completely repudiated. The advent of Christ was announced with the words: "Glory to God in the highest, and on earth peace among men with whom he is pleased."[55] The disciple of Christ believes with Charles E. Raven that this is nothing less than God's will for His children; that to regard the way of peace as irresponsibility is to repudiate Christ Himself.[56] Even as the incarnate God out of love accepted the status of sinful men and gave up His life at their hands, so must the disciple of Christ be prepared to lay down his life for his enemies. If we think the

53 Paul Ramsey, *Basic Christian Ethics*, 77.
54 *Ibid.*, 200.
55 Luke 2:14.
56 Cf. Charles E. Raven, *The Theological Basis of Christian Pacifism* (New York, 1951).

Christian life can be protected only by the hydrogen bomb, says Raven, it is time to examine our life to see if it is Christian. At the center of Christianity is not collective security but the cross. There is no resurrection without crucifixion; hence if we avoid the cross we deny the possibility of the resurrection.[57]

The heart of Christian ethics is love for the neighbor: "Let no one seek his own good, but the good of his neighbor."[58] In the story of the Good Samaritan the crucial question was, "Which of these three . . . proved neighbor to the man who fell among the robbers?"[59] The important question is not who is the neighbor, but whom do I serve as neighbor. I, the disciple of Christ, must be a neighbor. I must exercise love to those about me. Christian ethics is concerned with the neighbor's good, even as Christ gave His life for all men. Martin Luther sharpened up this great truth this way:

"Therefore, in all his works he [the disciple] should be guided by this thought and look to this one thing alone, that he may serve and benefit others in all that he does, having regard to nothing except the need and advantage of his neighbor. Thus the apostle commands us to work with our hands that we may give to him who is in need.[60] . . . And this is what makes it a Christian work to care for the body, that through its health and comfort we may be able to work to acquire and lay by funds with which to aid those who are in need. . . . I will therefore give myself as a Christ to my neighbor, just as Christ offered himself to me; I will do nothing in life except what I see necessary, profitable, and salutary to my neighbor. . . ."[61]

For the Christian who has given himself in utter abandon to the way of the cross, Christ's yoke is easy, and His burden is light.[62] The Sermon on the Mount and the entire Christian ethic are exceedingly strenuous, however, for him

57 *Ibid.*
58 I Cor. 10:24.
59 Luke 10:36.
60 Eph. 4:28.
61 Martin Luther, quoted in Ramsey, *op. cit.*, 142
62 Matt. 11:30.

who has not accepted this yoke. The original law of eye for
eye and tooth for tooth seems so harsh as to savor of barbarism. Consequently the Jews of the old covenant had softened
it down to a legalized suit for damages. This is carrying the
refinement far enough, however, for the man of the world,
even for many Christians. But Jesus goes the whole way and
forbids even legal resistance to the offender. To him who
strikes the right cheek the Christian is bidden to turn the
other also; and instead of filing suit for the recovery of his
coat, he is bidden to give away his cloak as well.[63] This is complete nonresistance, pouring out one's love without reserve,
even as Christ poured out His life completely on the cross for
His enemies. It is not nonviolent resistance which Jesus enjoins, for even this is but a technique, however mild its manner may be, to bring the enemy to the place where he will
cease to do you evil—where he will do you good. The ethic
of Jesus, however, enjoins the Christian to seek the enemy's
good, to do him good, even though the enemy may continue
to return evil for good. The disciple of Christ abandons all
claims on his brother, forgiving him unendingly, even until
seventy times seven.[64]

Jesus does not deal in broad generalities. He is pain-
fully specific. It is the neighbor's good that must be sought.
The other cheek is to be turned. We are to give to him who
asks. The Christian is to invite the poor to his house, and to
give a dinner to beggars, rather than to feast those who can
feast you again. Christ died on the cross, not that He might
thereby gain something for Himself, but that He might bring
life to men. So likewise must the disciple of Christ in his
relations with his fellow men have their welfare first in mind,
not his own.

Nowhere is the principle of nonresistance put to a sharper test than in the Christian's personal relations with his own
brethren. Military service and suits at law are institutionalized violations of the Christian ethic so obvious that nonpar-

---

63 Matt. 5:38-40.
64 Matt. 18:22.

ticipation in them can, with relative ease, be diluted to a mere legal code like that of the Pharisees, without entering into the deeper meaning of the law. Personal relations with members of his own family, however, or with members of the congregation or of the church, can not be institutionalized in the same way. Here the Christian finds himself in the midst of primary group relationships where his true character reveals itself. This is why it sometimes happens that those who are nearest to us, and whom we love most, receive the most unchristian treatment at our hands. In our organized secondary relationships the institutional code regulates our behavior in line with what we know it ought to be. In our primary group relationships, however, our real self becomes manifest. Here, if nowhere else, we really discover the extent to which we have been crucified with Christ. Here is the yardstick with which we can measure the degree to which we have given ourselves to the way of the cross. If we fail in this test it may well be questioned whether our conformity to the nonresistant way of love is genuine.

The Christian ethic is not based on rational grounds. It is rooted in the love which proceeds from the heart of the crucified, risen Lord. Therefore it is not possible to enumerate in advance all the details of conduct which that love requires. Some forms of conduct, to be sure, like carnal warfare and other types of violent retaliation, are so obviously out of line with the way of the cross that they can be ruled out with little discussion. The mere outward observance of the code is no guarantee, however, that the heart has been brought into complete subjection to the love of Christ. For this reason the Christian minister has a standing obligation, not merely to preach the strenuous ethic of Christ. More basically than this, he must warn against sin; he must bring men to the cross and lead them into experience in the way of the cross, until giving themselves in complete abandon to the love of Christ, they renounce their selfish ambitions, seeking first the neighbor's good. This is the life of the disciple. This is the way of the cross.

THE CHRISTIAN COMMUNITY: THE COLONY OF HEAVEN

The way of the cross is a way of life to be lived among people. The strenuous ethic of Jesus is a social ethic. The Christian Gospel is social as well as personal in its implications. When God became incarnate He came "down to earth," bringing the way of salvation to human society.

"Therefore to separate Christianity from social concern is to corrupt it at its roots. . . . When Jesus . . . walked the crowded ways and lovingly identified himself with the struggles and the miseries of men . . . it was a declaration that divine eternal truth and the tough concrete actualities of the human situation belong together. . . . It is an unholy divorce those Christians are aiding and abetting who separate 'spiritual' religion from such 'material' issues as feeding the hungry, rescuing the refugee, and enfranchising the racially disinherited. To prophesy smooth things, to preach a comfortable innocuous Gospel that leaves the crying injustices of life untouched, is a denial of Christ every whit as flagrant as Peter's 'I know not the man.' "[65]

The church, the body of Christ, must express the will and the purpose of God, both within and without the body. The Christian community must be a true brotherhood, its members walking in the way of the cross. It must be a continuous challenge to the world which surrounds it. The church must serve as the conscience of society, of the state, and of the social order. Paul told the Christians at Philippi they were a colony of heaven.[66] They were as a colony of settlers from another country, planted in a strange land, for the purpose of bringing to it the challenge of that better country.

The outstanding feature of the colony of heaven is its character as a community of saints knit together by the power of love. Paul, speaking to Christians of Gentile background, tells them they are no longer an alien people, but "fellow citizens with the saints and members of the household of

65 James Stewart, *A Faith to Proclaim*, 18, 19.
66 Phil. 3:20: "We are a colony of heaven" (Moffatt's translation).

God."[67] This is what the redemptive, reconciling work of
Christ does. It brings together Jews and Gentiles, Barbarians,
Scythians, slaves and freemen, white and black, brown and
yellow, the rich and the poor, the learned and the unlearned,
melting them together into one harmonious community in
Christ. If, as has been suggested, the Tower of Babel symbolizes a false religion producing confusion and disharmony,
Pentecost represents true religion bringing order out of
chaos, binding men together in love. Here were men of many
tongues and nations ranging from Mesopotamia to North
Africa and to Rome, men who did not understand each other
and whose nations had often been at swords' points. Under
the power of the Holy Spirit on that memorable day, however, they came first to know their Redeemer and Lord and
then to understand each other. Thus it was that the Lord
added together day by day those who were being saved. It
was not merely an addition of a few Gentiles to the Jewish
church. It was rather a fusion, an adding together as a literal
translation of Acts 2:47 suggests, of peoples of various tongues
and understandings into a colony of heaven.

The colony of heaven, the Christian community, is a
visible church. There have been times in history when the
church and the world were so confused that men invented
the concept of an invisible church to represent the faithful
who exist invisibly within the professing church. This concept has its value in thinking of saints who have gone to their
reward plus those on the earth, including some whose identity may not be known. Nevertheless, the picture in the New
Testament is that of a visible church on this earth, located
in a specific place, as the church at Rome, the church at Corinth, and the church at Philippi. Gerhard Kittel, in a study
of this question concludes that the Protestant idea of the
church visible and the church invisible is due to the influence of an unrealistic Platonism.[68] This view is also held

---

67 Eph. 2:19.
68 J. R. Coates (Ed.), *Bible Key Words from Gerhard Kittel's Theologisches
Wörterbuch zum Neuen Testament* (New York, 1951) 2:65.

by John Horsch, who says: "the early Mennonites held that when the church is invisible, it does not exist."[69] It has been suggested, perhaps correctly so, that the concept of the invisible church was conveniently borrowed from the pagan Plato when discipline in the church had declined to the point where the Christian and the world could scarcely be distinguished in the visible community. At any rate, the churches described in the Acts of the Apostles and in the Pauline epistles are visible communities of real people who in their harmonious relationship under the lordship of Christ constitute colonies of heaven on this earth.

In the Ephesian letter Paul uses various figures to characterize the Christian community. Its members are "fellow citizens," laboring together to promote the welfare of the divine commonwealth. They constitute the "household of God."[70] The Christian community is a heavenly family in which God is the Father, Christ is the Elder Brother, and the saints are brethren and sisters in the Lord. Or as Peter says, the saints are "living stones . . . built into a spiritual house."[71] The church is a temple in which every saint, be he Jew or Gentile, bondman or freeman, is an indispensable building stone, laid upon the foundation of the apostles and prophets, Christ Himself being the chief cornerstone. This building, with all the saints cemented together into an indissoluble union, is the "dwelling place of God."[72] This temple is the fountain of love from which alone can flow streams of healing for human society, for the social order, and for the nations.

In whatever way the New Testament writers choose to paint it, the picture of the Christian community is always one of unity, of brotherhood, and of co-operation, the individual members working together with God.[73] The church is not an association of individuals, each enjoying his personal salvation while simply using the church for whatever he can

69 John Horsch, *Mennonites in Europe* (Scottdale, 1942) 339.
70 Eph. 2:19.
71 I Peter 2:5.
72 Eph. 2:20-22.
73 II Cor. 6:1.

get out of it. Neither is the church a hierarchical society consisting chiefly of bishops and overseers. Christ did not say: Where the bishop is, there is the church; or where the conference is, there is the church. He did say: "Where two or three are gathered in my name, there am I in the midst of them."[74] This is the gathered community. This is the church: a group of saints in union with Christ, sharing in His common life.

It is true, some members of the body are assigned certain responsibilities of leadership. The only purpose of this, however, is to equip the entire body of saints for its ministerial function. Weymouth's translation of Ephesians 4:11-12 is as follows: "And He Himself appointed some to be apostles, some to be prophets, some to be evangelists, some to be pastors and teachers, in order fully to equip His people for the work of serving—for the building up of Christ's body." Phillips' translation says: "His gifts were made that Christians might be properly equipped for their service, that the whole Body might be built up." John A. Mackay insists[75] that this is the correct rendering of the passage; that the standard translations, including the Revised Standard Version, reflect an ecclesiological bias by inserting too many commas, making it read as follows: "And his gifts were that some should be apostles, some prophets, some evangelists, some pastors and teachers, for the equipment of the saints, for the work of ministry, for building up the body of Christ." This translation would make it appear that the prophets, apostles, evangelists, pastors and teachers are appointed: (1) to equip the saints; (2) to do the work of ministry; (3) to build up the body of Christ. Instead, their task is to equip the saints, in order that the saints may do the work of ministering, and that by their ministry the body of Christ might be built up. The saints are not the field of labor upon which the church leaders are to expend their energies. The leaders are to lead the

---

74 Matt. 18:20.
75 John A. Mackay, *God's Order: The Ephesian Letter and This Present Time* (New York, 1953) 149.

saints, in order that the Christian community, the colony of heaven, may expend its energies upon the general social order which is the church's field of labor.

This helps to explain the "universal priesthood of believers." Too long, says Mackay, has this doctrine been "interpreted as the mere affirmation of the rights and privileges of every Christian to approach Jesus Christ 'within the veil' and to enjoy the fullest share of spiritual blessing. It is time for Christians to become aware that priesthood means responsibility as well as privilege. . . . Members of the laity are under the same obligation as members of the clergy to be utterly Christian, to take seriously their Christian calling, and to follow in the steps of Him who said that 'He came not to be ministered unto, but to minister.' For the formation of their Christian spirit and the guidance of their Christian service, lay men and women must keep constantly before them the essential image of the Christian religion."[76]

This image, says Mackay, is found in the foot-washing scene in the thirteenth chapter of John, a scene in which Christ sums up in Himself what was "most distinctive of Israel, of manhood, and of Deity."[77] Israel had been called of God to a ministry of service to all peoples. In the incarnation God identified Himself with man. In His public ministry Christ poured out His life for His people. It was God Himself making the atonement, giving His life for man. Now, as His earthly life was drawing to a close, being intensely aware of His mission, "that he had come from God and went to God," looking back on His public ministry and forward to His death on the cross, in one dramatic moment He symbolizes the meaning of it all by girding Himself with a towel, and stooping to wash His servants' feet. "The sequel of the foot-washing," says Mackay, "and the goal of the lowliness that inspired it was the Cross. Water and a towel portray the victory of the God-man in life; a cross was His triumph in death."[78]

76 *Ibid.*, 150-52.
77 *Ibid.*, 82.
78 *Ibid.*, 82, 83.

"The physical blood which was lost by our Lord in his suffering and death, was but a symbol of real blood, of life poured out in anguish, during his whole public ministry. For, speaking in all reverence, the God-man had to qualify to be worthy of the final act of dying. . . . From the Temptation onwards to the Cross blood was literally drained from the soul of Christ. . . . To understand the Atonement let us remember that the crucified Christ who summed up in himself both God and man, summed up also in the supreme hours of his Sacrifice all that he had suffered for sin and from sin from the time that he stepped out of Jordan till the time he said, 'It is finished.' "[79]

If it is fitting and proper for Christians to memorialize the cross death of Christ by the observance of the communion service, it is equally fitting to memorialize His cross life by the observance of the foot-washing ceremony, as some Christian groups do observe it. But if the foot-washing ceremony is a fitting symbol, then the life of loving and devoted service which it symbolizes stands out all the more strikingly as the *sine qua non* of the Christian community. In the colony of heaven at Jerusalem, at Corinth, at Philippi, at Ephesus, the saints gathered for worship and fellowship and for mutual helpfulness in the material things of life. These were communities performing good works, showing forth their members as sons of God. This was as it should be, for it is the call of the Christian community to make the way of the cross effective in all of its social relations.

The members of the true Christian community have put off their old nature; they are renewed in the spirit of their minds; they speak the truth one to another, and are not deceitful; they labor with their hands that they may be able to give to those who are in need. Evil talk does not proceed from their mouths; bitterness and malice are absent; with kindness and tenderness they forgive one another. Covetousness is laid aside, and thanksgiving takes its place. They are not drunk with wine, but filled with the Spirit. Above all,

79 *Ibid.*, 86.

they are concerned for each other's welfare, and live in subjection one to another "out of reverence for Christ."[80]

One of the greatest sins of the Pharisees was their pride, their arrogance, and the condescending manner in which they regarded all who were less learned than they, or who did not occupy the seat of authority with them. They loved to enhance their prestige by having others recognize their own inferior status, saluting the superior Pharisee in the market place, and addressing him as rabbi, or master. But Jesus said to His disciples, "You are not to be called rabbi . . . . Neither be called masters."[81] In the Christian community only Christ is a master and He is the servant of all. He comes down to earth, living the cross life in submission to His fellow men. The foot-washing scene with Jesus and the towel stands as an everlasting rebuke to all who seek prestige, and who love to have others bow in reverence to them. The members of the Christian community in honor prefer one another out of reverence for Christ who is their great example in humble, loving service.

This spirit of love and subjection must be carried into every area of life. In the home, husband and wife, parents and children, live in subjection one to the other.[82] It is loving devotion and service in the name and spirit of Christ that bring husband and wife together in holy wedlock, enabling them to live for each other until parted by death. It is this same devotion which leads parents to beget and nurture children, to live and sacrifice for them, and to bring them up in the fear and admonition of the Lord. Children in turn submit to their parents, honoring them in reverence for Christ, whose spirit rules the Christian household.

Going beyond the family circle to the economic frontier the same spirit of submission prevails. The citizen of the colony of heaven does not steal from his fellow citizens. He labors, "doing honest work with his hands, so that he may

---

80 Eph. 5:21.
81 Matt. 23:8-10.
82 Eph. 5:22—6:4.

5

be able to give to those in need."[83] Employers and employees
live in subjection to each other, seeking not their own, but
each the welfare of the other.[84] Each must engage in honest
toil; but even under the complex conditions of twentieth-
century industrialism this toil must be carried on in the
spirit of love, without strife or ill will, out of reverence for
Christ who labored as the servant of all. Industrial management while entitled to a reasonable return on its investment
must first of all seek the welfare of those it serves; must do
justice in all things; must guard against every temptation
toward tyranny, even over ungrateful and inefficient employees; and must so administer its affairs as to respect and
to develop the personality of the worker. The industrial
worker while entitled to respectable working and living conditions and a reasonable wage must first of all seek the welfare
of his employer. Out of reverence for Christ he must render
a full day's work of first-rate quality. Even when management is unjust, the worker, though rightfully seeking to
improve conditions through methods of Christian love, is
never justified in doing inferior work. The Christian community does not think in terms of management and labor.
It thinks of itself as a brotherhood whose members are laborers together with God. Out of reverence for Christ who
was servant of all, in honor the members of the Christian
community prefer one another.

As the modern economy grows more highly industrial-
ized, and the social order becomes increasingly secular, the
importance of laymen and laywomen in the household of
saints becomes increasingly great. It is they who live and
work on the very frontier between the church and the world.
It is they, more than the prophet, the evangelist, or the pastor,
who must make the way of the cross effective in human relations. The prophet may proclaim the justice of God from
the housetop; and the pastor in his ministry may show forth
the way of love and mercy to the members of his flock. These

83 Eph. 4:28.
84 Eph. 6:5-9.

efforts will be fruitful, however, only in so far as the rank and file of the household of saints actually love mercy and do justice, and walk humbly with their God, making the way of the cross effective on the farm, in the shop, in the market place, in the schoolroom, and in the home. It is the body of saints who must make the way of the cross effective in the Christian community, thus enabling that community to make its impact for good and for righteousness upon the world in which it dwells. It is the citizens of the heavenly colony who must enlist as emissaries to carry the message of the cross to the outside world, planting new colonies wherever new citizens can be recruited, and thus extend the borders of the kingdom.

In this pragmatic age some practical-minded soul may well be expected to say: I understand the importance of the Christian community, but why must there be so much concern for the needs of others? Will not the needs and interests of the community be best served if each individual takes care of his own? Ramsey says that to people who think in this manner love for the other person is like two men alone on a desert island making their living by taking in each other's washing. Wouldn't it be better for each to wash his own? Ramsey replies, however, that in our complex modern economic structure men are so utterly dependent upon each other that "one man's good must serve another."[85] If this holds in the economic realm, it is infinitely more true in personal and spiritual relationships. When the colony of heaven at Corinth was torn by factionalism and fruitless controversy over personalities and secondary, even trivial issues, Paul told them that while all things are lawful for the individual, all things are not helpful for the building of the Christian community. In insisting on having his own way on these various points of controversy each one was seeking his own good. But Paul says, "Let no one seek his own good, but the good of his neighbour."[86] On another occasion he wrote

85 Ramsey, *Basic Christian Ethics*, 234.
86 I Cor. 10:24.

the saints at Galatia in a similar vein. Those who belong to Christ, he says, have crucified selfish ambitions. If a brother is overtaken in a fault, spiritual brethren should "restore him in a spirit of gentleness." The spiritual brother must examine himself, however, to make sure that none of his brother's weakness lies within himself. "Look to yourself, lest you too be tempted. Bear one another's burdens, and so fulfil the law of Christ."[87]

So revolutionary is the New Testament ethic, however, that men who have not surrendered to the way of the cross are ever substituting something of a lower value. Jeremy Bentham, utilitarian philosopher of nineteenth-century England, frankly advanced self-centered reasons for serving others. The wise statesman will, as much as possible, pursue that course which satisfies his own selfish ends. In doing so he will also incidentally serve others. If all citizens follow this course, the end result will be the "greatest happiness of the greatest number."[88] John Stuart Mill advanced a value-centered ethic, holding that when men focus their attention on the greatest value for its own sake the question of who receives the benefit from it, I or my neighbor, fades out of the picture.[89] Henry Sidgwick, another of the utilitarians, defines justice as "treating similar cases similarly," and gives love a position subordinate to that of justice. "Each one is morally bound to regard the good of any other individual as much as his own."[90]

It is obvious that each of these three approaches, whether that of self-love, love of value, or treating similar cases similarly, falls short of Paul's dictum not to seek one's own good, but that of the neighbor. Whereas utilitarian ethics gives primacy to the question, "What is the good?" Ramsey insists that in Christian ethics primacy must be given to the question, "whose good?" The good of other individuals must be regarded as *"more* than your own." "Moreover, instead of

87 Gal. 5:24—6:2.
88 Quoted in Ramsey, *op. cit.*, 237.
89 *Ibid.*, 237 ff.
90 Henry Sidgwick, *The Methods of Ethics* (London, 1913) 382.

benevolence being a sub-case of justice, for Christian ethics the reverse is true—love is always the primary notion, justice derivative, since justice may be defined as what Christian love does when confronted by two or more neighbors."[91]

It is significant that when Ramsey confines his discussion to the New Testament ethic itself he comes dangerously near to a repudiation of his own preferential ethic which is referred to in the following chapter.[92] He recognizes, or at least seems to imply, that the principle of regarding the good of others "more than your own" must be applied in the relationships of group to group and community to community as well as in the relationships of person to person. Once this point is conceded we may well ask on what grounds its application to the relationships of nation to nation may be denied. This is Ramsey's statement:

"The importance of keeping community intact can hardly be overestimated. Nevertheless, creating community among men where none now is, the task of reconciling man with man, is a still more important problem. As regards it, 'if you love those who love you . . . . And if you salute only your brethren, what more are you doing than others? Do not even the Gentiles the same?' (Matt. 5:46, 47). If you love only within societies held together by mutual self-interest, what more are you doing than others? Does not even Bentham the same? If you love only for the sake of some increment in value, loving yourselves and others alike, what more are you doing than others? Does not even Mill the same? If you follow natural rational intuition, uninstructed by Christ, in considering yourself and others each as similar 'cases' to whom distribution of goods should be given, what more are you doing than others? Does not even Sidgwick the same? These all alike assist perhaps in conserving life in community, but they can hardly bring an isolated or hostile man into community with you or you with him. 'But I say to you, Love your enemies and pray for those who persecute you' (Matt.

91 Ramsey, *op. cit.*, 243.
92 See below, pp. 60, 61.

5:44). Let love penetrate the barriers between man and man at which, by definition, all mutual self-interest halts, all concern for one another *over* concern for some good is bound somewhat to fail."[93]

Nowhere and at no time has love succeeded in breaking down so completely the barriers that separate man from man as in the case of the early Christian communities themselves. Here many individuals of varying backgrounds, and often opposing interests (Jews and Gentiles, masters and slaves), were so completely caught up in the revolutionary force of the cross-centered life and ethic that in utter forgetfulness of themselves and their previous interests they gave themselves completely to their risen Master and to their fellow saints in the Lord. Says C. H. Dodd:

"Here . . . was in actual being that holy commonwealth of God for which the ages waited. Here was a community created not by geographical accident or by natural heredity, . . . but coming into existence by the spontaneous outbreak of a common life in a multitude of persons. The free, joyous experience of the sons of God had created a family of God, inseparably one in Him: 'one person in Christ Jesus.' . . . A community of loving persons, who bear one another's burdens, who seek to build up one another in love, who 'have the same thoughts in relation to one another that they have in their communion with Christ.' . . .[94]

"In the very act, therefore, of attaining its liberty to exist, the Divine Commonwealth has transcended the great divisions of men. In principle it has transcended them all, and by seriously living out that which its association means, it is on the way to comprehending the whole race. Short of that its development can never stop. This is the revealing of the sons of God for which the whole creation is waiting."[95]

This is not to say that the Christian communities scattered from Jerusalem to Rome were communities of angels.

93 Ramsey, *op. cit.*, 243, 244.
94 This is Dodd's translation of Phil. 2:5, which is similar to that of the RSV: "Have this mind among yourselves, which you have in Christ Jesus."
95 Dodd, *op. cit.*, 140-45.

They were communities of saints, however, men and women who had been redeemed through the saving work of Christ. They were human of course, and there was stumbling and backsliding among them. It was for the redemption of men such as these that Christ came. It must also be remembered that Corinth and Ephesus were wicked cities in a pagan empire; and it was in cities such as these that the little colonies of heaven were planted. It was to the saints in immoral Corinth that Paul wrote the majestic thirteenth chapter of I Corinthians. It was the saints in Philippi who were admonished of Paul to have that same mind which was also in Christ Jesus. It was in idolatrous and materialistic Ephesus that the saints were asked to labor with sacrificial hands in order that they might be able to contribute to the welfare of the entire community. Finally, it was to the saints in Rome, the capital city of Nero's own empire, that Paul wrote those marvelous words portraying the way of the cross in love and nonresistance: "Bless those who persecute you; bless and do not curse them. . . . If your enemy is hungry, feed him; if he is thirsty, give him drink. . . . Do not be overcome by evil, but overcome evil with good."[96]

Even as Jesus gathered sinners unto Himself, so the apostle followed the example of the friend of sinners and planted the little colonies of heaven in the midst of a pagan and hostile world. It was the evil of this world that the community of saints was commissioned to overcome with good. That was the social task of the church in Paul's day; and it is the social task of the church in our own day. Christians are not called to the defensive, in a losing cause, only to be overcome of evil. They are called to the offensive, fighting the good fight of faith, overcoming evil with good—with love, nonresistance, and the way of the cross, even as Christ overcame the world by going to His cross.

While the social implications of the Gospel are numerous and detailed the fact still remains that the primary contribution which any man can make to the society in which

96 Rom. 12:14-21.

he lives is simply to be a Christian. In the third century Origen declared that it is Christians who are "the salt of the earth," and that they "are benefactors of their country more than others."[97] In recent times Arthur E. Holt, looking back through the pages of history, makes this significant remark: "The more one thinks about the early Christian communities and the Roman Empire, the more one is convinced that the only piece of permanent social building was that carried on by the Christian community in the face of the Roman Empire."[98] Elton Trueblood's books, especially his *The Predicament of Modern Man* and the *Foundations for Reconstruction*,[99] demonstrate in a remarkable way the absolute necessity of obedience to the Ten Commandments, with all their social implications, for the saving of our twentieth-century civilization. Power culture has failed. Individual religion, even individual Christianity if there is such a thing, is insufficient for the needs of our day. The crying need of our time is a "redemptive society" of saints which like those of the early Christian communities will establish little colonies of heaven in every corner of our world; thus with the spirit of evangelism and the Christian "habit of adventure" to bring the pagan, materialistic world of our day face to face with the claims of Jesus Christ and the way of the cross in human relations.

97 *Ante-Nicene Fathers* (Roberts and Donaldson, Editors, New York, 1925) 466, 468 (*Origen vs. Celsus*, 8:70, 73-75.

98 A. E. Holt, *Christian Roots of Democracy in America* (New York, 1941) 129.

99 D. Elton Trueblood, *The Predicament of Modern Man* (New York, 1944); *Foundations for Reconstruction* (New York, 1946).

THE WAY OF THE CROSS
IN CHRISTENDOM

3. THE MEDIEVAL CONCEPT

Christians are called to the way of discipleship, following the steps of Christ. This is not a call to be undertaken lightly. Personal egoism and the love of power are so deeply ingrained in human nature that only the redeeming love of God can bring about the surrender of the self to the point where it is willing and able to go the way of the cross. Returning good for evil, turning the other cheek, is not the way of sinful nature. It is the way, however, of those who have been crucified with Christ and who are risen with Him. To the early Christians discipleship meant crucifixion and martyrdom. It has meant the same to countless saints and martyrs since that time, even during the twentieth century. The disciple must ever be prepared for this if need be.

Since the time of the so-called conversion of Constantine, however, followed by a virtual identification of the church with the state and the invasion of marginal men and women into the church, those members of the church who follow the way of costly discipleship have been greatly outnumbered by those who regard this way as something which is not intended for this present world. Many say they are caught between the Christian ethic of love and the Christian sense of public responsibility, and that the greater their understanding of these two forces the greater their perplexity grows. It seems taken for granted that he who sincerely advocates the way of the cross must be lacking in an understanding either of what Christian love actually is, or of what social responsibility requires, or of both. Even if we knew what God's will is at any given moment, they affirm, it would be difficult for us to do His will. The perplexity is virtually insurmountable, however, we are told, because it is so difficult to know what that will is. The dilemma is implicit in Romans 13 itself where

Paul accepts the state as God's instrument for order in this world; and the more complex the disorders of our modern world become, the more necessary it is for the Christian to do that which is evil.[1]

It must be granted that when Jesus commanded His disciples to live the good life in an evil world He did not give them an easy task. He never claimed it to be such. Discipleship involves suffering and the cross. "If any man would come after me," says He, "let him deny himself and take up his cross and follow me."[2] "Blessed are you when men revile you and persecute you and utter all kinds of evil against you falsely on my account. Rejoice and be glad, for your reward is great in heaven, for so men persecuted the prophets who were before you."[3] These are not soft words; but neither are they spoken as if they were not meant to be kept. The early disciples understood that they were meant to be kept, and so did the Christian Church for nearly three centuries. What is more, they did keep them. The early church was a brotherhood in which those who were united in Christ dwelt together in love, following the way of the cross.

As soon as Christians began to find the way of the cross too difficult, however, their casuistic treatment of Christian ethics also began. With the secularization and the materialization of the church came its compromise with the state. The way of the cross was never lost sight of completely, but it was gradually modified to meet the exigencies of the new social situation. The first step in the modification of the New Testament ethic seemed innocent enough, in that it emphasized the importance of unselfishness on the part of the individual. Ambrose and Augustine both denied the right of the individual to defend himself, but upheld his right to protect or defend others, or to fight for the general welfare of society. To follow anything but a policy of nonresistance when oneself alone is involved would be selfishness. When others are

---

1 See John C. Bennett, *Christian Ethics and Social Policy* (New York, 1946) ch. 2.
2 Matt. 16:24.
3 Matt. 5:11, 12.

involved, however, unselfishness on the part of the individual requires a preferential ethic of protection.[4] At this stage in its development the nonresistant love of the New Testament was still the basis of medieval social ethics, the important modification being the idea that love required the protection and defense of the neighbor. While the way of the cross still required the individual to sacrifice himself out of love for his personal enemy, it now also required the individual to sacrifice himself out of love for, *and in defense of,* neighbors and brothers when they were confronted with their enemies.

In the high Middle Ages, however, when the kingdoms of the earth had supposedly been gathered up into the kingdom of Christ, the ethics of Aristotle and the corresponding theory of natural law were also accepted by scholastic theology to such an extent that they came to occupy the central position, while the nonresistant love of the New Testament was forced to play an increasingly secondary role within the Christian ethic. This assimilation of pagan philosophy by Christian thought has produced a theology enabling Roman Catholicism ever since to be more optimistic about man and the quality of the social order than the New Testament warrants, or the Protestant Reformers were able to admit. Society was no longer regarded as evil and its members spiritually dead, necessitating their resurrection into the kingdom of God or the colony of heaven. The social order was thought of rather as being sick, and as quite capable of restoration to health through the ministry of the church with which it had come to be identified.

Since this Christian society was sick, however, not all of its parts could be expected to function in a perfect manner. At the same time there were many saints with extraordinary spiritual health who were able and who were expected to maintain the strenuous ethic of love, nonresistance, and brotherhood which the New Testament proclaims. To these sensitive souls not only the sordid ways of the evil world, but even the normal and necessary engagements of everyday life,

---

4 Cf. Paul Ramsey, *Basic Christian Ethics* (New York, 1950) 172 ff.

were unholy occupations which must needs be avoided. Thus it was that within the universal church of western Christendom there emerged a dual system of ethics, providing two levels of Christian life. On the lower level was the mass of Christians who accepted the standards of the worldly society, including participation in "just wars" for the defense of the commonweal. On the higher level lived the special class of holy people, the priests, the monks, and the nuns who accepted the ascetic ideal, and whose holy life provided a vicarious substitute for the substandard Christianity of the worldly Christians of the lower level.

The holy class did not participate in war, not even in a just war. Its members gave up all personal property, whereas the ordinary Christian held property even as a man of the world; and yet not entirely as a man of the world, for it was to be held with a different inner attitude, "as if he had it not." Commerce and trade occupied a low position in the medieval ethic. The charging of interest was forbidden as a violation of the principle of Christian brotherhood. Loans were to be made for the purpose of helping the brother in need; not for the purpose of profit. It would seem that the medieval ethic was more strict in the economic area than in the area of the state and participation in war. If this is correct it is probably so because in the medieval world the Christian encountered fewer ambiguities in the economic order than he did in the political order, a situation which probably does not hold in the twentieth-century world. The simplest rural economy devoid of complicated ambiguities was not only the ideal; it was an ideal which found expression in the natural economy of the time, far more so than in imperial Rome in the time of the early church.

The dual ethic also carried over into the realm of sex and family relations. Sex life and the married state, that of the woman especially, had a low ethical rating, with a resulting general tendency to degrade womanhood. The ascetic ideal on the other hand which led many women as well as men into the monastic orders offset this tendency, while the worship of the Virgin Mary elevated womanhood to a very high place. Thus, while the married state rated a low ethical position, the elevation of womanhood through the Virgin and the sisters in the convent had a wholesome effect on family life and helped raise it to a high level.

Since in medieval society there was a sociological consolidation of the church with the social order, and since the actual forms of social life with the exception of the feudal wars approached the ecclesiastical ideal, the tension between the church and the social order which characterized the early church period was largely overcome. The lower level of society represented natural law in general. The upper level represented a mystical supernature pointing toward the blessedness of the future state. This made possible a new theory which recognized the value of the world while at the same time defining the limits of its claim. Thus the radical religious ethic was maintained as a goal to be aimed at, while at the same time lesser values were also drawn into the approved Christian pattern as a lower and preparatory stage. The Christian ethic became relative, while the radical Christian ideal itself was preserved.

Since society was regarded not so much dead as sick, it was thought of as in need of healing and progress toward a higher ideal. This progress was to be achieved under the direction of a patriarchal organism, the church. The lower classes were to be humble and grateful. Because of the fall the ruling classes must be paternalistic and exercise love and care. If paternalism were removed the way would be open for revolution; hence the patriarchal idea helps to keep the social order conservative. Catholicism does not condone the class struggle. The only conflict it recognizes is the conflict of truth and love against selfishness and error, all of which is kept under control by the paternalistic system.

The early church had regarded the social order as evil and incapable of being reformed, whereas the medieval church regarded it as the divinely appointed harmony of nature and grace which needed only the authority of the patriarchal church to make it secure. For the achievement of this task the monastic institutions always came to the rescue to perform vicariously that which the lower preparatory stage of the social order was unable of itself to achieve. Moreover, since the political order with its feudal wars was that aspect of the total social order farthest removed from the Christian ideal there developed an elaborate theory of the just war in which the moral responsibility for decisions was taken out of the hands of the individual and assumed by the church. The state, under the direction of the church, was responsible for the commonweal. When war was necessary for the defense of the state it was a just war, politically speaking; and from the point of view of the patriarchal church it was not sin. True, this required the suspension of the divine absolute will. Since the church with its papal head was the vicar of God on earth, however, the responsibility for this suspension was in the hands of God, not in the hands of man. Thus the individual was saved from the problem of the relation of the Christian ethic to the ambiguities of public life. The church did it for him; and his failure to measure up to the divine absolute will was overcome by the meritorious works of the holy class on the upper level of society and by the saving grace of the seven sacraments.[5]

5 For penetrating insights into the developments here discussed see Ramsey, *op. cit.*, and Ernst Troeltsch, *The Social Teaching of the Christian Churches* (London and New York, 1931) Vol. 1.

4. THE REFORMERS

Although the Reformation objected vigorously to the medieval division of the body of Christ into upper and lower moral strata, with the holy class at the upper level living vicariously for the worldly Christians beneath them, the Reformers nevertheless continued the concept of a universal church coinciding with the social order as a whole. This meant the acceptance of a sub-Christian social order; and for Luther the result was a dual ethic somewhat different from that of Romanism, but a dual ethic nevertheless. Luther had a high spiritual conception of religion. He represents not only a revival of salvation by faith, but also a renewed understanding of the primacy of Christian love. He saw clearly that resistance of an enemy and litigation, for example, were out of harmony with the Sermon on the Mount. He therefore hesitated on the use of force, but accepted it when it became clear that his ideal of a universal church could not be maintained without it. He therefore founded a state church, while continuing his ideal of subjective personal piety.

The result of this was the transfer of the medieval ethical tension "from the social community into the anguished breast of the individual Christian."[1] Since secular institutions, including the state, are ordained of God, the individual as a citizen must play his part in them, although as a Christian he must maintain the New Testament ethic. Thus the individual becomes a dual personality, a Christian and a citizen, a member of the colony of heaven and a member of the sub-Christian social order. He belongs to two orders with conflicting ideals and he must live at home in each of them. In

1 *Peace Is the Will of God: A Testimony to the World Council of Churches* (A statement prepared by the Historic Peace Churches and the International Fellowship of Reconciliation, Zeist, Holland, 1953) 10.

4

historic Lutheranism the organic element of Catholicism dis-
appears. The church simply brings men to faith in God.
Lutheranism "has no conception of the church as an ethical
organization of Christendom as a whole."[2] It submits to the
social order passively, neither rejecting it as the sectarian
does, nor becoming a determining factor in it as Calvinism
does. It is not active politically; it has no scheme of social
reform; and historically it has been of least social significance
among the major Christian types.

With his reversion to the Sermon on the Mount and the
nonresistant ethic of love, Luther found himself in practical
agreement with Ambrose and Augustine of the early Middle
Ages rather than with Aquinas of the scholastic era. He did
not defend his distinction between the individual and the
public ethic as a concession to sub-Christian society. He defended it rather as a distinction between what is right when
the Christian alone is involved, and what is right when responsibility to others is involved. That is, love for the enemy
forbids the Christian to defend himself when attacked by the
enemy; but this same love for others requires him to protect
the neighbor even with force when the neighbor is attacked.
Such protection is the purpose of the state and this is why the
Christian must do the bidding of the state when it calls him
to military service.

"As concerns yourself, you would abide by the Gospel
and govern yourself according to Christ's word, gladly turning the other cheek and letting the mantle go with the coat,
when the matter concerned you and your cause. . . .

"For in the one case you consider yourself and what is
yours, in the other you consider your neighbor and what
is his. In what concerns you and yours, you govern yourself
by the Gospel and suffer injustice for yourself as a true Christian; in what concerns others and belongs to them, you govern
yourself according to love, and suffer no injustice for your
neighbor's sake."[3]

2 Troeltsch, *op. cit.*, 2:540.
3 Martin Luther, *Secular Authority: To What Extent It Should Be Obeyed*
(*Works* 3:241, 242) quoted in Ramsey, *op cit.*, 185, 186.

Luther's view of the Christian ethic as here stated is also related to his view of natural law as mentioned in chapter I.[4] It was his view that the Decalogue and the Golden Rule are founded on the order of creation, and that their requirements are lodged in the conscience. As said before this view is supported by Paul when he says that the "Gentiles who have not the law do by nature what the law requires," thus showing that "what the law requires is written on their hearts."[5] The Pauline doctrine as followed by Luther may be thought of as a doctrine of "natural law" in the sense that it is a law which operates within the order of God's creation. It is quite different from the Greek view, however, which being largely based on pantheism was inclined to regard natural law as self-existent and self-determined rather than the creation of a supernatural, holy, and righteous creator. It was the assimilation of the Greek view by medieval theology which helped Catholicism to develop its optimistic view of the social order, and which enabled it to condone the sub-Christian ethic of those in the lower stratum of the Christian society. The Pauline doctrine of natural law revived by the Reformers, on the other hand, contained within itself the strict ethic of love and nonresistance.

What Luther, following Ambrose and Augustine, failed to see, however, was the Scriptural distinction between the natural and the supernatural orders for the correction of injustice.[6] Through the order of creation even the "natural man" understands the evils of injustice and proceeds to correct them by means characteristic of those who to a large degree have lost the image of God. The Christian, however, to whom the image of God has been restored through the reconciling work of Christ, seeks the correction of injustice through the supernatural order, the way of the cross. In interpreting the Christian ethic of love as forbidding the Christian to defend himself when attacked, while requiring him to protect

---

4 See above, p. 16.
5 Rom. 2:14, 15.
6 See above, pp. 17-21, 60.

the neighbor even with violence when the neighbor is threatened, Luther had not departed from the Scriptural doctrine of natural law as expressed in the order of creation. He did, however, allow the ambiguities of the social order as identified with his universal church to modify the Christian ethic of love so as to permit the use of violence in the defense of the neighbor. In so doing Luther, with Ambrose and Augustine, took the first step toward the rejection of the strict ethic as impracticable in a complex and ambiguous world in which the Christian is assumed to have responsibility for others. If a Christian has such responsibility for others how can he discharge this responsibility if he allows an enemy to destroy his life? Is he not obligated, therefore, by his love for family and those for whom he is responsible, to defend himself? So runs the argument; and when this point is reached the strenuous ethic of love and nonresistance is gone. It was a halfway house on this road that Luther erected for the Christian Church.

Having stated the double standard of Lutheranism for personal and public life, it would obviously be unfair to leave the impression that this double standard is characteristic of all that goes under the name of Lutheranism. John C. Bennett has reminded us that this is not characteristic of Scandinavian Lutheranism, and that many American Lutherans would reject it, although this attitude is encouraged by Lutheran theology. Bennett quotes the following statement from Paul Althaus, a German Lutheran theologian, rightfully challenging it as a dangerous doctrine: "Christianity has neither a political program, nor any inclination to control or censure the political life in the name of Jesus and the Gospels."[7]

Those of the Anabaptist tradition would agree with Lutheranism in declining to control the political order, but they would certainly be more in accord with Calvinism on the matter of censure. Never to censure is always to acquiesce, and this neither the Scriptures nor Anabaptist teaching would

7 Paul Althaus, *Luther in der deutschen Kirche der Gegenwart* (1940) 24-26, quoted in Bennett, *op. cit.*, 53.

condone; for the time eventually comes when Christians must draw the line of moral demarcation and say with the apostles: "We must obey God rather than men." Many times in the history of the church has the theology of the double standard signified approval or even active support of the most heinous practices. Bennett rightfully says: "Whatever may be the difficulty in applying the ethic of Jesus to political life, to withhold Christian criticism of social policy is to open the door to complete autonomy of a pagan or cynical political ethic."[8]

This dangerous position is seen in those Lutherans of Germany who in the name of Christ and the church supported the Hitler regime, or even those who supported uncritically the first World War. The following quotation from Frederick Naumann, a Lutheran of Germany during the first World War, illustrates the point:

"The Gospel is one of the standards of life, but not the only standard. Not our entire morality is rooted in the Gospel, but only a part of it. Besides the Gospel there are demands of power and right without which human society cannot exist. . . . The state rests upon entirely different impulses and instincts from those which are cultivated by Jesus. . . . Not every doing of one's duty is Christian. . . . Hence we do not consult Jesus, when we are concerned with things which belong to the domain of the construction of the state and of Political Economy."[9]

As said before, however, many Lutherans would reject this view. Moreover, during the second World War many German Lutherans actually departed from this tradition and broke with the state. A few took their stand for the nonresistant position and the way of the cross, although most of them no doubt went over to something more like the Calvinist position in an attempt to bring a change in the existing social order through the use of force.

---

8 Bennett, *op. cit.*, 53.
9 Quoted in Ray H. Abrams, *Preachers Present Arms* (New York, 1933) 71.

CALVIN

Because of its basic theological assumptions Calvinism and the Protestant groups of the Calvinist tradition have been of greatest significance as a social force in the western world. Of all the Reformers John Calvin was the greatest systematic theologian and developed the most complete theory of God's moral law and of its operation in human society. He saw most clearly the requirements of justice and righteousness, as found in the order of creation and taught in the Scriptures; and he understood the wrath of God as a corrective for injustice through the operation of the natural law and the agency of the state. Unfortunately, however, he failed to see that the Christian is not called to serve as an agency of the divine wrath. Human vengeance was recognized as unscriptural to be sure. In Calvin's view, however, the individual Christian who serves as a magistrate for the enforcement of law and order is not exercising the vengeance of man, but the vengeance of God. To Calvin, therefore, the administration of violence and punishment, even of the death penalty, is permissible to the Christian. So likewise is defensive warfare.

Calvin was familiar enough with the Anabaptist teaching that the shedding of blood is contrary to the will of God for the Christian. He had an answer to this objection, however, as follows: "If we understand, that in the infliction of punishments, the magistrate does not act at all from himself, but merely executes the judgments of God, we shall not be embarrassed with this scruple."[10] That section of the Sermon on the Mount setting aside the law of eye for eye and tooth for tooth, and commanding the Christian who is smitten on the cheek to turn the other also,[11] was interpreted as simply forbidding a desire for retaliation. This requires patience and a readiness to suffer injuries and reproaches. Calvin even goes so far as to say that Christians should be "so calm and

10 John Calvin, *Institutes of the Christian Religion* (Seventh American Edition, Philadelphia, 1936) 2:782.
11 Matt. 5:38, 39.

composed in their minds, that, after having suffered one affliction, they may prepare themselves for another, expecting
nothing all their lifetime but to bear a perpetual cross." He
also quotes Paul with approval when he says Christians must
"overcome evil with good."[12] Then he hastens to say, however, that this does not preclude, in the interest of the public
good, the bringing of a "pestilent offender to justice, though
they know he can only be punished with death."[13]

Calvin, like the other Reformers, rejected completely
the Thomistic dual ethic. What he did, however, was to re-
vert to the preferential ethic of Augustine which sanctioned
warfare and the use of force for the defense of others and for
the general welfare of society. Nonresistance and the way of
the cross is the correct way when the individual alone is involved. When others are involved, however, or even for the
good of the offender himself, the use of violence as a preferential ethic of protection is required. Calvin quotes with
approval the words of Augustine when he says that New Testament admonitions to love one's enemies "relate to the internal affection of the heart more than to the external actions;
in order that in the secrecy of our minds we may feel patience
and benevolence, but in our outward conduct may do that
which we see tends to the advantage of those to whom we
ought to feel benevolent affections."[14]

From this vantage point Calvinism developed a doctrine
of "sphere sovereignty," which teaches that human society
consists of distinct areas or spheres, such as the church, the
state, the family, education, or labor, each serving God
through the operation of its own inherent laws. According
to this view both the church and the state exist for the welfare
of sinful man, each contributing to his redemption, although
in different ways. The state is the agency of God's common
grace, which comes as a natural development within the order
of creation. The church, on the other hand, is the agency of

12 Rom. 12:21.
13 Calvin, *Institutes*, 2:794.
14 *Ibid.*, 2:794.

God's special grace, which is supernatural, having its origin outside the created universe.[15] At this point Calvinism and Lutheranism come very close together, in that each has two spheres, the church and the state, within both of which the individual Christian must operate. There is a difference, however. Luther's two spheres operate under opposing and contradictory principles, making the individual Christian a dual personality with a dual ethic.

The Calvinist spheres, on the other hand, operate under similar and complementary principles making for an integrated ethic on the part of the participating Christian. The church admonishes, warns, and persuades, with the assistance of the Word of God. In later Calvinism it became a voluntary brotherhood of love. It leads on to spiritual holiness. The state, on the other hand, deals with law and order, houses and lands, money and crops, food, guns, and ships. Its membership is compulsory and it restrains sin by the use of the sword. The Christian citizen may freely participate in these various functions since such of its methods as are out of harmony with the way of the cross in personal relations are necessary in public relations; it is only by these means that the third party or the general welfare can be defended and protected. Love and the way of the cross requires the individual to suffer at the hand of the enemy or even to lay down his life when he alone is concerned. Responsibility for the third party, or for the general welfare, however, requires action against the enemy even with force and violence if need be.

While original Calvinism favored a union of church and state, such as existed in Geneva and in colonial New England, the modified Calvinism of a later day favors a separation of church and state. While it believes that the state should be operated by Christians who defend and protect the interests of the church, the strictest Calvinism today does not believe that the church as an organized body should reach into the sphere of the state. Political pronouncements on the part of the church should be sparingly made, if at all; neither should

15 See C. Van Til, *Common Grace* (Phila., 1954).

there be much official interference by the church organization in such areas as education and labor. In other words, it is not the calling of the church to engage in various forms of social action. Individual Christians who are the children of the church, however, have an obligation to social action to the end that the general social order may as far as possible be Christianized. It is by this approach that Calvinism has been and still is a mighty force within the social order.

The social power of Calvinism derives from its theology. God is a majestic God who requires strict holiness on the part of man. Inasmuch as the Calvinist is one of God's elect, his salvation is settled and sure. He need not, as in the case of Lutheranism or Pietism, devote his time to a search for inner peace. His task is to show proof of his salvation; to reveal and to demonstrate his new creation. To achieve this task he is driven into the work of the world, charged with the responsibility of maintaining a holy society ordered to the glory of God. In its political aspect this has meant a state governed by righteous principles.

In spite of its original austerity Calvinism has always had a bent toward democracy. The Geneva government was actually republican in form. Beza found sovereignty to reside in the people, and his writings include the idea of the social contract and responsible rulers. To be sure, this is not the rationalistic social contract of John Locke, which springs from society itself. It is rather a covenant in which God constitutes one party, and the ruler and people the other, as in the case of the Old Testament covenant. This is not a philosophy which permits men to do as they please. It is a system in which the righteous govern by Biblical rule; but it also is a system in which the people do not bow to the dictates of a mere king. The king himself is bound by the Biblical rule, and when he exceeds his authority the people may exercise the right of rebellion, for God rules mediately through His people. The movement for independence in eighteenth-century America cannot be understood without taking into account the influence of Calvinism in New England and elsewhere. It is true that Franklin and Jefferson received much of their revolutionary inspiration from the eighteenth-century enlightenment; but if these Revolutionary leaders had not had a "prepared" people to appeal to, they would have been only empty voices in a barren wilderness. As it was, many of the people had been prepared for the Jeffersonian leadership by five generations of democratic indoctrination from Calvinist pulpits.[16]

For every legitimate work of this world Calvinism has meant diligence, thrift, and intense labor in the devotion of the individual's talents to the glory of God. Being one of the elect there was no question that he possessed the talents; and not to employ with success that with which God had endowed him would be to repudiate his heavenly calling. Before leaving for Massachusetts, therefore, John Winthrop said that "if he should refuse this opportunity, that talent which God hath bestowed upon him for publick service were like to be buried."[17] To the Calvinist businessman this point of view has meant discipline, frugality, and hard work. The primary objective of this diligence has been not so much the enjoyment of the fruits of his labors as it has the achievement of great things for the glory of God. This attitude and way of life has been referred to as a "worldly asceticism"; and as a characterization of the earlier Calvinism this is no doubt an apt expression. It is a well-known fact, however, that the hard-working, frugal ways of one generation frequently lay the economic foundation which enables future generations to become prosperous, wealthy, and materialistic, not to the glory of God, but rather for their own aggrandizement, and often at the expense of the general welfare. While Calvin certainly would have disapproved of many practices which have characterized modern capitalism, and of fortunes which have been amassed at the expense of the common man or

16 For a discussion of religious factors in the movement for American independence see Alice M. Baldwin, *The New England Clergy and the American Revolution* (Durham, 1928) and W. W. Sweet, *The Story of Religions in America* (New York, 1930) ch. 12.

17 Quoted in V. L. Parrington, *Main Currents in American Thought* (New York, 1930) 1:39.

even perhaps of unfortunate peoples in other parts of the world, the social and economic historians seem nevertheless to be on pretty safe ground when they hold that the social dynamic inherent within Calvinism has made a contribution to the development of the spirit of modern capitalism.[18]

This social dynamic was characteristic not only of sixteenth-century Calvinism; it has continued and remains true even of neo-Calvinism, both the conservative and the liberal varieties, of our own time. Certain types of nineteenth-century Calvinism, for example, showed a tendency to form organizations and societies for the promotion of pacifism, humanitarian rights, philanthropy, antislavery, feminism, and other reforms for the advancement of social justice. In the twentieth century Calvinistic influence is certainly evident in that type of Christian social strategy which John C. Bennett describes as tending to identify Christianity with particular social programs.[19] The social gospel of a generation ago had its Calvinistic roots; and the contemporary Christian Action school with its tremendous emphasis on social responsibility draws much of its strength from the same source.

18 For the influence of Calvin on the rise of capitalism see Troeltsch, *op. cit.*, Vol. 2; Max Weber, *The Protestant Ethic and the Spirit of Capitalism* (London, 1930), and R. H. Tawney, *Religion and the Rise of Capitalism* (New York, 1926).
19 Bennett, *op. cit.*, 46-51.

5. THE SOCIAL GOSPEL

Reference was made above to the social dynamic of Calvinism in both its earlier and later forms. At Geneva it was Calvin's purpose to establish a holy society, a kingdom of God on earth. This idea was brought to America by the Puritans and was shared by the Quakers and others who followed them. Seventeenth-century American Christianity had a social message. The details of its ethics varied to correspond with the different types of theology represented by the churches; but the fundamental nature of the kingdom as conceived by early American churchmen was the same. It was a kingdom into which men were brought, one by one, by the process of personal conversion. Once in the kingdom they lived as disciplined citizens under the sovereignty of God. Says H. Richard Niebuhr: "It was the rule of self-restraint in lives which had become repentant of their evil tendency."[1] This was the tradition of the American churches which continued until the middle of the nineteenth century. The Great Awakening, from Jonathan Edwards to Charles G. Finney, maintained an interest in Bible study combined with a conviction that the way of life taught in the Scriptures must be manifest in the life of the disciple. "The reign of Christ [was] . . . a rule of the knowledge of God."[2]

The era of Finney in the middle third of the nineteenth century was also the age of the common man, which witnessed the introduction of numerous social reforms, such as anti-slavery, peace, temperance, prison reform, and others. While it would be unfair to give the evangelists all the credit for these achievements, it is certain that the reforms of the era were in part the fruit of the great revivals. Finney preached

1 H. Richard Niebuhr, *The Kingdom of God in America* (New York, 1937) 105.
2 *Ibid.*, 110.

judgment upon the sin of slavery and pleaded with slaveholders to repent of their ways in preparation for the wrath to come. He did not preach mere individual salvation. Once men were converted and brought into the kingdom it was their duty to go forth "with all their hearts to search out all the evils in the world, and to reform the world, and to drive out iniquity from the earth. ... Religion is something to do, not something to wait for."[3] Finney was president of Oberlin College, the first coeducational college in America; and the progressive program and reforms associated with this institution are evidence enough that the statement quoted here was no mere set of empty words.

By the middle of the nineteenth century, however, the second Great Awakening had about run its course, and secular forces were slowly but surely gaining control of the American mind. John Calvin had insisted that the businessman must be honest because this is what God requires. In the eighteenth century, however, Benjamin Franklin was approving honesty as the best policy; and in the gilded age following the Civil War it seems that at least some businessmen were not sure that it was even the best policy. At any rate the exuberant prosperity of the new country with its unbounded opportunities, and a continuous flow of mechanical devices ministering to convenience and comfort, cast such a materialistic spell over the average American that if he thought of the kingdom of God at all he conceived it as a paradise of material delights. Since America was a chosen nation especially favored of God, why look any farther for the kingdom? The idea of progress advanced by the eighteenth-century philosophers was verified by nineteenth-century evolutionary optimism; and if the kingdom was not already here it was rapidly on its way. Judgment and catastrophe were outmoded ideas. Progress was the watchword. Man and human nature were good. There was therefore no need for repentance. Christ the Redeemer had become merely Jesus the teacher. "To be

3 Quoted in Liston Pope, "Religion as a Social Force in America" *Social Action* (May 1953) 19:6:8.

reconciled to God," says H. R. Niebuhr, "now meant to be reconciled to the established custom of a more or less Christianized society." It was a naive optimistic religion: "A God without wrath brought men without sin into a kingdom without judgment through the ministrations of a Christ without a cross."[4]

This new theology, as it was called, appealed to refined and wealthy Americans who wanted a religion which would leave them feeling comfortable, their complacency undisturbed, as they worshiped man and his material achievements. "Believe in yourselves and reverence your own human nature," said Phillips Brooks; "it is the only salvation from brutal vice and every false belief."[5] Those who practice this gospel are sure to prosper and need not concern themselves too much about those who are less fortunately situated. True, poverty merits our concern, but "actual suffering for the necessities of life, terrible as it is, is comparatively rare." At any rate, a certain amount of inequality is good; and if we will only let natural harmony have its way, the social problems of the world "will get settled somehow."[6]

The attitude of the Protestant clergy toward wealth and toward their poverty-stricken fellow men in the gilded age seems strange indeed alongside the admonitions of the prophets and the commands of Christ. Henry Ward Beecher, a "prince of the pulpit," was able to brush off the plight of the striking railway workers with the statement that a family unable to live on a dollar a day is not fit to live. At the same time Beecher was noted for his own showmanship and extravagant living. His handsome income from newspaper revenue and other sources besides his ministerial salary enabled him to indulge in fancy horses, and in handfuls of uncut gems which he carried in his pockets. The lack of good taste, not to speak of the distance which the ministry could go in its departure from the way of the cross portrayed in the New

4 Niebuhr, *op. cit.*, 181, 193.
5 W. S. Hudson, *The Great Tradition of the American Churches* (New York, 1953) 164.
6 *Ibid.*, 166.

Testament, is seen in the following "testimonial" advertisement which carried the heading, "Henry Ward Beecher's Opinion of *Pears'* Soap."

"*Cleanliness* is next to Godliness. Soap must be considered as a means of *grace* and a clergyman who recommends *moral* things should be willing to recommend soap.

"I am told that my recommendation of *Pears'* Soap has opened for it a large sale in the *United States.*

"I am willing to *stand by every word in favor of it, I have ever uttered.* A man must be fastidious indeed who is not satisfied with it."[7]

In those days the defense of wealth by the Protestant clergy seems to have been taken for granted. In 1885 Noah Porter, president of Yale, said God has given man the duty to acquire property, and to defend it, once it is his.[8] James McCosh of Princeton said: "God has bestowed upon us certain powers and gifts which no one is at liberty to take from us or to interfere with. All attempts to deprive us of them is theft. Under the same head may be placed all purposes to deprive us of the right to earn property or to use it as we see fit."[9] A widely used textbook on Christian ethics published in 1875 declared: "By the proper use of wealth man may greatly elevate and extend his moral work. It is therefore his duty to seek to secure wealth for this high end. . . . The Moral Governor has placed the power of acquisitiveness in man for a good and noble purpose . . . ."[10] Ralph Gabriel thinks the mood of the American middle class can be measured by the great popularity of Russell H. Conwell's famous lecture, *Acres of Diamonds.* Said Conwell, a Baptist minister of Philadelphia: "To secure wealth is an honorable ambition, and is one great test of a person's usefulness to others." Poverty, on the other hand, is a mark of sin. "To sympathize with a man whom God has punished for his sins, thus to help him

7 Quoted in *ibid.,* 178.

8 Noah Porter, *Elements of Moral Science* (1885) 362, 368, quoted in R. H. Gabriel, *The Course of American Democratic Thought* (1940) 147.

9 James McCosh, *Our Moral Nature* (1892) 40, quoted *ibid.,* 147.

10 D. S. Gregory, *Christian Ethics* (1875) 224, quoted *ibid.,* 148.

when God would still continue punishment, is to do wrong, no doubt about it . . . ."[11] In 1900 Bishop Lawrence of Massachusetts said: "In the long run, it is only to the man of morality that wealth comes . . . . Godliness is in league with riches. . . . Material prosperity is helping to make the national character sweeter, more joyous, more unselfish, more Christlike."[12]

These views and attitudes were so extreme, however, that they were bound to bring a reaction. The industrial revolution and the rapid urbanization which accompanied it were manifesting so many unwholesome features that many Christian leaders began to challenge the thesis of the morality of the rich and the sinfulness of the poor. The sweatshop, child labor, women in industry at starvation wages, and endless processions of men "out of work, out of clothes, out of shoes, and out of hope," caused more than one city pastor to conclude that something was wrong with a social order which produced such bitter fruit. As a result there emerged a new attitude toward the social order in most of western Christendom, an attitude which has affected Catholicism and all branches of Protestantism, both in Europe and America. While this new point of view expressed itself in various ways, depending on the religious group, the country, and the time, in general it recognized: (1) that continuous change in the social order is to be expected; (2) that the church has an obligation to make the Gospel meaningful and effective in this changing society; (3) that the church has a special obligation toward oppressed and neglected classes and races of people.

The most radical expression of this new point of view took the form of what came to be known as the social gospel, an American movement which got under way about 1865 and reached its zenith about 1915. While the movement included many sincere and sensitive souls who earnestly

---

11 R. H. Conwell, *Acres of Diamonds* (1890) 19, quoted *ibid.*, 149, and in Marquis W. Childs and Douglass Cater, *Ethics in a Business Society* (A Mentor Book, New York, 1954) 137.
12 Quoted in Gabriel, 149, 150.

sought to make the Christian ethic effective in industrial society, it is unfortunate that the basic theology of the social gospel was frequently no different from that of the liberal clergymen who spoke comforting words to the rich and the powerful. The social gospel did not think of the church as a colony of heaven within the sinful society as did the Apostle Paul. It was Calvinistic in its approach in that society as a whole was to be governed by Christian principles. It was a departure, however, from original Calvinism: (1) in its optimism, which assumed that everything within the social order would readily become Christian; (2) in the method by which the Christianization of the social order was to be achieved.

Central to the social gospel was its identification of the kingdom of God with the Christianized social order which Jesus supposedly had come to establish. The kingdom of God was not the church. It was not a holy society bringing judgment on the sinful social order after the manner of Edwards and Finney. At most the church was a fellowship for worship within the kingdom. Jesus was the founder of a new society providing for all human needs, which the law of human progress, undergirded by the newly discovered theory of evolution, was now surely bringing into fulfillment. The abolition of slavery was not an act of repentance. It was merely one stage in the evolution of the kingdom, after which the next stage would come. "Now that God has smitten slavery unto death," said Edward Beecher at the close of the Civil War, "He has opened the way for the redemption and sanctification of our whole social system."[13] To many of the social gospelers, however, redemption and sanctification meant nothing more revolutionary to the individual than a proclamation of "the glad tidings of progress." "What Christ meant to [Henry Ward] Beecher," says Winthrop S. Hudson, "was never wholly clear."[14] He had much to say about the noble

[13] Quoted in C. H. Hopkins, *The Rise of the Social Gospel in American Protestantism, 1865-1915* (New Haven, 1940) 9.
[14] Quoted in Hudson, *op. cit.*, 172.

example, the king of love, or the spiritual presence; but an examination of his sermons shows that he had never preached on "the passion and death of Christ upon the cross."[15] Lyman Abbott, Beecher's successor in Plymouth Church, said frankly: "We do not ask what men believe."[16]

Newell Dwight Hillis, Abbott's successor, followed the same line.

"Better times are coming. Good will is taking the place of hate. Even labor and capital are becoming better friends. Peace is going to succeed war. Wealth is becoming the almoner of universal bounty. Statesmen are trying to right the wrongs of the oppressed . . . . Literature is sharpening arrows against injustice . . . . Never were the libraries filled with wiser books; the press is sowing the land with the good seed of wisdom and knowledge . . . . For centuries the democracy of Jesus has slowly leavened the people, but the time is not far off when with one accord every knee shall bow, and every tongue confess that Jesus Christ is Lord . . . ."[17]

It is unfortunate, indeed, that a movement which saw so clearly the social implications of the Gospel should have gone so far astray in its theological assumptions. "Happy believers in divine benevolence and human goodness . . . ," says Hudson, "the majority of the preachers of the new theology found it difficult to conceive of a church which did not embrace humanity indiscriminately . . . . They believed that the mission of Christianity was largely accomplished."[18] This being the case, what real need was there for a church? William Newton Clarke's *An Outline of Christian Theology*, leading textbook of the new theology, did not even include a discussion of the church; and Hudson says that if the author had been asked about the omission he would likely have replied "that the proper place to discuss the church was in sociology, not theology."[19] If there was no need for the church, what need was there for Christ the foundation of the church or for the God who was in Christ?

15 *Ibid.*, 173.
16 *Ibid.*, 172.
17 *Ibid.*, 179.
18 *Ibid.*, 194.
19 *Ibid.*, 203.

"For anyone living in the troubled mid-twentieth century," says John A. Hutchison, "it is hard to comprehend the widespread acceptance of so blandly hopeful a faith a brief fifty years ago."[20] While much was said of social reforms to come, sin was ignored, and the "preliminary pessimism which the great religions of the world have all presupposed as their premise" was repudiated.[21] There was no cross death in the New Testament sense, much less the cross life which is a fruit of the new creation which follows the reconciling work of God who was in Christ. Hudson says: "It was as if God had been 'naturalized' and invited . . . 'to give a weekly editorial commentary' on the vagaries of a society, in the image of which he had been made."[22] Thus it would not be far wrong to say that the theological era prior to the first World War was a kind of fool's paradise in which it was believed that, "with the ever-kindly but often vague help of God, man could make his way by continuous progress into that ideal society which the social gospel called the kingdom of God."[23]

While this would seem to be a fair characterization of the movement as a whole, the story would not be complete without special reference to Walter Rauschenbusch, the greatest prophet of the social gospel. Rauschenbusch had an understanding of the social implications of the Christian faith beyond that of any of his contemporaries; and those aspects of the social gospel which have survived as of permanent value were largely his contribution. In this sense he was the best representative of the era. At the same time he had so much in common with the earlier evangelicals, such as Finney, or perhaps Edwards, that Winthrop S. Hudson calls him "a lonely prophet,"[24] atypical of his own age. Paradoxically, this atypical quality is what enabled him to be the best

20 John A. Hutchison (ed.), *Christian Faith and Social Action* (New York, 1953) 10.
21 W. L. Sperry, quoted in Hudson, *op. cit.*, 194.
22 Hudson, 194.
23 Hutchison, *op. cit.*, 10.
24 Hudson, *op. cit.*, 226.

representative of his era and to make his contribution one of permanent value.

Rauschenbusch was born in 1861 and was graduated from seminary in 1886, after which he became pastor of a small German Baptist Church in New York City, where his ministry to the people of the working class, victims of industrialism at its worst in the gilded age, provided the material for the development of his social message. From 1897 to the time of his death in 1918 he was a member of the faculty of Rochester Theological Seminary, where his father had taught before him. In the midst of his ministerial and professional duties he found time for several interludes of study and travel in Europe, which also made their contribution to the development of his concept of social Christianity. Rauschenbusch was influenced by the writings of Henry George, whose *Progress and Poverty* was published in 1879. While traveling in England he was much impressed by the co-operative movement in that country. He also followed the economic thought of Richard T. Ely and Franklin H. Giddings. Being greatly influenced by socialism he became a severe critic of the capitalist system, especially as expressed in the monopolistic corporations of the time, which he described as "an unregenerate part of the social order, not based on freedom, love, and mutual service, as they are, but on autocracy, antagonism of interests, and exploitation."[25] He called for a new economic order characterized by social justice, collective property rights, industrial democracy, approximate equality, and co-operation. Specifically, he proposed measures to limit the hours of labor, to increase wages, to protect the worker against accident and disease, to provide better housing, and to improve the care of the aged. Before this could be accomplished, however, he believed it necessary to socialize such natural resources as coal and iron and to convert all natural monopolies into public property. "My whole desire has been," he said, "to summon the Christian passion for justice and the

25 Quoted in Hopkins, 223.

Christian powers of love and mercy to do their share in redeeming our social order from its inherent wrongs."[26]

Rauschenbusch lived in the era when the theologies of
Schleiermacher, Ritschl, and Harnack were making their
greatest impact. He was born two years after the publication
of the *Origin of Species*; and when he began his ministry
Herbert Spencer was at the height of his influence. Rauschenbusch was too much a child of his age not to be deeply
influenced by these forces. Thus it is that nowhere in his
writings can one find a clear commitment to the doctrine of
the deity of Christ, or of the Incarnation as taught in the
Pauline writings. There is no question that Rauschenbusch
recognized the existence of sin and a kingdom of evil, but he
was content to leave Satan as a figure of speech; and he
referred to the "blessed skepticism of the age of Enlightenment and the dawn of modern science which saved humanity
from the furies of a theology which had gone wrong."[27]
While much is said about the need for redemption from sin,
both personal and social, the writings of Rauschenbusch
treat the atonement and the resurrection of Christ, and the
meaning of His life and death, in such a manner as to leave
with a deeply unsatisfied feeling those who find in the Gospel
message the way of the cross in human relations. When he
denounces the hypocrisy of the orthodox churchman who
amasses a fortune at the expense of his fellow men, he strikes
a chord to which we respond with gladness and sympathy;
but when he refers to heresy as a lesser evil,[28] a sinking feeling
comes to one's heart, especially if the heresy has to do with
the person and work of Christ which is the source of power
for the way of the cross.

On the other hand, Rauschenbusch did not share the
naive optimism of his contemporaries. He was more like a
prophet warning America of impending doom unless there is
repentance from the collective sins of the nation.

26 *Ibid.*, 215.
27 Rauschenbusch, *A Theology for the Social Gospel* (New York, 1917) 83-86.
28 *Ibid.*, 53, 54.

"The continents are strewn with the ruins of dead nations and civilizations. History laughs at the optimistic illusion that 'nothing can stand in the way of human progress.' It would be safer to assert that progress is always for a time only, and then succumbs to the inevitable decay. One by one the ancient peoples rose to wealth and civilization . . . and then began to decay within and to crumble away . . . . What guarantee have we, then, that our modern civilization with its pomp will not be 'one with Nineveh and Tyre'? . . .

"Will some Gibbon of Mongol race sit by the shore of the Pacific in the year A.D. 3000 and write on the 'Decline and Fall of the Christian Empire'? If so, he will probably describe the nineteenth and twentieth centuries as the golden age when outwardly life flourished as never before, but when that decay, which resulted in the gradual collapse of the twenty-first and twenty-second centuries, was already far advanced.

"Or will the twentieth century mark for the future historian the real adolescence of humanity, the great emancipation from barbarism and from the paralysis of injustice, and the beginning of a progress in the intellectual, social, and moral life of mankind to which our past history has no parallel?

"It will depend almost wholly on the moral forces which the nations can bring to the fighting line against wrong, and the fighting energy of those moral forces will again depend on the degree to which they are inspired by religious faith and enthusiasm. It is either a revival of social religion or the deluge."[29] These words were written seven years before the first World War; and when that holocaust finally came Rauschenbusch was not at all sure that these gloomy words were not in process of fulfillment. He was not swept away by the lighthearted thought that this was a Christian crusade for the ending of all wars.

Rauschenbusch believed that the cause of national decay is sin, and that sin consists primarily of selfishness and injus-

---

[29] Rauschenbusch, *Christianity and the Social Crisis* (New York, 1907) 279-86.

tice. In a day when others were making light of the idea of sin he declared his own belief in "original sin." True, he did not seem to be sure whether original sin stemmed from Adam's fall or from man's untamed animal nature. He was sure, however, that something was wrong with man and that this wrong was being transmitted from generation to generation, both biologically and by social transmission in the customs and institutions of society.[30] His writings are devoted to a call to repentance from sin and a turning to salvation. He recognized "the sinfulness of every human heart . . . and power of God to save every soul that comes to him . . . . Salvation of the individual is . . . an essential part of salvation. Every new being is a new problem of salvation. It is always a great and wonderful thing when a young spirit enters into voluntary obedience to God and feels the higher freedom with which Christ makes us free. It is one of the miracles of life."[31]

The great emphasis of Rauschenbusch's teaching, however, was that the concept of salvation must be enlarged. If the social order is sinful, then this must also be saved and redeemed; thus he had much to say of "social salvation." Many of his statements concerning social salvation appear to be an exposition of the way of the cross in social relations as set forth in the New Testament. He recognizes nonresistance as an essential part of Christ's teaching and of his conception of life.[32] Frequently he seems to approach the Anabaptist view of the social order, calling for a colony of heaven, a society of the redeemed, who make the way of the cross effective in all of their human relations. Indeed, Rauschenbusch seems to have been deeply influenced by the Anabaptists. "While the great churches were bitterly contending" over the nature of the Lord's Supper, he says, "the persecuted Anabaptists, who had neither the right to meet nor to exist, . . . returned to the original spirit of the Lord's Meal and realized

30 Rauschenbusch, *A Theology for the Social Gospel*, 57-72.
31 *Ibid.*, 5, 95.
32 *Ibid.*, 263.

that Real Presence about which others wrangled."[33] He recognized this Real Presence among them as the power which gave the Anabaptist communities their prophetic quality, making them forerunners of the modern world, standing "against war, against capital punishment, against slavery, and against coercion in matters of religion before others thought of it."[34]

The following statement of "social salvation" reads almost like a nineteenth-century version of sixteenth-century Anabaptist doctrine.

"If sin is selfishness, salvation must be a change which turns a man from self to God and humanity . . . . Complete salvation, therefore, would consist in an attitude of love in which he would freely co-ordinate his life with the life of his fellows in obedience to the loving impulses of the spirit of God, thus taking his part in a divine organism of mutual service. When a man is in a state of sin, he may be willing to harm the life and lower the self-respect of a woman for the sake of his desires; he may be willing to take some of the mental and spiritual values out of the life of a thousand families, and lower the human level of a whole mill-town in order to increase his own dividends or maintain his autocratic sense of power. If this man came under the influence of the mind of Christ, he would see men and women as children of God with divine worth and beauty, and this realization would cool his lust or covetousness. Living now in the consciousness of the pervading spiritual life of God, he would realize that all his gifts and resources are a loan of God for higher ends and would do his work with greater simplicity of mind and brotherliness."[35]

When Rauschenbusch says that the experience of Moses at the burning bush led him to the social task of delivering his people from bondage and when he says that Isaiah and Jeremiah were used of God to bring the way of salvation to

33 *Ibid.*, 205, 206.
34 *Ibid.*, 195, 196.
35 *Ibid.*, 97, 98.

their nation we readily give our assent. But when he speaks of social institutions as "lost" and "saved" one is compelled to raise a question.

"Super-personal forces are saved when they come under the law of Christ . . . . A state which deals with those who have erred in the way of teaching, discipline, and restoration, has come under the law of Christ and is to that extent a saved community . . . . A change in penology may be an evidence of salvation . . . . The fundamental step of repentance and conversion for professions and organizations is to give up monopoly power and the incomes derived from legalized extortion, and to come under the law of service, content with a fair income for honest work. The corresponding step in the case of governments and political oligarchies, both in monarchies and in capitalistic semi-democracies, is to submit to real democracy. Thereby they step out of the Kingdom of Evil into the Kingdom of God."[36]

According to the New Testament the kingdom of God is a brotherhood of individuals who have renounced the sinful world, and who have experienced individual salvation through faith in Christ. It is to this brotherhood of saved individuals that Jesus spoke the Sermon on the Mount and the doctrine of nonresistance. If a community is Christian it is because its members are Christian and follow the way of the cross in their social relations. Many of the social gospelers ignored the need for personal regeneration altogether, and devoted their energies entirely to the reconstruction of the social order, the community, the city, the state, and the international world. Since evil is the result of an unfavorable environment, they would change the environment, making it difficult to do evil, so that men would be Christians as a matter of course. Evangelism in the New Testament sense was ignored, the church becoming an agency for social reform, believing that when co-operatives, democracies, and decent housing had replaced private enterprise, monarchies, and slums, the kingdom of God would have arrived.

36 *Ibid.,* 113, 117.

To be fair to Rauschenbusch, however, it must be said that he did not go as far in this direction as some of the lesser social gospelers did. His understanding of sin was too deep to permit its dismissal as a mere environmental influence. His program for the Christianization of the social order included individual repentance from wrong attitudes and practices, and an entrance of the individual into a life of obedience to God. "The greatest contribution which any man can make to the social movement is the contribution of a regenerated personality . . . . The fundamental contribution of every man is the change of his own personality."[37] One cannot dispel the feeling, however, that his gospel of social salvation was vitiated in the first place by a low view of Christ, of the Incarnation, and of the Atonement. A man completely surrendered to the will of God can indeed be a great prophet and a mighty leader in the work of the kingdom. Our historic faith tells us, however, that Jesus was more than a man, yes more than a prophet with a message from God. He was God Himself, speaking with authority from heaven; and every creative age of the church has been characterized by a deep consciousness of this great truth. The theology of Rauschenbusch, however, is lacking in this dimension.

In the second place, one cannot escape the feeling that in Rauschenbusch's scale of values God and the divine are given too low a rating while that given to man is relatively too high. After all, Jesus said the first and great commandment is to love God, while love for one's fellow men comes second, and "is like it."[38] Rauschenbusch says, however, that "to love men . . . is an avenue to the living experience of God,"[39] and cites Biblical teaching to support his view: "He that loveth not his brother whom he hath seen, how can he love God whom he hath not seen?"[40] The fact is, of course, that these two commands are inextricably intertwined so that one cannot keep

37 Rauschenbusch, *Christianity and the Social Crisis*, 351, 412.
38 Matt. 22:37-39.
39 Rauschenbusch, *A Gospel for the Social Awakening* (edited by Benjamin E. Mays, New York, 1950) 125.
40 I John 4:20 (KJV).

the one without keeping the other also; and the nontheological mind might be excused if it does not fully succeed in placing them in proper order. It must not be forgotten, however, that in Biblical teaching the Christian's union with God is brought about as a result of the divine initiative in the first instance. It is the love of God as expressed in the self-emptying act of Jesus Christ which comes down and draws all men into Himself, and makes them capable of loving their fellows. It is not man's search through devious mountain paths, not even the noble path of human love, that leads him upward to the reality of God. Hence Rauschenbusch's statement, even though it contains an element of truth, does not ring quite true when he says: "It is by loving men that we enter into a living love for God. Social work may be a gateway to conscious religion. . . . There may be other paths that lead to him, such as the solitary search for truth, or the lonely way of mystic contemplation. But love is the surest way with fewest pitfalls. . . ."[41]

In the third place, despite his acceptance of personal regeneration and the rejection of the naive optimism of his contemporaries, the frame of reference for Rauschenbusch's kingdom of God was the general social order itself, rather than the New Testament colony of heaven. The emphasis was on a redeemed society rather than on a society of redeemed men, and the difference between these two concepts is a real one. Here again there is so much truth to what Rauschenbusch says that in laying the finger on his error one must needs take care lest he reject the good with the bad; or to use a Biblical figure, lest he pull up the wheat with the tares. When Christ told His disciples, "Ye are the salt of the earth," He did give expression to "a great historic mission to the whole of humanity."[42] Truly the Christian Church is the salt of the earth, the conscience of society, or whatever figure we may choose to express the idea. Surely the moral and ethical impact which Christianity has made upon western civilization has been nothing short of marvelous. Alongside of our vaunted material progress, the value of which is in many ways questionable, there has been genuine moral progress, especially in the area of social ethics. And there can be no doubt that this is largely the fruit of the Christian witness and its impact upon society as a whole. Were it not for the church and its influence the character of our sinful social order and of western civilization would be far less desirable than it is at present.

There is so much truth to this that the following outburst of Rauschenbusch is understandable: "If at this juncture we can rally sufficient religious faith and moral strength to snap the bonds of evil and turn the present unparalleled economic and intellectual resources of humanity to the harmonious development of a true social life, the generations yet unborn will mark this as that great day of the Lord for which the ages waited, and count us blessed for sharing in the apostolate that proclaimed it."[43]

Had Rauschenbusch's Christology and his eschatology been more Biblical, however, this statement would have been tempered and the author's vision more realistic. This dream, he says, "is not one tenth as hopeless" today as it was in the time when Jesus first announced it. "Under the circumstances at that time it was an utterance of the most daring faith,—faith in himself, faith in them, faith in what he was putting into them, faith in faith."[44] Indeed, if Jesus was only a "Nazarene carpenter speaking to a group of Galilean peasants and fishermen,"[45] this was a daring venture. If what has occurred in Christian history these 1900 years, however, is but a religious version of evolution, Jesus and His kingdom are on a lower level by far than the triumphant church of Jesus Christ portrayed in the New Testament. Evolution, says Rauschenbusch, "has prepared us for understanding the idea of a Reign of God toward which all creation is moving. Translate the evolutionary theories into religious faith, and

43 *Ibid.*, 422.
44 *Ibid.*, 415.
45 *Ibid.*, 415.

you have the doctrine of the Kingdom of God."[46] In the final analysis this view puts the whole kingdom idea on the human level, although admittedly God is back of it.

Happily, however, Jesus was more than an inspired prophet with faith in Himself and His followers. He was the Incarnate Son of God who had emptied Himself of His heavenly prerogatives to demonstrate the way of love and the cross in His life and in His death, in order that there might be one in whom men could have faith. He did not have faith in Himself. He was the Faithful One with authority not only to teach the way of the cross, but with power to create bornagain saints equipped to follow the way of the cross. It is this community of saints in subjection to the lordship of Christ which constitutes the kingdom of God. It is this kingdom which is the salt of the earth, the conscience of society, of the state, and of the social order. To the extent that men have come under the rule of the kingdom and in their ethics have accepted the way of the cross, to that extent the social order has been and will continue to be Christianized. Until Satan and his hosts have been destroyed, however, and sin rooted out of the earth, the general social order and the kingdom of God cannot be identical.

The eschatology of Rauschenbusch, however, required the identification of the kingdom and the social order, here and now. The Christian hope must be restored to theology, but it is a hope based on development, not upon catastrophe. "The future development of the race should have a larger place in practical Christian teaching. . . . As to the way in which the Christian ideal of society is to come,—we must shift from catastrophe to development. . . . An eschatology which is expressed in terms of historic development has no final consummation. Its consummations are always the basis for further development."[47]

Here again, there is much truth to what he says. The kingdom of God has experienced development in the past,

---

46 Rauschenbusch, *Christianizing the Social Order* (New York, 1912) 90.
47 *A Theology for the Social Gospel*, 223-27.

and it may be expected to do so in the future. Rauschenbusch's rejection of naive optimism also gives a necessary
warning that the development of the kingdom does not take
place without conflict and disappointment. "At best there is
always but an approximation to a perfect social order. The
kingdom of God is always but coming."[48]

Even though this theology of development is cautiously
stated it is nevertheless carried so far that it eliminates the
Biblical doctrine of the *Parousia* and of the Last Judgment.
Indeed, if there was no Christ who came from heaven and
returned to heaven, how could He come again in the *Parousia?* The evolution of a naturalistic kingdom cannot be disturbed by such supernaturalistic intervention. And yet, even
Rauschenbusch's eschatology warns us of an end to the earthly phase of His kingdom through the natural process of age
and decay. "Our race will come to an end in due time; the
astronomical clock is already ticking which will ring in the
end."[49] This would seem to be catastrophe enough, even
though realized only by degrees. As between this "hope" of
a slow but sure demise through naturalistic processes and the
hope of the glorious appearing of the King Himself finally to
bring all things under His lordship and to establish the kingdom in its fullness, the latter scheme would seem not only to
have New Testament theology on its side, but a satisfying
sense of well-founded Christian optimism as well.

In many ways Rauschenbusch seems to be very close to
the way of the cross in his social ethics. He refers to the nonresistance of Jesus.[50] He speaks of the cross: "Let the Church
of Christ fling in, not the sword, but the cross, not against the
weak, but for them!"[51] Salvation, he says, brings men together as the children of one Father, whereas sin divides men
"in war and hate, in pride and lies, in injustice and greed."[52]
Again, he says: "The sense of equality is the only basis for

48 *Christianity and the Social Crisis,* 421.
49 *A Theology for the Social Gospel,* 227.
50 *Ibid.,* 263.
51 *Christianizing the Social Order,* 39.
52 *Ibid.,* 327.

Christian morality"[53]; the Christian will regard all men as equals before God, be they black or white.[54] He recognizes that Jesus had superseded the customary ethics of Judaism in His insistence that the moral law of God must be fulfilled.[55] He has a keen insight into the collective sins of our society, pointing out how organizations formed for a good purpose "drift into evil under sinister leadership, or under the pressure of need or temptation . . . . A trade union fights for the right to organize a shop, but resorts to violence and terrorizing; a trust, desiring to steady prices and get away from antiquated competition, undersells the independents and evades or purchases legislation. This tendency to deterioration shows the soundness of the social instincts, but also the ease with which they go astray, and the need of righteous social institutions to prevent temptation."[56]

As mentioned above,[57] Rauschenbusch was impressed by the extent to which the Anabaptists had achieved a holy society, with righteous social institutions, which had succeeded in conquering collective sins within their own brotherhood. In spite of the fundamental difference between Anabaptism and the modern social gospel in their conception of the kingdom of God and its relation to the social order, Rauschenbusch admits that it is only sectarian groups such as they that have succeeded in making the principles of the kingdom effective in their way of life:

"The platform for ethical progress laid down in the Sermon on the Mount is a great platform. . . . Yet its fate is tragic. . . . Only small sections of the Christian Church have taken the sayings on oaths, nonresistance, and love of enemies to mean what they say and to be obligatory.[58]

"Only those church bodies which have been in opposition to organized society and have looked for a better city

53 *Christianity and the Social Crisis*, 247.
54 *The Social Principles of Jesus*, 27, 28, 33, 38, 39.
55 *Ibid.*, 89.
56 *A Theology for the Social Gospel*, 72.
57 See pp. 87, 88
58 *The Social Principles of Jesus*, 89. 90.

with its foundations in heaven, have taken the Sermon on the Mount seriously."[59]

Rauschenbusch was so near to the way of the cross and yet so far from it. There were conflicting elements in his thinking on the nature of the kingdom which was the heart of his theology. From one point of view he stands in the tradition of the earlier pietists and even of the American evangelicals with their emphasis on a holy society of men born into the kingdom through the supernatural experience of regeneration. From another viewpoint he was the heir of Anabaptist tradition which interpreted the kingdom as a holy society of redeemed men and women who took upon themselves the way of discipleship, in obedience to the Sermon on the Mount and the way of the cross. From yet another point of view, however, he was also the child of his own naturalistic age to such an extent that in many ways the foundations of these two great traditions were destroyed.

Despite his personal loyalty to the Sermon on the Mount which was given to men whom Christ had called out of the world, and which Rauschenbusch says has been taken seriously only by those who have stood in opposition to the social order, his own frame of reference remained the general social order. The admittedly sinful social order and the kingdom were identical. Despite all that he said about regeneration and the miraculous character of the kingdom, he nevertheless virtually identified the coming of the kingdom with the process of natural evolution. Even though he warned against a naive optimism, and had much to say about the sinful nature of the social order, the evolutionary philosophy which he endorsed virtually required the inevitability of progress, so that the inability of his contemporaries to take his words of caution seriously is not surprising.

Finally, despite his emphasis on the Sermon on the Mount, on love, and even at times on the cross, his concern for the achievement of social justice was nevertheless so great that in the final analysis the demand for justice stands out in

59 *A Theology for the Social Gospel,* 134.

sharper relief in his writings than does the doing of justice.
Jesus consciously cast His lot with the common people and
the poor, says Rauschenbusch: "He gave them a faith, a hope
of better days, and a sense that God was on their side . . . .
He saw them over against 'the rich' . . . took sides with the
group of toil. He stood up for them. He stood with them.
We cannot help seeing him with his arm thrown in protection about the poor man, and his other hand raised in warning against the rich. . . . It seems hard to escape the conclusion that Jesus was not impartial between the two."[60]

Great as the element of truth in this statement may be,
and severe as Jesus' denunciation of the selfish rich certainly
was, there is yet another dimension which Rauschenbusch
overlooks. This is the dimension of nonresistance, of self-
emptying, of the suffering of injustice rather than to violate
the law of love. In short, the dimension which is missing is
the cross life of Christ which led to His death on Calvary and
which constitutes the pattern of life for His disciples today.
With this all-important dimension missing, the ethic of the
kingdom is watered down so that ultimately the demand for
justice takes precedence over the doing of justice; Christian
nonresistance becomes Gandhian nonviolent resistance; and
the way of the cross becomes the class struggle. The divergence between Rauschenbusch and the way of the cross seems
inconspicuous, and at times it is almost indiscernible. It is
certainly not as great as the divergence between the way of
the cross and the preaching of many of his contemporaries;
but even so the ultimate result is two roads leading in radically different directions.

We return now to the social gospel as a whole to observe
some further developments, particularly its later history.
Although there was much pacifism within the movement, it
was a type of pacifism which looked for the elimination of
war through the operation of the law of progress and the
Christianization of the social order. As a rule it did not produce conscientious objectors who took their stand for the law

60 *The Social Principles of Jesus,* 39, 40.

5

of Christ and the way of the cross in the face of a society given to militarism. When the war came in 1914 many of the social gospel pacifists were caught off guard since they were not expecting a major war to occur. They recovered their composure, however, when they were assured that this was the war which would end all wars. Since it was merely one of those obstacles which the pilgrim on the progress road inevitably encounters, the best must be made of it. This point of view made it relatively easy for men like Newell Dwight Hillis and Harry Emerson Fosdick to support the war, and it helps to explain why many churchmen of the social gospel school virtually turned their pulpits into recruiting stations for the army.

Rauschenbusch died in 1918, at the age of 57. It is impossible to say what his final course would have been had he lived another fifteen years. We know, however, that during the war itself he was not overcome by the hysteria of the time. We also know that the disillusionment which followed the war, when it was discovered that the great crusade had not ended war as it was supposed to do, made for a generally better record on the part of the clergy and the churches during the second World War. Some who remained pacifists now became real conscientious objectors, as in the case of Fosdick. Others who finally rejected pacifism, as in the case of Reinhold Niebuhr, did so with a sobered theological outlook which at least enabled them to recognize war as the sin which it is instead of calling it a fulfillment of the Sermon on the Mount as some had done in 1918.

Present-day theologians of the Christian Action school have been very critical of social gospel pacifism, regarding it as shallow in its outlook, failing to understand both the towering heights of New Testament love and the abysmal depths of human evil. Especially have they charged it with watering down Christ's law of love to a mere nonviolence, which may not be Christian at all. Whereas Ambrose and Augustine justified participation in war for the defense of the neighbor and denied the right of self-defense, modern pacifism frequently does the exact opposite, denying the right to participate in war for the defense of the nation, while justifying litigation or other forms of nonviolent coercion for purposes of self-defense. The Augustinian position, says the Christian Action school, is an unselfish one, and therefore Christian, whereas certain forms of modern pacifism are essentially unchristian, for two reasons: (1) self-defense means a pursuit of self-interest, rather than a concern for the neighbor; and (2) refusal to participate in warfare for the national defense may be grounded on a horror for violence and bloodshed, which may also indicate a stronger love for oneself than for the neighbor. At any rate, they say, such a view has more in common with Indian religious ethics than with the Sermon on the Mount. In this they are no doubt correct.[61]

The Christian Action school has also charged social gospel pacifism with a lack of realism in race and industrial relations: It assumed that capital and labor, or black and white, in a sub-Christian social order would love each other sufficiently to obviate the use of force for the realization of justice. In apparently giving unrestricted endorsement to the cause of organized labor, the social gospel was certainly throwing its support to the underdog who was at that time the greatest sufferer of injustice in our industrial society. In doing so, however, it was condemning injustice on the part of industrial management without at the same time showing forth the way of the cross as the Christian way for both management and labor.

In an evaluation of the movement it must also be recognized that the social gospel came far short of accomplishing all that it had set out to do. Liston Pope says the movement "was largely middle class in character, urban in setting, and almost exclusively clerical in leadership. It never made really successful contact with the labor movement or with any large segment of the population other than middle class liberals. It relied principally on preaching, education methods, discussion groups, and fugitive publications to transform a society

61 See Ramsey, *Basic Christian Ethics*, 182, 183.

headed increasingly toward power conflicts and mass up-
heavals."[62] The social gospel did, nonetheless, make a lasting
impression. Churches were awakened to new ethical responsibilities; seminaries were led to revise their curricula; and
the movement gave support to secular reforms of various
kinds. Moreover, most of the larger denominations were led
to give official recognition to the social implications of the
Gospel by appointing social service agencies or social action
commissions. The first such agency of importance was the
department of Church and Labor of the Board of Home Missions of the Presbyterian Church in the United States of
America. In 1903 Charles Stelzle, a native of New York's
East Side, became superintendent of this department. Stelzle
had worked for eight years as a machinist, then studied at
Moody Bible Institute, after which he held successful pas-
torates in working-class congregations in several of the larger
cities. In 1910 he organized the Labor Temple in New York
City.

Following the organization of the Federal Council of
Churches in 1908 that body appointed a Commission on the
Church and Social Service, which concerned itself with the
problems of the working man and other social concerns of the
church. Four years later the report of the commission called
upon the churches to take their stand for humanitarian measures and reforms, such as the abolition of child labor; regulations for the safeguarding of the health of working women;
the protection of society from the evils of the liquor traffic;
and provision for the old age of workers and for those inca-
pacitated by injury. The report called for a new emphasis
on the application of Christian principles to the acquisition
and use of property, and for other reforms. The principles
of this report were widely adopted by Protestant denominations and were not modified by the Federal Council until
1932.

By the time that the social gospel cause was taken over
by the denominations and the Federal Council, the social

62 Liston Pope, loc. cit., 12.

gospel movement as such had about run its course. Rauschenbusch died during the war. Then after the war the movement began to break up, its leaders going in divergent directions, although the tradition was continued by Bishop McConnell, Charles Clayton Morrison of the *Christian Century,* and others. A few of the former social gospelers went so far to the left as, for all practical purposes, to exchange their religious faith for that of communism. Some gave up the ministry to enter the professional field of sociology. Others enlisted their energies in specialized types of social reform, such as pacifism, socialism, or prohibition. Some, like Reinhold Niebuhr, while retaining their social passion, gave it a more sober theological orientation and became leaders in the new theological movement commonly known as neo-orthodoxy. Others, like J. B. Matthews and Stanley High, moved even farther to the right socially and repudiated completely their former position.[63]

63 See *ibid.,* 10, 11.

6. CHRISTIAN ACTION

The dominant school of thought in higher theological circles in America today commonly known as neo-orthodoxy, or crisis theology, stands in the succession of the social gospel. It has cast aside the old optimism based on the idea of progress and the natural goodness of man; and it has moved to the theological right far enough to recover an orthodox anthropology and a doctrine of sin. Its weakness, as this writer sees it, is an insufficient emphasis on redemption, on the power of the Holy Spirit, and on the lordship of Christ. As in the case of the social gospel, the neo-orthodox theologians have identified themselves with the general social order, and their thinking is with that orientation. The difference is that whereas the social gospel would transform the nearly sinless kingdoms of this world into the kingdom of God with such ease that the help of God was barely needed in the process, their successors are so involved in the ambiguities of the hopelessly sinful social order that even God Himself is not powerful enough to enable a penitent soul to do more than to confess his sin and then keep on sinning.

In 1930 a group of disillusioned social gospelers under the leadership of Reinhold Niebuhr organized the Fellowship of Socialist Christians. The fact that they called themselves socialist Christians rather than Christian socialists indicates their attempt to find a more solid theological base for their socialism. By 1947 they had concluded that socialism was no real cure for the ills of society, and adopted a new name calling themselves the Frontier Fellowship. This does not mean, however, that the group had become socially reactionary. It remained severely critical of those sections of American Protestantism associating themselves with "Spiritual Mobilization, Christian Economics, and other movements

102

which identify the will of God with American destiny and *laissez-faire* capitalism with Christian freedom of spirit,"[1] and it regards itself as prophetic in the tradition of Amos and Isaiah. Since 1951 the movement has been known as Christian Action. In general, Christian Action criticizes the social gospel as shallow and unrealistic, in that it fails to comprehend "the towering heights of the New Testament ideal of love and the abysmal depths of human evil." Social justice in industrial and race relations can be achieved only with much greater effort and with more compulsive means than the social gospel had assumed to be necessary. Social gospel pacifism is criticized for assuming that Christianity is merely a matter of following Jesus; for scaling down the strict New Testament ethic of nonresistance to mere nonviolence; and for its blindness to the operations of egoism in human society. Thus the Christian Action group has rediscovered the Biblical evaluation of fallen man as a sinner. What has not been rediscovered, however, is the power of God unto salvation and redemptive living for the sinner who has been reconciled to Christ.

The secret for this failure seems to be the fact that the Christian Action group, and neo-orthodoxy in general, has chosen the sinful social order as its frame of reference for social action rather than the New Testament ethic itself. Paul Ramsey, for example, finds "in Jesus Christ perfect God and perfect manhood, the essential nature of the divine and the essence of human moral maturity." He acknowledges "Jesus Christ as the Lord of Life and the Sermon on the Mount as the perfect will of God," the encounter with which brings "about in us a combination of increasing achievement." "This has been the hallmark of Christian character in all ages," says Ramsey, and here he does not seem to doubt at all the possibility of a Christian discipleship which is obedient to the Sermon on the Mount. "Repeatedly moment by moment we discover from comparing ourselves with Jesus Christ and his teachings how to have humility increased in us with-

1 John A. Hutchison (ed.), *Christian Faith and Social Action* (N. Y., 1953) 7.

out sabotaging effort and how to make every effort without provoking pride. Hence we have whereof to glory, but are not tempted to glory save in the Lord."[2] Neither will Ramsey permit the Sermon on the Mount to be watered down to nonviolent self-defense in the form of litigation or similar forms of pressure, which he believes is Hinduism more than it is Christianity.[3]

Having recognized unselfishness as the heart of the Christian ethic, however, and having objected to watering it down in one direction, Ramsey proceeds to dilute it in another direction by means of what he calls "enlightened unselfishness." The kind of nonresistance which dispenses its love for the neighbor indiscriminately is "unenlightened." When the Christian's personal welfare alone is concerned complete nonresistance is the way of unselfishness, even if it means the laying down of one's life. When Jesus teaches the turning of the other cheek or the giving away of the cloak He is dealing with a two-person relationship. Jesus Himself died without defending Himself. So likewise must we decline to resist others in order to defend ourselves when we are the victims of injustice. But what shall the Christian do when his neighbor is the victim of a second neighbor's injustice? Here there is no longer a two-person relationship, but rather a multilateral relationship requiring an "enlightened" preferential ethic in which unselfish love must go out in defense of the helpless victim. "The same inner disposition which, so far as one's self is concerned, leads to a practice of the absolute demands of the Sermon on the Mount may, so far as others must be served, lead to the reverse action: in both, 'you govern yourself according to love.' "[4]

John C. Bennett accepts this premise and elaborates it at great length, using the general social order for which the Christian is "responsible" as his frame of reference. On the whole, his analysis of the difficulties which one confronts in

2 Ramsey, *Basic Christian Ethics.* 200.
3 *Ibid.,* 182.
4 *Ibid.,* 186.

applying the Christian ethic in this sub-Christian society is a valid one. It is a large-scale society in which social relations are secondary and impersonal in character. It is a mixed society with a cumulative disorder of prejudices and conflicting group interests. One's personal responsibility is diluted because this responsibility is shared by others. The making of sound ethical decisions is further complicated by the capacity of men to cloak their self-interest with a veneer of idealism, and by the fact that many issues are of a technical character calling for expert judgment which the untrained individual is unable to make.

These observations are so sound that the truth which they contain must be humbly admitted. There is no question that the problem of living the good life, the way of the cross, in our modern complex society is a difficult one. One cannot help feeling, however, that Bennett and the Christian Action group are making the problem more hopeless than it is. They consistently come up with the answer that the best the Christian can do is to choose between the lesser of two or more evils. After saying many fine things about the Sermon on the Mount they usually conclude that in this world some other course is necessary, despite the fact that Jesus said: "You, therefore, must be perfect, as your heavenly Father is perfect,"[5] and that Paul said: "Do not be overcome by evil, but overcome evil with good."[6] Bennett is greatly impressed with the literature of Christian resistance in Europe of the Nazi time which "is full of references to this problem of the lesser evil which at times seems to be commanded. How was it possible to resist without being ready to lie and to kill? This would be more obviously necessary where one had to choose between allowing other individuals to become victims of the Gestapo and defending them by deceit or violence." Then Bennett quotes with approval the following statement by an ecumenical leader who had studied with care the resistance movements in Europe.

5 Matt. 5:48.
6 Rom. 12:21,

"Problems which the ordinary textbooks on ethics at most treated as hypothetical limit-cases, have become part of the normal experience of many Christian patriots. The problems of lying and of killing traitors may be given as illustrative examples. Trying to find 'the more excellent way' in inextricable and unprecedented situations of moral conflict, many Christians in these years have rediscovered the profound truth that Christian conduct cannot be equated with an anxious, moralistic perfectionism or an angelic Utopianism, but rather means a lowly, dangerous obedience, trusting in the divine forgiveness of inevitable sins.[7]

Bennett goes on to speak of situations in which "every available alternative is evil, that to refuse to deceive or use violence in defending others may make one responsible for their becoming the victims of the most cruel atrocities." What is more, he receives powerful support for his position from the personal history of Dietrich Bonhoeffer whose *The Cost of Discipleship*, first published in German in 1937, was referred to in the previous chapter. In *The Cost of Discipleship* Bonhoeffer clearly rejects the view of the preferential ethic which forbids the Christian to engage in self-defense, and yet constrains him to use violence for the defense of those for whom he is responsible.

"If I am attacked am I not at once the father of my children, the pastor of my flock, and the ruler of my people? And am I not always an individual, face to face with Jesus, even in the performance of my official duties? . . . Jesus . . . tells us that it is just *because* we live in the world, and just *because* the world is evil, that the precept of nonresistance must be put into practice. Surely we do not wish to accuse Jesus of ignoring the reality and power of evil! . . . The passion of Christ is the victory of divine love over the powers of evil . . . . Once again, Jesus calls those who follow Him to share His passion. How can we convince the world by our preaching of the passion when we shrink from that passion in our

7 Quoted in Bennett, *op. cit.*, 26.

own lives? On the cross Jesus practices what He preaches, and at the same time, by enjoining this precept upon the disciples, He helps them to realize their share in the cross. The cross is the only power in the world which proves that suffering love can avenge and vanquish evil. But it was just this participation in the cross which the disciples were granted when Jesus called them to Him. They are called blessed because of their visible participation in His cross."[8]

No stronger statement than this of the case for nonresistance can be found anywhere; and yet what did Bonhoeffer himself do when he was put to the test during the second World War? Regretfully, it must be admitted that when the bitter trial came he changed his position. When Hitler's persecution of the church became too strong Bonhoeffer administered an underground seminary. Later through a friend who had some rank with the Nazis he became attached to an office which sent him as an emissary to Sweden and England where he engaged in espionage, giving information to foreign governments and falsifying his own reports. After his return to Germany his activities were discovered and he was imprisoned in April 1943. During his imprisonment he wrote his *Ethik* which represents a different view from that of *The Cost of Discipleship*. A letter from Pastor Harald Poelchau of Berlin, a close friend of Bonhoeffer who visited him in prison, says that as the situation in Germany grew more serious "Bonhoeffer . . . turned more and more strongly towards the responsibility for this world . . . . According to my personal knowledge Bonhoeffer was finally ready—in view of the great danger which Hitler represented—also to return violence for his violence."[9] Bonhoeffer was finally executed in April 1945, charged with complicity in the plot against Hitler's life. Poelchau says he could not have participated in this plot since he was in prison at the time, but he does say that Bonhoeffer had given his assent to violence against Hitler.

8 Bonhoeffer, *op. cit.*, 124, 125.
9 Letter, Harald Poelchau, Jan. 8, 1954.

To what extent Bonhoeffer's experience represents a complete reversal of a former nonresistant position, and to what extent it merely represents the two aspects of a Lutheran dualistic theology, it is difficult to say.[10] Whichever it is, Bonhoeffer is a striking illustration of sensitive Christians who like Ramsey and Bennett agree to the high ethic of the Sermon on the Mount only to set it aside in the end as an impossible choice in the present evil world. To the case of Bonhoeffer could be added other illustrations, including those of supposedly nonresistant Mennonites who broke down under the bitter test. Illustrations can be found among the Mennonite refugees from communist Russia who under pressure likewise resorted to dishonesty and deceit, and in some cases actual violence, as in the case of the youth organization known as the *Selbstschutz* in Russia in 1918. The matter of Mennonite lapses from the way of discipleship and the cross receives further attention in later chapters. Suffice it to say at this point, however, that such lapses are illustrations of Christians who failed in their calling of discipleship in a difficult situation. They are not illustrations, however, of the inapplicability of the Sermon on the Mount to the Christian life in the modern world. To admit this would be to disregard in a most ungrateful manner such stalwart Christian spirits as Pastor Wilhelm Mensching of Germany and André Trocmé, Henri Roser, and Philippe Vernier of France, who remained true to their nonresistant faith, without compromise, during the same Hitler time as that in which Bonhoeffer suffered. To accede to the arguments of Bennett and Ramsey would likewise mean the thankless repudiation of countless thousands of Christian martyrs, Anabaptists and others, who through the centuries have died for their faith in the face of a social order as evil as our own and through

10 Bonhoeffer came from an aristocratic German family, and it has been suggested that *The Cost of Discipleship*, instead of being accepted at face value, might possibly be interpreted "as a wistful retreat into a certain side of Lutheranism which borders on the romantic in which case there would be no basic change in Bonhoeffer's real practical point of view." J. Lawrence Burkholder, in a letter, Dec. 30, 1953.

whose death the price was paid for the freedom of conscience which we enjoy today.

This is not to suggest any disparagement of the members of the Christian Action group. They are men of the highest order. In addition the group must be given credit for an analysis of the social order so penetrating as to reveal our present world condition in its stark reality. Under the piercing searchlight of a Bennett or a Niebuhr the complacency of a superficial pacifist or of a self-righteous Mennonite will be seen for the nothingness that it really is. All of this is a most valuable contribution, which believers in the strenuous ethic must utilize to the full as a corrective to the danger of Pharisaism and complacency. Having said this, however, one must feel nevertheless that Christian Action is making the task of the Christian harder than it is, or than God intends it to be, both because it fails to lay hold of the redeeming, reconciling power of God with sufficient faith, and because it assumes social responsibility beyond that which God Himself has assigned to the Christian. When Bennett, for example, outlines his personal Christian strategy he would: (1) Rely upon Christian faith and ethics to control his motives and his goals. (2) Seek for humility which makes for self-criticism in the making of decisions. (3) Bring everything under the criticism of love. (This enables him to see the evil of tyranny which he thinks pacifists fail to see.) (4) Having been led by these guiding forces to do that which he must do as a citizen he now attempts to counteract the effects of this tragically necessary action by action of another kind. In time of war, for example, the soldier can deal with the enemy only as an enemy. If the soldier is a Christian, however, he will seek out his defeated enemy at the end of the war and deal with him as a person and thus counteract his former tragically necessary acts.[11]

However they choose to state it, members of Christian Action usually begin with the high ethic of the New Testament, and then by some process of tragic necessity they scale

11 Bennett, *op. cit.*, ch. 5.

it down, so as to make it conform to the sinful social order. Bennett finds an evil greater than war which must be dealt with in a manner not promulgated in the Sermon on the Mount. Then he would compensate for the compromise with further action of another kind. *Paul L. Lehmann even concludes that Christian ethics is a theological discipline which is not identical with New Testament ethics.* The primary question is not, What does God require? but What does God do? It is not the divine imperative that we seek, but rather the divine indicative. The basic answer to the question of Christian ethics is the will of God. But it is difficult to know how to arrive at the will of God; and when we have arrived it is difficult to know what the will of God is. Even so simple a matter as telling the truth about an automobile which is for sale, says Lehmann, presents almost insurmountable difficulties. What does it mean to tell the truth about the car? Even if the owner tells all that he knows, can he be sure that he is telling the truth about the automobile?[12]

After granting to the full the factor of human fallibility in even so minor an ethical question as this, one cannot help feeling that our Christian Action friends, in their effort to be honest and to examine every ethical standard with critical care, have brought this matter much too far; that they have carried the raising of problems for the avoidance of easy answers almost to a *reductio ad absurdum*; and that they are making it more difficult to be a disciple of Christ than our Lord intends it to be. One is reminded of the scribes and Pharisees who tried so hard by their good works to make ready for the Messiah and then failed to recognize Him when He came. Can it be that our friends who try so hard to be truly and perfectly ethical fail to see the ethical way when it lies before them? It is true that Jesus said, "If any man would come after me, let him deny himself and take up his cross"[13]; and a cross can be a heavy burden. But the same Jesus also

---

12 Paul L. Lehmann, "The Foundation and Pattern of Christian Behavior," in John A. Hutchison (ed.), *op. cit.*, 98, 101, 105.
    13 Matt. 16:24.

said: "Take my yoke upon you, and learn from me; for I am gentle and lowly in heart, and you will find rest for your souls. For my yoke is easy, and my burden is light."[14] It was this great truth that enabled the martyrs to go to their death, a truth which Christian Action seems to overlook.

It was suggested earlier that neo-orthodoxy has recovered something of an orthodox anthropology, but that it is lacking in a doctrine of redemption. The basic difficulty would seem to be that its outlook, like that of the old social gospel, is too much man-centered. The difference is that whereas the social gospel concentrated on man's inherent goodness, its successors concentrate on man's predicament from which there is no escape. John H. Yoder has given us a penetrating analysis of Reinhold Niebuhr's theology as it affects the Christian doctrine of pacifism and nonresistance.[15] In this analysis Yoder lists four major objections to Niebuhr's thought:

(1) The doctrine of the lesser evil involves two fallacies: (a) A false judgment that war is less harmful than tyranny. (b) A moral fallacy in not distinguishing between agents. Even if it could be assumed that tyranny is worse than war, the tyranny is the tyrant's sin, not the Christian's. But when the Christian engages in war to counteract the tyrant's sin the new sin is his own. The Christian's responsibility is to overcome evil with love, not one evil with another, not even a greater evil with a lesser one, assuming that it is possible to distinguish the lesser from the greater. George M. Gibson is correct when he says the only choice which the Christian Action group has to offer is the choice between two evils. This would seem to be rather far removed from the Biblical concept of the broad and the narrow way. And as Gibson says, it is a serious oversimplification to state categorically as the Christian Action group does, that war is a lesser evil than tyranny. It would be nearer the truth to say that they belong

14 Matt. 11:29, 30.
15 John H. Yoder, *Reinhold Niebuhr and Christian Pacifism* (Zeist, The Netherlands, 1954).

together and reinforce each other, and that the Christian can
have nothing to do with either. The fact that this doctrine
in its present form emerged during the second World War
as a means of destroying pacifism, and as a justification of the
compromise which the church was making with war, is sufficient cause in itself to make the doctrine suspect.[16]

(2) Niebuhr's ethical reasoning includes certain presupposed axioms which must be submitted to critical examination. (a) We are told that our involvement in the complexities of the social order is such that there is no escape from the
necessity of doing evil. To this Yoder replies that "nothing
is necessary in itself as far as ethics is concerned." Necessity
has to do with ends, not with ethics. It is not necessary to eat
unless we want to live. It is not necessary to defend ourselves
unless we feel that we must survive. It is not necessary to
fight for the perpetuation of our social order unless we
believe that this order must be perpetuated. There is no
necessity to give up the way of love and nonresistance unless
we want something else more than we want love and nonresistance. If there is a moral value higher than love we should
find it necessary to seek this higher value. But if love is the
highest value, it is necessary for everything else to give way
to love. True, this may mean suffering and death, and this
is exactly what it did mean to the Christian martyrs. The
apostles found it necessary to lay down their lives in order
that they might follow the way of love. Above all Jesus Christ
lived the cross life and died the cross death that men might
be reconciled unto God and so become worthy of being called
Christian. It may well be that there is a tragic, or perhaps a
glorious, necessity to suffer that the way of love may be realized. The modern doctrine of the tragic necessity to do evil,
however, would have us cast all this aside so that the social
order may be saved from tyranny. Actually, as Yoder says,
the doctrine of tragic necessity "is but a camouflage for some
personal or group egoism, whether the survival instinct itself,

16 George M. Gibson, *Critique of the Dun Report* (Commission on Christian
Conscience and War of the Church Peace Mission, 1950, Mimeographed) 4.

unwillingness to surrender advantages, or something more abstract and less overtly selfish."[17] Gibson adds that "if this argument could be made convincing, it would dispose of the conscientious objector, and indeed, would effectively silence all conscience. Moral responsibility requires freedom; under a doctrine of total necessity, there is obviously no moral problem." That the Christian Action group has not gone the whole way of total necessity is evident, however, from its emphasis on repentance and sorrow for sin. On the other hand, Gibson is no doubt right when he says that it does not use the term "repentance" in the Biblical sense of "turning around," but rather "as the continuing attitude of one who, though sorry for his sins, expects to continue in them under the sheer necessity of his own nature and of social compulsions." [18]

(b) The Christian Action group assumes it to be the Christian's responsibility to guarantee the survival and improvement of the social order, not by means of the love ethic through which Christ reconciles the world unto Himself, but rather by those means which the sinful social order itself dictates. The New Testament ethic and program makes the Christian responsible to bring the way of love and the cross as a challenge to the conscience of society, the state, and the social order. This responsibility is rejected, however, in favor of a spurious responsibility to accept the norms and the means which the sinful social order itself provides.

(3) Niebuhr's new ethical norms of necessity and responsibility which cancel out the way of love and the cross are based on three deeper and more basic errors: (a) It is assumed that "ought" is derived from "is." The Christian must answer, however, that an indicative does not make an imperative; that a fact does not constitute a value. Kinsey's statistics, however reliably they may describe the ways of the American people, do not provide ethical norms, nor a pattern of tragic necessity for family life. (b) The selfish motive of self-

17 John H. Yoder, *op. cit.,* 18.
18 Gibson, *op. cit.,* 3, 4.

preservation is given the status of a norm. From this base it is possible to proceed to any compromise, no matter how extreme. The necessity and the responsibility arguments "may be used in any country to approve any foreign policy," in Russia as well as in the United States. This kind of reasoning will call good any policy chosen for selfish purposes anywhere.

(c) This constitutes a doctrine of ethical pluralism which denies "that God's will can be known and that right action can be identical for all." In other words, it is the doctrine of relativity which holds that what is right for one person may be wrong for another. Thus Niebuhr is able to endorse nonresistance as an ethical norm for some Christians if they in turn are willing to endorse an opposite ethic for Niebuhr. As Yoder states it, this view assumes "that there is no one knowable good and that conflicting actions carried on with good intentions or in the awareness of their imperfection are all equally right. It goes without saying that if this is really true there is little point to any talk about ethical considerations."[19] And Gibson says: "The distinctions between right and wrong, so clearly defined in the New Testament and in the great creative Christian eras, are blurred in the welter of conflicting opinions. . . . . There is no apparent difference between Christians and secularists. . . . . The crisis theologians have consistently made common cause with liberal, radical, and nationalistic political positions which make no pretense of basing themselves on any theology or religion. This over-accent on relativity is a definite mark of our times and may be regarded as one of the poisons now destroying western culture. Its philosophic derivation is not from the Bible through the main stream of Christian thought, but it is distinctly a product of the secular mind under which our era has fallen."[20]

J. Lawrence Burkholder[21] has pointed out the significant fact that in rejecting the absolute ethic of the New Testa-

19 Yoder, *op. cit.*, 19.
20 Gibson, *op. cit.*, 2.
21 J. Lawrence Burkholder, letter, Jan. 16, 1954.

ment in favor of a doctrine of relativity, the Christian Action group has virtually established a new absolute in its concept of social responsibility, a concept which if not given New Testament limits seems to demand the use of whatever means the evil social order itself approves for its own defense and perpetuation. Accompanying this new absolute there seems to be "an uncritical conformism to American patterns of conduct and thought" which Burkholder correctly describes as socially dangerous.

(4) Niebuhr's answer to man's predicament is not the New Testament answer. Whereas the New Testament ethic is based upon the fact of God's redemptive work, Niebuhr derives his ethic from the predicament of man itself. In so doing he slights, or transfers to a realm beyond history, or dismisses "as mythological expressions of man's capacities for transcendence," four cardinal teachings of the New Testament: (a) *The doctrine of the cross in the light of the resurrection.* Whereas the Bible admonishes those who have been raised with Christ "to seek the things that are above," thus "opening new ethical possibilities," Niebuhr practically omits all consideration of the resurrection, regarding enabling grace as a temptation to pride, and considering forgiving grace only as related to man's sinfulness, giving him peace as he continues in his sin.

(b) *The church as the body of Christ and the bearer of the meaning of history.* Niebuhr thinks in terms of the social order, of the American body politic. It is this order for which we are responsible and it is this order whose compounded ego is greater than the total of its individual egos, which in turn determines the tragic necessity of Niebuhr's sub-Christian ethic. When God invaded history in the person of Christ, however, He established the church as His body through which the meaning of history would be realized. This body of Christ is not like ordinary social bodies, subject to sociological laws alone. It is not less moral than its individual members; it is a divine-human society which is better than the sum of its members. "If being a perfectly loyal

American, a freemason, or a bourgeois, identifies a man with that group egoism in such a way as to make him less loving than he would be as an individual," says Yoder, "the contrary is true of being a member of Christ. Thus the thesis of *Moral Man and Immoral Society* falls down in the crucial case, the only one which is really decisive for Christian ethics."[22]

In addition to this it must also be remembered that the church is a universal body transcending all boundaries of nation, race, or class. Thus when Christians for whatever reason accept the ethical norms of the social order and act upon them, as in the case of international war or class conflict, we have Christians killing Christians which is "the greatest possible offense against the unity of the body of Christ." Because of this fact one would suppose that those Christians who are deeply involved in the ecumenical movement of our day would be the Christians who would see this point most clearly. Unfortunately, however, in many instances this is not the case. In the case of Niebuhr himself, as Yoder says, "this argument is meaningless . . . because, despite his participation in the ecumenical movement, the church as distinguished from society has no significant place in his ethical thought."[23]

(c) *The doctrine of regeneration.* The Bible teaches that there is a significant difference between the saint and the sinner; that the ethics of those who are born again are different from those who are not. The strait and narrow way leads to life eternal; the broad way leads to destruction. With Niebuhr, however, the doctrine of regeneration is almost completely ignored. He grants that it is there, to be sure, but he considers it ineffective, for even the born-again saint is in some sense still a sinner. This fact, together with the ambiguities of the social order, takes the high ethic of the New Testament literally out of this world in so far as effectiveness is concerned.[24] While granting that saints like the Apostle Paul,

22 Yoder, *op. cit.*, 20.
23 *Ibid.*, 21.
24 Reinhold Niebuhr, "The Christian Witness in a Secular Age," *Christian Century* (July 22, 1953) 70:841.

though pressing toward the mark, never fully attained unto it, and granting that the complexities of modern society make the Christian's problems more difficult, Niebuhr's chief difficulty nevertheless consists in attempting, as Yoder says, to construct an ethic for an unregenerate society, based on its own terms, and then insisting on calling it Christian. Such an ethic is not Christian, however, because "the doctrine of regeneration means that ethics for Christians and ethics for unregenerate society are two distinct disciplines." The attempt to construct a Christian ethic for unregenerate society is to effect an "illegitimate union of Christian and non-Christian elements,"[25] from which union there comes only an illegitimate offspring.

(d) *The doctrine of the Holy Spirit.* Finally, Niebuhr neglects the doctrine of the Holy Spirit whose power is manifest in the resurrection of Christ, in the growth and the healing influence of the church, and in the regeneration of the sinner, empowering him to live a life of holiness before God and among men, even in the midst of a sinful society. That the way of holiness and the triumph over sin is never complete, is readily conceded. There is no doubt, however, that it is real; and the testimony of the martyrs of all ages is proof, written in blood, that men and women born of the Spirit receive power from on high enabling them to choose the ethic of Christ and the way of His cross, refusing to escape by an easier way on the ground of tragic necessity. "The triumph of love over sin is not reserved for some Platonic realm (such as Niebuhr's 'superhistory') where the eschatological judgment takes place. Sin is vanquished every time a Christian in the power of God chooses the better instead of the good, obedience instead of necessity, love instead of compromise, brotherhood instead of veiled self-interest."[26]

Gibson reminds us with telling effect that this life of the Spirit is the reality of which the Scriptures speak.[27] The

25 Yoder, *op. cit.,* 21.
26 *Ibid.,* 21, 22.
27 Gibson, *op. cit.,* 5.

momentary afflictions of this life are but a preparation for
the eternal, the real which is to come. "We look not to the
things that are seen but to the things that are unseen . . . .
For we know that if the earthly tent we live in is destroyed,
we have a building from God, a house not made with hands,
eternal in the heavens."[28] The things which can be seen are
unreal. Reality consists of the unseen, the eternal. This is
precisely the opposite of the view taken by the crisis theologians. They would have us face the realities of life, and by
reality they mean power politics, the sensate, and the material. Christians who decline to follow the power way are looked
upon as unreal, as romantic, and as utopian. Sin is real, to
be sure, in the sense that many people are in bondage to it.
But the Gospel of Jesus Christ is more real than sin; for "it is
the power of God for salvation to every one who has faith."[29]
Our sin is ever before us, yes; but not that we should surrender to it. We confess our sin and the sordid things of this
life, not that we may continue in them, but that we may turn
from them to the realities of God and His Spirit.

28 II Cor. 4:18—5:1.
29 Rom. 1:16.

7. THE COUNCILS OF CHURCHES

The ecumenical movement, as represented both by the World Council of Churches and the National Council of Churches of Christ in the United States of America, and its various predecessors, has given a considerable amount of attention to the social implications of the Gospel. On the question of war, the ecumenical movement has reflected the various points of view which have characterized the history of Christendom; and at present, as one would expect, it has a strong coloring of crisis theology with its emphasis on the lesser evil, the tragic necessity, and the responsible society. It would seem correct to say, however, that the World Council is more receptive to Christian pacifism and the strict New Testament ethic than is the National Council. Section IV of the Amsterdam Assembly of the World Council (1948) was concerned with the church and the international disorder. The report of this section says: "War is contrary to the will of God . . . incompatible with the teaching and example of our Lord Jesus Christ. The part which war plays in our present international life is a sin against God and a degradation of man." The report then describes the character of total war, as now waged with atomic and other new weapons rendering widespread and indiscriminate destruction, as so serious that "the tradition of a just war, requiring a just cause and the use of just means, is now challenged. Law may require the sanction of force, but when war breaks out, force is used on a scale which tends to destroy the basis on which law exists." This fact, the report says, brings us face to face with the inescapable question: "Can war now be an act of justice?" The Amsterdam Assembly, unable to answer this question unanimously, then set forth three broad positions, representing three points of view, held by members of the World Council. These three positions are as follows:

119

"1. There are those who hold that, even though entering a war may be a Christian's duty in particular circumstances, modern warfare, with its mass destruction, can never be an act of justice.

"2. In the absence of impartial supra-national institutions, there are those who hold that military action is the ultimate sanction of the rule of law, and that citizens must be distinctly taught that it is their duty to defend the law by force if necessary.

"3. Others, again, refuse military service of all kinds, convinced that an absolute witness against war and for peace is for them the will of God and they desire that the church should speak to the same effect."[1]

The last of these three positions is that of the conscientious objector. That the World Council should have recognized this as a possible Christian position is significant, considering the spirit of the time. Moreover, the general secretary of the World Council subsequently invited the historic peace churches to present a statement of their antiwar position in a form suitable for study by the 1954 Assembly of the Council at Evanston. The historic peace churches accepted this invitation and a 24-page document, *Peace Is the Will of God*[2], was published in October 1953. Although this is a hopeful development, and an illustration of the kind of testimony which Mennonites and others should give more frequently than they do, it is obvious that the historic peace church document represents a minority point of view.

Among those responsible for the report of Section IV on the church and the international disorder was John Foster Dulles, now United States Secretary of State, Emil Brunner, the Zurich theologian, O. F. Nolde, and others. The personnel of Section III, dealing with the church and the disorder of society, included Reinhold Niebuhr, John C. Bennett, Emil Brunner, and others. It is not surprising therefore to

---

1 W. A. Visser 't Hooft (ed.), *The First Assembly of the World Council of Churches* (New York, 1949) 89, 90.
2 See above, p. 65n.

find the report filled with references to the will of God for peace and order in this world, while frankly acknowledging a "deep sense of perplexity in the face of conflicting opinions" regarding the Christian attitude toward war, urging theologians to continue wrestling with the problem, and in the meantime admonishing the churches to "continue to hold within their full fellowship all who sincerely profess such viewpoints as those set out above and are prepared to submit themselves to the will of God in the light of such guidance as may be vouchsafed to them."[3] Thus while the World Council in 1948 did not deny conscientious objection to war as a possible Christian position, it was still far from ready to make it the Christian position.

In the meantime the National Council of Churches also concerned itself with the problem of war. In 1950 the Department of International Justice and Goodwill of the NCC published a report of a special commission on *The Christian Conscience and Weapons of Mass Destruction*. The chairman of the commission was Bishop Angus Dun of Washington, D.C., an Episcopalian, and the report is commonly known as *The Dun Report*. This document reflects the Niebuhrian position more fully than does the Amsterdam report, largely no doubt because at Amsterdam the church, although concerned for the welfare of society, was after all earnestly trying to be the church, whereas the Dun commission seems to have been a group of church representatives whose primary concern was responsibility for the social order. The report says that "serious Christians of every name now see in war a grievous disclosure of man's lostness and wrongness," and then it turns and finds its tools for Christian action in the equipment of this very same lost and wrongful society. Instead of bringing the way of the cross as a mighty rebuke and challenge to the sinful social order, it identifies itself with that order and uses its own methods. Even though war is an evidence of lostness and wrongness, yet the majority of Christians have always agreed that "there are times when

3 Visser 't Hooft, *op. cit.*, 90.

Christians should take the sword and fight as very imperfect
servants of God's justice." The important exception was in
"the earliest days when the Christian community was a little
persecuted minority in a pagan society, without political
responsibilities." We, however, are responsible, says the
report, "not only for peace within the church, . . . but also
for the maintenance of order and justice in civil society."
Most Christians "have recognized the tragic necessity for
coercive restraints on 'the unruly wills and affections of
sinful men,' including their own."[4] Yes, there are pacifists
to be sure, who "believe that the refusal of all kinds of military service and an unqualified witness against war and for
peace is for them the will of God. . . . But most of us find
ourselves called to follow a course which is less simple and
which appears to us more responsible because more directly
relevant to the hard realities of our situation. And we believe
it is the way in which most Christians must go."[5]

The Dun report recognizes that past efforts to subject
war to some restraint in its methods have not been successful.
It recognizes that modern weapons of mass destruction make
the prospect of future wars more terrible than the mind of
man has yet conceived; and yet all it is able to suggest that
might be done about it is that our government use atomic
weapons, "with all possible restraint." There is no moral
distinction as between weapons. The moral difference comes
in the motive or purpose with which they are used. We
should search for an agreement among the nations to prevent
the manufacturing of weapons of mass destruction. But since
there is no hope for this, Christians must support their use,
with all possible restraint to be sure, for to do otherwise
would be for Christians "to share responsibility for the world-
wide tyranny that might result." "Even if as individuals we
would choose rather to be destroyed than to destroy in such
measure," says the report, "we do not believe it would be

---

4 The Department of International Justice and Goodwill, *The Christian Conscience and Weapons of Mass Destruction* (The Dun Report, New York, 1950) 6, 7.
5 *Ibid.*, 8, 9.

right for us to urge policies on our government which would expose others to such a fate."[6] In this last statement the report does suggest the way of the cross as a possibility for the Christian, but rejects its possibility for the state. With this distinction we could agree providing our friends would then retain the distinction between the church and the state and as churchmen actually follow the way of the cross and so bring the Christian challenge to the state. But no, the responsibility for cross bearing even for Christians and the church is cast aside in favor of the church's unscriptural responsibility for the evil social order with all its evil methods.

It would be unfair not to mention that the Dun report has many constructive suggestions for the improvement of international relations, through such means as efforts to reduce armaments through the instrumentality of the United Nations, the relief of suffering and need throughout the world, and other means. This is all very good but the report is primarily concerned with the use of weapons of mass destruction; and this is condoned as justifiable for a society for which the church is responsible—this instead of the way of the cross. In October 1953 the Department of International Justice and Goodwill which sponsored the Dun report held its Fourth National Study Conference on the Churches and World Order. The published report of this conference, *Christian Faith and International Responsibility,* is really an enlarged version of the Dun report. It likewise contains many wholesome proposals for improved international relations, especially through the nonmilitary functions of the United Nations and by other means. On the crucial question of armed force, however, that part of the American church which spoke at the Cleveland conference emphatically declared its support of, and made itself responsible for, the present security system as represented by Article 51 of the United Nations Charter, NATO, the Rio and Pacific pacts and other similar defense arrangements.[7] It should be add-

---

6 *Ibid.,* 14.
7 National Council of Churches, *Christian Faith and International Responsibility:*

ed, however, that there were minority reports attached to both the Dun and the Cleveland conference reports.

The executive director of the Department of International Justice and Goodwill of the National Council of Churches is Walter W. Van Kirk. In 1934 Van Kirk said: "The churches of the world are determined to combat the whole war system . . . mankind will no longer pin its faith to any religious system that is helpless to stay the hand of the militarist. . . . Either religion will put an end to war or war will put an end to religion . . . . Not until the full implication of this sovereign truth registers indelibly in the thinking process of all who lift their faces Godward will any permanent advance be made in the crusade for a warless world."[8] So spoke Van Kirk in 1934. As in the case of others, however, the Hitler era and the second World War had their effect on his emphasis, so that in 1953 he was able to quote with approval an action by the General Board of the National Council which said: "We must come to grips with the issue of collective security. Either the United Nations will develop a system of law under which unprovoked military aggression can be resisted by the joint endeavor of all peace-loving states, or it will become impotent and wither away. The choice before us is that of supporting collective action against aggression in the name and for the sake of the world community, or giving aid and comfort to the aggressor." Then Van Kirk continues and says: "Let it be said again, Christians will have to deal with this issue. They have not always been willing to do this . . . . The choice before Christians is a choice between law and lawlessness."[9]

Report of the Fourth National Study Conference on the Churches and World Order (New York, 1953) 40. In 1951 the Church of Scotland published a *Report of the Special Commission Anent the Just War.* This report came to conclusions similar to those of the Dun and the Cleveland reports. Even though the terrible weapons of mass destruction will be used, the report concludes "that if a Christian nation is faced with the terrible choice of allowing aggression, tyranny, and lawlessness to triumph, and entering upon war in defense of a free and ordered society, the resort to arms may be considered legitimate and just" (p. 750). A minority report was also attached, saying that "modern warfare, with its mass destruction, can never be an act of justice" (p. 751).

8 W. W. Van Kirk, *Religion Renounces War* (Chicago, 1934) 253.

9 W. W. Van Kirk, "Korea: Thoughts After Storm," *Christian Century* (Aug. 26, 1953) 70:961.

Reference was made above to *Peace Is the Will of God*,[10] the statement of the historic peace churches published in 1953 in response to an invitation by the World Council of Churches. In 1955 in *Christianity and Crisis* Angus Dun and Reinhold Niebuhr published a rejoinder to this statement under the title, "God Wills Both Justice and Peace."[11] The rejoinder simply challenges the peace church statement with a restatement of the responsibility-tragic necessity argument. "Pacifism distorts the command of love," say Dun and Niebuhr, and it "tries to apply an individual ethic to a collective situation." A substantial portion of the statement is devoted to the concept of the just war. It is granted that the intricacies of modern international relations, complicated as they are with the new weapons of mass destruction, make it difficult for the nonpacifist to find a policy which is an "easy way or foolproof guide." The authors are certain, however, that modern atomic weapons are not a sufficient cause for ruling out the concept of the just war. Established international law and the vindication of an essential Christian principle, such as the defense of victims of wanton aggression or the securing of freedom for the oppressed, are suggested as criteria for the determination of the justice of a given war. The criteria may be difficult to discover, of course. In the final analysis the individual conscience must be the guide. The complexities of the situation, however, do not rule out the feasibility of a just war; for God wills justice as well as peace. So runs the argument of Dun and Niebuhr, but as always the frame of reference is the social order rather than the lordship of Christ and the way of the cross.

Happily, not all Christians are ready to accept this point of view; and not all pacifists have shifted their position with Walter Van Kirk as cited above. There were critical reac-

10 Page 65n.
11 Angus Dun and Reinhold Niebuhr, "God Wills Both Justice and Peace," *Christianity and Crisis* (June 13, 1955) Vol. 15, No. 10. Since then the HPC and the IFOR have replied to the Dun-Niebuhr rejoinder in "God Establishes Both Peace and Justice." The three documents were then to be published as one pamphlet with the general title, *The Christian and War: A Theological Discussion of Justice, Peace and Love* (The Historic Peace Churches and the International Fellowship of Reconciliation, Zeist, 1958).

tions to his article in the *Christian Century*, as there were minority statements attached to the Dun and the Cleveland reports. One objector said Van Kirk was "unwittingly calling on every Christian to follow the spirit of nationalism and the mind of militarism instead of following the Spirit and the mind of Christ." Another said there was a great difference between the writings of Van Kirk and those of Amos, Isaiah, and Jeremiah. "Could the difference be," he asked, "that Amos and company used the plumbline of the moral law, and therefore possessed 'the insight required of unerring judgment,' while Van Kirk fares forth into the chaos which is international politics with his plumbline safely tucked away in his tool kit?"[12]

There is no question that in the decades following 1930 the ranks of pacifism within American Christendom were thinned. The rise of totalitarianism and the reaction to the obviously shallow character of the social gospel type of pacifism had caused many erstwhile pacifists to fall by the wayside. Many former pacifists were now aligned with the crisis theologians and the Christian Action group. On the other hand, there were many who had retained their antiwar position, and who with the chastening of the time had modified their theology and established their pacifism upon more solid ground than that on which it formerly stood.

Granting the sincerity of those who adhere to the social responsibility doctrine of the crisis theologians it would seem that to many discerning minds this identification of the church and its program with that of the social order is ultimately nothing less than the identification of the ethics of the kingdom with that of the same sinful social order. True, the Christian who rejects this view and adheres to the high ethic of the New Testament can be in danger of self-righteousness. As George M. Gibson said, however, in an address at the 1953 Detroit conference on the church and war: "I would rather run the risk of being a little self-righteous than to run the risk of giving myself over to approval of the political immorality that is war."

12 "Correspondence," *Christian Century* (Sept. 16, 1953) 70:1055.

8. FUNDAMENTALISM

By the time the social gospel had reached its zenith a new Protestant force known as fundamentalism had emerged on the American scene. The new movement came as a reaction to the theological liberalism of the social gospel which was much in need of correction. Had fundamentalism been broadly conceived; had it returned to the theological foundations of the earlier American Protestantism with its social message and its view of the kingdom; and had it then capitalized on the positive social gains and insights of the social gospel, the history of American Protestantism during the past half century might have been quite other than that which it has been. Had it brought the combined evangelical theology and the social vision of Finney under the intellectual leadership of men whose creative thinking could have put the constructive work of Rauschenbusch on solid foundations and moved forward with it, the leadership of creative Protestant thought today might be in evangelical hands.

Unfortunately, however, fundamentalism was narrowly conceived and became increasingly so as time went on. Its doctrinal position included little of social ethics; there was little emphasis on the church; and with the time it became increasingly negative in its emphasis. Although it obtained a large following under outspoken leaders so that American Christianity appeared to be divided into two great camps, the fundamentalists and the liberals, there was a large body of evangelical Protestants which could not properly be classified under either of these categories, and which was more balanced in its theology than either of them, but which for lack of aggressive leadership was sometimes lost sight of.

The outstanding evangelist during the second half of the nineteenth century was D. L. Moody. Moody was a lay preacher, not an educator or intellectual leader like Finney or Rauschenbusch. His work did, however, combine the promotion of evangelical Christianity with the social implications of the Gospel in a manner similar to that of Finney. Moody's work falls in the era of urbanization and his mission, like that of the social gospelers, was carried on in behalf of the industrial working class. He came to Chicago in 1856 and organized a Sunday school for the working classes in a needy section of the city. From 1856 to 1869 he was president of the Chicago YMCA, and he collected funds for the erection of the first YMCA building in the country. The YMCA was a Christian institution designed to meet the needs of the working classes. The movement began in England in 1844 and then spread to America where there were 200 YMCA's by 1861. From 1871 Moody gave full time to evangelistic work, preaching to large crowds in the industrial cities. In 1886 he founded the Moody Bible Institute whose purpose it should be "to raise up men and women who will be willing to lay their lives alongside the laboring class and the poor, and to bring the Gospel to bear upon their lives."[1]

In this connection it is also important to remember Moody's attitude toward war. Much as he believed in abolition, and strong as the pressure was to induce him to enlist in the service of his country during the Civil War, Moody did not join the Union army; for the fact is that Moody was what today would be called a conscientious objector. He did bring a spiritual ministry to the soldiers at Camp Douglas near Chicago and elsewhere, through the organized YMCA, but he consistently refused enlistment in the army. The biography of Moody by his son says "a company was also raised among his friends and former associates in business, and on all sides he was urged to enter the service of his country. . . . In spite of all this he could not conscientiously enlist." When questioned, Moody answered as follows: "There has never been a time in my life when I felt I could take a gun and shoot down a fellow being. In this respect I am a Quaker."[2]

1 Quoted in S. G. Cole, *The History of Fundamentalism* (New York, 1931) 43.
2 William R. Moody, *The Life of Dwight L. Moody* (New York, 1900) 81, 82.

These social aspects of Moody's ministry, including his anti-war position, are of great importance in view of the later history of the Moody Bible Institute and of the fundamentalist movement which is commonly supposed to fall within the Moody tradition. Here, as in the prewar period, evangelical Christianity and an insight into the social implications of the Gospel went hand in hand, and were not antagonistic to each other.

By the time the Moody Bible Institute was founded, however, the social gospel movement of the universities and seminaries, with its liberal theological orientation, was already under way. Darwinism, the higher criticism, and the new theology with which it was associated were so great and so serious a threat that conservative ministers and church leaders began to organize their forces to stop the liberal movement. In doing so, however, they rejected good features of the social gospel along with the bad.

A Bible conference held at Swampscott, Massachusetts, in 1876 was the forerunner of the well-known Niagara Bible Conference and others with a continuous history, such as the Winona Lake and Rocky Mountain conferences. In 1895 the Niagara conference set forth its well-known five points of doctrine: (1) The inspiration of the Scriptures. (2) The deity of Christ. (3) The virgin birth. (4) The substitutionary atonement. (5) The second coming of Christ. About the same time R. A. Torrey, then head of the Moody Bible Institute, sounded a new note when he announced it a major objective of the school "to increase the spirituality of the church" in view of "the advancing apostasy predicted in the Bible."[3] In due course numerous other Bible institutes were established on the Moody pattern, and sounding this same anti-apostasy note. In 1909 an organization was effected for the publication of a twelve-volume manifesto, known as *The Fundamentals*; and in 1919 the World's Christian Fundamentals Association was organized for the effective propagation of the faith. The difficulty with fundamentalism has not

3 See Cole, *op. cit.*, 43.

been the five points of doctrine outlined at Niagara in 1895. There was nothing here that had not been included in evangelical Christian doctrine all along. The chief difficulty at this point was the omission of all reference to a doctrine of the church, or of Christian ethics, or of discipleship.

Moreover, as time went on these omissions were supplemented with active opposition to certain essential ethical teachings of the New Testament; and to these were added new positive doctrinal emphases, some of them extremely erroneous. The *premillennial* second coming of Christ soon became a required essential of the faith. The next step was a more radical form of millennialism known as dispensationalism to which were added an emphasis on nondenominationalism and the doctrine of eternal security. To many evangelical Christians this combination of ideas, eternal security, dispensationalism, and nondenominationalism, was no more acceptable than the social gospel.

Eternal security, of course, has its roots in the Calvinist doctrine of election. Calvin's body of the elect, however, was a vigorous social force promoting good works to the glory of God within the present world. Fundamentalist eternal security, on the other hand, promises salvation (which cannot be lost) upon the acceptance of the so-called fundamental doctrines, including that of the imminent ushering in of the new dispensation, the kingdom of God on earth. It was Christ's intention to establish this kingdom at the time of His first coming, says dispensationalism. When the Jews rejected Him, however, Christ postponed the kingdom to a later date which is now to be expected at any moment. In the meantime an intermediary makeshift, known as the church, was arranged for. Because of its temporary character the church is of little importance at best. The Gospels, which include the ethical teachings of the Sermon on the Mount, and even other ethical portions of the New Testament, have to do with the future kingdom and are therefore inapplicable to the present dispensation. What is more, the organized denominational churches are apostate so that the true Christian cannot have anything to do with them.[4]

The program of the dispensationalist, therefore, is a simple one: Preach salvation through faith in the atoning work of Christ; ignore the denominational church; and wait for the ushering in of the kingdom. Negatively this has meant an aggressive denunciation of apostasy: first the higher criticism, then the social gospel and modernism, and more recently pacifism and the National and World Councils of Churches. Christian ethics is for the most part narrowly defined as personal morals requiring the avoidance of alcohol, tobacco, gambling, card playing, dancing, membership in secret societies, and attendance at theaters. This is not to suggest that these items are unimportant, and that none of them involve social ethics. They are important; but the significant fact is that fundamentalism largely ignores the even greater social issues of war, labor relations, race relations, and social justice in general.

It is also significant that a number of items here mentioned as accepted by fundamentalism had first come to be accepted by American Christianity as Christian ethical principles after a more socially minded church of an earlier day had made an issue of them. The temperance question is perhaps the best illustration. In colonial days the use of alcohol was practically universal. As its harmful effects came to be generally recognized, however, a socially minded church launched the temperance crusade, and total abstinence came to be accepted as a Christian virtue by practically all of those churches who had come under the influence of the revivalistic preaching of the second Great Awakening prior to the Civil War. Then when the fundamentalist movement emerged in the post-Civil War period this earlier social gain was included in its system. Fundamentalism seemed unable, however, to make social gains of its own. Once the apostate social gospel had been discovered, movements and ideas savoring of social

4 For an exposition of this extreme view see Lewis Sperry Chafer, *Dispensationalism* (Dallas, Texas, 1951).

change or social improvement were open to suspicion as a scheme to reduce Christianity to mere humanitarianism. Although fundamentalist colleges are evidence that there were many who valued education, there were also many who felt that education beyond Bible study would replace personal regeneration and the Holy Spirit with worldly wisdom. Even on the foreign mission field medical service and education were often frowned upon as substitutes for true evangelism. What fundamentalism demanded was the preaching of the Gospel of personal redemption, looking to the coming of the kingdom, and trusting God in His own way to supply any necessary additions. For these additions social action was unnecessary and uncalled for.

Fundamentalism, however, embodies a strange inconsistency. While disparaging Christian social service and social action on the one hand, it has proved itself capable of most vigorous, and in extreme forms of fundamentalism even vicious, social action on the other hand. Its tendency toward militarism is one illustration; and the tendency toward racism on the part of certain fringe groups is another. When the World's Christian Fundamentals Association was organized in 1919 the United States had just emerged from the first World War. The fact that they were already engaged in a war against an apostate German theology seems to have enabled fundamentalist preachers to engage in the war against the German Kaiser with more than ordinary zeal. Stewart G. Cole has suggested that the greatest support for fundamentalism and the corresponding opposition to the social gospel has come from the south and from the rural sections of the north.[5] There is perhaps some truth to this observation, if for no other reason than that these regions were farthest out of touch with the changing social situation of the industrial city which was the occasion for the social gospel movement. When it is remembered that the south has a strong military tradition, the roots of which go back to the planter aristocracy of the old south, we may have yet another

5 Cole, *op. cit.*, 26, 27.

factor contributing to the militarism which is often found in fundamentalism today. The deletion of the Sermon on the Mount from the church age in the dispensational scheme of theology, of course, removed an important deterrent to this militaristic ethic. When necessity required it, however, some fundamentalists have even succeeded in interpreting the Sermon on the Mount itself so as to support a militaristic ethic.[6]

Reference was made above[7] to the biography of Moody by his son, which describes the evangelist as a Quaker in his convictions with respect to war and military service. This must have caused no little embarrassment to more than one militaristic fundamentalist who regarded himself within the Moody tradition. In course of time, however, the biography became out of print and when a new and revised edition was published in 1930 this information was rewritten so as to give it quite a different interpretation.[8] Whether the revision was consciously designed to remove the embarrassment the present writer is unable to say. In any case it is symbolic of what has happened with respect to an important question of Christian ethics within fundamentalist circles. There is considerable doctrinal variation within fundamentalism; hence it would be unfair to cite the extreme right wing as typical of fundamentalism as a whole. At the same time one cannot help being impressed by what has happened in fundamentalist circles from the time of Moody to that of Carl McIntire whose American Council of Churches represents the extreme position on militarism and related social questions. In 1951, for example, the American Council resolved that should the American people believe that Russia is preparing to wage war, America has "a moral responsibility . . . to strike first." The American Council is an ardent promoter

6 E.g., see Henry Ostrom, *The Christian and War* (Grand Rapids, Mich., 1941). Fundamentalists have not been alone, however, in such interpretations. During World War I, for example, W. Douglas Mackenzie of Hartford Seminary declared that "nowhere has the Sermon on the Mount, the embodiment of the Spirit of Christ, exercised more visible and amazing power than in the matter of war." Quoted in Ray H. Abrams, *Preachers Present Arms* (New York, 1933) 66.

7 Page 128.

8 William R. Moody, *D. L. Moody* (New York, 1930). The 1930 edition says: "Moody had zealously championed the cause of the Union and vigorously expressed

of universal military service as "absolutely indispensable," and boasts of its support of the "armed camp" point of view.[9]

Like many other Protestants, fundamentalists have objected to an American ambassador at the Vatican as a violation of the principle of separation of church and state. *United Evangelical Action*, the organ of the National Association of Evangelicals, has often expressed itself on this issue. In April 1951, however, the annual convention of the NAE happened to be in session at the time when President Truman dismissed General MacArthur as commander of the forces in the Far East. The convention then departed from its separation of church and state position by an amazing action in which it condemned the dismissal, and officially supported General MacArthur as the Christian statesman whose principles and policies were those of Christ and the church, which must be promulgated by the national government. Certain convention delegates even went so far as to demand the impeachment of the President for his action although this demand was not included in the official resolu-

his allegiance to Abraham Lincoln. To prove the genuineness of his profession did not duty demand that he enroll as a soldier in defense of his principles? On the other hand, having dedicated himself to Christian service, could he morally take up arms? Moody made his decision in the light of what he believed his immediate duty and continued in the service of peace instead of war" (84, 85).

This version would suggest that Moody declined military service because of his more urgent immediate call to ministerial service, rather than because he was a conscientious objector. The statement in the earlier edition, however, that Moody "could not *conscientiously* enlist," together with the direct quotation, "There has never been a time in my life when I felt I could take a gun and shoot down a fellow-being. In this respect I am a Quaker," would argue rather strongly that Moody refrained from military service not merely because of other duties, but because he considered the taking of human life as wrong in itself.

The 1900 edition includes another incident in Moody's life (also omitted in the 1930 edition) which lends support to the same interpretation. When Moody was on his deathbed (he died Dec. 22, 1899) he spoke to his son about the Boer War then in progress. "I know what I would do if I were old Kruger," said Moody. "I would just send a message to Lord Salisbury, and state that there have been so many hundreds killed on the Boer side, and so many on the English side. And I would say that, as an old man, I would soon have to stand before God, and that I didn't want to go before Him with all this blood on my conscience, and I would tell England to make her own terms of peace." When it was suggested that England also was guilty, Moody replied: "That's quite so; but if Kruger placed himself in that position after showing the fight he has, England would have to make the best of terms, or answer for it to the best element in her own land, as well as the entire civilized world" (p. 550). Certainly this point of view is not unlike that of the Quaker.

9 Ralph L. Roy, *Apostles of Discord* (Boston, 1953) 217, 218.

tion. The action of the convention was vigorously protested by the Christian Reformed delegation which held that while it is proper for the individual Christian to engage in political action, the church as an organization should refrain from doing so. Later the Christian Reformed church withdrew from the NAE, although this is not to suggest that the action on the MacArthur case was the only reason for doing so.

Fundamentalists have been severe in their criticism of the social action program of the National Council of Churches, as being out of harmony with the Gospel message and program. Some of these same persons have been very active themselves, however, in supporting and even promoting the work of congressional investigating committees, especially that directed against churchmen of the National Council. The February 1, 1954, issue of *United Evangelical Action* carried an article on "The Truth About Those UAC Probes," by Gordon Scherer, a member of the House Un-American Activities Committee. The article had much to say about the investigation of Bishop Oxnam, and the periodical gave the article and the policies of the Un-American Activities Committee strong editorial support. It is also known that officials of the American Council of Churches, the extreme right-wing fundamentalist organization, were in touch with the House Un-American Activities Committee in connection with its investigation of Bishop Oxnam, and that some of them by special arrangement occupied front seats at the Oxnam hearing.[10] This is a case where a group of churchmen professing separation of church and state came dangerously close to a concordat with the state for the prosecution of an opposing school of churchmen.

In order to see how far social action can be carried by certain extreme sections of fundamentalism which claims to have nothing to do with a social gospel, one need only read Ralph L. Roy's *Apostles of Discord,* a recent book describing the Protestant fringe which is exploiting the Christian religion to justify racial or religious hate, discord and dissen-

10 *Christian Century* (Nov. 4, 1953) 70:1272.

sion, and economic or political extremism. There is Gerald
L. K. Smith who carries on a Christian Nationalist Crusade
for various causes including the abolition of the United Nations, and in 1952 to prevent the nomination of Dwight D.
Eisenhower for president because of his alleged Jewish ancestry. The Christian nondenominationalism of the late
Gerald B. Winrod was so real that "the entire United States
and Canada are his congregation." The shepherding of this
large flock was done from the headquarters in Wichita, Kansas. One of his contributions was the promotion of an anti-
Semitic crusade, using the forged *Protocols of the Learned
Elders of Zion* as evidence of a supposed plot of international
Jews to rule the world. For a time Winrod was joined in the
crusade against the *Protocols* and its supposed authors by
W. B. Riley, who was the leading figure behind the World's
Christian Fundamentals Association. In 1938 Winrod entered the Kansas primaries seeking the nomination for United States Senator on the Republican ticket on a platform
of high tariff, states rights, private enterprise, and isola-
tionism. "Let's keep Christian America Christian. Let's keep
America safe for Americans," was his slogan.[11] In order to be
fair we must hasten to say that Smith, Winrod, and Carl Mc-
Intire represent the extreme right wing of fundamentalism,
which must be distinguished from what Roy calls the "legitimate fundamentalist movement," represented by Charles E.
Fuller, John W. Bradbury, and Paul S. Rees. The evidence
is clear, however, that neither extreme nor legitimate fundamentalism are averse to certain forms of social and political
action.

R. L. Roy quotes an anonymous fundamentalist document which repudiates the social gospel in the following
language: "We are sent to preach Salvation, not Society; Evangelism, not Economics; Redemption, not Reform; Conversion, not Culture; Pardon, not Progress; a New Birth, not a
New Social Order; Regeneration, not Revolution; Revival,
not Renovation; Resurrection, not Resuscitation; a new

11 Roy, *op. cit.*, 31, 32.

Creation, not a new Organization; the Gospels, not Democracy; Christ, not Civilization; to be Ambassadors, not Diplomats."[12] This is a forceful statement of the fundamentalist case against the social gospel and against the social action programs of the liberal churches. And yet, the evidence is overwhelming that many of the fundamentalists themselves are steeped in social action. Unfortunately some of this action is not too commendable.

In 1953 during the days of the McCarthy investigations the Presbyterian General Council published *A Letter to Presbyterians Concerning the Present Situation in Our Country and in the World.*[13] Following its appearance James D. Murch, the editor of *United Evangelical Action,* published a critique of the *Letter.*[14] The *Letter* deals with current political questions in a manner that is quite in line with the traditional Presbyterian approach to political and social questions. It manifests a concern because of communism in the world and in America, and it offers suggestions as to what the United States should, and should not, do about it. Murch's critique does the same, except that his proposed remedy is different from that of the Presbyterian *Letter.*

The *Letter* frankly recognizes "that many of the revolutionary forces of our time are in great part the judgment of God upon human selfishness and complacency, and upon man's forgetfulness of man." All forms of feudalism and imperialism are foredoomed, the *Letter* says, and then suggests by implication that American foreign policy must be conducted in a way that will clear the United States of charges of adherence to these outmoded ways. The *Letter* suggests that society should be organized "in accordance with the everlasting principles of God's moral government of the world," as the best means of discouraging the growth of communism; that the post-communist mood which seems to be developing

---

12 *Ibid.,* 214.

13 *A Letter to Presbyterians Concerning the Present Situation in Our Country and in the World* (Philadelphia, Oct. 21, 1953). The *Letter* was reprinted in *The New York Times,* Nov. 3, 1953, p. 20.

14 James Deforest Murch, " 'This Nation Under God' and a 'Liberal' Ideology," in *United Evangelical Action* (Dec. 15, 1953) 4-6.

in the world should be encouraged; and that everything possible should be done to improve world relations through negotiation and by means of organizations such as the United Nations. Negatively, the *Letter* warns against the "almost exclusive concentration of the American mind upon the problem of the threat of communism," and says that "some congressional inquiries have revealed a distinct tendency to become inquisitions . . . [which] constitute a threat to freedom of thought in this country." "Treason and dissent are being confused," the *Letter* says. Then it warns that this "purely negative" approach to the situation can lead "the American mind into a spiritual vacuum" within which a fascist tyranny may easily develop.

Murch's critique, on the other hand, says the authors of the *Letter* did not understand the seriousness of communism which is in imminent danger of destroying our whole civilization; and that congressional investigations as currently conducted do not interfere with civil liberties and basic freedom; that they do not savor of inquisition. The Presbyterian *Letter* and the Murch critique reflect similar attitudes toward the basic question of social action, as such. The difference is in the political and social views of the men engaged in action. The Presbyterian *Letter* considers "McCarthyism" a dangerous program. The fundamentalist Murch thinks it is a good program. This writer must conclude, therefore, that the fundamentalist is not only favorable to social action as much as is the Presbyterian, but that in this case his kind of action is the less desirable of the two. To this writer it also seems that the tone and spirit of the Murch critique is too much that of the "apostles of discord," which by innuendo, and by something which approaches name-calling, attempts to attach a subversive label to the authors of the Presbyterian *Letter*. Even though admitting that capitalism is not mentioned in the *Letter,* Murch says it "implies that the American capitalist system is foredoomed to destruction." When the *Letter* speaks of organizing society in line with the principles of God's moral government he suspects that it actually means "reorganization," and so he feels sure that the *Letter* is promulgating dangerous socialistic doctrines.

Despite the above fundamentalist statement that Christians are called to preach "evangelism, not economics," President V. Raymond Edman of Wheaton College has an article on "Facts and Fallacies in Public Affairs," in a recent issue of *United Evangelical Action*.[15] This is a critique of the policies of the American government evidently following rather closely the arguments of a publication of the American Economic Foundation. While Dr. Edman is certainly within the Calvinist tradition when, as a Christian citizen or educator, he speaks on social, economic, or political questions, the article appearing as it does in the official organ of the National Association of Evangelicals, it certainly cannot be said that this fundamentalist organization rejects political and social action as a legitimate task of the church. Here the NAE is engaged in the same kind of action as the National Council of Churches is. And the fundamentalist *United Evangelical Action* is giving voice to its own variety of "social gospel" as much as is the *Christian Century* which has long been the spokesman for the old liberal social gospel. Although its basic theological presuppositions are more true to the New Testament teaching, fundamentalism seems no more, and in some cases less, able than does liberalism to grasp the ethical dimensions of the Gospel which it proclaims.

It was said earlier that the social gospel movement never succeeded in making real contact with the American working class; that it was largely a liberal middle class movement. What has fundamentalism achieved in this respect? It was noted that an original purpose of the Moody Bible Institute had been to train ministers who would be "willing to lay their lives alongside the laboring class and the poor, and to bring the Gospel to bear upon their lives." Even though other objectives have been added to this one, there is no doubt that the Moody Bible Institute and the "legitimate

---

15 V. R. Edman, "Facts and Fallacies in Public Affairs," *United Evangelical Action* (Jan. 1, 1954) 3, 4 ff.

fundamentalist movement" have extended a genuine ministry to the poorer classes. Roy says: "Where other Protestants
have failed, the fundamentalists have succeeded. They have
reached America's 'disinherited'—the poor, the uneducated,
the social outcasts. Untold millions have found life's meaning through this 'old time religion.' "[16] Even though Protestantism on the higher organizational level within the denominations and in the Federal and National Councils has
maintained a progressive, liberal approach to social questions, the parish church too often has reflected a bourgeois
character to such an extent that the laboring classes have been
repelled rather than attracted. Here is where fundamentalism with the tabernacle, the radio, and similar methods has
moved in and obtained a substantial following. The founding
of the Assemblies of God in 1914 and its growth to a membership approaching a half million in half a century is an illustration of what is meant. In a recent statement Henry P. Van
Dusen has described the "fringe sects," which must be included in the broad pattern of fundamentalism, as constituting a
New Reformation which next to the ecumenical movement
is "by all odds the most important fact in the Christian history of our times . . . in many respects startlingly analogous to
the most vital and dynamic expressions of the sixteenth-century Reformation."[17]

Unfortunately, however, this frequently means merely
that the working classes have been reached by a section of the
church. Often the preaching which these people hear contains little of the social implications of the Gospel. Frequently considerable emphasis is placed upon personal morals,
which is certainly the place to begin. Too frequently, however, it ends at that point and questions of far-reaching social
significance, such as the issues of war and peace, and of economic, racial, and social justice, are untouched. In 1947
Carl F. H. Henry considered this matter serious enough to

16 Roy, *op. cit.*, x.
17 Henry P. Van Dusen, "Caribbean Holiday," *The Christian Century* (Aug.
17, 1955) 72:948.

warrant a book on *The Uneasy Conscience of Modern Fundamentalism*. Using the term "fundamentalism" to cover all of conservative Protestantism to the theological right of neo-orthodoxy, Henry, a staunch fundamentalist himself, deplores an "apparent lack of any social passion in Protestant fundamentalism . . . . The picture is clear," he says, "when one brings into focus such admitted social evils as aggressive warfare, racial hatred and intolerance, the liquor traffic, and exploitation of labor or management, whichever it may be."[18]

During the past generation, says Henry, the great majority of fundamentalist ministers have become "increasingly less vocal about social evils." He refers to the campus newspaper of a fundamentalist college which devoted much space to the question "whether it is right to play 'rook,' while the nations of the world are playing with fire," and then declares it "a question whether one can be perpetually indifferent to the problems of social justice and international order, and develop a wholesome personal ethics."[19]

In its reaction to the social gospel, fundamentalism fell into the trap of attacking the reformers instead of the social problem. As a result, its own Gospel message has been narrowed. "Whereas once the redemptive gospel was a world-changing message, now it was narrowed to a world-resisting message. Out of twentieth century fundamentalism of this sort there could come no contemporary version of Augustine's *The City of God* . . . . Fundamentalism in revolting against the Social Gospel seemed also to revolt against the Christian social imperative.

"It was the failure of fundamentalism to work out a positive message within its own framework, and its . . . despairing view of world history, that cut off the pertinence of evangelicalism to the modern global crisis. The really creative thought, even if in a non-redemptive context, was now being done by the non-evangelical spokesmen . . . . [While

---

18 Carl F. H. Henry, *The Uneasy Conscience of Modern Fundamentalism* (Grand Rapids, 1947) 17.
19 *Ibid.*, 18-22.

condemning the leftist tendencies of the Federal Council of Churches fundamentalism has been silent] about the evils of a Capitalistic system from which the redemptive reference is largely abstracted . . . .

"The troubled conscience of the modern liberal, growing out of his superficial optimism, is a deep thing in modern times. But so is the uneasy conscience of the modern fundamentalist, that no voice is speaking today as Paul would, either at the United Nations sessions, or at labor-management disputes, or in strategic university classrooms whether in Japan or Germany or America. For the first protracted period in its history, evangelical Christianity stands divorced from the great social reform movements.[20]

This is a remarkable statement by an outstanding leader of an emerging school of fundamentalists which is earnestly trying to chart a new course, with its faith and program established on a broader base than that which has characterized the movement up to now. In an effort to clear the atmosphere and to divest legitimate fundamentalism from the extreme tendencies and influences described above Henry is proposing to replace the name "fundamentalism" with that of evangelical Protestantism. Indeed, the name used by the National Association of Evangelicals would seem to be an indication that legitimate fundamentalism as a whole is joining in this effort.

Henry's statement quoted above says that creative social thought in recent times has been the contribution of nonevangelical spokesmen, and that "for the first protracted period in its history, evangelical Christianity stands divorced from the great social reform movements." It was suggested earlier that if from its beginning fundamentalism had combined evangelical theology and the social vision of Finney under the intellectual leadership of men whose creative thinking could have put the constructive work of Rauschenbusch on a solid foundation and moved forward on it, the leadership of creative Protestant thought today might be in

20 *Ibid.*, 30-36.

evangelical hands. The publication of Carl F. H. Henry's *Uneasy Conscience* has been called the turning point in the social outlook of fundamentalism. Does the new development give promise that that which did not occur in the older fundamentalism is about to emerge in the new evangelicalism? This writer is one among a number who have been hopeful that such might be the case.

Occasionally one finds cause for encouragement in this hope. Evangelical Protestantism seems more sympathetic to the way of the cross as defined in this book than was the case a generation ago. One finds an occasional leader among them who is fully committed to nonresistance and the renunciation of war. Culbert G. Rutenber, the author of *The Dagger and the Cross*,[21] must certainly be classified as an evangelical. There are other members of faculties of evangelical seminaries and colleges, some of whom would be classified in the distinctly fundamentalist group, who are likewise committed to the Christian pacifist position.

An important illustration of a fundamentalist who has come to this position is James R. Graham, a minister and foreign missionary of Calvinist background, who for years had accepted the traditional fundamentalist position on war. Study of the Bible convinced him, however, that dispensationalism is a fallacy; that "the Sermon on the Mount is the heavenly jurisprudence of the Christian"; and that a theology which "invalidates it for Christians of this age is an insult and iniquity against the person of Christ." His evangelical theology makes it impossible for Graham to endorse a liberal type of pacifism or a social gospel which ignores the divine work of regeneration; but he can sympathize even less with the fundamentalist who is too busily engaged in the saving of souls to be occupied with social concerns—until a war comes along when he says, "Okay, call on me," and walks off to the slaughter leaving the souls of men to shift for themselves.[22]

The most popular and generally influential representa-

---

21 C. G. Rutenber, *The Dagger and the Cross* (New York, 1950).
22 James R. Graham, *Strangers and Pilgrims* (Scottdale, 1951) 34-38.

tive of American fundamentalism at its best today is Billy
Graham, the evangelist. That his has been a positive influence in western Christendom there can be no doubt. Having read his writings and heard his preaching, both in person
and by radio, this writer shares the universal esteem of Billy
Graham "as a humble, straightforward Christian." Moreover, it cannot be said that Graham does not have a social
consciousness. His views on economics, industrial relations,
and race, for example, seem to be enlightened.

One of the eighteen chapters of Graham's book, *Peace
with God,* is devoted to "Social Obligations of the Christian."
Here he says: "If Christ could prevail in all labor-management relations, we would not have any strikes. . . . Management would treat employees with generosity, and employees
would be eager to put in a full day's work . . . . A man of real
Christian concepts cannot help being concerned about safety
precautions, good working conditions, and the well-being of
those in his employ. He will not only see his workers as 'man
power,' but also as human beings . . . .

"*The Christian looks through the eyes of Christ at the
race question* and admits that the church has failed in solving
this great human problem. We have let the sports world, the
entertainment field, politics, the armed forces, education, and
industry outstrip us. The church should have been the pace-
setter. . . . The closer the people of all races get to Christ and
His cross, the closer they will get to one another."[23]

Here Graham seems to uphold the way of the cross in
race and industrial relations. Furthermore, there has been a
growing clarity of his pronouncements on the race question.
There was no racial segregation at the Graham meetings in
Richmond, Virginia, in 1956. Many Negroes sang in the one-
thousand-voice choir back of the speaker's stand. Graham
has been criticized by Reinhold Niebuhr and others for not
speaking out strongly enough on social issues. On the race
question, however, Carl F. H. Henry would seem to be correct when he says that in the wholly integrated New York

23 Billy Graham, *Peace with God* (Garden City, 1953) 194, 195.

crusade, "for thousands of Christians it was a new experience to share a hymnbook in worship with a member of another race. From Madison Square Garden, quite unpublicized, rose outlines of a new working relationship between believers of all races. Gain was registered, therefore, in the very realm that concerned some of Mr. Graham's critics."[24] It is also reported that Graham has declared his willingness to conduct a campaign in South Africa only on condition that the audiences be mixed, white and colored, a condition which the Dutch Reformed Church in South Africa has refused to consider.[25] Henry also reports that the "executive director of the Protestant Council of New York told a news conference that he did not know another clergyman in the city who had spoken as forcibly from the pulpit as Billy Graham during the crusade on areas of social responsibility."[26]

It seems ungrateful to be critical of any good work because it is not good enough, especially in a case like that of Billy Graham who has had more than his share of critics. Nevertheless, it does seem to this writer that if the leadership of creative Protestant thought and action is to pass into evangelical hands the evangelical leadership will need to be more boldly imaginative, and will need to remove itself farther from what Bonhoeffer has called "cheap grace," and to become more thoroughly steeped in the way of the cross and discipleship than is the case at present. In the quotation cited above Graham himself admits that in the solution of the race question the church has not been the pace-setter, but has followed in the wake of sports, entertainment, politics, the army, and industry.

It is recognized, of course, that in evangelism and the preaching of the Gospel there is a New Testament order, first acceptance of the redemptive work of Christ and then a following in His steps and the way of the cross. No doubt some of Graham's critics are placing too much emphasis on social justice as such, and not enough on social justice as a

24 Editorial, *Christianity Today* (Washington, Sept. 16, 1957) 1:24:5.
25 *Gospel Herald* (Scottdale, July 10, 1956) 49:672.
26 *Christianity Today* (Sept. 16, 1957) 1:24:5.

fruit of the redemptive work of Christ. On the other hand, it is clear that the eighteenth-century Wesleyan and Evangelical movements in England, and the first and second Great Awakenings in America, while keeping the Gospel and social reform in proper order, were nevertheless aggressive in their attack upon social evils. The revivalists did not follow in the wake of the reforms. The reforms followed in the wake of the revivals. Some of them, moreover, represented real trail blazing in the face of tremendous opposition, not the belated espousal of a cause which had become more or less popular. The same was true to an even greater degree of the work of the sixteenth-century Anabaptists discussed in the following chapter.

It is the conviction of this writer that if Christendom is to find its way through the crisis of the mid-twentieth century it will need to produce another creative movement as "momentous and significant" as that of the Anabaptists, and that such a movement demands nothing less than a complete break with the war system, a deep and unqualified commitment to Christian pacifism. Neo-orthodox theologians may reject New Testament ethics as inferior to Christian ethics[27]; but evangelical theologians must accept New Testament ethics alone as valid for the Christian in this age. Nothing short of full commitment to renunciation of war, the world's greatest social evil, can satisfy the demands of Christian discipleship and the way of the cross. And anything less than this would almost seem to remove Christendom's last hope for winning the peoples of Africa and the Orient for Christ and the church.

It has been this writer's happy privilege to exchange views on Christian pacifism and the Christian's relation to the state in sessions of the social action section of the National Association of Evangelicals presided over by Carl F. H. Henry. This writer is also highly appreciative of the sympathetic hearing and discussion of the nonresistant point of view on the part of both the leader of the session and the

27 See above, pp. 105, 110.

audience in attendance. It should be pointed out, however, that even James M. Gray, representing an earlier generation of fundamentalist leaders generally lacking in social consciousness, had an equally sympathetic understanding of the New Testament peace position—also without commitment to it himself. It would seem, therefore, that the leaders of the new evangelical social consciousness should take the next step of positive committal to the way of the cross.

In a day when Catholic theologians like Pater Stratmann of Cologne and Johannes Ude of Austria, without departing from Augustinian or Thomist theology, find themselves completely committed to nonparticipation in war on the ground that in the day of atomic weapons and intercontinental ballistic missiles there is no longer such a thing as a just war;[28] and when a fellow evangelical like James R. Graham believes a theology which invalidates the Sermon on the Mount to be "an insult and iniquity against the person of Christ," it is disappointing to see other evangelicals following from afar, speaking only gently against "aggressive war." If evangelicals who would base their faith and life on what "the Bible says," wait to renounce all war until others have first done so, what reward have they? Do not even non-Christians the same? And if Christian evangelicals use the social order as their frame of reference to such an extent that they can do no more than to choose between the lesser of two evils, what are they doing more than others? Does not even Niebuhr the same?

Billy Graham's statements on the Christian's obligation to the state and participation in war illustrate how difficult it is for Christians to divest themselves of the dualistic ethic which comes down in the tradition of Augustine and the Reformers. First in his list of social obligations is that of good citizenship. To the obligation to be law-abiding, pay one's taxes, love and seek the welfare of one's country, and support the welfare institutions of the community, one can readily agree.

28 See J. Ude, *Du Sollst Nicht Töten!* (Dornbirn, Austria, 1948); F. M. Stratmann, *Krieg und Christentum heute.*

Beyond the recognition that there might be unjust laws which the Christian has a right to criticize, however, the discussion leaves the impression that the Christian's relationship with the state is mostly sweetness and light. As if the state and its program were altogether lovely he complacently says: "We ought to seek and work for the good of our country. Sometimes we may be called to die for it. We are to do it gladly—as unto God. We are to be conscientious in our work as good citizens."[29] On another occasion Graham said: War "is certainly not the Christian way of settling either individual or global problems. On the other hand, we must accept our responsibilities as citizens. . . . A Christian would find it hard to be a loyal citizen in a nation that promoted warfare. We can thank God that we are part of a nation that seeks to solve all problems by peaceful means."[30]

Obviously, Graham is far from being a militarist. If all men were of his spirit wars would not be started. On the other hand, when an evil society wages war he has nothing better to offer than to support it. There can be little doubt that in our day war is the world's greatest collective sin. How then is it possible to call on America to repent from her sins and at the same time indicate a readiness to engage in this greatest of sins?

It is admitted that war is "not the Christian way of settling problems." Is it possible then to appeal for repentance from sin on the basis of what "the Bible says," and at the same time grant that in spite of what the Gospel says the Christian has other obligations? John C. Bennett whose frame of reference is the social order rather than the Bible admits an anguish of soul because of his precarious position between the New Testament ethic and the terrible necessity of meeting the requirements of the state in the sinful social order.[31] But Graham simply says that if called upon to die for one's country one should do it gladly. When the question

---

29 Billy Graham, *Peace with God*, 191.

30 Quoted, Paul Peachey, "Billy Graham on Nonresistance," *Gospel Herald* (Oct. 22, 1957) 50:896.

31 See below, p. 194.

of killing other Christians is raised his answer is that "if they are killed through the ravages of war, it is because they are members of a warring society and incidentally Christians."[32] Is it possible for members of the body of Christ to destroy each other with no more anguish of soul than to dismiss one another as incidentally Christian?

André Trocmé, the French Protestant pastor, has laid his hand on the great social issues and the sin of our society and has lifted them up where they can be seen in their stark reality. Coming from the pen of one who has seen his country overrun in two wars and who has suffered in prison for his loyalty to the Gospel, these words are a clear proclamation of what it means to be a good soldier of Jesus Christ: "The world habitually lies? The Christian will always tell the truth. . . . The world cheats and exploits? The Christian does not steal, but shares his goods. . . . The world returns evil for evil? The Christian does not resist the evildoer. The world kills? The Christian saves. The world seeks to end aggression and exploitation by war? The Christian will begin with himself. He will prefer the risk of being killed to killing, of being exploited to exploiting, of being deceived to deceiving. And what is 'worst' in this method of defense, so discouraging in its simplicity, is that it is the good way, the only true way, and therefore the only effective way. . . . There are no Christian politics; but the repentance of Christians and the change of conduct that springs from it can profoundly modify the course of political events."[33]

It seems to this writer that Graham on the other hand, in spite of his good intentions, plays directly into the hands of the militarists. General Norstad of the NATO forces has admitted that the United States would never permit the Russians to surround it with military bases as it has surrounded them. Nor is it a secret that some men in and out of the Pentagon are saying that if and when the present war is extended beyond the cold stage the United States must strike

---

32 Paul Peachey, *loc. cit.*, 896.
33 André Trocmé, *The Politics of Repentance* (New York, 1953) 66, 75.

first. It is the deep conviction of this writer that Billy Graham does not give adequate consideration to the true nature of the military power of the state as the outworking of the wrath of God in an evil society, which under "normal" conditions serves as a "minister for good, for the punishment of evil and the praise of them that do well," but which under other circumstances becomes the beast of the book of Revelation.

As Christians our great obligation is to bring the Gospel of Jesus Christ to those who have it not. As we bring the Gospel to the people of Africa and Asia can we at the same time assume and say that "we are part of a nation that seeks to solve all problems by peaceful means"? Can we really expect the people of Africa, India, and Japan to believe that this is so? Even if we could grant that the nation state is doing the best that it can, is it possible for Christians to place the obligation to serve the state above the obligation to follow the way of Christ? And if they do so can the people of Africa and the Orient in this day be expected to respond to the Christian invitation? It is the deep conviction of this writer that unless preachers of the Gospel, ambassadors of the Prince of Peace, divest themselves completely from western militarism, with unequivocal commitment to the way of the cross, we need not be surprised if instead of winning these people for Christ they will be driven into the arms of Buddhism or communism.

This writer would join with Paul Peachey in urging "the Graham team to a soul-searching study of war in the light of the Gospel at the earliest possible date, at least before the next overseas campaign. Millions are waiting for a clear word from the Gospel in the atomic age, and Billy Graham could be in position to say it."[34] To this appeal we would add another: that the editorial policy of *Christianity Today*, as it aspires to be the spokesman of evangelical Christianity, likewise divest itself of all nationalistic connections with full committal to the way of the cross. As an illustration of what

34 Paul Peachey, *loc. cit.*, 897.

is meant, the second issue[35] of this in many ways promising and excellent journal carries an article by Senator William F. Knowland on the issue of admitting communist China to the United Nations. Various arguments against admission are offered, but none of them is related to the Christian faith. This writer can agree with Paul Erb when he says: "It seems unfortunate to us that a magazine which should become a leading voice of evangelical Christianity should speak on a purely political question in such a way as to equate Christianity and American nationalism for readers in Europe and Asia. American self-protection is not the Gospel of Christ."[36]

In the mid-twentieth century evangelical Christianity is at the crossroads. The older fundamentalism seems on the way out. A new leadership with a nobler spirit and a deeper social consciousness seems to be emerging. Where will it lead us? Could it send to the foreign mission field thousands of missionaries who accept the evangelization of the world as the primary task of the church and who are committed to the lordship of Christ over the whole man in personal and social life as an integral part of the evangel which is preached; could it see that such commitment requires the complete renunciation of war as the world's greatest social evil and as a mockery of the faith of all professed Christians who engage in it; could it see that nothing less than the way of the cross in the human relations of the Christian can win the hearts of people who have come to identify Christianity with a despised western imperialism; could evangelical leadership everywhere unite in an unreserved commitment to the way of the cross, there would be hope that evangelical Christianity would find its rightful place in the arena of social reform, and that leadership in creative Christian social thought would be in evangelical hands. If, on the other hand, there is to be a complacent assumption of "other obligations," are we not obliged to ask: What do ye more than others? Do not even the crisis theologians the same?

35 *Christianity Today* (Oct. 29, 1956).
36 *Gospel Herald* (Dec. 4, 1956) 49:1143-44.

ANABAPTISM

9. ANABAPTISM AND THE SOCIAL ORDER

In surveying the history of Christendom and the various adaptations and compromises of its ethic as represented by Catholicism and the major Protestant types, it is important to remember that down through the entire stream of that history there has been a continuous succession of protest against these forms of compromise. This protest has been the contribution of small groups of earnest Christians, commonly referred to as the sects, and represented by the Montanists and Donatists in the earlier period, the Waldensians in the high Middle Ages, and the Anabaptists in the Reformation. Generally speaking, the sects rejected the division of the body of Christ into two classes, the holy and the worldly. Thus they declined to accept the medieval dual ethic. They insisted that the Christian was one individual whose ethic as a citizen of the state must be no different from his personal ethic as a Christian; and in so doing they rejected the ethic of Luther. Their strict adherence to the Sermon on the Mount and the New Testament ethic also made it impossible for them to accept the Calvinist doctrine of the sphere of common grace which enables the Christian to serve as an agency of the divine wrath.

The sects stressed the way of the cross in all of their relationships. They emphasized inward perfection, the way of brotherhood, and close personal relationships within the group. They did not build their church coterminously with the general social order and then modify its ethic to fit this lower level. They built their church on the New Testament pattern and invited men and women to leave the world; to take up their cross and follow Christ into the life of the holy community, the colony of heaven, which was planted within the pagan world. The strenuous ethic of Jesus was accepted without question. They were not aggressors before the courts of law; they did not use the oath; they did not engage in war; they were indifferent toward the state; and they kept themselves largely separate from the economic struggles of the time. Their emphasis on brotherhood made for equality and simplicity of life, for the sharing of material possessions, and in some cases for actual community of goods. The pre-Reformation sects were short-lived for the most part, however, because of the tremendous opposition of the all-powerful medieval state church. The Reformation sects, on the other hand, obtained a wide following in spite of opposition and persecution, and their influence was destined to be a great and far-reaching one.

Of all the reforming groups of the sixteenth century there was none which saw the distinction between the Christian order and the pagan disorder more clearly than did the Anabaptists. So sharp was their discernment of the New Testament ethic and its meaning; so fundamental was their challenge to the general social order; and so vigorous their dissent from it, that they brought down upon their heads one of the severest persecutions which the Christian Church has witnessed in all its history. Even though all of the major groups, Protestant and Catholic alike, regarded the Anabaptists as the greatest of heretics, threatening not only the purity of the church but the very structure of society itself, strangely enough many of the principles for which they stood have come to be generally accepted in our western world, and others, while not generally accepted, have come to be tolerated and recognized as a worth-while contribution to the culture of our time. This is a vindication of the truth that the law of God written in the heart of every man will ultimately bring a sub-Christian or even a pagan society to recognize the way of the cross when it is consistently demonstrated by the disciples of Christ who make their impact upon that society.

The significance of the Anabaptist movement was stated as follows by Walter Rauschenbusch more than forty years ago: "These radical bodies did not produce as many great individuals as we might have expected because their intellectuals and leaders were always killed off or silenced. But their communities were prophetic. They have been the forerunners of the modern world. They stood against war, against capital punishment, against slavery, and against coercion in matters of religion before others thought of it. It was largely due to their influence that the Puritan Revolution had its prophetic elements of leadership. The Free Churches throughout the world, consciously or unconsciously, clearly or dimly, have passed beyond the official types of orthodox Protestantism and have taken on some of the characteristics of the early radicals. Great church bodies now stand as a matter of course on those principles of freedom and toleration which only the boldest once dared to assert. The power of leadership is with those organizations and movements which have some prophetic qualities and trust to the inner light."[1]

Precisely then, what was the Anabaptist movement? It was a plain announcement that the way of the cross was real, and that those who walked that way proposed to maintain the high ethic of the New Testament in every phase of life, existentially. Specifically this meant loyalty to the Scriptures as the sole and sufficient authority for faith and practice, with recognition of the New Testament as having superseded the Old. It meant the way of discipleship, bringing the whole of life completely under the lordship of Christ. It meant the Christianization of all social relationships by the application of the strenuous ethic of love. This meant nonresistance in personal and group relationships, the renunciation of vengeance, of litigation, and of violence, war, and bloodshed. It meant an economic life which was harmonious with the ethic of love. It meant simplicity in every manner of life: simplicity of speech, requiring the renunciation of the oath whether legal or profane; simplicity in personal appearance and household furnishings, and simplicity in eating and drinking, with abstinence from alcoholic beverages.

1 Walter Rauschenbusch, *A Theology for the Social Gospel* (New York, 1917) 195, 196.

The Anabaptists were not reformers like Luther and Calvin. They were *restorers* who searched the Scriptures to discover the New Testament pattern of society. And having found it they sought the restitution of the true colony of heaven. To the Anabaptists the church "must be a community of the saints whose members, though not perfect, yet aspire to perfection and strive mightily."[2] There is no question that to a high degree they achieved that to which they aspired and for which they strove. Even their opponents testified that they did so. Zwingli said their conduct appeared "irreproachable, pious, unassuming, attractive, yea, supermundane. Even those who are inclined to be critical will say that their lives are excellent." Bullinger, Zwingli's successor, says members were received into the Anabaptist fellowship "unto repentance and newness of life. They henceforth led their lives under a semblance of a quite spiritual conduct. They denounced covetousness, pride, profanity, the lewd conversation and immorality of the world, drinking and gluttony."[3]

Catholic opponents found in the Anabaptists: "No lying, deception, swearing, strife, harsh language, no intemperate eating and drinking, no outward personal display . . . , but humility, patience, uprightness, meekness, honesty, temperance, straightforwardness. . . . They call each other brethren and sisters, . . . they do not use weapons. . . . They do not go to law before the magistrates; they bear everything in patience, as they pretend, and in the Holy Ghost."[4]

"Now a community leading such a noble, blessed life as these Anabaptist heretics I should have liked to establish within the Roman Catholic Church, for, as far as I can see, it surpasses even the monastic life."[5]

How was it that the Anabaptists to such a high degree achieved that for which they sought? Clearly it was not their own achievement. It was an achievement of the Holy Spirit through the redemptive work of Christ. "A genuine Chris-

2 R. H. Bainton, *The Reformation of the Sixteenth Century* (Boston, 1952) 96.
3 Quoted in John Horsch, *Mennonites in Europe* (Scottdale, Pa., 1942) 294.
4 Quoted in *ibid.*, 295, 296.
5 Quoted in R. J. Smithson. *The Anabaptists* (London, 1935) 117.

tian," says Menno Simons, "is a man that is born of God after the Spirit; one who has become a new creature in Christ."[6] It is as a new creature in Christ that a man is able to crucify the flesh, hating ungodliness and sin, bringing forth fruits unto righteousness. Nonresistance and the rejection of war are not human achievements, for it is "the regenerate" who "put on Christ and manifest his Spirit, nature and power in all their conduct"; who "know not hatred and vengeance"; who "do good to those who despitefully use them, and pray for those who persecute them"; who "have beaten their swords into plowshares and their spears into pruning hooks, and know war no more. . . . Their sword is the sword of the Spirit, which they wield in a good conscience through the Holy Ghost."[7] Thus, by their own testimony, the life of the Anabaptist community was one of complete subjection to the person and the work of Christ, in full recognition of Him as Prophet and Saviour, and Lord of their lives.

To the Anabaptists, the church was the body of Christ, the temple of God. It was a voluntary society of personally committed members. It was a fellowship of believers; an ethical community of brotherly love, frequently meeting for prayer and fellowship. To them the church was not coextensive with the general social order, a fusion of disciples and worldlings. It was a disciplined spiritual brotherhood in which every member was significant, the leadership widely distributed, with an abundance of "lay" responsibility. To the Anabaptists the Christian brotherhood was a new social order, composed of those called out from the semipagan disorder. Their community was the colony of heaven in the midst of the society of this world. The task of each was to strive for the perfection of that community. The church was the final goal of all its endeavor, challenging the chaotic disorder of this world, warning the sinner, wooing him into the fold, there to be united with the body of Christ for the communion of the saints and the glory of God.

---

6 Menno Simons, *The Complete Writings of Menno Simons* (Scottdale, 1956) 600.
7 *Ibid.*, 93, 94.

The character of the Anabaptist brotherhood and the nature of its communion and fellowship is characterized as follows by Rauschenbusch: "While the great churches were bitterly contending over the question whether their Lord was physically or spiritually present, and if physically, whether by transubstantiation or consubstantiation, the persecuted Anabaptists, who had neither the right to meet nor to exist, had the spirit of the original institution among them. As in the primitive church, their service was preceded by searching of heart and reconciliation, so that all might be one in Christ. As in the upper room at Jerusalem, they acted in full view of death, and their main thought was to gain strength for imprisonment and torture by once more touching the garment-hem of their Lord. They often dwelt on the fact that many grains of wheat had been crushed and had felt the heat of the oven to make this bread, and many berries of the vine had been pressed in the wine-press to make this wine; in the same way the followers of Jesus must pass through affliction and persecution in order to form the body of the Lord. Thus these poor proletarians, hunted by the tyrannical combinations of church and state, Catholic and Protestant alike, returned to the original spirit of the Lord's Meal and realized that Real Presence about which others wrangled."[8]

As this graphic statement affirms, there was a significant relationship between the hostility of the outside world and the presence of the Lord within the fellowship of the saints. In a day when other churches considered themselves coextensive with the general social order, frequently accepting its sub-Christian standards as normal or at least permissible for the Christian, the Anabaptists refused to conform themselves to that order. They subjected the social order to the critique of the Christian ethic. They were a remnant called out from the world, sitting in judgment upon that world, and disturbing its conscience. The world never likes to have its conscience disturbed, however. When Ahab and Jezebel had their consciences disturbed they struck back at the prophet

8 Rauschenbusch, *op. cit.*, 205, 206.

in an effort to cut him down as a troubler of Israel. The prophet replied in no uncertain terms, however, that it was they who had troubled Israel in forsaking the commandment of the Lord.[9]

The Anabaptists were the Elijahs, the Isaiahs, and the Jeremiahs of their time, and theirs was the task of testifying to the Ahabs and the Jezebels of the sixteenth century. The unregenerate world has never understood the way of the cross, however, and it could not be expected to understand it now. Thus the drama recorded in the eleventh chapter of Hebrews, with its graphic account of the prophets and saints who were persecuted and tortured, was re-enacted in sixteenth-century Europe. Furthermore, the experiences of the persecuted saints came to be accepted as the normal experience of Christians in this world, so that the Anabaptists developed a theology of martyrdom. Hebrews eleven with its description of mockings and scourgings, chains and imprisonment, of wanderings over deserts and mountains and in dens and caves of the earth, by men of whom the world was not worthy, was the pattern which the Anabaptists were destined to follow and which they took for granted. Conrad Grebel in his well-known letter to Thomas Müntzer said: "True Christian believers are sheep among wolves, sheep for the slaughter; they must be baptized in anguish and affliction, tribulation, persecution, suffering, and death; they must be tried with fire, and must reach the fatherland of eternal rest, not by killing them bodily, but by mortifying their spiritual enemies. Neither do they use worldly sword of war, since all killing has ceased with them. . . ."[10]

Not only did the *Martyrs' Mirror*[11] come to be the most highly prized Anabaptist book. The Anabaptist hymns, of which there are many, are also filled with the martyr theme.

9 I Kings 18:17, 18.

10 H. S. Bender, *Conrad Grebel, the Founder of the Swiss Brethren* (Goshen, 1950) 284, 285.

11 T. J. van Braght, *The Bloody Theatre, or Martyrs' Mirror of the Defenseless Christians, who baptized only upon Confession of Faith, and who suffered and died for the testimony of Jesus, their Saviour, from the time of Christ to the year A.D. 1660.* (First published in the Netherlands, in the Dutch language in 1660.)

7

The true church has always been a suffering church. The disciple follows his Master in the cross life and need not expect to be excused from suffering even as his Master suffered. The martyr is the "true soldier of God," fighting against the power of darkness.[12] "Therefore, dear Christian," says one of their tracts, "do not be disappointed that the world hates you, but only continue, be patient, wait on the great God with joy, for blessed are those who weep here, for it is only for a short time."[13] "Whoever will not suffer with Christ also will not rule with Him, and whoever doesn't have this holy spirit is no Christian."[14]

Menno Simons said: "The martyrdom of Stephen, in which there appears the Christ-pointed situation, is today relevant and primary. It shows not only that the disciple must undertake to follow the vision of Christ's suffering and death, but *how* he must do it. He cried in the way and manner of his Master on the Cross, Father do not count these sins unto them! That is according to Christ's mandate the new concept with which the elect conquer their fate, their opponents."[15]

The martyr theme among the Anabaptists was not a cry of despair. It was a shout of triumph. Through martyrdom the saints would conquer their fate and their foes. The time of suffering would not be long. God was more real than the world. In the end the followers of Christ would reign with Him and the persecutors would stand before Him whom they had pierced.[16] The Anabaptist theology of martyrdom was a theology of triumph and of aggressive evangelism. While the fearful authorities persecuted them because they believed their doctrine and their program threatened the integrity, yes the very existence of society itself, the Anabaptists were

12 Ethelbert Stauffer, "The Anabaptist Theology of Martyrdom," *Mennonite Quarterly Review* (July 1945) 19:200.
13 Robert Friedmann, "Concerning the True Soldier of Christ," *Mennonite Quarterly Review* (April 1931) 5:95.
14 Quoted in Franklin H. Littell, *The Anabaptist View of the Church* (1952) 109.
15 Quoted in *ibid.,* 111.
16 Rev. 1:7.

just as sure that they were the emissaries of God, proclaiming the message which alone had power to bring salvation to men and to society. With this conviction they went forth, coming directly to grips with the world, taking their stand regardless of consequences. To the Anabaptists, persecution and the evil social order were a challenge to preach the Word and to witness to the truth. They attacked the social order to evangelize it. Theirs was a corporate witness in which the life of the entire community was a demonstration of the power of God to create a colony of heaven on earth. Their preaching mission was a demonstration of every member evangelism. Roland H. Bainton says: "Every member of the group was regarded as a missionary. Men and women left their homes to go on evangelistic tours. The established churches, whether Catholic or Protestant, were aghast at these ministers of both sexes insinuating themselves into town and farm."[17]

When the state churches divided European territory among themselves and gave the ruler of each region power to determine the religious faith of his subjects, the Anabaptists quoted the twenty-fourth Psalm which says "the earth is the Lord's and the fulness thereof."[18] Since they were His emissaries, they were commissioned to go into all of the Lord's territory. Wherever they could they went, heedless of any worldly prince who may have claimed a given territory as his own. The Great Commission[19] was an authoritative command; so into the world they went, preaching to all who would hear, and baptizing whoever would receive the Word. George Blaurock baptized 150 people at one service and on another occasion he entered a chapel and preached to the assembly before the appointed minister arrived.[20]

Under the Anabaptist influence the medieval pilgrim who carried his penance from shrine to shrine was transformed into a fiery evangelist who walked into the jaws of death with the Gospel message. In 1542 an imperial edict forbade every man to receive Menno Simons into his house,

17 Bainton, *op. cit.*, 101.
18 Psalm 24:1.

19 Matt. 28:19, 20.
20 Littell, *op. cit.*, 101.

to give him food or drink, or even to speak to him. Whoever found him was to capture him and turn him over to the authorities and receive the reward. Whoever disobeyed the edict was himself liable to pay the penalty of death. But this did not stop Menno. On one occasion he entered a church and talked to the priest so effectively about the errors of the Catholic faith that the priest resigned his office.

The sixteenth-century Anabaptists were a Christian community which was definitely not of this world. It was very much in the world, however, and certainly not afraid of the world. It recognized an inevitable tension between the church and the pagan disorder, and believed its mission to be that of pressing upon the world the claims of the Christian order. Bainton says the Anabaptists were the awakeners of their time, arousing men from their lethargy, summoning them to forsake the pagan social order and join the order of God, the Christian community, the colony of heaven. The Anabaptists did not claim sinless perfection for themselves, nor for their communities. What the Bible called sin, however, they called sin; and to them repentance meant forsaking that sin, not a continued involvement in it because of tragic necessity. They taught that the church must be perfect in the sense that the perfection of Christ is accounted unto them; and they said it must be blameless in that its teaching and its practice are founded on God's Word. It was recognized that there had been a Judas among the original twelve disciples and that this could and would happen again. On the other hand, it was also recognized that the Christian community must exercise discipline, purge out the dross, and strive toward perfection, never condoning that which is evil. The Christian community must in deed and in truth be a Christian social order with a high ethic, based on the pattern of God's own design. It cannot be a semipagan disorder which compromises with evil. Its members are crucified with Christ, living the cross life and ready to die the cross death if necessity requires it.

10. ANABAPTISM AND THE STATE

The Anabaptists regarded temporal government as ordained of God, and recognized both the police and the welfare functions of the state. The Swiss Brethren addressed their magistrates as ministers of God, even while being persecuted by them. They recognized, however, that the police function was an expression of the wrath of God operating within a social order which did not follow the way of the cross. Their earliest confession of faith adopted in 1527 says: "The sword is ordained of God *outside the perfection of Christ* . . . for the punishment of the wicked and . . . to be used by the worldly magistrates."[1] The Dordrecht confession of 1632 says "that God has instituted civil government, for the punishment of the wicked and the protection of the pious; and also further, for the purpose of governing the world . . . and . . . to preserve its subjects in good order and under good regulations."[2] The Ris confession, an eighteenth-century Dutch statement, says that the original nature of man gave no room for violence in human society. Because of man's later "great corruptness," however, government which uses force and coercion was ordained of God, "first through His divine providence in general"; then was authorized for Israel under the old covenant; and is likewise necessary today in the general social order.[3]

Since the police function of the state employs coercive methods out of harmony with the New Testament ethic and since these methods are designed for use within the sub-

---

1 John C. Wenger, "The Schleitheim Confession of Faith," *Mennonite Quarterly Review* (October 1945) 19:250.

2 The Dordrecht Confession of Faith (Art. XIII, "The Office of Civil Government"). The entire Confession appears in John F. Funk, *Confession of Faith and Minister's Manual* (Elkhart, 1917). Articles XIII and XIV appear in Guy F. Hershberger, *War, Peace, and Nonresistance* (Scottdale, 1953) 317, 318.

3 Cornelis Ris, *Mennonite Articles of Faith* (a translation, Berne, Ind., 1925) 51, 52.

Christian disorder, it naturally followed that the Anabaptist faith stood for a separation of church and state. Especially objectionable was compulsory membership in a state church. As early as 1523 the Anabaptists opposed Zwingli's decision to submit to the Zurich council for final decision the matter of the reformation of the church. Here, says Harold S. Bender, "are the crossroads from which two roads lead down through history: the road of the free church of committed Christians separated from the state, with full religious liberty; and the road of the state church, territorially fixed, depending on state support, and forcibly suppressing all divergence, the road of intolerance and persecution."[4]

The Anabaptists believed that no one could be a true disciple of Christ unless of his own free will he chose to be a disciple. To compel a man to join the church was therefore useless. It was more than that, however; it was wrong. Christians must never use force for the coercion of their fellow men for any purpose, least of all for bringing them into the kingdom of heaven. The Anabaptists insisted that the New Testament church was a voluntary association of regenerated believers, who through their experience of personal salvation were drawn together for fellowship with one another and with Christ, without any outward compulsion by the state.

Menno Simons, the leader of the Dutch Mennonites, asks the pointed question: "Where do the Holy Scriptures teach that in Christ's kingdom and church we shall proceed with the magistrate, with the sword, and with physical force and tyranny over a man's conscience and faith, things subject to the judgment of God alone?"[5]

In an age when the laws of Calvin's Geneva ordered heretics to "be sent before the consistory to be rerpimanded, or before the council to receive punishment, according to the exigencies of the case,"[6] which in some cases meant death,

4 H. S. Bender, "The Anabaptists and Religious Liberty in the 16th Century," *Mennonite Quarterly Review* (April 1955) 29.

5 Menno Simons, *Complete Writings*, 537.

6 Quoted in Georgia Harkness, *John Calvin, the Man and his Ethics* (New York, 1931) 105.

Conrad Grebel, the first leader of the Swiss Brethren, said: "Go forward with the Word and establish a Christian Church with the help of Christ and His rule, as we find it instituted in Matthew 18 and applied in the epistles. Use determination and common prayer and decision according to faith and love, without command or compulsion, then God will help thee and thy little flock to all sincerity. . . . Moreover, the Gospel and its adherents are not to be protected by the sword, nor are they thus to protect themselves."[7]

Within certain limitations, the Anabaptist-Mennonite tradition has always emphasized a general attitude of obedience or submission to the state. Taxes are to be paid. Laws are to be obeyed so long as they do not require a violation of the laws of God; and prayers are to be offered in behalf of those in authority. Romans 13:1-7; Titus 3:1, 2; I Peter 2:17, and similar Scriptures are cited in recognition of the Christian's obligation to the state. The Dordrecht confession says the Christian must be subject to the government "in all things that do not militate against the law, will, and commandments of God; yea, 'to be ready to every good work'; also faithfully to pay it custom, tax, and tribute; thus giving it what is its due; as Jesus Christ taught, did himself, and commanded his followers to do. That we are also to pray to the Lord earnestly for the government and its welfare, and in behalf of our country, so that we may live under its protection, maintain ourselves and 'lead a quiet and peaceable life in all godliness and honesty.' And further, that the Lord would recompense them (our rulers), here and in eternity, for all the benefits, liberties, and favors which we enjoy under their laudable administration."[8]

Along with this obligation of submission, support, and prayer, however, there is always the limiting factor. When Jesus granted that to Caesar should be given what belongs to Caesar, He also added: "And [render] unto God the things that are God's." The negative of this statement would be:

---

7 Grebel's letter to Müntzer; see Bender, *Conrad Grebel*, 284.
8 Funk, *op. cit.*, 24, 25; Hershberger, 317.

Do not give to Caesar the things that are God's. There are some things which do not belong to Caesar. The state may legitimately increase its functions along certain lines for the promotion of the general welfare. But this extension of function has a limit. When it reaches into the realm of religion, conscience, and the home, and attempts to control these, the state is demanding what does not belong to it. Modern totalitarian states attempt to dominate the whole of life. They seek to impose on all citizens a uniform philosophy and way of life. Education, up to a certain point, is a legitimate function of the state, but totalitarian states make an illegitimate use of education when they seek to create a particular type of man with a totalitarian world view.

It is the duty of the church and of the individual Christian to be on guard against such illegitimate encroachments on the part of the state. If the state enters this realm and makes demands that are in conflict with the will of God, the Christian must have the courage to say: "We must obey God rather than men." So far America has been mercifully spared from totalitarianism as it is found in some parts of the world. There is, however, a secularizing tendency in American affairs, which, together with the expanding powers of the federal government, may constitute a greater threat to religious liberty than many people realize. In our concern to restrain communistic totalitarianism in other parts of the world, policies and programs are sometimes promoted which not only encourage the spread of communism abroad instead of diminishing it, but which also increase the trend toward totalitarianism at home. Most serious of all is the fact that many well-meaning people equate Christianity and the American way of life to such an extent that they are able to endorse and support and participate in the program of the state to a degree quite out of line with Scriptural teaching as well as with that of the sixteenth-century Anabaptists who were pioneers in the promotion of freedom of conscience and the separation of church and state in modern history.

Mennonites of the twentieth century have had their share

of suffering at the hands of communism and other forms of totalitarianism in Europe and Asia. They are in as good a position as anyone to understand the evils of totalitarianism, both the sixteenth- and the twentieth-century varieties. They are persuaded, however, that they dare not compromise their principles through an unqualified allegiance to one sub-Christian state as it opposes another sub-Christian state, even though the latter is more unchristian than the former.

In line with this conviction one Mennonite group in 1937 adopted a fresh statement of its position, in which the following paragraph appears: "If our country becomes involved in war, we shall endeavor to continue to live a quiet and peaceable life in all godliness and honesty; avoid joining in the wartime hysteria of hatred, revenge, and retaliation; manifest a meek and submissive spirit, being obedient unto the laws and regulations of the government in all things, except in such cases where obedience to the government would cause us to violate the teachings of the Scriptures so that we could not maintain a clear conscience before God (Acts 5:29). We confess that our supreme allegiance is to God, and that we cannot violate this allegiance by any lesser loyalty, but rather must follow Christ in all things, no matter what it cost. We love and honor our country and desire to work constructively for its highest welfare as loyal and obedient citizens; at the same time we are constrained by the love of Christ to love the people of all lands and races and to do them good as opportunity affords rather than evil, and we believe that this duty is not abrogated by war. We realize that to take this position may mean misunderstanding and even contempt from our fellow men, as well as possible suffering, but we hope by the grace of God that we may be able to assume, as our forefathers did, the sacrifices and suffering which may attend the sincere practice of this way of life, without malice or illwill toward those who may differ with us."[9]

---

9 "Peace, War, and Military Service: A Statement of Position adopted by the Mennonite General Conference in 1937." See the complete statement in Hershberger, 319-23.

It is obvious that the way of the cross, of love, and of nonresistance will not permit participation in those functions of state which require the use of violence. Military service was rejected by the early church and by the sixteenth-century Anabaptists. It has also been rejected by Quakers and other pacifist groups. Even some of our Christian Action friends admit that the New Testament ethic excludes this type of service. The extent to which this excludes the performance of other state functions, however, is a question on which even pacifists are by no means agreed. Many pacifists make a sharp distinction between the military and the police. They would say that the Christian can perform the latter function, perhaps should do so, but in a more Christian manner than it is generally performed, reducing the use of violence to a minimum, and avoiding the taking of life altogether. Many of these pacifists also feel that in a modern democratic government which has come under Christian influence, the Christian has an opportunity and an obligation to perform a service and to advance Christian principles through the operation of the state. In many cases, no doubt, this view represents a social gospel type of pacifism which identifies the kingdom of God with the general social order. On the other hand, there are evangelical Christian pacifists who do not share the social gospel view who nevertheless feel that the Christian who follows the way of the cross should carry this way into the administrative affairs of the pagan or semipagan state, thus bringing the challenge of Christianity and the way of the cross to the general social order. Among those who hold this view are a few Mennonites.

On this question we have little direct New Testament teaching. One reason for this is the fact that the political system of the first century offered little opportunity for government service on the part of Christians even if they had desired it. Even so, Paul refers to the saints of Caesar's household, and to Erastus, a city treasurer.[10] The sixteenth century likewise provided little opportunity for Anabaptists to serve

10 Phil. 4:22; Rom. 16:23.

in the government, even if they had desired such service. They were not full citizens, hence could not have held public office. They were regarded as heretics and could not have exercised the franchise, even where such would otherwise have been possible. In most places it was only the wealthy property-owning classes who were able to participate in the affairs of government, and this did not include the great body of Anabaptists who for the most part came from the lower classes. Some of the early leaders, to be sure, came from socially more prominent classes, but these were soon killed off, or at least stripped of their social standing.

Pilgram Marpeck is an illustration. He came from a prominent family in the Tyrol, and was an engineer by profession. At one time he was a mining magistrate and a member of the city council at Rattenberg. In 1527, however, he became an Anabaptist and soon thereafter he was driven out of the town and territory, whence he fled to the more liberal region of Alsace and the city of Strasbourg where he was employed as an engineer. In this capacity he gave notable service in the construction of waterways for the floating of logs and lumber from the forests on both sides of the Rhine to Strasbourg. His activities as an Anabaptist minister soon got him into trouble with the city council, however, so that he left the city early in 1532 after having labored there less than four years. In one of his last letters to the council in December, 1531, Marpeck said he would leave the city, but reminded the council that he had not received all of his pay for his engineering services.[11] Marpeck's experience would suggest that the sixteenth-century Anabaptists were willing to accept employment in the civil service. Since their faith was not tolerated, however, they were far from secure even in this employment. Marpeck was explicit in his teaching that a true Christian could not wield the power of the sword in the kingdom of this world, not even in Strasbourg. If this was his position, and if he insisted on teaching this doctrine to his

11 J. C. Wenger, "The Life and Work of Pilgram Marpeck," *Mennonite Quarterly Review* (July 1938) 12:153.

followers, the council seems to have reasoned, he could not
be used even in the civil service. He was therefore forced to
leave the city.

Toward the end of the century the Anabaptists experienced a degree of toleration in the rural villages of Alsace,
although at times they seem to have been asked to do service
as "watch or guard in village, field, wood, or forest." At any
rate the Strasbourg conference of 1568 gave its consent for a
brother to perform such service, "if it is for the best . . . but
not to anyone's harm, and he may not carry any weapon such
as spear and the like."[12] Swiss, German, and Dutch leaders
alike rejected the magistracy as unsuited to the nonresistant
Christian, since it required the use of force. Some of Menno
Simons' statements have been interpreted as suggesting the
possibility of "Christian magistrates";[13] but he certainly did
not consider the magistrates and princes of his own day as
falling within this category. The Dordrecht confession of
faith, adopted in 1632, assumes the sword as an essential instrument of the magistracy and clearly says that its use is forbidden to Christians.[14] The Ris confession, a Dutch statement
of the mid-eighteenth century, says: "When we consider that
the Lord Jesus seems everywhere to warn his disciples against
bearing rule according to the manner of the world . . . , as
well as against all vengeance . . . , we consider it a very difficult matter to administer this office according to faith."[15]

The approach of the Ris confession to the question of
participation in political life is somewhat different, however,
from that of the earlier Dordrecht confession. The Dordrecht
confession simply states the Christian's duty to honor, respect,
and obey the government, without so much as raising the
question of participation in its functions. It is assumed that

12 H. S. Bender, "The Discipline Adopted by the Strasbourg Conference of
1568," *Mennonite Quarterly Review* (January 1927) 1:66.
13 See below, p. 191, the quotation from Menno's *Writings*, 206. The exhortation to magistrates to "hear, believe, fear, love, serve, and follow" the Lord seems
to suggest that such obedience and service would constitute a Christian magistracy.
14 See the articles on "The Office of Civil Government" and "Defense by
Force," in Funk, *op. cit.*, 24-26, and in Hershberger, 317, 318.
15 Ris, *op. cit.* (Art. XXVIII) 53.

the Anabaptists are subjects, not rulers. The Ris confession, however, raises the question of participation. "Should . . . such an office be conferred upon us, we would hesitate and would not dare to accept it, not knowing the will of Christ as to how such office should be administered." Then follows the above statement that it would be "very difficult" to administer such offices in harmony with the nonresistant faith. The doctrine of nonresistance itself receives a clear and positive statement in a separate article. The article on government then closes by saying: "We consider ourselves fortunate to be exempt from this most important and at best dangerous service . . . while at the same time we can live in peace and quiet under the protection of such a benign government, who, though not recognizing for themselves the difficulties mentioned (but rather seeing in their office a divine calling), have yet granted to us such great privileges and exemptions . . . for which we cannot thank God enough . . . and owe our government all reverence and love."

11. LATER MENNONITISM AND THE STATE

Whether the Ris confession simply represents a more intellectual and objective approach to the question than that of the earlier Dordrecht confession, or whether it reflects an early stage of the cultural assimilation of the Dutch Mennonites which eventually smothered the doctrine of nonresistance itself, is not clear. It is clear, however, that by this time the Dutch Mennonites had been well assimilated into the economic life of their country. They were prosperous businessmen and merchants with commercial connections in the Baltic, the Mediterranean, and the Far East. Their wealth gave them social standing, with a corresponding decline in religious earnestness. Then in 1795 the Dutch Mennonites were granted full rights of participation in the political life of the state. Evidently since the time of Ris they had also learned more about "the will of Christ as to how such office should be administered." At any rate they now began to take full advantage of their new opportunity, and during the nineteenth century they came to occupy a place of major importance in the political life of the nation.

In an earlier day persecution had failed to break down the faith of these people and their loyalty to the principle of nonresistance. What adversity and persecution had failed to accomplish, however, prosperity and toleration now achieved with relative ease. The membership of the church steadily declined from 200,000 in 1700 to 30,000 in 1820. Loyalty to the doctrine of nonresistance declined at about the same pace, so that when a new military law was passed by the Dutch parliament in 1898, making no provision for the exemption of nonresistant Mennonites, the leaders of the church did not so much as protest. In course of time members of the Dutch Mennonite church came to occupy such prominent posts as

174

burgomaster of Amsterdam, judges of the highest court, governor of the East Indies, and minister of the navy. What had seemed "very difficult" in 1750 was taken for granted in 1915; and so far had the church departed from its original principles that during the time of the first World War only one of the Dutch Mennonites conscripted for military service took his stand as a conscientious objector. Although the story of the North German Mennonites is less dramatic, it is much the same story of prosperity, accommodation, toleration, participation in political life, and the eventual decline and virtual demise of nonresistance and conscientious objection to war. Even in agricultural south Germany, France, and Switzerland during the same period there was a gradual decline of nonresistance among the Mennonites so that by the time of the first World War it was practically gone.

One question raised by this story is whether assimilation into the economic life of the nation must ultimately mean renunciation of the principle of nonresistance; whether the way of prosperity and the way of the cross are mutually exclusive. This question will be dealt with further in the following section.[1] The question at the present moment is whether participation in the political life of the nation and the way of the cross as expressed in the doctrine of nonresistance are mutually exclusive. Even the Dutch Mennonite confession of the eighteenth century found political participation "very difficult." Then when participation was accepted nonresistance departed. Must the outcome of the Dutch experience, however, be necessarily repeated?

In modern democracies such as those of England, Canada, and the United States, conscientious objectors to war may exercise the franchise freely without danger of interference by the government. In England occasional seats in Parliament are occupied by conscientious objectors who state their position openly. Even among the Dutch Mennonites in recent years there has been a significant revival of nonresistance and conscientious objection to war, with young men of draft

1 See below, chs. 14-21.

age giving alternative civilian service, but without absten-
tion from all political activity as in the time of the Dordrecht
confession. Many pacifists in the United States are far more
active politically than Mennonites are. And even among
nonresistant Mennonites there is a surprising amount of variation on this point. What course of action with respect to
government service, the franchise, and office holding is the
consistent course for the nonresistant Christian to take if he
would follow the way of the cross?

In the United States during the second World War approximately 12,000 conscripted conscientious objectors, 4,665
of whom were Mennonites, were assigned to civilian public
service camps. Practically all of the Mennonite objectors to
every form of military service accepted some form of civilian
service, whether agricultural, forestry, or hospital service, as
consistent with the way of the cross. Since 1952 another 7,000
conscripted men have engaged in direct government service
or in other approved services to which the government assigned them. Of this number more than 60 percent were
Mennonites whose church had officially accepted the program. Besides this, many American Mennonites not under
conscription are regularly employed by the state in various
civil service capacities such as the educational, postal, health,
agricultural, communication, and numerous other welfare
functions of the state.

Although certain "absolutist" conscientious objectors refuse every form of service under conscription, very few Mennonites have taken this position. Mennonites generally have
taken the position that government service under conscription, if it does not contribute to the military, or if the form
of service in itself is not in conflict with the New Testament
ethic, is permissible. Indeed, in CPS days, such service when
given without remuneration was interpreted as "going the
second mile" as taught by Jesus in the Sermon on the Mount,
and as such was a concrete demonstration of the way of the
cross. Under the postwar conscription program many Mennonites feel that the way of the cross is best found in volun-

tary service projects, under church agencies, which demand a greater degree of personal sacrifice than do the more remunerative government assignments. This does not change the fact, however, that in our time employment in various forms of civil service within the welfare state has come to be accepted by the majority of Mennonites as not inconsistent with Christian nonresistance and the way of the cross.

The fact that such civil service is possible for believers in New Testament nonresistance, and is even provided as an alternative to military service for conscripted conscientious objectors, is an indication of how tolerant many modern governments are, as compared with those of the sixteenth and seventeenth centuries. The franchise as well as legislative, executive, and judicial functions are also open to all citizens without religious discrimination. From the time of the founding of Pennsylvania in the seventeenth century, for example, Quakers, Mennonites, and other Christian pacifists of that province have had political privileges which came to the Dutch Mennonites for the first time in 1795, after two and one-half centuries of persecution and discrimination. What have the American Mennonites done with these privileges? It seems clear that the use of the franchise was common among the Mennonites of colonial Pennsylvania where they generally supported the Quaker government at the polls. Following this precedent Mennonites in the newer settlements of Pennsylvania, Ohio, and westward commonly exercised the franchise. Office holding, however, with the exception of minor offices on the local level not involving the use of force, was generally avoided.

In a general way this pattern prevails to the present day among the Mennonites representing the descendants of the eighteenth-century immigration. The experience of World War I, however, and the resulting tension with the state, brought a reaction against voting in some quarters with the result that the franchise was probably less generally exercised at the middle than it was at the beginning of the twentieth century, although there was a wide variation in practice from one community to another. The Mennonites representing the nineteenth-century immigration have generally taken a more liberal view, the exercise of the franchise being taken for granted among them and minor office holding at least being a common practice. Some of their number have occupied seats in state legislatures. Two of them have been in the United States congress, and one served for a time as federal judge.

Every conscientious objector to war must somewhere draw a line beyond which he cannot go in his participation in the affairs of state. The least he must do is to decline the operation of weapons of destruction. One might arrange a graduated scale of modern government functions and activities, locating each item in its proper place on that scale from the feeding of starving children to the manipulation of atomic weapons, and then attempt to draw the line which separates those things which he can do from those which he must decline. No matter where one objector draws the line, however, another might feel that he is illogical or inconsistent at some point. Since the state exercises the use of force and engages in war one might conclude that it is not consistent to co-operate with it in any way, thus refusing to exercise the franchise, to submit to conscription even for civilian service, or even to pay taxes. A very few absolutists do go to this extreme on all of these points. Or one might conclude that since he cannot escape involvement in the unchristian acts of government in some manner he might as well participate in its functions to the full, all along the line. This is the point at which our Christian Action friends with their doctrine of tragic necessity and of full responsibility find themselves.

One historic difference between Anabaptism and Quakerism on the relation of the Christian to the state has been their view of the police. Anabaptism has regarded the magistracy and the police as different from the military only in degree, whereas Quakerism has thought of the two as being different in kind. C. G. Rutenber reminds us, however, that there is a point at which a difference in degree becomes a difference in kind: "No one is wholly free from active participation in coercion and violence. Perhaps a straight line runs from spanking a child, through police action against criminals, to international war. But, for some of us, the difference in degree acquires decisive significance by the time the end of the line is reached. Spanking may be justifiable, but war—no! The position cannot wholly be rationalized. All the methods of seeking the will of God that are opened to a Christian must be involved in the decision that says: 'Thus far, but no farther.' Each man takes his own stand, at the place where he must."[2]

Most American Mennonites have taken their stand somewhere between spanking and the police force. Many Quakers have taken theirs at a point between the police and the military. If the line is drawn at the latter position, however, he who draws it must then decide whether he can participate in an international peace force, which presumably is the same in essence as the local or state police, only on a larger scale. Were the United Nations forces in Korea a police force? If so, could one actually draw a line between MacArthur's police force in Korea and Eisenhower's army in western Europe in 1944? Obviously those who would draw the line between the police and the military have a very difficult task.

Drawing the line between acceptable and unacceptable forms of civil office, however, presents its difficulties also. A generation ago the Mennonite Peter Jansen, a member of the Nebraska legislature, drew the line personally between the state legislature and the governorship because the governor is commander in chief of the militia. Many Mennonites have drawn the line before reaching the state legislature because this body appropriates funds and authorizes their expenditure for the militia, and because through the legislative process it is responsible for coercive action in various forms. If the nonresistant Christian accepts office holding at all, where

2 C. G. Rutenber, "Applying the New Testament" (Area 1, Paper 3), *Study Materials Conference on the Church and War* (New York, 1950) 7.

is the line to be drawn? Perhaps a conscientious objector could win election to congress and then abstain from voting in favor of military appropriations, concentrating his attention upon nonmilitary matters. Theoretically he might even be elected president and then, as commander in chief, order the navy into storage and ground the air force.

However fantastic this may seem it must be admitted that the ease or difficulty of such a course will vary from state to state and from time to time. The Danish alternative service program for conscientious objectors, for example, was inaugurated almost singlehandedly in 1917 by a minister of defense who was virtually a pacifist. While it is difficult to forget the case of the Mennonite mayor who publicly congratulated a factory in his city upon its receipt of an army-navy award for outstanding performance in "providing vital war materials," knowing that the "men in the armed forces . . . will be cheered to receive this information," it must be admitted that Mennonite mayors would not in all cases necessarily get themselves involved in this way, and that many lesser office holders might continue in their work for years without such extremely embarrassing inconsistencies.

12. POLITICAL RESPONSIBILITY

Occasionally one finds a sanguine Mennonite with sufficient optimism to argue for political participation on all levels, local, national, and international.[1] He generally argues that according to Romans 13 government officials are ministers of God; that the early Christians as well as the early Anabaptists were political nonparticipants because they were social outcasts; that in their day the state was an undemocratic police state, whereas modern states are democratic welfare states. The democratic welfare state, moreover, is a fruit of the Anabaptist effort. Therefore Anabaptists should enter into their own heritage. It is not enough to be an independent voter, it may even be argued. Mennonites should become active party members where they can help to shape party policies. If they have righteous principles they should exercise political responsibility; for if the righteous withdraw from such responsibility only the unrighteous will remain to formulate policies and to direct the affairs of government. Those Mennonites who hold this view seem to think that the chief objections offered to political participation are its rough and ready ways and its corruption, reinforced by prejudice against political participation which has grown out of former years of Mennonite persecution. Their answer to this is that there is nothing evil in government as such; that we now live under a tolerant democratic government; that crookedness in politics is based on crookedness in business; that Jesus condemned economic evil more than He did power politics. Therefore, to be a consistent political nonparticipant would also require nonparticipation in the general economic order,

1 This general point of view is reflected in John J. Gering, *After Fifty Years* (Marion, S. Dak., 1924), especially chapter 7; for helpful discussions of the question see *Mennonite Life* (North Newton, July 1956) 11:139-44; Hans Hillerbrand, "The Anabaptist View of the State," *MQR* (April 1958) 32:83-110; Elmer Neufeld, "Christian Responsibility in the Political Situation," *MQR* (April 1958) 32:141-162.

perhaps the establishment of an exclusive communal society like that of Hutterites.

Mennonite advocates of political activity generally will say that the Christian should not accept offices in which he would need to compromise his pacifist principles, but they seem optimistic enough to believe that most offices are not necessarily of this character since the state of today is primarily a welfare state rather than a police state. They cite cases of sheriffs and policemen who use the gun sparingly; of Chester Bowles who did a remarkable job as ambassador to India; and ask what the Germantown, Pennsylvania, Mennonites would have done if the Quakers had not been on hand to take over the government when the Mennonites relinquished it in 1707. They cite the real case of the Mennonites, first in Russia and now in Paraguay, who find it necessary to operate their own government, inasmuch as they constitute a kind of Mennonite state within the larger state. A Mennonite of ability, character, and conviction in the United States congress, they feel, would be a mighty force for good, and in a position to give a powerful testimony for peace and wholesome international relations as well as clean morals in domestic government. Political nonparticipation they say is a form of asceticism, abandoning its social responsibilities to the unscrupulous. How valid is this point of view?

It must certainly be admitted that the modern state, to a far greater degree than the ancient one, is more than a police power. It is a welfare institution performing many humanitarian functions which in themselves violate no principle of Christian ethics. Some of these services, indeed, such as the care of the sick, for example, and the education of the young, are in full harmony with the way of the cross and were a function of the church long before they were assumed by the state. Furthermore, in our western democracies the Christian is able through the exercise of the franchise and by other means to give his testimony for justice and righteousness to an extent that would have been impossible under the more authoritarian governments of New Testament times or of the sixteenth century. Even in the New Testament church a few Christians seem to have been employed by the state. On one occasion Paul mentions Erastus, the city treasurer[2]; and on another he refers to the saints "of Caesar's household."[3]

The argument offered above fails to recognize, however, that when Romans 13 speaks of the government as ordained of God it is the police function that is referred to as instituted through God's order of creation "to execute his wrath on the wrongdoers." Since it is certain that the early church was nonresistant it may also be assumed that such government service as Christians in this period may have accepted was detached from the police or punitive functions of the state. Furthermore the book of Revelation portrays the state as a totalitarian leviathan, which as an enemy of God has abused its power and seeks the destruction of the church. Under such a situation surely the tension between God's people and the state is a great one; and to a greater or lesser degree such a tension always exists between the state and the disciple of Christ who would follow the way of the cross, even in our western democracies in our so-called Christian civilization.

In stressing the welfare functions of the modern state the argument above passes too lightly over the fact that modern governments are often more dangerous police states than the Roman Empire was; and that their efforts to build the welfare state are in part responsible for making them police states. The Anabaptists were not political nonparticipants because they were social outcasts. They were social outcasts because the way of the cross which they espoused did not permit them to participate in the violent methods of the state. The Anabaptists produced their fruit by challenging the social order, not by accepting its way.

Those Mennonites who have had religious scruples against political activity have had them not primarily because of the rough and ready ways of politics, but rather because they declined responsibility for serving as an agency of

2 Rom. 16:23.
3 Phil. 4:22.

the divine wrath. They believed their responsibility was that of bringing men to repentance, of leading them to the way of the cross which brings reconciliation with God and men. The Christian does not exercise vengeance to obtain justice. The way of vengeance, the Anabaptists believed, was outside the perfection of Christ. The Christian rather suffers, even lays down his life if need be, in order that he might do justice. It was the Anabaptist belief that the magistracy meant involvement in the way of vengeance which made them non-participants, and which in turn brought persecution down upon their heads. It was not persecution which in the first instance caused them to question the validity of political activity for them. Persecution was the result of their attitude, not the cause.

It should be recognized, however, that in the vast welfare service of a government like that of the United States, many positions are of such a kind that compromise on the question of nonresistance need not be made. It might even be conceded that this is true of many positions in various sections of the state department—positions providing opportunity for a constructive contribution to international relations. On the other hand, in a day when 75 per cent or more of the federal budget is devoted to defense and military expenditures in one form or another, and when every department of the government is in some manner geared into the defense program, it is difficult to see how one could hold a responsible policy-making position in the executive or legislative branch of the federal government without becoming involved in the nation's defense and security program in a manner that would be difficult to reconcile with nonresistance and the way of the cross in which Mennonites profess to believe.

It is true, the proposal is that only those offices not requiring compromise would be accepted. The proposal seems much too sanguine, however, as to the number of such offices which could be found. Following the example of the prophets, the early Christians, and the Anabaptists, the Christian today must serve as a continuous challenge to the semipagan social order which includes the state. The proposal assumes that the electorate would honor pacifist representatives in public office if they proved themselves honest and sincere in their views. While cases could no doubt be found where this would be true, one must nevertheless question how long the American public would tolerate executive and legislative officials who in the spirit of Isaiah, Hosea, and Jeremiah, or of Menno Simons and the New Testament, would seriously strive to take the American nation down the way of the cross in the face of other nations led by a contrary spirit. To raise the question is only to answer it in the negative, and yet this way of the cross is precisely the road which a Christian nation would have to take, and it is the road toward which the New Testament Christian in public office would necessarily lead his people and his state. While the present writer would be the first to give approval to any Christian who could actually follow this course in government, he has no illusions as to the outcome. While the effort would serve as a witness to the way of Christ and the cross, the term of office would no doubt be short, while force of circumstances would compel the incumbent to direct his energies into other channels.

The above argument for political participation fails to grasp the heart of the problem. Government service in peripheral matters relating to the welfare state is one thing. The basic problem of the Christian's relation to the police state, however, goes much deeper than this. The argument that some Mennonites are involved in economic practices which violate the New Testament ethic is no argument for political involvement which does the same thing. Those who are so involved need to bring their economic practices in line with the New Testament ethic, not their political practices in line with a non-Christian economic ethic. As to the Mennonites formerly in Russia and now in Paraguay, who comprise a kind of state within a state, suffice it to say that this type of community pattern is hardly that of either the New Testament colony of heaven or of the Anabaptist communities. These were communities in the world, challenging the

world, evangelizing the world, and also making it possible
for their own backsliding members to slide out into the
world where they preferred to be. The Russian colonies,
however, were isolated to such a degree, both physically and
spiritually, that their challenging, evangelizing prerogatives
were too much curtailed; and the Paraguayan colonies have
to contend with the same problem. The Russian Mennonites
were too much a world· unto themselves, and when some of
their members forsook the way of the cross while remaining
within this Mennonite world, in course of time it had the
effect of making the Mennonite world too much like that
which surrounded it. The colony of heaven, if it is to remain
that, needs to be surrounded by a world, so that it may live in
the world; so that it may have a world to evangelize; and so
that there may be a world to which its own backsliding members, who will not follow the way of the cross, can go. It
would seem that if these conditions do not exist the colony
of heaven itself will eventually become the world.

If the question of political action for the way-of-the-cross
Christian is ever solved, the solution will probably be found
at a point which coincides neither with that to which the advocates of full participation would direct us, nor with that at
which the extreme nonparticipants have taken their stand.

Those pacifists who advocate full political participation
are inclined to take the coercive function of the state too
lightly. William Penn is an illustration of this tendency. He
stressed the welfare functions of the state and painted a glow-
ing picture of how it would operate had Adam never fallen.
Having seen this vision he seems to have believed that Pennsylvania was Eden restored, only to discover that many of the
participants in his holy experiment remained sons of the
fallen Adam. Before he realized it, therefore, Penn himself
was doing some surprisingly non-cross-like politicking. Emil
Brunner is right when he reminds us that after all has been
said about the importance of the welfare functions of the
modern state, the ultimate essence of statehood as taught in
Romans 13 has to do with the problems of justice, and "takes

criminal law . . . as the paradigm of the legal system of the state as a whole."[4] If ours were not a sinful society the state would at most be a center of social co-ordination. Since it is a sinful society, however, it is far more than that.

Our Christian Action friends are right when they tell us that in such a sinful society the police state with its exercise of violence will continue to be with us. In the view of this writer their mistake consists of renouncing the Christian's high responsibility for obedience to the law of love and the way of the cross in favor of a pseudo-responsibility for participation in the coercive functions of the police state. Those pacifists, on the other hand, who enter the political arena too blithely fail to comprehend the true nature of the way of the cross and the tension which must exist between it and the coercive ways of the state. From this situation one of two results is likely to follow. Either their pacifism will succumb, perhaps unconsciously in the beginning, to compromise until eventually the principle has vanished; or the participants will experience disillusionment, eventually resulting either in abandonment of the experiment or in renunciation of the ideal.

A recent study of Mennonites and Quakers in government shows that neither of the two Mennonites who have served in the United States congress has anything in his voting record which would so much as indicate that he was a pacifist. The congressman who was in office in 1917 voted for the declaration of war against Germany, even when fifty-six of his non-Mennonite colleagues voted against the declaration. He voted in favor of every defense bill that came up and even introduced a bill for the registration of all males aged 16 to 60 for military and industrial service for the duration of the war and one year thereafter.[5] It is freely granted that this particular Mennonite was probably not a believer in nonresistance even before entering congress, and that the

4 Emil Brunner, *Justice and the Social Order*, 220.
5 Betty Ann Hershberger, *A Pacifist Approach to Civil Government: A Comparison of the Participant Quaker and the Non-Participant Mennonite View* (ms. thesis, Swarthmore College, 1951) 153-56.

record of a thorough Christian pacifist in government could certainly be far better than that here described. It would seem a fair conclusion, however, that however correct the optimistic political participant among the pacifists may be in theory, the necessary tension between the way of the cross and the coercive functions of state will make it very difficult to prevent the theory from falling down in practice. The reading of a book like Paul Hutchinson's, *The New Leviathan*,[6] should be helpful to anyone with doubts as to the true character of the modern state and the tension which exists between it and the way of the cross.

Having said this, however, it must also be said that complacent aloofness bordering on indifference to the political life of the nation, such as characterizes some Mennonites, is equally far from the point to which New Testament teaching and Anabaptist history would seem to lead them. Erland Waltner has reminded us that complete aloofness, even to the rejection of the franchise and of minor office holding, is probably going farther than the New Testament would warrant, whereas the disillusionment experienced by some Mennonites in the failure to realize their hopes for a warless world, or permanently to advance the cause of temperance through legislative and political means, should help them to see that the Christian has a higher responsibility than political action and legislation.[7]

In attempting an answer to the question before us we might well ask: What would Menno Simons do if he were here today? Political action in the modern sense was impossible for the sixteenth-century Anabaptists, but this did not keep Menno from directing his message to rulers and the governments of his day. When he and his people suffered persecution he did not say with William Penn and the Quakers that there is no "business wherein the people of England [or of the Netherlands and Germany] are more

6 Paul Hutchinson, *The New Leviathan* (Chicago, 1946).
7 Erland Waltner, *An Analysis of the Mennonite Views on the Christian's Relation to the State in the Light of the New Testament,* (ms. dissertation, Eastern Baptist Theological Seminary, Philadelphia, 1948), especially Ch. VI.

concerned than in that which relates to their civil and religious liberties."[8] Menno was not a nonviolent resistant fighting an aggressive fight in an insistent demand for justice on the part of the government toward the governed. He did not base his appeal on the Magna Charta, as Penn did, and proclaim the three fundamental rights of man: the ownership of property; a share in legislation; and a share in the judiciary, or trial by jury.[9]

Instead Menno begins one of his most important writings, *The Cross of the Saints,* with the quotation from the Sermon on the Mount: "Blessed are they which are persecuted for righteousness' sake; for theirs is the kingdom of heaven."[10] Since the children of God have always been persecuted and always will be, he encouraged his brethren to "take the crucified Jesus as your example and the righteous apostles and prophets of God. Learn through them how they all crept in at this very narrow gate and have left all things hanging at the entrance. . . ."[11] Persecution is as a chastening of the Lord that Christians may be enabled to "hear and obey him in his holy word." "For this reason, James says: My brethren, count it all joy when you fall into divers temptations, knowing this, that the trying of your faith worketh patience. . . . For even as gold through the fire's heat separates itself from the dross and by the flames becomes more and more pure, so the man of God who is susceptible to it is humbled, purified, and cleansed in the oven and fire of tribulation in order that he may be an everlasting praise, honor, and glory to Christ. . . ."[12]

But Menno Simons does not stop with this. Even though he grants that in this world Christians must suffer, he is not for this reason afraid of the world, nor does he hesitate to speak out to its leaders. If the Anabaptists were the prophets

8 See C. M. Case, *Non-Violent Coercion: A Study in Methods of Social Pressure* (New York, 1923) 100.
9 William Penn, *Works* (1726 ed.) 1:672-704.
10 Menno Simons, *Complete Writings,* 582.
11 *Ibid.,* 598.
12 *Ibid.,* 616, 617.

of their day Menno was a major prophet whose joy and delight was proclaiming the way of the cross to all men, including kings and princes and all in high places. In his *An Admonishing Request to the Magistracy,* Menno entreats rulers to "humble yourselves in the name of Jesus, that your poor souls may be excused . . . sheathe your sword. For as the Lord liveth you do not fight against flesh and blood, but against him whose eyes are as a flame of fire . . . who hath on his vesture and on his thigh a name written, *King of kings and Lord of lords.* . . .

"We resist neither the emperor, the king, nor any authority in that to which they are called of God. . . . But so much mercy we request that under your gracious protection we may live, teach, conduct ourselves, and serve the Lord according to our consciences so that to you and many with you, the Gospel of Christ may be rightly set forth and the gate of life swing open. . . . Therefore humble yourselves under the mighty hand of God . . . awake, and repent, for it does not become the creature to rise up against the Creator. . . ."[13]

In his *Exhortation to the Magistrates* Menno says to kings and princes: "O highly renowned, noble lords, believe Christ's word, fear God's wrath, love righteousness, do justice to widows and orphans, judge rightly between a man and his neighbor, fear no man's highness, despise no man's littleness, hate all avarice, punish with reason, allow the Word of God to be taught freely. . . . O my dear sirs, what are you doing? Where in the world is the sword of righteousness, of which you boast, given and entrusted to you? You have to acknowledge that you have put it in the sheath, and in its stead you have drawn the sword of unrighteousness. . . . Therefore, dear sirs, take heed wisely, rightly to execute your responsible and dangerous office according to the will of God. . . .

"They who are baptized inwardly with Spirit and fire, . . . according to the Word of the Lord, have no weapons

13 *Ibid.,* 117-19.

except patience, hope, silence, and God's Word. . . . Our weapons are not weapons with which cities and countries may be destroyed. . . . Christ is our fortress; patience our weapon of defense; the Word of God our sword; and our victory a courageous, firm, unfeigned faith in Jesus Christ. And iron and metal spears and swords we leave to those who, alas, regard human blood and swine's blood about alike. He that is wise let him judge what I mean. . . .

"Pharaoh, with his entire host, was destroyed in the Red Sea by the righteous judgment of God. . . . Ahab was shot through with an arrow. . . . Jezebel was thrust out of the window. . . . Herod . . . exalted himself in his heart against God, and . . . he was smitten by the angel of the Lord. . . . O God, what escape? Dear noble sirs, what escape? How will it stand with your poor souls in the day in which the heavens shall pass away? . . . Therefore cease flying in the eyes of the Lord, for he that toucheth his saints toucheth the apple of his eye. . . . Do not usurp the judgment and kingdom of Christ, for He alone is the ruler of the conscience, and besides Him there is none other. . . .

"Hear, believe, fear, love, serve, and follow your Lord and Saviour, Jesus Christ, for He it is before whom every knee shall bow: God's eternal Word, Wisdom, Truth, and Son. Seek His honor and praise in all your thoughts, words, and actions, and you shall reign forever."[14]

This was the prophetic witness of Menno Simons to the state and those in authority in the sixteenth century.

14 *Ibid.,* 193-206.

13. THE PROPHETIC WITNESS TODAY

When Jesus commissioned His disciples to live in the world without being of the world He made no pretense of giving them an easy task. Throughout the New Testament the emphasis is one of tension in which the Christian stands as a witness against the evil of the world even if it must be in the face of persecution. When one examines the reality of the world and its evil, however, and looks upon the frailty of man, it is not difficult to understand why Christendom has been so faltering in its prophetic witness. Today Christians of every tradition are found wanting in one way or another when their witness to the way of the cross is measured by the New Testament standard or by their own tradition.

Traditional Protestantism generally recognizes the high ethic of the New Testament as valid for personal relations, but in one way or another finds it inapplicable to the wider social relationships. Carl F. H. Henry in a recent treatment continues the old interpretation that the Sermon on the Mount "gives an individualistic articulation of ethics—dealing with my relations to the person at my side, and not with the larger question of my duty to social groups in the order of economics and politics, or to humanity as a whole." It deals only with obligations to God, not with obligations to Caesar which are dealt with elsewhere in the New Testament where "additional responsibilities to those of neighbor-relations" are given to the Christian. The Sermon on the Mount is not decisive on the question of war. To the Old Testament command Jesus does not add a command against war. "If that is the sense of the commandment, it must belong to the Old Testament conception. But the Old Testament record cannot be reconciled to this alternative," for there God often commands participation in defensive warfare.[1]

192

To a Christian of the Anabaptist tradition this seems too much like an interpretation of the New Testament in the light of the Old. He would reverse the order, interpreting the Old in the light of the New. Most serious of all, in the mind of this writer, is the ease with which Henry seems to accept war as sometimes a Christian obligation. One receives the impression that here an old-line Protestant theologian, while taking the Scripture as his frame of reference, nevertheless underestimates the sinfulness of the social order even as described within Holy Scripture itself. War itself, in a time when even some Catholic theologians say the day of just wars is past, is accepted with less anguish of soul than in the case of those who take the social order as their frame of reference.[2]

Even though he cannot accept their interpretation of Christian ethics, this writer feels that the church owes a debt of gratitude to our Christian Action friends for the thorough manner in which they have exposed the sinful nature of man, as well as the complex nature of the modern social order. Failure to recognize the reality of sin is not only folly; it is the assumption of an unscriptural view as well. Long before Christian Action was heard of the first two chapters of the epistle to the Romans gave us a picture of sinful society, just as real, and no doubt more authentic, than that which

---

1 Carl F. H. Henry, *Christian Personal Ethics* (Grand Rapids, 1957) 305, 324, 325.

2 At one point Henry seems to misunderstand the Anabaptist view of the Sermon on the Mount and its relation to the Old Testament. This view holds that Jesus abrogated or modified the ceremonial and civil laws of the Old Testament and that the New Testament ethic is a fulfillment or restoration of the moral law as found in the Decalogue. The Anabaptist view is not that Jesus "raised the moral law itself to higher ground" (p. 304), or that He "set Himself in antagonism to the Decalogue" (306). It is rather that He placed the New Testament ethic on the level of the moral law (Decalogue), a goal which had been achieved neither by the interpretations of the contemporary Jewish teachers nor by the Mosaic civil code itself. At times Henry seems to identify the civil code with the moral law of the Decalogue (306), although in his interpretation of Matt. 19:8 he seems to agree with the Anabaptist view that polygamy and divorce were "temporary concessions made to human weakness of what the Old Testament clearly condemns as wrong in its specifically formulated ethical teaching. At most it might be said that polygamy and divorce were tolerated by way of sufferance or forbearance, as a concession to man's weakened condition in sin, in order to prevent a more radical abuse through the hardness of his heart. The New Testament provides some encouragement for so regarding divorce in the older economy (Matt. 19:8). . . . It

our friends are giving us. What some of our friends seem to overlook, however, is the fact that the same St. Paul in all of his epistles, and notably in that to the Colossians, speaks to the colony of heaven which the Holy Spirit planted within this sinful order, informing its members that they have been raised with Christ and that their calling is to live above the sordid ways of the pagan order.

One is impressed by the humility with which many of our friends present their view of social responsibility and of the lesser evil. John C. Bennett, for example, while convinced that as a Christian he must support the war against tyranny, frankly admits the anguish of his own soul at the thought of large-scale obliteration bombing. "I could never dispel the suspicion," he says, "that if I had been an eyewitness of the effects of the bombing . . . I would have been forced to say that . . . these deeds are . . . so utterly abhorrent to the conscience of any Christian . . . that they must be rejected."[3] The Dun report on *The Christian Conscience and Weapons of Mass Destruction* is written in much the same spirit.

When one considers the positive assurance with which the way of peace and nonresistance is nevertheless rejected as unrealistic and utopian, one cannot help feeling that this spirit of humility is more than offset by an attitude of condescension in which mere rational man presumes to tell the early Christian Church, yes even Jesus and the New Testament writers themselves, that their message is not for our

is not only the New Testament that views monogamous marriage as the divine ideal. The Biblical revelation, on the basis of creation and the revelation of Sinai and the Sermon on the Mount, provides no ethical validation of either polygamy or divorce as the Divine ideal. . . . With the progress of redemptive revelation, man in sin was more and more enlightened about the implications of the moral law. At last the moral law was perfectly incarnate in Jesus Christ. Christians are more and more enabled to approximate its requirements through the subjective dynamic of the Spirit following Pentecost" (328, 329).

This is an excellent statement of the present writer's concept of the Anabaptist view on the relation of the New Testament ethic to the civil code of the Old Testament, not only with respect to polygamy and divorce, but to war as well. This approach would seem to solve the problem of the supposed "issuance of contradictory moral commands" which concerns Henry (305), as well as the concern for the "continuity of Biblical ethics" (306). This view and approach is presupposed throughout the present volume as well as in Guy F. Hershberger, *War Peace, and Nonresistance* (Scottdale, 1944; revised, 1953).

3 John C. Bennett, *Christian Ethics and Social Policy* (New York, 1946) 20

time. It is as if they said: We know very well what you have instructed us to do and what you did in your time. Even though we are your followers we are sorry that we cannot follow you, because you were after all only "a little persecuted minority in a pagan society, without political responsibilities."[4] Since we have assumed the responsibility for the moral structure of the sub-Christian social order we must reject your colony of heaven as not sufficiently "down to earth" for our purpose, although we are still your followers.

We Christians cannot afford to forget that when God became incarnate in Jesus Christ He literally came "down to earth"; that the New Testament colony of heaven was planted in the very midst of the pagan social order for the purpose of challenging its evil, and of calling its members to repentance and to the acceptance of a new social order which is based on the way of the cross. The way of the cross and of the resurrection was intended for this world and is valid for that purpose today. In the Christian society, order is brought out of chaos. Those who have been gathered into the way of the cross from east and west, whether white or black, ignorant or educated, poor or rich, are bound together in one community of saints, equipped for the ministry, empowering it to direct its energies outwardly upon the general social order which is its field of labor. Even as Christ poured out His life for the redemption of sinful man, so must the church, the body of Christ, pour out itself in redemptive living for the reconciliation to God of sinful man and of the social order in which the sinner lives and moves and has his being.

The modern doctrine of social responsibility speaks of a preferential ethic which requires the individual to lay down his own life for an enemy when he is involved in a two-person relationship, for in this way he does good to his neighbor or enemy. As soon as the Christian has two or more neighbors to deal with, however, so the argument goes, and as these neighbors are in conflict with each other, the requirement to

4 The Dun Report, 6.

do good makes him responsible to defend that neighbor who is being abused by the other. When the abused neighbor is a member of his own household the Christian has a special responsibility to protect him against the enemy. When the abused neighbor is an oppressed social class, or a nation victimized by aggression, the ethic of love requires the Christian to come to the rescue of the oppressed, even with force if need be. Thus would our Christian Action friends have us bear one another's burdens and so fulfill the law of Christ.[5]

In the colony of heaven, however, as we find it in the New Testament, it is the entire Christian community, the body of Christ as one unit, which pours out its corporate life in redemptive living, and if need be lays it down in obedience to Christ the head. There are two societies in our world, the Christian order and the pagan disorder. Here is true Christian responsibility: to keep the Christian order Christian, in order that it may bear witness to the world's disorder, and if need be make a sacrifice for it. A classic illustration of how it works is the case of the Jacob Hochstettler family on the Pennsylvania frontier in pioneer days. When hostile Indians surrounded their cabin one night, the family took counsel and the agreement was not to use the rifle in self-defense. They paid for their decision with their lives. The father might have reasoned that in this complex society of multi-relationships a preferential ethic demands the defense of the family against the onslaughts of the enemy. Or the entire family might have reasoned that since they are settlers in a British colony they are hopelessly involved in the evils of British and French imperialism, in a culture which is war; that by virtue of the very fact that they live in British territory they are sinners; that the best they can do is to confess

5 Carl F. H. Henry has not spelled it out in the same rational manner, although apparently he arrives at the same practical conclusion. The difference is that Henry is able to interpret the New Testament in a manner that fits this conclusion, whereas Paul L. Lehmann, for example, while granting that this is not New Testament ethics, concludes that New Testament ethics and Christian ethics are not identical. Cf. John A. Hutchison (ed.), *Christian Faith and Social Action* (New York, 1953) 98. Henry's book is *Christian Personal Ethics*. A treatise on social ethics is planned for the future.

their sin and penitently accept the tragic necessity of fighting the Indians which is a lesser evil than to allow oneself and others to be subjected to tyranny.

They chose rather to believe, however, that even as an individual lays down his life for his neighbor or his enemy, so must a family, a miniature colony of heaven, lay down its life for an enemy nation. If the enemies are not Christians, to destroy them would be to send to Christless graves souls for whom Christ died; and if they are Christians, to destroy them would be to commit murder within the very household of Christ. In our day when members of the body of Christ are to be found in every nation, how is it possible for a Christian in the name of social responsibility to take up arms for the destruction of his fellow Christian on the other side of the national boundary line? Does not the way of love and the cross transcend all national and other man-made boundaries; and does it not demand that the body of Christ corporately lay down its life in sacrificial service and even death if need be? The way of the cross requires the Christian community as well as the individual to turn the other cheek, to go the second mile. The Niebuhrs and the Bennetts have done good service in showing that the collective ego in an unregenerate society is greater than the individual ego; in pointing out the shallowness of much of modern pacifism; and in emphasizing the responsibility of the Christian to others. They overshoot the mark, however, when they insist that in order for the Christian to exercise love to his neighbor he must violate the Christian ethic and the Gospel order. If we think of the Christian community as the colony of heaven, the entire body of which transcends national boundaries corporately practicing the ethic which our friends approve for the individual—then the idea that the Christian ethic must be sacrificed for the sake of the neighbor whom we love, falls to the ground. In the body of Christ it is the *collective love* which exceeds the individual love, and as it does so it overcomes the collective ego of the unregenerate society.

But our friends would ask us, Can we think of an entire community, or a state or nation, taking the way of the cross and laying down its life for the neighboring state, friend or enemy? The answer is yes, to the extent that the community, state, or nation is Christian, this is what we should expect. Would not such a course result in sure destruction? It might. The body of Christ is not promised salvation from trouble in this life. It is rather promised persecution and suffering. On the other hand, experience also tells us that nations who take up the sword are not assured of safety; and the Old Testament prophets declared that Judah's destruction came because of her evil ways, including the use of the sword and her military alliance with Egypt.[6] Who knows but that a nation Christian enough to take the self-sacrificial way might not release such a stream of spiritual power as to bring many people into the way of Christ, even as the way of the cross in the time of Christ and the early church brought life to countless thousands of souls gathered into His church, the body of Christ, the colony of heaven?

However, since no nation, not even Judah itself, is Christian, we must ever bear in mind the fact of the two social orders in our world, the Christian order and the pagan disorder; and the individual Christian must find his place and his work with the Christian order. The Christian order must live in the midst of the pagan disorder, and must ever serve as a goad and a challenge to that disorder. The order must never be identified with the disorder, however, nor adopt its ways and its means. The individual Christian must never leave the sphere of his own order for that of the disorder. The New Testament recognizes the existence side by side of the order and the disorder, and the church has recognized it ever since. The medieval church recognized it and assigned the monks to the order and relegated ordinary Christians to the disorder. Luther unfrocked the monks, reducing them to the status of ordinary Christians, allowing them to live orderly

6 Cf. Isa. 31.

one day and disorderly the next as necessity might require. Calvin tried to keep his followers within the order but his reliance upon Old Testament concessions for the modification of the moral law tended to introduce disorder into the order. The social gospel attempted to transform the disorder into order without benefit of personal regeneration. And now Christian Action has penitently resigned itself to the hopelessly permanent disorder from whence there seems to be no escape.

Herman F. Reissig is correct when he says that God did not disdain to become mixed up in mundane affairs; that the fact of the incarnation obligates Christians to get into the fray of human affairs.[7] The performance of the God incarnate within that fray, however, and the performance of the early Christians as well, was something quite different from that which Reissig advocates for Christians today. Theirs was the way of the cross which applied the ethic of love in every situation regardless of consequences. They stressed the doing of justice, and looked for ultimate justice as a fruit of the way of love. But they did not sacrifice the way of love as a means for the obtaining of justice.

The bias of this writer requires him to accept sixteenth-century Anabaptism as one of the closest approximations to New Testament Christianity in the history of the church. Not only did it measure up to the New Testament standard in a remarkable way, both in theory and in practice. Considering the opposition which it encountered, the impact of Anabaptism on modern Christendom has been nothing short of remarkable. Fritz Blanke has reminded us that the Swiss Brethren of 1525 were "the first forerunners of the free church conception." "In Zollikon a new form of church constitution began to show itself—that of the free church. Zollikon is the cradle of this idea, from whence it set out on its triumphal march through four centuries and through the

---

7 Herman F. Reissig in an address at the Fourth National Study Conference on the Churches and World Order (Cleveland, 1953).

whole world."[8] Ern'est A. Payne comments that while this is a bold claim, "it can be substantiated,"[9] and the present writer is ready to accept this statement as a valid evaluation of sixteenth-century Anabaptism.

We must be reminded, however, that to recognize the significance of Anabaptism is one thing, while finding the way of the cross at work in an equally significant manner today among those who stand in the Anabaptist tradition is quite another matter. To what extent are those who stand in the Anabaptist-Mennonite tradition true exemplars of that which they represent; or to what extent have they modified their own ethic even as Christendom in general has modified that of the New Testament? This is the crucial question which Mennonites must face in all seriousness today.

Christendom having been influenced by Anabaptism to the extent that it has, the western world is less hostile to its ideals than was the case several centuries ago. In many instances, indeed, it is remarkably tolerant of them, or even friendly in its attitude. On the surface this would seem to provide a favorable situation for a prophetic witness in our day, and in many ways it does so. On the other hand, it is also true that the modern world has a more subtle way of opposing the way of the cross than was formerly the case, with less conscious but perhaps equally devastating results. Once persecution was relaxed, the struggle for existence gave way to the problem of a more or less friendly social order. Frequently the economic factor was responsible for the new tolerance, bringing with it a temptation in two opposite directions.

The first temptation was in the direction of too much accommodation, first to the economic order and then to the political and the cultural order generally, resulting in virtual assimilation and the removal of practically all distinction between the Anabaptist descendants and their neighbors of the major Protestant traditions. The outstanding illustration of

8 Fritz Blanke, "Zollikon 1525. Die Entstehung der ältesten Täufergemeinde," *Theologische Zeitschrift* (Basel, July-August 1952) 8:262.

9 Guy F. Hershberger (ed.), *The Recovery of the Anabaptist Vision* (Scottdale, 1957) 312.

this tendency is the Mennonites of Holland and north Germany in the nineteenth century. The second temptation was in the direction of too little accommodation, frequently expressed in retirement to a geographic frontier where the once prophetic community was degraded into an isolated enclave primarily concerned with the preservation of its ethnic culture. E. K. Francis, speaking of the situation in south Russia, suggests that instead of the church-centered community maintaining a sense of mission, challenging the world in which it lived, it was transformed into a secular world order of its own of which the church was only one of its institutions.[10] In either case, whether of secularization by accommodation and assimilation, or secularization through isolation, the Anabaptist vision with its sense of mission and prophetic witness is lost. In commenting on both of these tendencies, Littell says: "When we survey both historically and dogmatically the ways of 'nestling back into the world,' we are forced to the conclusion that cultural enclaves which have lost their missionary passion and sense of a new world to come are hardly more true to original Anabaptism than those who have acclimated themselves to commerce and warring."[11]

Happily, there remains between these extremes a large body of Anabaptist-Mennonites whose contact with the world is sufficient to provide opportunity for a prophetic witness and who have not succumbed completely to the process of assimilation. Happily also, the past two generations have experienced something of a recovery of the Anabaptist vision in world Mennonitism, a renewed understanding of its meaning, and a challenge to a vital experience in the way of the cross after the manner of the first- and the sixteenth-century Christians. The rise of a new Mennonite missionary movement, a revival of educational interests, the recovery of and renewed commitment to the principle of nonresistance, an expanding social service program, and a growing social consciousness and a deepened concern for Christian social ethics

10 *Ibid.*, 254.
11 Franklin H. Littell, *The Anabaptist View of the Church*, 93.

are indications of the presence of a "continuously created fellowship of the people of God in Christ through the Spirit."

The great question, however, is whether this presence is real enough and vital enough to enable the church of the twentieth century to do for its time in a reasonably comparable measure what the church of the sixteenth century did for its time. There are among us those who are hopeful in this respect and some who are not. Whatever degree of optimism or pessimism may be ours, all can agree with Paul Peachey when he says: "If our study of the Anabaptist vision can serve as a schoolmaster to lead us to Christ, if the Anabaptist heritage can decrease that Christ may increase, this . . . can mean much to troubled men in a troubled world. If instead we transform the vision into a terminal cultural value we shall all go down with the other Pharisaisms of history."[12]

In America in the mid-twentieth century conscientious objection to war is so well recognized as to make it respectable. In contrast to the situation of an earlier day, therefore, it is relatively easy for an individual objector to avoid serious conflict with the state. If in addition to this he is also nonpolitical in thought and action while comfortably situated he may never experience a situation in which he is stimulated actively and aggressively to challenge the sub-Christian state as the Anabaptists did, or even the Christians of the early church. It is possible that many American Mennonites have reached the point where they must arouse themselves to rethink their political and social relationships lest they settle down in complacency of life so inactive as to lose its witness, eventually to become sterile and, as Peachey says, go down as one of the Pharisaisms in history.

Certainly anyone accustomed to the easy circumstances of the American conscientious objector cannot fail to be impressed by the circumstances which have compelled Christian pacifists like Wilhelm Mensching of Germany and André Trocmé of France to stand out in direct challenge to the state. Mensching's first conflict with the state came during World

12 Hershberger, op. cit., 340.

War I when as a German Christian missionary in south Africa he was arrested by British authorities and interned in India where he had an opportunity to study the caste system and to become something of an authority on the race question. This experience helped to develop his pacifist convictions in such measure that in the Hitler time he was able to stand, fearless as an oak, amidst the storms of the Nazi terror. The Nazis early suppressed his book on race relations, destroying all the copies they could find. The secret police seemed continuously to be on his trail. Mensching says that in those days he read his New Testament much in order that he might know what his attitude toward the Nazis ought to be. He concluded that he must be neither timid nor bitter, and that he must strive to see in every Nazi a child whom God loves. From what I have been able to learn I am convinced that Mensching definitely loved the Nazis, while always fearlessly opposing Nazism. This is an achievement which comes only by the grace of God. When urged to join the local Nazi organization he firmly told his solicitor: "My dear friend, I will join your organization when you take National Socialism out of it."

On one occasion a representative of the Gestapo and a local police official came to see him, perhaps to take him. When Frau Mensching informed them that her husband was not at home the Gestapo accused her of lying. But the local police said: "No, the Menschings are truthful; they do not lie." During all these years Mensching voted "no" at every Nazi election. He never said *Heil Hitler;* he never gave the Hitler salute. Even when many of his best friends urged him to take the Nazi oath of loyalty, to save the lives of himself and his family, he consistently refused to do so. On one occasion late in 1944, when Himmler issued a special order for everyone to take the oath, Mensching brought the local authorities a signed statement in which he said he would be obedient to the *Führer* in all that conforms to the law of Christ, and they took it. There were times when the area director of the *Schutzstaffel*, Hitler's private police, issued orders that Mensching must be imprisoned; that he had so many foreign connections as to make him dangerous. But it seems that persons who knew him always testified that Mensching was an absolute pacifist, that he would take no part in the war on either side, and therefore was not dangerous. Finally, it seems, the local Gestapo received orders from above to leave him alone until ordered to do otherwise. Thus they never took Mensching, although he and members of his family were continuously giving aid to persecuted Jews, and in other ways violating the program of the Hitler regime.

It was difficult for me to piece this story together, even after two lengthy conversations with Mensching. There are many details which the world will never know because of the humility of the family, and the reluctance of its members to speak of themselves, or to put the story into written form. It is certain, however, that they suffered much; and years after the war the health of several members of the family was not good, as a result of this experience. It is equally certain that this was a case of an entire family standing unitedly for the principles they believed and suffering for them. On one occasion Mensching gave me these significant words: "I was well and favorably known for a long time in Petzen, and I had a very brave wife." Then he told me the stories of several men who resisted the Nazis successfully past the point where their own lives were threatened, but who broke down and signed the Hitler oath when the officials threatened to shoot their wives and children. "My wife," said Mensching, "was more brave than I was and would never let me down."

There were many Christian pacifists who stood out with equal courage against the Nazi state. Johannes Ude of Graz, Austria, and author of a pacifist book, *Du Sollst Nicht Töten!*,[13] was sentenced to be shot. The sentence not having been executed when the war ended, however, his life was spared. Edwin Gross, a baker in Stuttgart, was notified of the day when he would leave his prison cell for execution, but for some unexplained reason he was given a discharge instead.

13 Johannes Ude, *Du Sollst Nicht Töten!* (Dornbirn, Austria, 1948).

Professor F. Siegmund-Schultze of Münster was compelled to live in exile in Switzerland during most of the Nazi time. A few others remained alive at the end of the war, but no doubt most of the Christian pacifists in Hitler's Germany paid for their faith with their lives. The Dominican Franziskus M. Stratmann of Cologne, who also served time in prison, tells the story of one of these martyrs, a priest named Franz Reinisch, who refused to take the army oath, and then was denied communion by the military chaplain and finally executed. In commenting on this story, Stratmann says: "If millions of Germans had refused to follow Hitler in his criminal plundering wars, that would have been the most powerful and noblest patriotic deed in history. It was not Fr. Reinisch who had the erroneous conscience, but the Brandenburg chaplain, along with millions of others. Their error lay in assuming the duty of obedience even in cases where the state ordered something evil, and hence too when it ordered them to invade neighboring lands, plundering them and murdering their citizens in droves."[14]

Equally impressive is the quality of Christian pacifism found in the French Protestant school represented by André Trocmé, Henri Roser, and Philippe Vernier. When it is remembered that France has a strong military tradition; that there is no legal recognition of conscientious objectors; that there are only about 1,000,000 French Protestants in a total population of 44,000,000; and that the Roser-Trocmé-Vernier group represents only a tiny section of French Protestantism, it is clear that this is a very small remnant which in the midst of a hostile nationalistic culture is giving a mighty witness for Christ and His kingdom today. Practically all of the members of this group have spent some time in prison or in concentration camp, and they take for granted that this is the price which must be paid for the faith which they hold.

Roser was graduated from the Sorbonne in 1918, then completed the required three years of military training, followed by theological studies in preparation for the mission

14 See *I.F.O.R. News Letter* No. 91 (London, December 1955) 7.

field. He began his training with idealistic enthusiasm, but before it was over he had been convinced that military service is incompatible with the Christian's duty to the kingdom of God. As he pursued his theological studies this conviction deepened, with the result that he finally returned his military papers to the ministry of war and renounced his commission in the reserves. This caused his theological professors and his friends to turn against him, and the missionary society refused him an appointment. Undaunted, he began a Christian ministry in the slums of Paris and became a traveling secretary of the Fellowship of Reconciliation. In 1933 while visiting friends in Germany he was arrested by the Nazi police, charged with being a danger to the German state, and was escorted to the French border. On September 4, 1939, the day after France declared war on Germany, his own government arrested him, after which he was sentenced to four years' imprisonment for refusing obedience to military orders. When France was invaded in 1940 Roser and his fellow prisoners were freed before the Germans reached Paris. He then joined his wife and children who had previously fled to Le Chambon-sur-Lignon. Duty soon called him back to Paris, however, in order that he might minister to his little flock which could not escape from the conquering tyrant. Here he presented himself to the German authorities, officially identifying himself as a conscientious objector who could neither collaborate with the invader nor engage in underground resistance against him, only asking for the privilege of resuming his ministry with the poor people of Paris.

During the war years Henri Roser carried on his ministry of reconciliation, conscious of the call of Christians to be "laborers together with God." To be a colaborer with Christ in Nazi-occupied France was no easy task: "Such is the mass of injustice and oppression that nothing can any longer be done about it. You can no longer publish, the platform is forbidden you, the pulpit must be prudent, even conversation becomes dangerous now that fortunes are offered for denunciation. What is the use of persevering further? The world, plunging into violence and lying, no longer has ears for our messages."[15] Roser admits a constant temptation to quietism, to be satisfied with merely "shining in one's own corner," there to await the return of Christ. But no, he says, this temptation must be resisted. For "so long as we remain the church of Christ" we cannot "refuse to judge the world, its institutions and its laws, its dispensations and its spokesmen, to the end that the world may be saved."[16]

With this conviction Roser and his associates firmly said "no" to the persistent demand that they take the collaborator's oath of loyalty. No one can serve two masters, he says, "and, having sworn complete loyalty to Jesus Christ, how can I swear absolute loyalty to another person?"[17]

If the severity of French military law has reduced the number of pacifists to the minimum, it has also helped to raise the quality of French pacifism to something approaching a maximum. The French Protestant school is no group of visionary idealists. These men have a realistic view of society. They have no illusions of a possible nonviolent state. They know that the state tends to abuse its power and they realize that the more powerful it becomes the more totalitarian in character it tends to be. They are convinced that democracy is the fruit of nonconformity.

"Alas for the state which does not count nonconformists among its citizens!" says Trocmé. "The church owes it to the state to bear testimony to a God who requires society, individual and church alike to repent. In carrying out this ministry the church is bound to be misunderstood. It will be taken for a political opponent to the public order. But it is simply serving a higher order of which the state is only an imperfect and temporary image. . . . The state must frequently choose between two evils, but never the church. It is not the church's part to assume the functions of the state. If it does, it loses its savor. . . . The state needs the church, but not as an ally, as Constantine thought. The state needs the salt of

15 Henri Roser, *Reflections of a Pastor in Occupied France* (N. Y., 1945) 20.
16 *Ibid.,* 21.
17 *Ibid.,* 21.

civil disobedience—which is Christian obedience witnessing to that divine order ʼto which the state, according to God's plan, will one day too be captive."[18]

André Trocmé's pacifism is the kind which stands undaunted even after three invasions of his native land in less than a century. With him the question is not whether pacifism is practicable, as men count practicability. The question is rather, What is the Christian's duty before God? Convinced of his calling as a herald of God's truth he welcomes every opportunity to give his witness to that truth. The French political system makes it possible for almost any citizen to form a party, adopt a platform, and stand as a candidate for public office. Using this situation as a means of witness to the truth Trocmé at one time announced himself a candidate. Standing squarely on the nonconformist platform outlined above he spoke forth prophetic words befitting an uncompromising disciple of Christ. Not measuring his words for the calculation of votes, he goaded the French populace to follow him in the nonconformist way of Christ. When asked whether he expected this political oratory to win him a seat in the French assembly he smiled and said: "Of course not, but it provided an excellent opportunity to testify to the truth."

In the mind of Trocmé the question whether pacifism is practicable, or whether a pacifist state is a possibility, or even whether Christian pacifists should assume political responsibility on all levels, is born of a superficial Christianity which takes the pagan social order as its frame of reference and which fails to understand the true nature of Christian discipleship and the way of the cross. The question is not one of practicability, not of responsibility, as men use those terms. The question is rather, What is right in the sight of God? Even so, Trocmé is equally certain that the militarist's case for practicability and responsibility is a spurious one. For was not the German Kaiser removed from the scene only to make room for Adolf Hitler? And was not Hitler eliminated only to raise the specter of a communist invasion? And now,

18 André Trocmé, "The Politics of Repentance," *The Christian Century* (Dec. 30, 1953) 70:1526, 1527.

even if a communist regime should be liquidated by hydrogen warfare, is there any assurance that the future status of France or of the world would be a less fearful one than that which went before? The frame of reference of the French Protestant school of pacifism is not that of political practicability or of social responsibility as those terms are commonly used today. The French school is called to make clear the way of the Lord as found in the New Testament ethic, and thus to serve as the conscience of the state. This is the true doctrine of Christian responsibility.

André Trocmé has described this call of the church in a striking interpretation of the parable of the widow and the unjust judge as given in Luke 18. The exploited widow is the church, the elect, buffeted by Satan the enemy who has corrupted the judge, the state. As the widow pestered the judge until he vindicated her against her adversary, so the church must press the claims of Christ and prick the conscience of the state until it responds with appropriate acts of justice. Not that the state will repent and fall at the feet of the Master. No, the state cannot repent; but even though it does not fear God nor regard man, the persistent efforts of the church result in a measure of justice. For even "the worst tyrant feels some mysterious respect for the man of courage." So "the judge yields. He does not proclaim next morning that henceforth the Sermon on the Mount will be adopted as the state's constitution, but he has given in on one point, and other plaintiffs, and the widow herself returning to the attack, will be able to invoke the precedent to obtain justice once again. In this way the church will fulfill its function in society. The church does not itself govern, but it is the cornerstone of divine justice, and the state must either build on it or else stumble over it to its own condemnation. . . .

"Its position is a precarious one between God who holds it in his hand and judges it from on high, and the church which it persecutes but whose senseless prayer will be answered. For the judge will be obliged to yield, so persistent are the widow's pleas. Our prayer is a level, its fulcrum God.

Bearing down on it with all its weight in the name of divine justice, the church moves the mountain of injustice which is called the world. . . ."[19]

Trocmé ends his interpretation of the parable with an imaginary scene at the last judgment where God asks the state for an account of its evil doings, its exploitation of the poor, its persecutions, and its murders. Then the state admits its guilt but asks for pardon because the church which "was placed by you in my body to serve as an eye for me" failed to prophesy and to show the state the way. Instead the church grew rich and became involved in all manner of secular concerns, thinking that concessions to the state would lead to better understanding. Then the judge turns to the church and declares that it has failed in its mission. "You were my elect, but you have renounced your vocation. You thought you were of the world, and you were not; or rather, you were the little flock in the world and inseparable from it because you were charged with a special mission for it. Like Jonah, you have failed in your mission. Through your fault . . . the ship has almost foundered. . . . [Then] like the man of the parable, the church will bow its head. It will be speechless. The divine judgment against it will be far more severe than against the state."[20]

Forty-five years ago Rufus M. Jones pronounced Anabaptism "one of the most momentous and significant undertakings in man's eventful religious struggle after the truth . . . , the spiritual soil out of which all nonconformist sects have sprung, . . . the first plain announcement in modern history of a programme for a new type of Christian society which the modern world . . . has been slowly realizing. . . ."[21] If these words are a true statement of the place in history of the Anabaptists, then the words of Trocmé quoted above are a warning to their twentieth-century descendants that they keep that place in history, and that they continue to make the way of the cross effective in the world today.

19 André Trocmé, *The Politics of Repentance* (New York, 1953) 86-88.
20 *Ibid.*, 92-94.
21 Rufus M. Jones, *Studies in Mystical Religion* (London, 1909) 369.

THE WAY OF THE CROSS
IN ECONOMIC LIFE

14. THE DIVINE ORDER IN ECONOMICS

Nowhere do justice and love come into sharper focus in their mutual relationship than in the Scriptural teaching on the economic life; and nowhere, perhaps, is the Christian in greater danger of losing the way of the cross than in his economic relationships. There are good reasons why the apostle called the love of money the root of all evils,[1] and why Israel was warned to take heed when vineyards are productive and when houses are filled with good things, lest love be lost so that even the God who gave deliverance from the injustice of Egyptian bondage be forgotten.[2] On the economic level men are very sensitive to injustice when they happen to be on the receiving end; but they are often quite insensitive to injustice when they become involved in the delivering end of the process. For this reason Christians need to give special attention to justice as found in the order of creation, and to love as expressed in the way of the cross in economic relations.

By the order of creation, certain economic rights are given to every man. The fourth commandment not only dedicates one day out of seven to rest from one's labors. It also dedicates six days to that work to which every man has a natural right. The eighth and the tenth commandments declare it a violation of God's fundamental law to take from any man, yes even to covet, that which he has acquired through the efforts of his labors.[3] Stealing is wrong because it deprives another of that which he has produced by his God-given powers of work. Child labor under the old sweatshop system is wrong because it is a means by which one man for purposes of selfish gain robs another of the opportunity for

1 I Tim. 6:10.
2 Deut. 6:10-12.
3 Ex. 20:8, 15, 17.

that natural development which will enable him eventually to enjoy the fruits of his own labors.

Work, the drawing of one's living from the earth, is an order of creation. As Emil Brunner correctly says, toil is not a result of sin, for in the story of creation man was first placed in the garden "to till it and keep it," and only afterwards did sin appear.[4] Furthermore, the Bible stresses the right of *every* man to draw his living from the earth. Thus property and economic opportunity are a social and not merely an individual concern. When concentration of land was carried too far and some men lost their holdings, or were even reduced to slavery, the Levitical law provided a year of jubilee in which liberty was proclaimed "throughout the land to all its inhabitants."[5] Families who had been deprived of land and the opportunity of making a living had it returned to them again. There can be no liberty without property. Slavery and the absence of property go together. Property and the human welfare which it represents are thus not merely the concern of the individual, but of the entire community. The Levitical law provided that when a man became poor and unable to maintain himself he was to be taken in by his brethren and kept by them as they would entertain a guest. Money was not to be loaned to him for interest, nor food given him for profit. As God had led Israel out of Egypt so should Israel extend mercy to her helpless poor.[6]

Personal property and the drawing of one's living from the earth are rights which belong to every man by the order of creation. However, since the manner in which a man makes his living affects his fellow men; and since the amount and kind of property which he owns, and the manner in which he disposes of it do likewise, each man's individual economic life becomes the concern of the entire society of which he is a part. Each man has a right to own property

    4 Gen. 2:15-17. See Emil Brunner, *Justice and the Social Order* (New York, 1945) 148.
    5 Lev. 25:10.
    6 Lev. 25:35-37.

and to make a living, but this right is not unqualified. In the order of creation it is ordained that when sinful men abuse this right the wrath of God, operating through the process of natural law, proceeds to correct the abuse even as it seeks to correct all forms of injustice. For the Christian, however, the way of the cross, seeking to do justice and standing ready to suffer injustice rather than to violate the higher law of love, must here as always prevail. What, then, are some of the requirements which the doing of justice and which walking the way of the cross lay upon the Christian today?

First there is the matter of inheritance and the relation of property to the family and to the community. If personal property is an essential to freedom then the right to transmit property from one generation to the next is an essential to the integrity of the family. One reason for the instability of family ties among the industrial proletariat, no doubt, has been the absence of property to be transmitted from one generation to the next. Tangible property, a homestead in particular, provides a rallying point for family sentiments which bind the group together. The value of the property need not be great. Indeed, when it becomes too great much harm is done both to the family and to the community. Be it ever so humble, however, there is no place like home. Naboth might have exchanged his vineyard for one of greater value, but he chose to keep the lesser one since it was the inheritance of his fathers. When Ahab and Jezebel took the inheritance from him they not only committed murder and theft; they also struck a blow at the integrity of the family and of the community.[7]

Throughout most of human history the sociological community has been principally an extension of the family or of groups of families. From the New Testament point of view, likewise, the Christian community is a brotherhood, the family of God, sharing a common life which affects the property of its members in a real way. When Moses num-

7 I Kings 21.

bered the people each tribe was given an inheritance suitable for its numbers.[8] This does not mean that there must be strict equality in the amount of land holdings or of other forms of property. Variation in the amount of property held, or of wealth possessed, need not constitute an injustice. Indeed, by virtue of the fact that men's gifts and talents differ the amount of property suited to their needs and services must necessarily differ. This difference must not be too great, however, and the Christian community has an obligation to avoid the extremes of concentrated wealth and of poverty, for such always tend to vitiate the spiritual life of the brotherhood. The important thing is that each man have sufficient to supply his personal and family needs and to enable him freely to use his gifts and talents for the service of God and man, of society and of the church.

The French, the Russian, the Chinese, and other great revolutions in history were manifestations of the wrath of God seeking, through the operation of natural law within a sinful social order, to correct the injustices which followed the concentration of land and the means of production in the hands of the few. Oppressed peoples will always attempt to free themselves from injustices which follow the monopolization of power and the means of production, especially when the monopolists are foreigners who do not share the intimate life of the local community. When Isaiah condemned those in Israel who joined house to house and field to field, who devoured the vineyards of the common people and ground the face of the poor[9]; when Amos upbraided those who stooped so low as to sell into slavery a man unable to pay a debt equivalent to the price of a pair of shoes, while they themselves lived securely and luxuriously in mountain resorts,[10] he was crying for the correction of economic abuses on a small scale which since that day have often existed on a much larger scale, and which even now are far from eliminated.

8 Num. 26:53, 54.
9 Isa. 3:14, 15; 5:8.
10 Amos 2:6; 6:1-6; 8.

Amos gives an ironic picture of the pious hypocrite who devotes the Sabbath to waiting for its close when there will be a renewed opportunity to "deal deceitfully with false balances," to sell a diminished ephah of wheat for a shekel of enlarged value.[11] This religious materialist has his counterpart in the modern "Christian" businessman who contributes his thousands to the church where on Sunday morning he soothes his mind with the aid of stained glass, ritual, and music as he concentrates on the business deal scheduled for consummation the coming week. According to Micah, however, the Lord will not be pleased with such even though they offer thousands of rams, or ten thousands of rivers of oil, or millions of dollars. The time will come when their sins will bring desolation, when they will eat and not be satisfied, when they will sow and not reap.[12]

The remedy for this sorry situation, says Micah, is that men must do justice, and love kindness, and walk humbly with their God.[13] When God was in Christ reconciling the world unto Himself He took the way of the cross and showed us the meaning of justice and love and humility. The way of the cross is to seek the kingdom of God and His righteousness, and not to be anxious about food to eat and clothing to wear.[14] It is to labor with one's hands, that we may be able to give to those in need.[15] It is to aid the poor without concern for interest or even for the return of the principal.[16] It is to beware of covetousness, and not to engage in strife because of the family inheritance.[17] It is to be rich toward God, even as Lazarus, and not to feast sumptuously as the rich man did.[18]

It is to go all the way with Christ and His Gospel even if it means economic loss, and not to demur the heavenly call as did the Ephesian silversmiths.[19] For Zacchaeus and his kind it is to come down from the tree to dine with the

---

11 Amos 8:5, 6.
12 Mic. 6.
13 Mic. 6:8.
14 Matt. 6:31.
15 Eph. 4:28.

16 Matt. 5:42.
17 Luke 12:13-15.
18 Luke 16:19-31.
19 Acts 19:23-27.

Master, to restore that which has been taken by fraud, and to minister to the poor.[20] For employees it is to do an honest day's work as servants of Christ doing the will of God.[21] For employers it is to treat their employees justly and fairly, knowing that they also have a Master in heaven.[22] For all it is to love one another with brotherly affection, in honor preferring one another.[23]

The book of Acts gives a dramatic picture of what actually happens when the Spirit of God descends upon men and brings them into the way of the cross. Here the disciples "devoted themselves to the apostles' teaching and fellowship, to the breaking of bread and the prayers." Daily they attended the temple for worship and continued in their homes, eating the meal of Christian fellowship "with glad and generous hearts." This was no formal worship designed to soothe the distraught mind in preparation for strenuous days of bargain driving. It was true worship and genuine fellowship which brought the fear of God into men's hearts so that many signs and wonders were performed among them. Men actually sold their possessions so as to be able to assist those who had need. For a time some of them even practiced what is sometimes called community of goods. Instead of using religion for the furtherance of personal economic ends, their religion led them to use their assets for the welfare of the entire Christian community. They "were of one heart and soul, and no one said that any of the things which he possessed was his own, but they had everything in common. And with great power the apostles gave their testimony to the resurrection of the Lord Jesus, and . . . there was not a needy person among them, for as many as were possessors of lands or houses sold them, and brought the proceeds of what was sold and laid it at the apostles' feet; and distribution was made to each as any had need."[24]

This is not to say that Christian economics requires the

20 Luke 19:1-10.
21 Eph. 6:5, 6.
22 Eph. 6:9; Col. 4:1.
23 Rom. 12:9, 10.
24 Acts 2:42-47; 4:32-37.

renunciation of private property, for the Scriptures do not teach us so. The "everything in common" of the Jerusalem church here referred to was a spontaneous sharing of *private* property to meet the needs of the group, not an organized social system requiring group ownership. The property of Ananias and Sapphira, while it remained unsold, was their own; and even after it was sold it was at their own disposal. Their sin was not a rejection of group ownership. It consisted in falsely pretending to share their private property for the welfare of the group.[25] Both the Old and New Testaments give strenuous warning against materialism and the concentration of wealth. While recognizing the "ownership" of property from a human point of view they also teach that in a more real sense ownership belongs to God alone, and that men are mere stewards of God's possessions. From this it follows, both logically and Scripturally, that the Christian steward may acquire and use earthly possessions only to the glory of God and in an amount and manner that will be beneficial to the society of which he is a part.

25 Acts 5:1-11.

15. ANABAPTISM AND THE ECONOMIC ORDER

When it is remembered that sixteenth-century Anabaptism was a restoration movement it is not surprising to find within it an emphasis on economics much like that of the early church. The Anabaptists aimed to restore the early Christian community, the colony of heaven in all of its aspects, including the material. An examination of the economic views of Menno Simons and Peter Rideman[1] shows that both of these leaders believed and taught that: (1) Materialism is unchristian. (2) Material goods, neither good nor bad in themselves, are to be used by Christian stewards as a means of doing good, to the glory of God. (3) Christians should trust in God who supplies the necessities of life. (4) The unfortunate state of the world is largely due to an unchristian attitude toward material possessions. (5) Extremes of luxury, riches, and the concentration of wealth on the one hand, and poverty on the other, are both wrong, among other reasons because they break the Christian fellowship. (6) True Christian fellowship involves something approaching economic equality, since Christian brotherhood has a material as well as a spiritual basis. (7) This requires an intimate Christian community life in which mutual aid and generous sharing and co-operation in economic matters are freely practiced.

For Rideman and the Hutterian Brethren this meant actual community of goods and the elimination of private property. Rideman developed his case at length, arguing that the communion of the saints must be in material as well as in spiritual things. The body of Christ as described by

1 See Donald Sommer, "Peter Rideman and Menno Simons on Economics," *Mennonite Quarterly Review* (July 1954) 28:205-23.

Paul[2] is not complete unless the entire life, including material goods, is literally incorporated within the body. This completion, Rideman believed, was actually achieved in the early Jerusalem church where community of goods was practiced.[3] Menno Simons, however, did not accept this extreme view. While granting that the Jerusalem church did have community of goods for a time, he also asserted that this economy was later abolished.[4] Nowhere among the Anabaptists was group ownership of property established as an institution outside the Hutterian circle. Except for this point, however, there was little difference among the Anabaptists in their economic views. All of them placed great emphasis on Christian brotherhood, holding that the Christian is the owner of his property in a limited sense only; that he is in fact but a steward of that which he is permitted to use for the glory of God and for the welfare of his fellow men, with whom he must ever be ready to share his goods as need may require. In some instances the baptismal vow itself included a pledge of willingness to give up earthly possessions for the sake of the brotherhood if need required it.[5]

Their enemies seemingly were unable or unwilling to distinguish this practice from group ownership of property, resulting in frequent charges of communism, which the Anabaptists were quick to refute. Some of the Anabaptists seem even to have used the term "community of goods" in describing their practice of mutual aid and then found it necessary to explain that this did not mean group ownership. Felix Manz, for example, said he understood community of goods to be a willingness to help those who are in need.[6] George Blaurock when questioned regarding his idea of "community of all things" explained that by this he did not mean group

2 I Cor. 12:12-27.

3 Peter Rideman, *Account of our Religion, Doctrine and Faith; Given by Peter Rideman of the Brothers whom men call Hutterians* (Suffolk, 1950) 43, 90.

4 Menno Simons, *The Complete Writings of Menno Simons* (Scottdale, 1956) 559, 560.

5 A. Hulshof, *Geschiedenis van de Doopsgezinden te Straatsburg van 1525 tot 1557* (Amsterdam, 1905) 216.

6 See Harold S. Bender, *Conrad Grebel, the Founder of the Swiss Brethren* (Goshen, 1950) 159, 205, 254, 276.

ownership of property. What he did mean was that "He who is a good Christian should share what he has, else he is none." This, says Robert Friedmann, "was the traditional attitude of Anabaptists everywhere toward worldly goods."[7]

Balthasar Hubmaier expresses a similar view when he says: "Concerning community of goods I have always taught that a man should have a concern for the other man, that the hungry be fed, the thirsty receive drink, etc. For we are not the masters of our possessions but stewards and distributors only. No one would say, take away what a man has and make it common. Rather he would say, let the coat go together with the mantle . . . ."[8] The following description by Sebastian Franck, a contemporary historian, is a fair characterization of the Anabaptists generally, using the term "things in common" in the sense that Manz, Hubmaier, and others use it: "It seems they taught nothing but love, faith, and the cross. Under trial they showed themselves patient and humble. They broke bread with each other as a manifestation of unity and love. They helped each other faithfully, . . . lending, borrowing, giving, and taught that all things should be common, called each other brothers. . . ."[9]

This is a fair statement of Menno Simons' own views. In his *Reply to False Accusations* (1552), in which he clearly rejects group ownership of property, Menno is most severe in his condemnation of materialism, and upholds the principle of brotherhood in a most vigorous fashion. He says: "All those who are born of God, who are . . . called into one body and love in Christ Jesus, are prepared by such love to serve their neighbors, not only with money and goods, but

7 Robert Friedmann, *Mennonite Encyclopedia* (Scottdale, 1955) 1:659.

8 Balthasar Hubmaier, in *Gespräch auf Meister Zwinglis Taufbüchlein* (1526), quoted by Friedmann, *ME*, 1:659. The testimony of Ambrosius Spitelmeier as given before the authorities at Cadolzburg in 1527 would seem to have a similar meaning, since the recognized ability to buy or sell implies possession of property: "True Christians shall have all things, be they spiritual or material, in common . . . since God has permitted all things to grow in common for all men. Christians shall not buy anything from each other but give it without charge (Read Acts 2, 3, 4 whether the Christians in Jerusalem did not have all things common)." K. Schornbaum, *Quellen zur Geschichte der Wiedertäufer: II. Markgraftum Brandenburg* (Leipzig, 1934) 64.

9 Sebastian Franck, *Chronica, Zeitbuch und Geschichtbibel* (1531) ccccxliiii.

also after the example of their Lord and Head, Jesus Christ, in an evangelical manner, with life and blood. They show mercy and love, as much as they can. No one among them is allowed to beg. They take to heart the need of the saints. They entertain those in distress. They take the stranger into their houses. They comfort the afflicted; assist the needy; clothe the naked; feed the hungry; do not turn their face from the poor; do not despise their own flesh. . . . Behold such a community we teach . . . . God be thanked forever that although our property has to a great extent been taken away from us and is still daily taken, and many a pious father and mother are put to the sword or fire, and although we are not allowed the free enjoyment of our homes as is manifest, and besides the times are hard, yet none of those who have joined us nor any of their orphaned children have been forced to beg."[10]

The brotherhood emphasis of the Anabaptists was no mere expression of loyalty to the social in-group. It was an expression of evangelical love which went out to all men whether brother or stranger, whether friend or foe. A practical demonstration of this fact was the incident which occurred at Wismar in North Germany in December 1553, where Menno Simons lived in hiding with a small congregation at the time. It so happened that a group of Protestants who had been driven out of England by the Catholic Queen Mary had sailed for Denmark. Since they were not Lutherans, however, the Danes did not permit them to land. As the refugees were fleeing from Denmark one of their ships found itself frozen in the sea a short distance from Wismar. When the authorities of Wismar failed to help them Menno and his followers, who themselves were barely tolerated in the Lutheran city, took steps to rescue the fleeing Calvinists.

Obviously, it was a most courageous act for a group of persecuted Mennonites to bring a group of persecuted Calvinists into a Lutheran city which was inclined to tolerate neither the rescuer nor the rescued. This was the kind of

10 Menno Simons, *Writings*, 558, 559.

action which the brotherhood faith of the Mennonites required, however, and they did not hesitate because of the difficulty. When they were informed of the plight of the refugees, Menno says: "They were moved by Christian mercy . . . as was proper. They talked it over and concluded to lend them assistance and help them out of the ice and escort them to the city in an orderly way without any commotion as they also did—although they suspected that it might cause trouble with the government as indeed it did." Food was taken to the ship and after the refugees had been brought to the city the Mennonites made up a collection for them "out of their poverty." The refugees declined to accept the money, however, saying they did not need it, but asked the Mennonites to assist some of their number in finding employment, which they did.[11] This incident provides an excellent illustration of the Anabaptist-Mennonite faith in action. First, they extended help to the needy stranger. Second, they did so at considerable risk to themselves. Third, those who received the aid were members of an intolerant religious group at whose hands the Anabaptists had suffered much in Switzerland, in Germany, and in the Netherlands.

This doctrine of Christian stewardship with its corresponding emphasis on brotherhood economics included some positive ideas regarding the amount of wealth which the Christian might possess, the manner of obtaining it, and the purpose for which it should be used. Menno spoke out in a most vigorous fashion against the snare of riches. Possession of great wealth, he says, tends to make men "proudhearted, ambitious, and covetous of honor." He says there was good reason for Jesus' statement that it was easier for a camel to go through the eye of a needle than for a rich man to enter the kingdom; and he quoted James who tells the rich to weep and howl for the miseries which are to come upon them.[12] Living in luxury and bedecking oneself in finery were an inexcusable misuse of that which God has

11 *Ibid.*, 842.
12 *Ibid.*, 642.

given for better purposes. He says there is no doubt that if the rich "would apply to the support of the poor their silk, damask, the abundance of their clothes in which many of them go about so gloriously, the great and beautiful ornamentations of their houses, the golden and silver necklaces, the useless, costly leggings, gold chains, earrings, silver- and gold-plated swords, besides the booty of the distressed which probably may be found in the houses of some, then the poor would not suffer in the least from want."[13]

In his treatise on *The True Christian Faith,* in which he cites the faith of Zacchaeus the publican, Menno has only words of woe for unrighteous men who ignore the requirements of God in the conduct of their business.[14] Rideman especially emphasized the need for engaging only in such trades and professions as are consistent with the way of the cross which Christians profess. Three occupations definitely ruled out for the Christian were the making of implements of warfare; the making of fashionable clothing which could not consistently be worn by the Christian; and the manufacture and sale of alcoholic beverages.[15]

On these points, and in the matter of brotherhood economics generally, the views of the Anabaptists were in full accord with their basic principle of Christian discipleship. Being men of their age, however, they did not anticipate the technological changes which the coming centuries were to bring forth. Hence some of their views with respect to economic techniques were dated. They seem to have believed that agriculture and the crafts were worthy of a place within the Christian brotherhood, whereas commerce, trade, banking, and the paying of interest were outside the pale. This view was held in part because agriculture and the crafts of their day were simple operations, whereas commerce and trade were more complex, involving greater opportunities and temptations to engage in unchristian practices.

13 *Ibid.,* 658.
14 *Ibid.,* 368.
15 Rideman, *op. cit.,* 111, 112, 127.

Rideman said in so many words: "We allow none of our number to do the work of a trader or merchant, since this is a sinful business."[16] Menno spoke of "wicked merchants and retailers (I say the wicked, for I do not mean those who are righteous and pious), . . . so bent on accursed profit that they exclude God wholly from their hearts. They censure what they should properly praise, and praise what they should censure. They lie and swear; they use many vain words, falsify their wares to cheat the people, and strip them of possessions; they sell, lend, and secure the needy at large profit and usury, never seriously reflecting or taking to heart what is written, Let no man go beyond and defraud his brother in any matter."[17] Menno then quotes with approval the statement from the apocryphal book of Ecclesiasticus: "A merchant shall hardly keep himself from doing wrong, and a huckster shall not be freed from sin; many have sinned for a small matter, and he that seeketh for abundance will turn his eyes away. As a nail sticketh fast between the joinings of the stones, so doth sin stick close between buying and selling."[18]

While Rideman seemed to consider it quite impossible for a Christian to engage in trade, Menno Simons left the door slightly open for this occupation, granting that some merchants and retailers were God-fearing and righteous. Since the sinfulness of man had its roots in greed and materialism, however, and since commerce and trade seemed to increase this greed, the emergence of modern capitalism which he witnessed was full of evil forebodings. While Menno was much nearer the truth here than many of his twentieth-century followers would be willing to admit, it clearly would be difficult for us to draw the line so sharply at the point where he drew it, placing agriculture and the crafts on one side, and commerce and trade on the other.

16 *Ibid.*, 126.
17 Menno Simons, 368.
18 *Ibid.*, 369, quoting Ecclesiasticus 26:29; 27:1-3.

16. THE MEDIEVAL AND THE MODERN
ECONOMIES

In our time ordinary merchants and retailers, especially in the smaller communities, would be placed in the category of those engaged in the simpler aspects of the economic order. For many of them competition is so strong that their business would not long survive the practice of adulteration and price lifting which Menno describes. Meanwhile the industrial revolution has replaced the old-time craftsmanship with the modern factory system and its powerfully organized industrial associations and labor unions. Moreover, in America particularly, agriculture has been mechanized with a corresponding increase in the average size of farms. The American farmer is a commercial farmer, a businessman with a capital investment and a volume of trade involving organization, credit, and other procedures which would make many tradesmen of Menno's day look small by comparison. The coercive methods and powerful maneuverings of modern agricultural organizations, labor unions, and industrial corporations are of such a nature that today Menno would hardly classify them as innocent procedures of men with an essentially Christian calling. The ethical teachings of Menno are basically sound, and none of them is closer to the truth than that in which he holds that materialism and the love of riches are at the root of many social evils. Today, however, it should be recognized, first, that Menno did not fully succeed in avoiding the confusion of basic principles and economic techniques; and second, that no occupation or profession is immune from the temptations and perils against which he warned.

On the matter of confusion between basic principles and economic techniques, one should note first the question of interest, or usury as it was called in an earlier day. The medieval church prohibited the collection of interest on money loaned. Luther also opposed it to some extent. Menno Simons and Peter Rideman left no room for it whatever in their scheme of things. Today Mennonites occasionally refer to the charging of interest as unchristian, and point out that in the earlier history of the brotherhood it was not practiced. When one understands the medieval concept of money, however, opposition to the payment of interest on loans is easily understood. The theory was that money is unproductive, a mere medium of exchange. Hence when money was loaned to help someone in need of food for his family, for example, the lender was supposed to be satisfied if the borrower merely returned the principal. If the money had not been loaned it would not have produced anything. Why then should a poor man pay for the use of money which produces nothing?

On the other hand, the medieval church did approve the payment of rent, and indeed received such payment on its own lands. Following the argument used against the charging of interest it might have been argued that it was unfair to require the poor tenant to work on the land and pay rent besides, while the rich landowner should be paid for doing nothing. The difference was, however, that the land was regarded as something productive. The owner had acquired it through his labors, and now it was working for him. Renting it to someone else was putting the land to work for the tenant. The work which the land did for the tenant should be paid for, the same as if the owner had labored personally for him. The medieval church had no objection to the payment of rent, and there is no evidence that the Anabaptists objected to it.

The reason for the difference between the medieval and the modern view of interest is that money has come to be productive in a sense that it formerly was not. Money is the fruit of one's labors, the consumption of which has been postponed. Or it may be thought of as seed wheat which is not consumed, but planted that it may produce more wheat. Thus money works and produces for its owner just as the land does. Therefore, when the owner makes a loan his money goes to work for the borrower who should pay for the service rendered just as he would pay the owner if he had rendered his personal service, or if he had given a lease on his land. This is the justification for the payment of interest on money borrowed for productive purposes. It is really a form of wages paid for labor, or for services rendered.

However justifiable as a business procedure the charging of interest on capital loans may be, it is often in danger of abuse in practice. The person who pays the interest is also entitled to a fair remuneration for his contribution, and the problem is to find the correct balance between these two just claims. The poor man who has no capital must depend upon a fair wage for his labors in order that he may live; and, as Emil Brunner says, from the standpoint of justice this claim must take precedence over the return upon invested capital.[1] On the other hand, if there is no satisfactory return upon the investment, saving and lending tend to come to an end and the entire economic system is in danger of breaking down. Finding the way of strict justice is therefore a technical problem, and an intricate one, in modern industry.

The Christian, however, cannot be content with mere justice in economic relations. He must go beyond justice to find the way of love and the cross. Justice accords the lender a payment of interest upon his investment. On occasion, however, love may require him to forego this right. Unlike Anabaptism, Calvinism is commonly said to have made a positive contribution to the development of the spirit of modern capitalism. It must be remembered, however, that true Calvinism always placed capitalism under the restraining influence of Christian love. Calvin himself said: "It may happen that a man cannot make the smallest profit by interest without sin against God and wrong to his neighbor."[2]

Jesus describes situations for us in which this would be the case. He says: "Give to him who begs from you, and do

---

1 Brunner, *Justice and the Social Order*, 163.
2 Quoted in *ibid.*, 163.

not refuse him who would borrow from you."[3] Again He says: "Give to every one who begs from you; and of him who takes away your goods, do not ask them again. . . . And if you lend to those from whom you hope to receive, what credit is that to you? Even sinners lend to sinners, to receive as much again. But love your enemies, and do good, and lend, expecting nothing in return; and your reward will be great, and you will be sons of the Most High; for he is kind to the ungrateful and the selfish."[4]

These words from the Sermon on the Mount are not given as a statement of economic laws and techniques. They are a statement of the law of love which always stands ready to go beyond economic principles. When men are sick and destitute, Christians with means have an obligation to "lend" aid, hoping not only to receive no interest; there are times when it would be wrong to receive even the principal again. Christian charity often demands an outright gift of one's goods to the needy. Love and the way of the cross also forbid retaliation. If a man takes your coat give him your cloak also. If you suffer loss in an automobile accident do not sue the offender at law for the vindication of your rights. The way of love at work in the Christian community must find a better way, whether in a simple economy in which money is a mere medium of exchange, or under modern conditions in which it is productive capital.

In the Old Testament also certain passages forbid the taking of interest. Take, for example, this one from the book of Exodus: "If you lend money to any of my people with you who is poor, you shall not be to him as a creditor, and you shall not exact interest from him. If ever you take your neighbour's garment in pledge, you shall restore it to him before the sun goes down; for that is his only covering, it is his mantle for his body; in what else shall he sleep?"[5] Again, this is not a statement of economic principles and procedures. It is not

3 Matt. 5:42.
4 Luke 6:30-35.
5 Ex. 22:25-27.

a discussion of productive capital loaned for business purposes. It is a command to perform deeds of mercy, without hope of remuneration, for the aid of the brother who is in need. If this command was in order in both Old and New Testament times there is no question that Christians in our day as well have frequent obligations to lend and give of their means without thought of remuneration.

The Christian is not necessarily out of order when he pays or receives interest on productive capital in a business transaction. The command of love requires, however, that in all of his economic relations the principle of Christian love and brotherhood take precedence over the principle of "sound business practice." While it is hazardous to fix any figure as a "just" rate of interest applicable under all circumstances, the five per cent proposed by John Calvin and the Geneva council as the highest rate has stood the test of time remarkably well. The theory was that if a man's capital were consumed in one generation this would mean a certain percentage annually to which should be added something for the risk involved in making the loan.[6]

Even though Calvinism is supposed to have made its contribution to the growth of the spirit of capitalism, the latter has gone wrong not because of the economic techniques which Calvin recognized, but rather because it is no longer directed by the ethical principles which governed Calvin's own capitalistic endeavors and teachings. Calvin recognized work as a duty. He opposed concentration of wealth, luxurious living, and the unscrupulous business practices of his time. His denunciation of merchant princes in commercial cities like Antwerp and Venice was as severe as Menno Simons' denunciation of the mercantile life with which he was familiar. Certain kinds of crafts were taboo with him as they were with Peter Rideman, as for example when he ruled out the manufacture of playing cards.[7]

---

6 See Brunner, *op. cit.*, 162.
7 See Troeltsch, *The Social Teaching of the Christian Churches* (London, 1931) 2:641, 642.

Calvin did not follow Rideman and Menno, however, in insisting on a strictly agrarian economy for the Christian. He recognized the productive character of money and was ready to go along with a capitalistic economy including credit and interest. In Geneva he helped to introduce, with the aid of a state loan, the manufacture of cloth as a means of providing work for the unemployed. When competition from Lyons made the continuation of this program impractical, Geneva introduced the manufacture of watches.[8]

While recognizing the nature of trade as justifying greater profits for it than for agriculture, Calvin himself would have been horrified at the excesses which came to characterize a later capitalism. For him labor was actually a form of asceticism to be performed, not for personal gain, but for the glory of God. He considered the businessman a steward whose duty it was to increase his capital and to use it for the welfare of society, and especially for the good of the church. He should retain for himself only what is required to supply his needs.

Troeltsch further describes Calvin's economic program as follows: "Thus the Genevese assessed themselves to the furthest possible limit for special cases of need, and gave regularly in support of the local poor as well as for the numerous refugees. . . ."

"Only 'productive credit' for business purposes is allowed, not 'usury credit,' which is simply used for living on interest. From poor men, or people who have been otherwise harassed by misfortune, no interest is to be taken; loans also were not to be refused for lack of securities. Arrangements of that kind are only to be carried out with reference to the good of the community as a whole. The debtor ought to gain just as much from the money as the creditor. The law of cheapness ought to prevail everywhere, in accordance with the principle of the Gospel and of the Natural Law, that 'whatsoever ye would that they should do unto you, do ye also unto them.' Finally, the rate of interest ought not to exceed a maximum, which is to be legally fixed according to the needs of

8 *Ibid.,* 2:642

the situation. This was the theory. In Geneva practical life was regulated in accordance with these principles. The fight against usury and the exploitation of the poor fill the protocols of the Council and of the Consistory, and these Christian-Social elements of Calvinistic doctrine have also left their mark upon ethics. Thus we can understand how it is that within Calvinism, in the face of the modern development of capitalism, there has always been, and still is, a tendency to merge into a form of Christian Socialism. . . . A Socialism of this kind was contained, from the very outset, in the Genevan ideal of the Holy Community. . . .

"The Christian Socialism of the English people at the present day is essentially of Calvinistic origin, and the activity of the American churches is often of a Christian Socialist kind directed against the abuses of Capitalism. . . . This also is the basis of that intense self-consciousness of Calvinism, the sense that it is the only form of Christianity adapted to modern life, because, on the one hand, it is able to justify modern forms of economic production before the tribunal of conscience, and because, on the other hand, by means of Christian Socialism, it strives to rectify the abuses of the system when they occur."[9]

The abuses have often been greater, however, than Calvin anticipated. For as Troeltsch continues to say: "Once capitalism had been accepted, even with many precautions, given the right *milieu,* everywhere it led to results which increased its power; while the specifically Calvinistic habits of piety and industry justified its existence and helped to increase its strength, which gave it in the Calvinistic communities a special character and a peculiar intensity."[10] If capitalism could have been confined to truly Calvinistic communities of the Genevan variety it would no doubt present a different character than it does today. Unfortunately, however, every form of power is fraught with danger; and the power of even a Calvinistic capitalism is no exception. As

9 *Ibid.,* 2:648, 649.
10 *Ibid.,* 2:644.

Troeltsch further admits, such capitalism can "easily glide
into a purely secular conception, once the religious motives
had weakened and the religious atmosphere had begun to
evaporate. From the time of Adam Smith, indeed, the classical economic theory has constructed the foundations of economics in precisely the opposite sense, in pure hedonism."[11]

A century and a half before Adam Smith, John Cotton
and John Winthrop had planted the doctrines of Calvin on
the shores of New England. In the early eighteenth century
the former's grandson, Cotton Mather, was telling his congregation that a Christian had two callings: (1) a general
calling, "to serve the Lord Jesus Christ"; (2) "a certain *Particular Employment,* by which his usefulness in his neighborhood is distinguished."[12] Samuel Sewall (1652-1730), the best
representative of the twilight period of American Puritanism,
was faithful in his attendance at church and in meeting his
religious obligations; but the dominant ambition of his life
is said to have been the acquisition of wealth and the occupation of a dignified position among his fellow citizens. "From
commerce and land speculation and money lending and the
perquisites of many offices, he accumulated steadily until his
wealth entitled him to be regarded as one of the first citizens
of Massachusetts. He did not forget his prudence even in his
generosities, but set down carefully in his diary what his benefactions cost, that there might be no mistake when he came
to make his reckoning with the Lord. He knew his rights and
upheld them stoutly; and in the petty quarrels and litigations
in which he found himself involved, he stuck to the letter of
the law and usually won his point. He did not misuse his
official position to feather his own nest, but what might be
got legally from public office he took care to get."[13]

With the passing of Sewall and New England Puritanism
the point of transition from an economy largely influenced by

11 *Ibid.,* 2:646.
12 R. H. Gabriel, *The Course of American Democratic Thought* (New York,
1940) 147, 148.
13 V. L. Parrington, *Main Currents in American Thought* (New York, 1930)
1:90.

Christian principles and ideals to a secular economy emphasizing individualism and freedom from all restraint, whether of church or of state, had arrived. The emergence of an age of materialism which John Calvin and Menno Simons would have condemned with equal vigor was now at hand.

17. MODERN CAPITALISM

Vernon L. Parrington calls Samuel Sewall "the progenitor of a practical race that was to spread the gospel of economic individualism across the continent."[1] This characterization shows how subtle, but how sure, can be the transition from the Christian capitalism of a Calvin to the hedonistic capitalism of today. By the time Adam Smith had published the *Wealth of Nations* in 1776 the New England Puritan was gone and the new American had emerged in the person of Benjamin Franklin and the men of his age. Franklin had had a share in the making of Adam Smith himself and in the development of his economic theory. Having substituted the philosophy of deism for the theology of Calvin, the new American was free to promote *laissez-faire* capitalism without the inconvenience of religious restrictions. If honesty was to be pursued it would be because it is the best policy, not because it is the will of God. The undeveloped resources of a vast new continent provided unlimited material substance with which to put the neo-hedonistic theories into effect; and for some of Franklin's successors, it would seem, honesty was not even so much as a good policy.

Almost two centuries have passed since the time of Franklin and Smith, and their economic philosophy seems to have come to its full fruition. What, we may ask, are the manifest fruits thereof? Our civilization, we are told on every hand, is sensate and materialistic. In America the last third of the nineteenth century has even been called the age of the economic robber barons. In 1871 Charles Francis Adams, referring to the Goulds, the Drews, the Vanderbilts, and the Cookes, said his time had "witnessed some of the most re-

---

1 Parrington, *Main Currents in American Thought,* 1:97. (See above, p. 234).

markable examples of organized lawlessness, under the forms of law, which mankind has yet had an opportunity to study."[2] So overwhelming was the materialistic spell which the giants of industry had cast over the American public, however, that Andrew Carnegie was able to publish a book entitled *The Gospel of Wealth*, the philosophy of which was widely accepted. The foundations of our society, says Carnegie, are individualism, private property, the law of accumulation of wealth, and the law of competition. These are the principles which cause wealth to come to those who are superior in energy and ability. They are "the highest result of human experience, the soil in which society, so far, has produced the best fruit. Unequally or unjustly, perhaps, as these laws sometimes operate, and imperfect as they appear to the idealist, they are, nevertheless, like the highest type of man, the best and most valuable of all that humanity has yet accomplished."[3]

In order to evaluate Carnegie and his school fairly it must be recognized that they did have a sense of responsibility to society. Carnegie was opposed to bequeathing large family estates which would ultimately bring no benefit either to the heirs or to society. Instead, the man of wealth should, while he lives, administer his surplus wealth for the building of universities, libraries, hospitals, and other institutions which will help to raise the level of all the people. Thus millionaires in becoming rich do not make others poor. Their wealth and the industry which produces it make it possible for the poor to improve their lot, enabling those with ability through struggle to rise to the top.

Within proper limits Carnegie's "trusteeship of the poor" idea has its merits. Like most industrialists of his generation, however, his low view of the common man, together with his philosophy of the "advantages of poverty," stood between him and ordinary justice in such elementary mat-

---

2 Gabriel, *The Course of American Democratic Thought*, 144.

3 Andrew Carnegie, *The Gospel of Wealth and Other Timely Essays* (New York, 1900) 7.

ters as fair wages and decent working conditions. His program for the building of universities and libraries was motivated in part by a worthy sense of responsibility to society in
general. It was also motivated, on the other hand, by the
less worthy fear lest his surplus earnings be wasted through
the payment of too high wages to workingmen incapable of
using them properly. The better way was for the laws of
individualism, competition, and accumulation to do their
work, permitting the fittest to rise from their poverty and
build great fortunes the benefits of which would then trickle
down from the hand of the benevolent despot to those not
fitted for leadership and who cannot be trusted to make good
use of better wages. While the law of competition "may be
sometimes hard for the individual, it is best for the race, because it insures the survival of the fittest in every department"
whose benefactions will then indirectly find their way to the
less fit. "Such, in my opinion, is the true gospel concerning
wealth, obedience to which is destined some day to solve the
problem of the rich and the poor and to bring 'peace on
earth, among men good will.' "[4]

Sincerely as Carnegie may have believed this philosophy
it seems too much like a blasphemous proposal to bring in the
kingdom of God through the law of the jungle. It has too
little confidence in the common man and too little regard for
his rights. And it is certainly a far cry from the brotherhood
spirit of the New Testament, or from the economic teachings
of either the Anabaptists or of John Calvin. It is amazing,
however, the extent to which American educators and even
the clergy accepted this doctrine. James McCosh of Princeton, Noah Porter of Yale, Mark Hopkins of Williams, and
D. S. Gregory, author of a textbook on Christian ethics—all of
them—took for granted that acquisitiveness and the search for
wealth were a God-given gift and an obligation which must
not be neglected. While there were occasional references to
the need for honest acquisition, it seems for the most part to

4 *Ibid.*, 4, 18, 19.

have been assumed that this was a matter which would take care of itself. The important thing was to get the wealth.

The great popularizer of the idea was Russell H. Conwell whose lecture-sermon, *Acres of Diamonds,* delivered 6,000 times and published with a wide circulation to yield the author an income of $8,000,000, urged men to get rich: "Money is power. Every good man and woman ought to strive for power, to do good with it when obtained." Conwell agreed that money needs to be obtained honestly, but he was sure that "98 out of 100 of the rich men of America are honest. That is why they are rich."[5]

John D. Rockefeller's organization of the Standard Oil Company by the process of squeezing numerous small competitors into bankruptcy and out of existence has come to be the classic example of robber baronism; and yet this faithful Baptist layman told the first graduating class at the University of Chicago that "the good Lord gave me my money, and how could I withhold it from the University of Chicago?"[6] The University students, not to be outdone, gave their expression to the same sentiments by singing, "praise John from whom oil blessings flow." It was left to Bishop William Lawrence of Massachusetts to state the gospel of wealth in its finished form, however, when he declared godliness to be in league with riches to make the national character "sweeter, more joyous, more unselfish, more Christlike," by means of material prosperity.[7]

This is a splendid illustration of the dilemma so clearly seen by John Wesley in the eighteenth century. Christianity makes for frugality, and the frugal man accumulates wealth, observed Wesley. Then wealth generates pride and indifference to religion, so that religion tends to destroy itself.[8] No form of Christianity seems to be immune from this process,

---

5 Russell H. Conwell, *Acres of Diamonds* (1890) 19. Quoted in Gabriel, *op cit.,* 149; and in M. W. Childs and D. Cater, *Ethics in a Business Society* (Mentor book, 1954) 137.
6 Quoted in Gabriel, 149.
7 See *ibid.,* 149, 150.
8 Cf. Childs and Cater, *Ethics in a Business Society,* 83.

whether Calvinism, Methodism, or Quakerism. Wesley's contemporary, John Woolman the Quaker merchant-minister, did his best to cope with the problem, first by avoiding aspects of business in themselves ethically questionable, such as the writing of wills involving a bequest of slaves; and second, by retiring from business altogether. "The increase in business became my burden; for though my natural inclination was toward merchandise, yet I believed truth required me to live more free from outward cumbers. . . . In a while I wholly laid down merchandise. . . . I found it good for me to advise poor people to take such things as were most useful and not costly."[9] The gulf between this point of view, which proceeds from Calvary's brow, and that of the modern advertisers who insist on putting television in every home, and who would put two new cars a year in every garage, is so great that one can only stand in amazement, if not despair.

Even Woolman did not give up his business connections without an inner struggle, and most of his fellow Quaker merchants did not give them up at all. Samuel Fothergill, the eighteenth-century minister, spoke of the first-generation Quakers who came to Pennsylvania in its infancy, "and bought large tracts of land for a trifle; their sons found large estates come into their possession," enabling them to live "in ease and affluence, . . . whilst they made the barren wilderness as a fruitful field." They became rich in this world's goods. They lived in ease and security. They became independent, self-sufficient, and worldly in their outlook. Fothergill says it is true they had beaten their swords into plowshares, but they did so, he says, "with the bent of their spirits to this world" so that they were unable to "instruct their offspring in those statutes they had themselves forgotten."[10] This bent of their spirits to the world reflected itself in numerous ways, including the mansions which they built on their estates, so that even a poet wrote of them:

9 *Ibid.*, 84.
10 Frederick B. Tolles, *Meeting House and Country House: The Quaker Merchants of Colonial Philadelphia, 1682-1763* (Chapel Hill, 1948) 4.

> Strangers do wonder, and some may say,
> What mean these Quakers thus to raise
> These stately fabrics to their praise?
> Since we well know and understand
> When they were in their native land
> They were in prison trodden down,
> And can they now build such a town?[11]

By the nineteenth century the spirit of Adam Smith and Benjamin Franklin had permeated the thinking of American Christians to such an extent that the instruction which influential ministers gave their congregations was quite other than that dispensed by Wesley and Woolman in their day. Horace Bushnell, for example, admonished his businessmen parishioners to manage their affairs strictly on business principles, "and never let . . . operations be mixed up with charities. . . ."[12] American businessmen have given good heed to this advice, enabling *Fortune* magazine to say that "by the end of the [nineteenth] century . . . God was no longer in business in any real sense."[13] As a result of a survey conducted by A. Dudley Ward, the director of studies of the department of the church and economic life of the National Council of Churches, which sponsored a series of books on ethics and economic life, it was concluded that "religion plays little part, at least at the conscious level, in the decisions made by the thousand or more individuals included in the study." Childs and Cater refer to this as an "anemia of the religious experience." These people were not necessarily irreligious. "Many of them were churchgoers. It was simply that their religious experience did not seem to be relevant to the problems confronting them in earning their living. One gathered from their remarks that religion is something to one side, a social experience that is sometimes consoling and pleasant but one that does not strike very deep."[14]

11 Judge Thomas Holme, quoted in Carl Bridenbaugh, *Cities in the Wilderness* (New York, 1938) 99.
12 Childs and Cater, *op. cit.*, 138.
13 *Ibid.*, 86.
14 *Ibid.*, 173, 174.

When Christianity is virile and effective the way of love and brotherhood prevails; and where love and brotherhood prevail there is justice as well. When Christianity grows weak and anemic, however, love and brotherhood fade away, and injustice creeps in to take its place. This is precisely what happened in the nineteenth century when the leaders of the anemic Christian church began to preach a doctrine derived more from Adam Smith and Benjamin Franklin than from the Hebrew prophets and the New Testament. When the poor farmers of Israel suffered at the hands of the well-to-do classes, Amos in no uncertain terms pronounced woes upon the oppressors who idled their time in luxurious mountain retreats, sleeping on beds of ivory. In 1877, however, when the eastern railroads suddenly cut the wages of their employees by ten per cent and precipitated a violent labor battle, American Protestantism presented what Henry F. May calls "a massive, almost unbroken front in its defense of the social *status quo.*"[15] *The Congregationalist,* a leading denominational periodical, did not hesitate to advocate capitalist violence for the suppression of labor violence: "Bring on then the troops—the armed police—in overwhelming numbers. Bring out the Gatling guns. Let there be no fooling with blank cartridges. But let the mob know, everywhere, that for it to stand one moment after it has been ordered by proper authorities to disperse, will be to be shot down in its tracks. . . . A little of the vigor of the first Napoleon is the thing we now need."[16]

So far had Protestantism departed from the way of Christian brotherhood that the *Christian Advocate* had only words of condemnation for the thought that employers should be expected to confer with their employees. For the state to require such conference would be "despotism or Bellamyism,"[17] this being a bad name equivalent to that of communism today. It would seem that churchmen a century after

15 *Ibid.,* 139.
16 *Ibid.,* 140.
17 *Ibid.,* 140.

Adam Smith were promoting the selfish interests of business to a degree that even the supposed father of *laissez-faire* capitalism would not have thought of promoting them. Smith himself had warned that legislation sponsored by business interests "ought never to be adopted" without careful and even suspicious scrutiny, since it comes "from an order of men whose interest is never exactly the same with that of the public, who have generally an interest to deceive and even to oppress the public and who accordingly have upon many occasions both deceived and oppressed it."[18] A century later, however, it seems to have been assumed that "pure self-interest and nothing else would make society run at the peak of greatest efficiency for the greatest good of all concerned."[19] Here was a dangerous situation filled with evil forebodings.

18 *Ibid.*, 39.
19 *Ibid.*, 43.

18. THE ORGANIZATIONAL REVOLUTION

By the order of creation, however, a society not governed by the law of love finds other means for redressing its wrongs. When the way of the cross is not pursued the wrath of God moves in to correct the injustice, even with violence if need be. This is precisely what happened in the last quarter of the nineteenth century when three great series of strikes occurred throughout the United States: in 1877 a series of railroad strikes; in 1886 a nation-wide series culminating in Chicago's Haymarket bomb explosion; and in 1892-94 a series beginning in the steel industry and culminating in the Pullman railway strike. The very fact that the workers were able to carry through this series of strikes with success is indication in itself that a new industrial age had arrived. Just as the rise of the middle class and the commercial revolution had brought about the emancipation of the serfs and the end of the Middle Ages, so now the industrial revolution brought a new technology and an increased productivity destined to emancipate the proletariat and to usher in a new era of industrial relations.

As early as 1890 the United States had passed all of its competitors to occupy first place among the nations of the world in the value of its manufactured products. By 1901 the United States Steel corporation alone had something like 168,000 men in its employ; and Kenneth Boulding tells us that today General Motors alone constitutes an empire with an income almost as great as that of the entire state of Yugoslavia.[1] These new technological developments affected every aspect of American life; and nowhere did they bring about a more far-reaching revolution than in the field of agriculture.

1 Kenneth E. Boulding, *The Organizational Revolution: A Study in the Ethics of Economic Organization* (New York, 1953) 35.

At the beginning of the nineteenth century nineteen American farm families were required to produce the food for themselves and one lone family in the city. Today, however, modern mechanization makes it possible for one lone farm family to feed seven or eight nonagricultural families besides itself. Moreover, holdings have been enlarged and capital investments have increased so that the farmer today is a businessman operating on a scale the size of which many merchants of an earlier day did not even dream.

The industrial and the agricultural revolutions were followed in the twentieth century by an equally significant organizational revolution so that in America today the various sections of the economy have a relationship to each other quite different from that which formerly prevailed. Big business, instead of having its own way as did the robber barons two generations ago, now finds itself confronted with an organized labor force which has become big labor, and which is supported by a friendly government. The organization of the capitalist farmers, supported by an equally friendly government, has confronted big business and big labor with big agriculture so that the various sectors of the economy are kept in reasonable balance.

If these contending forces have served to keep each other in balance and to establish a reasonable degree of economic equity, so that America has no oppressed proletarian and peasant classes, it does not follow that the love of money and its attendant evils have been eradicated. It may even mean that many who might have remained humble through their poverty, if in no other way, have had even this incentive removed, so that today most Americans, regardless of their occupational classification, have possessions and power and prestige in sufficient abundance to devitalize their Christianity to the point where the way of the cross becomes exceedingly difficult. There may be a closer approach to economic equality than was formerly the case; but instead of making for brotherhood it may mean that we are simply developing a society bent on enjoying its economy of abundance while manifesting no more brotherhood within that society, nor any more love for the less favored peoples of the world than the rich man had toward Lazarus, or that the folks who slept on ivory beds in the day of Amos had toward the peasants whom they crushed under their heels.

Kermit Eby's writings reveal a sense of disillusionment as he contrasts the approachable winsomeness of the dedicated young dreamers who organized the CIO in the 1930's with the same men, twenty-five years older, now powerful labor executives sitting on the throne of the giant structure which they have created. Then they were workers among workers, tramping from home to home sharing the misery of the poor, singing with them in union halls, zealous evangelists in the cause of economic brotherhood. Today they are lonely men wielding power *over* men instead of *with* them. No longer are they men among men. They are "demigods among acolytes aspiring to be demigods." They must be as inaccessible as possible, with protesting secretaries on every hand. Keeping the boss isolated perpetuates the power to which he is now dedicated, and incidentally improves the secretary's status as well. The union movement and many of its leaders have been corrupted by the materialism of the very society which they once undertook to reform. "In order to compete in such a society, labor must itself dine and wine if it would win friends and influence people. And if the president of a corporation is paid $25,000 a year, should not the president of the union be paid as much? If the officer of the corporation has rich carpets on the floor, has glass-topped desks, and drives a black limousine, should not the union officer display these same symbols of prestige?"[2] Having come to this state, once idealistic labor leaders can be and sometimes are as unjust in the treatment of their own employees as are the employers of the workers they represent. They can be just as unscrupulous in their use of other people's money, and just as antisocial and undemocratic in general. All of which leads Eby to pray God

2 Kermit Eby, *The God in You* (Chicago, 1954) 64. See also Eby's unpublished ms., *Why Labor Leaders Are Lonesome*.

that "when you are protecting the labor movement from the insidious and corrupting Left, also protect it from its too-high salaries, excess expense accounts, and its too-soft beds at conventions. . . . And God, please protect our country from the belief that its servants must be paid by corporation standards and that $20,000 a year is inadequate to support a family in Washington, D.C."[3]

The organizational revolution has engulfed every sector of the American economy so that everyone is affected by it in some manner, whether he be a businessman or an industrialist, a factory laborer or an artisan, a farmer or a member of one of the professions. Temptations to sin may be more numerous and more compelling in some situations and occupations than in others, but they are great in all of them; and in our day one cannot divide occupations into safe and dangerous classes as conveniently as Menno Simons and Peter Rideman thought they could in their day. To be sure, there are certain occupations whose end products in themselves are such that the way-of-the-cross Christian must reject them. When it is known, for example, that cigarette smoking contributes nothing to the health and welfare of its users, that at best it is spending money for a narcotic, and that at its worst it contributes to the incidence of cancer and may have other deleterious physical if not moral effects, it is difficult to see how anyone claiming commitment to Christian discipleship and the way of the cross can be engaged in the production and distribution of such an article of merchandise. The same can be said of the production and distribution of other harmful products, such as intoxicating beverages and habit-forming narcotics, as well as numerous questionable products such as certain forms of cosmetics whose only function is to enable the purchaser to wear a symbol of paganism. Most objectionable of all from the viewpoint of Christian nonresistance would be the production of materials and instruments of warfare.

Besides remaining clear of occupations objectionable in

3 *Ibid.,* 65.

themselves the Christian who would follow the way of the cross has the further responsibility of maintaining in practice the highest Christian ethic within those economic pursuits which in themselves are legitimate. The complex character which the organizational revolution has given to every phase of economic life makes this a very difficult task, however, requiring a sensitive conscience and a high degree of spiritual acumen.

Let us take the case of the large business or industrial corporation. Should or can the Christian with executive and administrative ability enter the service of such a corporation where he might conceivably rise to a position of major executive importance? The ethical practices of large corporations in the past have been such that the American government has found it necessary to regulate and restrict their operations to the point where Kenneth Boulding even calls its attitude an unfriendly one.[4] In many cases the argument of inefficiency and the dangers inherent in concentration of power would be sufficient in themselves to make a decision against association with big business. On the other hand, it cannot be denied that it would simply be impracticable for certain types of industry, such as railway transportation and the manufacture of automobiles, to operate otherwise than on a large scale. It is also true, as Boulding says, that in the more superficial or obvious aspects of morality such as honest statements regarding the nature, quantity, and quality of the product, or punctuality in the meeting of obligations, American business does operate on a high level. In fact, Boulding feels that this high standard is a direct fruit of the evangelical Protestant faith, and that the type of religious faith which begets confidence in the fulfillment of contracts has made a genuine contribution to the remarkable development and productivity of American and north European business and industry. In the Latin countries where religion does not place so much emphasis on personal integrity, honesty, and punctuality, the nature, the quality, and the price of goods must continually

4 Boulding, *op. cit.*, 138.

be questioned, necessitating the continued use of bargaining and haggling, which are both an illustration and a symptom of profound business inefficiency.[5]

The ethical problems confronting large corporations, however, are more subtle than this. Boulding believes the nature of big business organization militates against its becoming a creative, satisfying experience. To have such an experience there must be a sense of mission, a feeling that one is engaged in the promotion of a great and good "cause." A church, a reform movement, a labor union seeking for justice, or even a political party can provide this sense of mission, but a mere business enterprise has more difficulty in doing so. Those who engage in business must find this satisfaction elsewhere, or in the relation of their business in some logical way to a higher cause to which they are attached. Thus the only incentive for greater endeavor within the business itself is increased salaries and the prestige attached to the various rungs in the executive hierarchy, each separated from the other by substantial salary differentials.[6] In addition to the resulting undesirable social stratification this situation likely creates some of the same kind of lonesomeness which Eby finds at the apex of the labor pyramid.

Theodore Quinn is an illustration of this experience. In 1935 Quinn had reached the position of vice-president of the General Electric company and was in line to succeed Gerard Swope in the presidency. Then when only a little past forty he resigned, and said: "I began to realize that I was serving no socially worth-while purpose in helping a giant to become even bigger." In his book, *Giant Business,* Quinn says it is intolerable that a small number of great corporations should have it within their power to determine whether or not numerous smaller businesses may or may not live. His chief criticism, however, is directed to what the giant corporation does to the individual, making for impersonality, subordination, and regimentation. Here it is no longer possible, says

5 *Ibid.*, 140.
6 *Ibid.*, 142.

Quinn, to live one's life "in the company of people who really know each other, deep down, and who, living in one community, usefully face together social discipline, integration, and maturity. The absorption of human lives in industrial centralization, and in the techniques of less responsible mass movements, belittles the individual. The loss of conscience, mutual respect, consideration, and wholesome humanity becomes greater than any possible gain."[7]

In addition to the ethical problems of the giant business executive, there are also those of the individual stockholder. Can the Christian be a stockholder in a typical modern industrial corporation, and if so under what circumstances? The Christian is a steward. He is responsible to God not only for a satisfactory return on his capital investment, but also for the manner in which the investment is used. When the investor is only one stockholder among thousands, with no executive responsibility, he is in no position to determine the ethical practices of the corporation. He should therefore have some assurance that the corporation in which he is a stockholder operates on a higher level than many of them do. He should be assured, in the first place, that his capital investment is used for the kind of production with which the Christian conscience can be at ease. Some years ago, for example, the Mennonite Board of Education, a body of responsible Christians committed to the peaceful Anabaptist tradition, reinvested certain of its funds when it was discovered that they were being used in the manufacture of war materials. There is the well-known story of the social workers of Trinity church parish who became greatly concerned about certain tenements in New York City's slums, only to learn that these miserable residences were actually owned by Trinity church, whose funds had been invested through a fiduciary company without the parishioners concerning themselves about the investment except to be sure that it brought adequate returns. The story is also told of a pious Mennonite who was very

---

7 Theodore Quinn, *Giant Business* (1953), quoted in Childs and Cater, *op. cit.*, 89, 90.

much chagrined some years ago to discover in a similar un-expected way that he was the owner of stock in a theater cor-poration, a concern whose product he did not approve at all. A similar illustration is that of the ardent temperance worker who discovered to her surprise that she was the owner of stock in a whiskey distillery.

Even though the end product of the business is consistent with the ways of Christian discipleship there still remains the important question of the character of its financial opera-tions. Do the officers of the corporation vote bonuses to its directors at the expense of noncommunicative, absentee stock-holders? Do they permit employees (meaning chiefly officers of the corporation) to purchase stock at a discount, enabling them to obtain substantial blocks of stock at advantageous prices at the expense of other stockholders? By this procedure some years ago the president of a large corporation was en-abled to purchase nearly 10,000 shares of stock at $25 each when the market price was $112, thus at one stroke adding $870,000 to his income to the grossly unfair disadvantage of other people.[8]

Does the management of the corporation in which one owns stock find ways of operating to the advantage of the stockholders at the expense of the company's laboring em-ployees and of the consuming public? Does the corporation water its stock to inflate its capitalization, causing unwarrant-ed increases in the cost of services to the public, as has at times occurred in the case of public utility stocks and rates of serv-ice, requiring drastic action by the Federal Trade Commis-sion? Does the corporation management, by means of its com-plicated holding company relationships, "squeeze" minority stockholders to the advantage of a select and privileged few? Are the labor policies and the labor-management relations of the corporation such that the Christian conscience of the in-vestor can rightfully feel at ease? Indeed, the operations of

8 See Carl Kreider, "Christian Ethics and the Organization of Business, In-dustry, and the Professions," *Report of the Study Conference on Christian Com-munity Relations held at Laurelville Mennonite Camp* (Goshen, 1951) 45.

large corporations are so complex that unethical and illegal procedures are frequently uncovered only with great difficulty even by the Federal Trade Commission. As a result, the ordinary stockholder, however sensitive his conscience, would have great difficulty in discovering unethical or illegal practices on his own, and would experience even greater difficulty in attempting to carry through remedial measures.

While this complex and difficult character of American business cannot be denied, it should be remembered on the other hand that *Fortune* magazine and others are heralding a revolution in business management in which the emerging new type of business manager with a keener sense of social responsibility is striving to maintain "an equitable and working balance among the claims of the various directly interested groups." This new type of manager is bringing to the fore a new art of human relations which promises to restore to the human cog in the industrial machine his rightful status as a person once again. Childs and Cater suggest that this new character, if not "steadfastly pursuing the Quaker goal of service to God," is at least attempting to achieve a Quaker-like "sense of the meeting," thus to restore a greater semblance of justice and equity to the American business scene.[9]

While the Christian certainly welcomes every good work which the managerial change is able to accomplish it must still be remembered that its success will depend largely upon the character of the men in managerial positions; and that the individual stockholder remains as helpless as ever for the correction of inequities and injustices if he does not have the co-operation of character and of high ethics in positions of power. Moreover, the recent experience of the Studebaker corporation seems to indicate that in the giant industry field even the lesser giants are not yet secure from the outstretched tentacles of the super giants. This particular situation is the more to be regretted because the Studebaker corporation has provided an outstanding example of managerial policy which promotes the better type of human relations.

9 Childs and Cater, *op. cit.,* 90, 91.

Without discounting the importance of big business, however, it is well to remember that small business still occupies an important place in the American economy. Moreover, many economists are critical of even the supposed economic advantages of large-scale business. Following a comprehensive study several years ago the Federal Trade Commission concluded that in many types of industry the medium-sized or the small organization is more efficient than the larger one. Many sociologists likewise are stressing the importance of the small community for the sociological health of the nation. What is more logical then, than for Christian businessmen concerned for the social applications of the Christian faith to put their energies into the building of small community industries? Such men are not absentee stockholders in corporations whose policies are none of their concern. They are responsible owners and managers with the opportunity of making Christian social ethics the major objective and the determining factor in their operations. A small community with an economy well balanced as to agriculture, business, and industry, and with an adequate educational and cultural program, the whole being church-centered and well integrated with a Christian orientation, would seem to be the best possible situation for making the way of the cross effective within the contemporary economic order.

The mere presence of an opportunity, however, is not sufficient for the achievement of results. The opportunity must be used, and fundamental objectives must ever be kept in the foreground by a consecrated and dedicated leadership. Selfish materialism can operate within the small as well as in the larger community. Moreover, the organizational revolution which serves the materialistic world so effectively is also operative within the smaller community. Whether these organizational techniques are devoted to mere materialistic ends, or whether they are enlisted to make the way of the cross effective, will depend upon the quality of the people who constitute the Christian community.

19. THE ORGANIZED ECONOMY

Do trade and business associations, and farm, labor, and professional organizations serve a Christian purpose as defined in these pages or do they not? In order to arrive at a satisfactory answer it is necessary to observe the nature of these organizations and to recognize points of similarity and difference among them. Labor organizations represent what may be called a "movement," carrying a moral tone. They have been created specifically for the correction of injustice, and as such they make aggressive use of various devices designed to compel such correction. To a lesser degree, the same may be said of certain phases of organized agriculture. This aggressive "movement" feature is less conspicuous in the trade, and least of all among the professional, organizations.

TRADE ASSOCIATIONS

The evils of organized big business are inherent within the individual firm or corporation itself more than within the trade association in which the corporation may hold membership. With the rise of big business and its accompanying abuses in the last half of the nineteenth century the United States government developed a policy of regulation and restriction. Despite all that has been said about the alliance of business and government, it is probably true that during the past seventy-five years the American government has actually been more friendly to agriculture and labor than it has to business. Government has actively encouraged the farm and labor movements, whereas business has been continually on the defensive, as far as government attitude and public opinion is concerned. Whereas the more socialistic governments of Europe have frequently sponsored monopolistic organizations and cartels, the American antitrust laws have operated in the opposite direction. Interestingly enough, Kenneth Boulding thinks that this policy is in part responsible for the high productivity and efficiency of American industry. Having been denied special government favor, business was driven to the development of technical improvements which have made for a productivity equaled in no other country.[1] It is this high productivity which has made possible the growth of the giant American industrial corporations, despite governmental regulation; and it is within the organization of the corporation itself, its policies as to prices, labor relations, ownership of stock, and its varying degrees of monopolization, that serious ethical questions reside, more than in trade associations as such.

Boulding estimates that there are about 1,500 American trade associations, most of them small organizations with small staffs, some with only a part-time secretary. These organizations collect and disseminate information about their respective businesses. Most of them have some kind of legislative program as well as a program to promote their particular industry. Some set up standards for the conduct of business and serve their member firms with statistics, cost surveys, and similar services. As a part of their promotional program many associations have annual meetings for the direct and personal exchange of information, or for the exhibition of their products to the purchasing public, or both. Much of the information provided or service rendered would seem to be what is needed for an intelligent operation of a business, not unlike agricultural information provided by agricultural experiment stations. It is the individual firm or corporation that puts this information and these services to use, however, and each such firm is free to use it in an ethical or an unethical manner as it may choose. There is a real sense, therefore, in which a firm which itself operates on ethical principles may not be involved in unethical practices through membership in trade associations to the same degree that the

1 Boulding, *op. cit.,* 138.

owner of stock in a corporation is so involved if that corporation devotes its information, its services, and its powers to unethical ends and means; or to the extent that a labor union member is involved in unethical practices if the policies of his union are not in line with the way of the cross.

Social power is neither ethical nor unethical in itself. It is the manner and purpose of its use that makes it one or the other. The temptation to misuse power for unethical purposes is ever present, however, so that concentrations of power are always dangerous. In the case of labor the power lies primarily within the organization. Hence it is the manner in which it uses its power that determines the relation which the way-of-the-cross workingman will have to the labor organization. In the case of capital and management the power lies chiefly within the capital structure itself, and it is the manner in which a given corporation uses its power that determines the relation of the Christian to it. Corporations can use cost surveys, statistics, price and production information, and other services provided by trade organizations as means to unfair competition, or for the management of production in a manner that is detrimental to their employees or to the public, but they need not do so. Some trade associations have been known to circulate labor black lists or even to provide espionage services which were then employed by corporations in fighting organized labor, using such methods as the lockout, and the employment of strike-breaking "scabs," or even of munitions. Every corporation whether a member of a trade association or not is free, however, to employ such unethical devices or not to employ them. Indeed, during the 1930's, when General Motors and the Ford Motor company were making extensive use of these coercive methods in their effort to prevent the unionization of their plants, only to see them unionized in the end, other corporations such as the Lincoln Electric company were moving on a higher ethical level, taking a more socially responsible attitude toward their employees, with the result that the Lincoln company is not unionized even today because the employees do not believe that with this corporation anything is to be gained by unionization. This better policy pursued by the Lincoln company was not due to the absence of membership in a trade association, but rather to the policies of the corporation itself, and to the more ethical use it has made of the services which it may have received from trade associations.

While all this is true it is also true, on the other hand, that the legislative program of trade associations may include lobbying for protective tariffs and other selfish and harmful class legislation, altogether inconsistent with the way of the cross. Another function of the trade association is advertising which can be and sometimes is carried on in an extremely unethical manner. In addition to the various trade associations there are also national federations such as the National Association of Manufacturers in the United States and the Federation of British Industries in England. These federations engage in a great amount of propaganda and lobbying, much of it of a questionable character, although Boulding considers their efforts more expensive than impressive, and feels that "they have been rather ineffective politically over the long pull in the social-democratic countries."[2] They have been unable to achieve either intellectual respectability or public sympathy, with the result that there has been a noteworthy failure of communication between organized businessmen and the remainder of society, especially the academic group. Boulding considers this a major cause for the turning of European countries to socialism and believes that if this situation continues indefinitely it will mean the ultimate breakdown of our business civilization. Boulding also feels that the new Committee for Economic Development organized by Paul Hoffman and others may be the beginning of a movement leading to better relations between business and the remainder of the national community.[3] The purpose of this organization is discussion and understanding

2 *Ibid.*, 149.
3 *Ibid.*, 150.

10

rather than propaganda, and if it achieves the end which Boulding hopes it will, it will no doubt do so because it approaches more nearly the brotherhood concept, and is not as far removed from the way of the cross as are numerous other business and trade organizations chiefly concerned with selfish class interests.

It was suggested earlier that to provide a true inner satisfaction the individual must be attached to a cause, with a sense of mission, something which business pursued for its own sake cannot provide. Business not subordinated to the Christian ethic and the way of the cross leads to pure materialism; and nothing is more deteriorating to the spiritual life of the Christian than continually to be subjected to materialistic influences or to live in an atmosphere of materialism. More than anything else, perhaps, it is the atmosphere of materialism prevailing in the modern business world which makes affiliation with business and trade associations a dangerous thing for the Christian. Theoretically, for the most part, the organization leaves the individual and his firm free to conduct his own business in line with the Christian ethic if that is his wish. In practice, however, the pressure of materialism is so great that the casualties are numerous. Menno Simons' fear of business and trade was not unfounded, not because business in itself is evil, but because business pursued for its own sake creates an atmosphere of materialism which is dangerous to the spiritual life. Even so-called "service organizations" such as Rotary and Kiwanis, which are an attempt on the part of businessmen to provide an idealistic source of satisfaction which business alone cannot provide, frequently have such a thin veneer of near-Christianity covering their materialism that even though they do not bind their members to any unchristian policies they do little to help them bring their businesses under the way of the cross, and often simply continue the atmosphere which prevents this very thing.

The only social group capable of providing a source of

satisfaction which actually gets to the root of the matter, and a source of strength enabling the Christian to resist the corroding effects of materialism and to serve as the conscience of the economic order, is the Christian brotherhood itself when it is disciplined to the way of the cross. The businessman who lives and moves and has his being within the Christian brotherhood may not necessarily be entirely detached from all trade associations or even "service clubs." In his relation to them, however, three things would seem to be obvious: (1) If he lives and moves and has his being in the Christian brotherhood, sheer limitation of time itself will necessarily prevent a great absorption in the work and program of these organizations. (2) The relationships maintained with the association will be such as contribute to the legitimate needs and services of his business without participation in unethical practices. (3) Being a Christian first, and a businessman second, he will use his organizational relationships as an aid in his Christian mission to act as the conscience of the economic order, continually confronting that order and its agencies with the claims of Christian discipleship and the way of the cross.

AGRICULTURAL ORGANIZATIONS

Agricultural organizations are of two types: (1) organizations for promoting the general welfare of agriculture; (2) organizations serving the interests of agricultural specialists, as dairy farmers, fruit growers, or poultry producers. The principal general organizations are the Grange, the Farmers' Union, and the Farm Bureau Federation. While each of the three has social, business, and legislative functions, the Grange has emphasized social functions more than either of the others has. In its beginning in 1867 this organization was patterned after that of the Masonic order and even today it retains certain features of the lodge. The Farm Bureau has the most extensive business operations of the three. In some states it works very closely with the county agent, the latter being at least partially employed by the Farm Bureau. Through this agency the organization combines educational and business functions. The Farm Bureau co-operative is well known, and in many states it is the leading farmers' co-operative, supplying its members with feed, fuel, lumber, farm machinery, and other supplies, as well as providing a market for the farmers' grain crops.

The legislative functions of the large farm organizations are directed to the enactment of legislation for the regulation of production and prices for the maintenance of a healthy agricultural economy. Improvement of technology is constantly increasing agricultural productivity so as to permit a continuous decline in the farm population. Since this decline in the agricultural population does not keep pace with productivity, however, farm prices frequently find themselves in a precarious situation. For this reason parity prices have become a symbol of that which farm organizations seek through production control, export marketing, government crop loans and purchases, price supports, and other devices.

Following the organization of the Grange in 1867 numerous "Grange laws" were enacted, particularly for the regulation of freight rates. During the depression of the 1890's Grangerism culminated in the Populist party movement which sought to restore prosperity by means of monetary inflation in the form of greenback currency and free silver, a graduated income tax, government ownership of railways, the popular election of United States senators, and other reforms. The agricultural depression of 1920 and 1921 inspired a new agrarian movement which culminated in the passing of the famous McNary-Haugen bill in 1927, and in modified form again in 1928, only to have it defeated each time by a presidential veto. The effects of the great depression of the 1930's were such, however, as to convince most people that some kind of relief for farmers was necessary. The result was legislation setting up the Agricultural Adjustment Administration and providing for crop reduction, followed by continuous legislation to the present time providing such measures as cash subsidies to supplement the market price of the crop, crop loans and purchases at a parity level, foreign marketing plans, the soil bank, and related programs. Back of all this legislation was an enormous amount of effort on the part of the farmers themselves and of their organizational representatives.

Legislative action to obtain the desired regulation of production and prices is the principal device of farm organizations for the promotion of agricultural welfare. This procedure is quite different from that of labor unions using compulsory membership and the strike techniques as means for achieving their ends. While organized agriculture is by no means free from unethical practices it has been relatively free from monopolistic and coercive techniques such as those frequently used by both trade and labor organizations. It is true that occasional outbursts of violence have characterized American agricultural history, such as the Shays' and the Whiskey rebellions in the eighteenth century and the violent attempts to stop judicial mortgage foreclosure proceedings and the "penny sheriff auctions" during the depth of the agricultural depression in 1932 and 1933. While the radical fringe of organized agriculture, represented by the Farmers' Union and the Farm Holiday Association, must share some of the blame for the extreme action of the 1930's, this as well as the earlier rebellions was for the most part a spontaneous uprising of desperate, embittered farmers, without any necessary connection with farm organizations.

Farm organizations have generally been characterized by order and dignity, and their leaders have been men of integrity. Their propaganda for the most part is straightforward and the success of their program depends on their ability to convince the public of the justice of their cause and to muster the required number of congressional votes in support of it. Kenneth Boulding is no doubt correct when he characterizes farm organization as "relatively free from the

personal vices which so often plague the labor movement,"
and that racketeering is virtually unknown among them,
"with the possible exception of occasional troubles in milk,
and even these are generally connected with strategic labor
unions. . . . There is nothing like the conflict of loyalties . . .
which exists in the labor movement; there is practically no
problem of violence except in rare cases of 'milk strikes' or
resistance to foreclosures. . . . Even the lobbying is carried on
with a minimum of deceit and, as far as I know, without
bribery. Nothing like the scandalous story of the business
influence in congress is here visible."[4]

Granting the validity of this description of the general
situation, there were warnings in 1958 that the "rare cases" of
milk strikes and corruption in farm organizations might become more common. In April of that year the press[4a] reported
the merger of 3,500 dairymen in the tri-state area, New York,
New Jersey, and Pennsylvania, with the New York State
Teamsters Union in an effort to put the farmers in a stronger
bargaining position with the dairy corporations to whom they
sell their milk. The new move was reportedly designed to
transfer the weighing of milk, the testing of butterfat, and
other prerogatives from the control of the corporations to
whom the milk is sold to that of the new farmer-labor union.
When the farm leaders were warned that their business might
come under the control of racketeers, their reply is supposed
to have been: "There are crooks in all big organizations.
We'll help the Teamsters clean up their organization. We
need someone with strength and they have it." To be sure,
corrupt organizations can be reformed. Apparently, however, the tri-state dairy farmers were interested in economic
power to the extent that they were willing to place their ethical future into the hands of an organization which at the
time was being denied membership in labor's own federation
on the ground of unethical practices. If this development is
an indication of the future direction of organized agriculture,

4 *Ibid.*, 123.
4a *Between the Lines* (New York, April 15, 1958) 3.

Christian farmers who would follow the way of the cross will wish to seek some other means for the promotion of their economic interests and concerns.

It might be added that there is nothing wrong with lobbying as such. Lobbying simply means conversing with legislators in the hall, or lobby, or elsewhere, to express one's views on legislation. Under a democratic government this is necessary if the democratic process is to work effectively. It is not the lobbying process itself that has given the term its bad name. It is rather the objectives and the methods of any given lobby which determine whether it is good or bad. It may as well be recognized that one of the functions of the National Service Board for Religious Objectors, for example, is a lobbying function. The historic peace churches and other peace groups who are represented by this organization need not apologize for its lobbying function so long as they are assured that the objectives pursued by the NSBRO and the methods employed are in harmony with the New Testament ethic; so long as their purpose is to testify concerning the way of the cross, and to find ways and means for themselves and others to follow this way more perfectly, and not to seek some selfish advantage. It must be the way of the cross which is sought, however, and the methods used must exemplify that way, if the organization and those whom it represents are not to fall under condemnation.

It is at this crucial point that the legislative program of the farm organizations when weighed in the balances is often found wanting. It is true enough that agriculture in the 1920's and the 1930's was suffering from depressed prices. On the other hand, it is also true that the promoters of the McNary-Haugen bills frankly asserted their aim to protect agriculture from industrial domination, to stop "the industrialization of America at the expense of agriculture."[5] The strategy of George N. Peek, the real leader of the McNary forces, was to convince the farmers that they would never re-

5 Gilbert C. Fite, *George N. Peek and the Fight for Farm Parity* (Norman, 1954) 130.

ceive a square deal until they had sufficient organized strength to force the government to acquiesce to their demands. This may indeed have been an effective method of obtaining a measure of justice for the farmer; but it was hardly the way of the cross which seeks first the welfare of the brother or neighbor, or for a social class other than one's own. In fact Peek was a high tariff protectionist who frankly put the national interest first regardless of what the international effects of the national policy would be; and who placed agrarian interests first regardless of what the effects of the agrarian policy on other economic groups within the nation would be.

As Kenneth Boulding states it, "farm organizations have felt less interest in the welfare of the larger society of which they are a part than in the struggle for the 'rights' of their own constituency. This is astonishingly true even in wartime, when the farm organizations seem to be much less willing even than labor organizations to transfer their struggle from an internal to an external one. Consequently farmers in wartime are apt to become a highly privileged class, in regard to the impact of conscription, of price control, and even of taxation. There is a striking contrast, for instance, between the acceptance of the 'little steel' formula by labor during World War II, grudging as it may have been, and the insistence of the farmers on 110 per cent of parity. In international relations also the attitude of the farm organizations has been one of irresponsibility, or at least indifference, to anything but the obvious and apparent interests of their own group. . . .

"The attitude of the farm organizations in this respect is no different from, and no worse than, the attitude of most special interest groups affected by international trade policy, in both labor and business. . . . The ethical problem for the leaders of these groups is an acutely difficult one. Each group represents, as it were, a nation within the nation, striving for its own ends against the others, with the legislative process as the battleground. . . . The farm leader therefore faces the same dilemma as the labor leader, that if he is too virtuous he will lose his job. The role of the farm leader is to get things for farmers, not to serve the general interest."[6]

This does not mean that farm leaders are vicious, in the commonly accepted meaning of that term. They would all say that it is their duty and desire to serve the general interest, and they would rationalize their pressure programs by regarding them as a necessary counter pressure against that of other groups so that the resulting balance will serve the general interest. Using one selfish program as a check against another may indeed keep the economy from getting too far out of balance, but it is clear that it is not the way of the cross which keeps the welfare of the brother, the neighbor, and the neighboring group in the foreground. It is a manifestation of the wrath of God operating within a sinful social order which does not understand the way of love and the cross. This discussion has concerned itself chiefly with the legislative program of the general farm organizations, because it would seem that here is where the way of the cross is most likely to suffer at the hands of organized agriculture. For that reason Christians who profess the way of love and the cross in all human relations will need to examine with critical care their relationship with this aspect of the agrarian movement.

For example, how far can the Christian go in co-operating with the government's program of farm price supports which includes the purchase of wheat at a price which is profitable for the American farmer and then selling it on the foreign market at a lower price, a form of the foreign marketing practice known as dumping? While it is recognized that this sale at a lower price under certain (but not under all) conditions may be beneficial to countries making the purchase, farmers in other wheat-growing countries, as Canada for example, consider it unfair competition, since it tends to harm their market. In May 1958 the American ambassador to Canada testified to the Senate Foreign Relations Committee on this very point, saying that American economic policy was contributing to a deterioration of Canadian-American

6 Boulding, 123-25.

relations.[6a] Coming as it did at the time of the anti-American demonstrations in South America during Vice-President Nixon's visit, which were also occasioned in part by the economic policy of the United States, this should cause the following question to be asked with all seriousness: Can the Christian farmer help to promote the welfare of agriculture in his own country at the expense of foreign agriculture?

There remain then the business and educational aspects of organized agriculture. The county agricultural agent is a government agency which works closely with the state agricultural colleges and experiment stations in bringing to the farmers the latest and best information concerning scientific agriculture. A similar government agency is the soil conservation service which is engaged in an effort to rescue the soil from the depletion process and to restore its usefulness for the maximum service to mankind. Since these agencies promote no selfish interest and their services contribute to the welfare of all, good stewardship would seem to commend a wholehearted co-operation with them on the part of the Christian farmer.

The origins of the Farm Bureau are associated with the establishment of the county agent and, as mentioned earlier, in some states even today the two work very closely together, the agent being employed in part by the Farm Bureau. In other areas marketing co-operatives are important, as in the case of the fruit and dairy marketing business. In evaluating the agricultural co-operatives, including that of the Farm Bureau, the same standards of measurement must apply as are used in evaluating any other business, for businesses is what they are. Owning stock in a co-operative in itself is ethically no different from owning stock in any corporation, unless it can be shown that the co-operative operates its business on a higher or lower level than others do.

In many circles the participation feature of the co-operative is assumed to make it ethically superior. It is for

6a *The New York Times* (May 17, 1958) 1, 6.

this reason perhaps that some church bodies have supported the co-operative as a particularly Christian form of business organization. It may be granted that under certain conditions the participation ideal will attract a high quality of human time and energy, enabling the co-operative to function on a high level. On the other hand, this writer would agree with Boulding that the co-operative form of business organization has no virtue of itself.[7] Furthermore, contribution to the welfare of the community should not be confused with participation in particular forms of organization. Forms of participation ethically satisfying to some persons merely consume time for others which should be devoted to forms of service making a greater contribution, both to the kingdom of God and to the immediate community. It is also questionable whether co-operatives are more efficient than other forms of business organization. Even an assumed greater efficiency in any given case would be no guarantee in itself that the co-operative would not be just another form of big business enterprise, dominated by the same cold calculating materialism, which disqualifies its members from following the way of the cross which the Christian professes. In fact a few of the giant marketing co-operatives, especially in the fruit and milk industry, have shown a tendency to develop monopolies capable of abusing their power in much the same manner as other monopolies do.

Specialized agricultural associations like those of the dairy farmers, the fruit growers, and the poultry producers not only combine business and educational features; they assume something of the character of a professional organization as well. A county dairy producers' association may function as a dairy testing organization employing a staff of testers whose services help to insure maximum health and production of the county's dairy herds. Associated with the general dairy organization may be a number of breeders' associations, each of which may conduct an annual show and sale of its par-

7 *Ibid.*, 150-58.

ticular breed of dairy cattle. The dairy show is designed as a
"window display" and an educational program where qualified judges evaluate the quality of the herds. Overall may be a
community dairy council composed of representatives of the
breed associations and the milk distributors and processors.
The council may have general supervision of the dairy shows
and sales and of the 4-H club junior activity, and may have
meetings held perhaps bimonthly for the planning of its
various activities and the settlement of any related questions
which may arise. Poultry, fruit, and other agricultural specialties have similar organizations for the promotion of the
professional, educational, and business aspects of their special-
ty. All of these are legitimate functions; most of them are
performed on a high level, and all of them can be. It is important to recognize, however, that they can also be carried
on in an objectionable manner and sometimes this is what is
done. The approach to all of these activities and functions
can be a purely materialistic one. It is possible for 4-H clubs
and related junior activities to produce scientific, materialistic farmers who engage in questionable social practices and
fail to integrate their agricultural science with Christian discipleship and to bring it under the way of the cross. The relation of these matters to Christianity is similar to the relation of formal education to Christianity. The subject matter
in each case is a worthy one. In each case the important question is whether the subject matter is pursued with a Christian orientation and a Christian motivation. To make sure
that this will be the case requires eternal vigilance on the part
of all.

LABOR ORGANIZATIONS

The objectives and programs of business and agricultural
organizations are so many-sided and so varied that ethical or
unethical practices which characterize one organization may
not be true of another at all. Moreover, the unethical practices which do exist are often so subtle in character as to make
their detection difficult for the superficial observer. While

the unethical practices of labor may be fundamentally no more serious than those of business and agriculture, it is nevertheless true that organized labor in America is more single-minded, having as its one great purpose the obtaining of better wages and working conditions for the laboring man. Since it strives to achieve this end largely through the single process of collective bargaining and compulsory membership, reinforced by the strike if need be, its questionable ethics are readily seen by even the untrained casual observer.

For the correction of social injustice within the economic order the rise of organized labor was a natural development. When the industrial revolution produced giant corporations employing thousands of men, the individual industrial worker was no longer free to bargain with his employer on a basis of equality. The giant labor union now emerged to restore the balance, the power of one group serving to offset that of the other. That this has been a means of correcting injustices there can be no doubt. But here, as in the case of the agrarian legislative program, the organization seeks the welfare of one group regardless of how this may affect other groups. The emphasis is placed upon the demand for justice whereas the way of the cross always places its emphasis upon the doing of justice. The relentless pursuit of justice for oneself or one's own group is always inimical to the way of Christian love, and it is difficult to see how the right to strike as claimed by all unions, with but few exceptions, can be reconciled with the way of the cross, however effective it may be as a means of bringing about a more just social order. Moreover, the insistence upon compulsory membership is nothing less than a form of totalitarianism; and demanding submission to the formal union obligation, from which some unions are very reluctant to grant immunity, seems too much like compelling the worker to bind himself body and soul to an agency with power to determine his policies and actions regardless of what his own convictions may be.

As pointed out elsewhere,[8] after American Protestantism

8 See above, 79, 80 ff, 242.

had far too long given a one-sided support to capital as opposed to labor, the social gospel turned the tables and gave
what seems to have become a one-sided support of labor. At
any rate Charles Clayton Morrison, notable surviving representative of the old social gospel school, several years ago
called for a re-examination of the church's social ideals. Morrison believes that the social action leadership of many
churches in supporting the labor movement fails to take account of the social experience of the past fifty years. During
this time many of the old injustices have been corrected, but
labor goes on increasing its strength until it is now the greatest power bloc in our economy "and, under its autocratic
leadership, appears to be willing even to disrupt the national
economy in order to gain ends which, many believe, are not
good for the country as a whole and thus, in the long run, not
good for labor itself. . . . Any proposed law designed to limit
the autocratic power of their leaders in the interest of the nation as a whole, is fought relentlessly and, if enacted, the sub-
servient executive dare not enforce it."

The churches must change their orientation, says Morrison, because labor is no longer fighting the *laissez-faire* industrialism of two generations ago. Capital has been brought
well under the control of a regulatory government, so that
the present American economy is no longer a capitalist economy, but rather a capitalist-labor economy with the two powers balanced against each other "in a state of precarious tension. . . . The faults and evils in the operation of this system
are flagrant and intolerable. Unless they are corrected, society
will surely turn upon it with 'a plague on both your houses'
and fall into the pit of dictatorship. The Christian responsibility of the churches in the present situation cannot now be
defined in partisan terms for either labor or capital, but in
terms of stabilizing this new capitalist-labor economy. It now
operates on the basis of sheer brute force and irresponsible
power. This, I say, is intolerable."[9] Morrison follows this
analysis by mentioning two evils to which the church must

9 C. C. Morrison, "Re-examine the Social Ideals," *The Christian Century*
(Jan. 21, 1953) 70:75-78.

direct its critical attention. First, the church can no longer condone the strike, but must condemn it "as morally and socially vicious." Second, the church must focus its "critical concern upon the irresponsible power now wielded by the official leadership of the labor unions." If Morrison in 1953 was able to see things beyond the comprehension of most observers, the Senate investigating committee's subsequent revelations of corruption and abuse of power should by 1958 have enabled even the ordinary observer to grasp the merits of his analysis and proposals.

As was to be expected, however, Morrison's statement brought sharp rejoinders from the side of labor and from its friends within the church. Francis W. McPeek, for example, denied that labor is the most powerful economic and political bloc in the country, asserting that this "doubtful honor is shared by business and agriculture." The denial of the right to strike on moral grounds he declares a "last straw," which must be utterly rejected.[10] Other friends of labor, however, were saying things in recent years not altogether out of line with Morrison's comment. As mentioned earlier,[11] Kermit Eby, Christian idealist, after entering the labor movement with a sense of mission to lift the oppressed workingman from his desperate state and devoting many years to his work as labor organizer, lobbyist, officer, and educational director, confesses to a certain disillusionment in discovering that labor, once it grows powerful and its leaders are comfortably situated, can be as unchristian as powerful business is. Regardless of whether labor, business, or agriculture constitute the greatest and most dangerous power bloc in the American economy it should be clear that in their political relationships all of these powerful organizations are motivated by something other than the New Testament ethic, and that they are traveling on a road which is something other than the way of the cross.

---

10 See Francis W. McPeek, *Labor Letter* No. 222 (Council for Social Action, Congregational Christian Churches) March 13, 1953.
11 See above, p. 246.

Apparently Eby's own disillusionment is due in part to a confused awareness that, however just the cause may be, the coercive methods of organized labor are not in harmony with the basic Christian ethic as it was understood and taught by his Brethren-Mennonite forebears. The nonresistant teaching of his boyhood Brethren church and community, and even the preaching of the Gospel teams of his Brethren college, may have been naive at times in their understanding of justice and of the social implications of the Gospel of peace which they proclaimed.[12] With all of their supposed naiveté, however, Grandfather Schwalm and his fellow ministers preached a Gospel which gave love its rightful priority over justice, as the New Testament also does. No Brethren preacher ever had more evangelistic fervor than has Eby himself. The difference lies in the content of the Gospel which is preached. For, once Eby found himself marching down the road of organized labor, with justice as his goal, the vision of the higher law of love became obscured.

The relentless pursuit of justice carries the seeds of its own destruction, however, as he discovered when he found the lonely giants at the apex of the labor pyramid as capable of injustice as were the giants mounted at the peak of the industrial pyramid. Then when he accompanied a group of CIO workers to a training conference at the Brethren service center in New Windsor, Maryland (the conference was held here because white and colored could participate without segregation), another discovery was made. In the hot midsummer weather the Brethren voluntary service workers vacated their cross-ventilated dormitory rooms to make room for the guests, moving to less comfortable quarters for the duration of the conference. When the guests learned of what had happened they asked their leader for an explanation of this unusual performance, so different from that to which they were accustomed. Sensing something which had its roots in the faith of his fathers, Kermit Eby now began to examine that faith in a new and fresh way. From this point

12 See Kermit Eby, *The God in You*, 71 ff.

onward his pamphleteering, while basically the same, nevertheless included new elements. Labor's cause was championed as ardently as ever, but with a more subdued and chastened tone, interspersed with sharp words of criticism for labor's leaders.

Most important of all, there has emerged an undisguised, wistful nostalgia, inspired by his own Brethren-Mennonite background, for a more pristine economy based on Christian brotherhood, with all hands joined in helpful co-operation, where justice is the fruit of Christian love rather than the offspring of a balance of economic powers. "Is a labor organization using traditional methods essential for the achievement of fair and just employer-employee relations in industry?", asks an inquirer. "Not at all, if Brethren-Mennonite principles are put to work on both sides," replies Eby. It would almost seem that this is a return to the kingdom. And yet, when confronted with actual conflict situations, methods of power apparently continue to take precedence over the way of the cross, so that one must ask in all seriousness whether it is not Grandfather Schwalm's red beard and other superficial cultural accouterment which the nostalgic Eby has grasped, rather than the basic principles for which the grandfather stood.

PROFESSIONAL ORGANIZATIONS

Virtually all professions have some kind of organization for the promotion of their particular concerns. Perhaps those in least danger of promoting unethical programs are the learned societies. Each academic discipline represented on a university campus has its particular society or association, the chief concern of which is the pursuit of learning. During the year the members pursue their academic specialties and then come together in annual meetings to inform each other, as it were, of things newly discovered since they last met. Papers are read, followed by discussion. It is as if classrooms from hundreds of colleges and universities were brought to a central location for half a week of stimulation to prepare its

19

members for another year's work. Members of the learned societies pay an annual fee to defray expenses, including the cost of publishing the organization's journal which regularly reviews the literature of this field of learning and reports the work of the members of the profession.

The learned societies seldom if ever attempt to control or influence the opinion of their members. On the contrary, variety of opinion is welcomed on the theory that this is an important means for the promotion of learning. Reports to legislative bodies are seldom made, and when this is done full recognition is given to minority and dissenting views. It would seem that the learned societies permit complete freedom of thought and action, aiming only to stimulate the production of learning and the exchange of its fruits, which serves no selfish ends, but the welfare of all. This does not mean that the program and influence of learned societies could not be misdirected. Indeed, the American Chemical Society has been criticized for unwarranted interference with undergraduate programs of chemical education in liberal arts colleges. No doubt grounds for criticism could be found in other organizations as well. Neither is it intended here to suggest that the rank and file of members of these organizations is committed to the way of Christian discipleship. It is merely to say that in the learned societies organized interference with the way of the cross on the part of individual members would seem to be at a minimum.

There are other organizations in the educational field, however, whose programs are more questionable. The American Federation of Teachers is, for all intents and purposes, a labor union; it is affiliated with the American Federation of Labor, and it makes use of all the techniques of the labor union, including the strike. The American Association of University Professors is primarily a pressure group which aims to defend the rights of its members, particularly in such matters as academic freedom. The National Education Association and the various state teachers' associations serve the needs of the teaching profession in much the same way that the learned societies serve the needs of scholars. While their primary concern is the improvement of instruction, and while they operate for the most part on a high level, their program does involve a philosophy of education which the Christian educator must constantly subject to the criticism of the Christian faith. In addition, there are action programs, which in some instances have been known to descend to a rather low level of political pressure, especially with respect to teachers' salaries and tenure legislation. In a few cases they have been known to threaten or even to use the strike. When this occurs the situation is no different from that of the questionable aspects of some agricultural organizations.

Associations for the accreditation of schools and colleges in the United States are not action groups in the ordinary sense of the term, neither are they concerned with a philosophy of education, as such. They are primarily concerned with the quality of the academic performance of the school, operating under its own philosophy and within the limits, objectives, and purposes which it has prescribed for itself. So long as they continue to be concerned only with the quality of the educational performance, leaving to the school the formulation of the content and philosophy of its own program, the accrediting agencies need be no hindrance, and can indeed be a great help, to the cause of Christian education.

A professional organization of a slightly different character is the American Medical Association. It serves as an accrediting agency for medical schools and even has an approved list of premedical schools. Its weekly journal, its semiannual convention, and the periodic meetings of the regional and local branches of the association serve the profession in the same manner as the learned societies serve the various groups of scholars which they represent. Local medical societies or hospital medical staffs, or both, also set standards for the operation of hospitals, and serve to maintain a rather high level of professional ethics. All of this is as it should be, for the profession itself should be the best judge of the quality of medical practice.

On the economic side of its activities, however, the American Medical Association during the 1940's was subjected to a considerable amount of criticism, not wholly without cause. Medical and hospital costs are high, and without the aid of some kind of mutual aid plan many people find it difficult to cope with emergency situations which may arise involving expensive hospital and surgical costs. The criticism had to do with inadequate encouragement of such plans, in some cases even opposition to them, on the part of the organized profession. In 1943 the American Medical Association and the Medical Society of the District of Columbia were found guilty by the Supreme Court of illegally obstructing the Group Health Association, a voluntary organization in Washington. In 1947, when a voluntary plan known as the Health Insurance Plan open to the public was organized in New York City the AMA opposed it. The organization of the Permanent Health Plan in California brought the same reaction, as did similar efforts in other parts of the country.[13]

The slow development of voluntary plans, due at least in part to the kind of opposition here described, was then responsible for the introduction in congress of a number of bills looking toward some kind of government-sponsored health insurance program. The AMA now took up the matter in earnest and in December 1948 ordered an assessment of $25 on its membership to raise $3,500,000 in order to fight what it called "socialized medicine." It is probably true that a few individuals in the government were interested in socialized medicine, but certainly the plans mentioned above and no plan likely to be passed by congress at the time were socialized medicine at all in the sense that physicians would become employees of the state as in Great Britian; hence in this instance the efforts of the AMA could hardly pass the test of ordinary honesty. Then in December 1949 the payment of the $25 assessment was made mandatory, with the possibility of expulsion from membership in the national association if it was not paid by January 1, 1951.

13 James H. Means, M.D., "The Doctors' Lobby," *The Atlantic* (October 1950) 186:4:59, 60.

Physicians with high ethical standards, both professionally and in economic matters, must have experienced no small amount of embarrassment by this performance. In October 1950 Dr. James H. Means of the Harvard Medical School publicly denounced the methods used by the AMA as "insulting to the intelligence both of the doctors and the people." This had particular reference to the wide use of a campaign poster showing a sick child, a frustrated doctor, and despairing parents beneath which appeared the slogan: "Keep politics out of this picture." Means described the appeal as purely emotional and on the same level as advertisements of tooth paste. "If organized medicine would drop its obstructionist tactics," said Means, and "devote its energy and money to the creation of adequate [voluntary] health plans ... it would more effectively forestall government medicine than it will with its present costly propaganda campaign and Washington lobby."[14]

As early as 1947 the Raymond Rich Associates, public relations counsel, which had been employed by the AMA, resigned, stating that its "position had become professionally untenable." Dr. Means contended that many physicians, especially the younger ones, were opposed to the policies of the older leadership and it was openly stated that the real reason for the resignation of Rich Associates was the conviction that the AMA leadership did "not honestly represent the doctors of America." Dr. Means looked to the younger physicians to bring about a change in policy, but in the meantime he deplored a situation which could result in expulsion from membership, "which would cut off, in considerable measure, the doctor's opportunity to keep in touch with his professional brethren—and without such contact the doctor rapidly stagnates intellectually. Also loss of hospital appointments might follow expulsion, which might make it difficult for a doctor to earn a living."[15]

In the end Dr. Means' courage was vindicated and his

14 *Ibid.*, 58, 60.
15 *Ibid.*, 58, 59.

hopes to a large degree were realized. His own efforts no doubt made their contribution to the change which he anticipated. Today most of the state medical associations sponsor or approve voluntary health plans, such as Blue Cross-Blue Shield, some of them having done so before the events of 1948-49. There were many physicians who would not be intimidated by the leadership of the national association and who declined to pay the unethical compulsory assessment for propaganda against proposed health plans, and they were not expelled from membership in the association, nor excluded from hospital appointments. One physician of the author's acquaintance who was president of his county medical society at the time objected to the assessment on ethical grounds and wrote the national organization declining to pay, giving reasons for his refusal, and nothing happened. In the case of the American Medical Association, it seems, membership in the national organization is more or less contingent upon one's standing in the local society. Thus a local group, led by a president with positive convictions on an ethical question, can have a healthy influence upon the organization as a whole. It is an illustration of the practical application of the principle which requires the Christian in his relations with the organized social order to follow a course which is in harmony with the way of the cross.

In course of time the national organization found a new leadership. In the end the counsel of Rich Associates was largely followed and today the promotion of voluntary health plans is part of the official policy of the national AMA. All of which illustrates the fact that while professional organizations sometimes go astray ethically they need not do so, and when they do go astray their ways can be mended.

THE DILEMMA OF ORGANIZED SOCIETY

The organizational revolution and the multiplicity of conflicting elements which are its fruits have placed the Christian into a very complex situation, indeed. That the possession and use of private property are an order of creation there can be no doubt. It is equally clear, however, that an unbalanced concentration of property is a violation of the same order of creation. Modern technology, moreover, tends to augment the process of concentration and to increase the economic power which can be wielded by individuals and by groups, while returning to the handicrafts of the Middle Ages is an unrealistic and impossible solution. To be sure, a Christian society should be able to find ways and means for controlling the economic processes and directing them in the way of Christian love and the cross. But when human society is less than Christian, lesser means and lesser procedures will also be used.

In our present world situation the social order seems to have the choice of two alternatives: either large-scale private capitalism, or bureaucratic state capitalism. Whether or not we eventually go the full way of state capitalism will depend in part upon the degree to which Christian idealism is able to mitigate the unchristian aspects of capitalism; the extent to which the Christian community succeeds in bringing business and industry into the way of the cross. Unfortunately, however, the approach to this great issue is too often the wrong approach. Instead of placing one's own economic and political interests under the searchlight of the cross, the tendency, even for many nominal Christians, is to become involved in a hysterical conflict between communism and "the American way," which is erroneously equated with Christianity. In this conflict the one side exploits the evils of capitalism, which are many, doing everything possible to discredit capitalism as such, and to move the nation forward on the road to state socialism. The other exploits the specter of godless communism to discredit legitimate efforts on the part of the state to regulate and control business and industry in its attempt to bring about at least an approximation of justice in the economic order. Those who take the latter position are simply attempting to reopen the door to an irresponsible capitalism which probably would hasten the day when totalitarian state capitalism would take full possession.

It is unfortunate, indeed, that many well-meaning Christians today are caught in this very trap. Instead of striving to arouse the Christian conscience so as to bring the economic order under the way of the cross, they have allied themselves with a reactionary individualism for the promotion of an outmoded and unchristian capitalism in the name of Christianity. In recent years this alliance has taken the form of concrete organizations some of whom have managed to mix religion and economics in their very titles. The Christian Freedom Foundation publishes a periodical, *Christian Economics,* to which ministers in all parts of the country receive free subscriptions. *Christian Economics* is critical of labor and friendly to business, and regards that government as Christian which keeps its intervention in business at the absolute minimum. A similar organization is Spiritual Mobilization which publishes *Faith and Freedom* and conducts conferences for discussion of economic questions along "old deal" lines, couched in religious language. The Committee for Constitutional Government, the National Economic Council, and the Foundation for Economic Education have similar objectives and make a similar appeal to ministers, as well as to professional people, although with less use of religious language and Biblical allusions. These organizations receive most of their support from large business corporations and wealthy individuals. The National Economic Council has also manifested anti-Semitic tendencies. Its leadership has maintained connections with Gerald L. K. Smith, Elizabeth Dilling, and others of similar persuasion.[16]

That the Christian Church has a responsibility for the character of the economic order there is no question. It is a responsibility to bring that order into the way of the cross, however, not to trim the Christian faith to meet the standards of the pagan economy. Had the Christian Church from the time of the industrial revolution exercised a prophetic ministry, in an effort to point industrial leadership to the way of

16 See *Social Action* (New York, May 15, 1951) Vol. 17, No. 5; Ralph L. Roy, *Apostles of Discord* (Boston, 1953) chs. 10, 12.

the cross instead of dismissing the miseries of the industrial proletariat with a reminder that Jesus had said the poor would always be with us, perhaps the economic abuses which ushered in the new era of government regulation could have been mitigated sufficiently to prevent the growth of the "welfare state" to the point where it has become dangerous.

As Emil Brunner has so aptly said, the rise of the modern totalitarian state is a judgment on the failure of the Christian Church to direct the moral forces of society to the creation of a just economy which accords with the order of creation. "Let us take as an example the welfare work of the state, which has already assumed monstrous proportions. This would not have been necessary if the family in the narrower and wider sense of the word, the social community, the Christian community, and the economic community of labor had not so conspicuously broken down. If, for instance, industry in its heyday had not, on the basis of an erroneous conception of property, diverted the proceeds of industry, in the form of high dividends and employers' profits, one-sidedly to the owners of capital but, after deduction of the necessary reserves and capital investment, had transformed it into just wages and welfare institutions for their workers, the state would never have had to take over these crushing burdens. If the Christian Church, at a time when its standing and authority were still intact, had more effectively reminded its wealthy members of their social duties in the sense of the requirements of justice, not of charity, and had used church discipline to give effect to its admonitions, a proletariat would probably never have come into existence. The social budget of the state, which has swelled to its present huge dimensions in all countries, is the consequence of a moral deficiency which we rarely have the courage to face squarely. The undesigned bias toward the totalitarian state, which seems like fate, and is present, not in some, but in all countries, not excluding those with democratic ideals, records like a barometer a moral depression."[17]

17 Brunner, *Justice and the Social Order*, 206, 207.

20. IF THE SALT HAS NOT LOST ITS SAVOR

The quotation at the close of the previous chapter is Emil Brunner's way of saying what Jesus said when He called His disciples the salt of the earth, and added: "But if the salt have lost his savour, wherewith shall it be salted?" When this occurs, says Jesus, "it is thenceforth good for nothing, but to be cast out, and to be trodden under foot of men."[1] Many have been the times in the history of the church when the salt has lost its savor. In the providence of God, however, there have always been times of renewal, when fresh salt has been created, or perhaps on occasion the savor of the old salt has been restored.

PIETY AND RICHES

Certainly Calvin and Wesley represent new salt in their time. But, as we have seen, frugality begotten of piety accumulates wealth, and wealth tends to generate indifference to faith and piety.[2] That which followed Calvin and Wesley in the wake of Adam Smith and Benjamin Franklin was no exception. Indeed some of it was more than indifference to the mission of the church as the conscience of society. It was rather a spurious faith, promoting injustice, even pagan materialism in the guise of Christianity. Some of it was worse than saltless salt which fails to bring healing to the world. It was a poisonous concoction doing positive harm to the social order, which if not cast out would eventually destroy even the church itself. Hence it was that numerous antibiotics in the form of state socialism and power blocs representing special economic and social interests emerged as counter agents to the poisonous evil. Antibiotics may be a necessary emergency

1 Matt. 5:13 (KJV).
2 See above, pp. 239-40.

measure for the counteracting of infection. At best, however, their contribution is a negative one, bringing necessary destruction to the evil, but without positive resources for good. For this reason the Christian, recognizing and accepting social antibiotics for what they are, must direct his energies to the way of the cross which alone can nourish the good life, bringing health and harmony to the whole social body. Or to return to Jesus' figure of speech, he must be genuine salt, full of strength for the good of the earth.

Among the exemplars of genuine salt in Christian history have been the Anabaptists and the Quakers of the sixteenth and the seventeenth centuries. Indeed they were a special variety with crucial elements not included in ordinary salt, which accounts for the superior quality of life which they brought to the church of their time. Even the best of salt, however, can lose its savor as the later history of the Quakers and the Anabaptists so clearly shows. While John Woolman was "laying down merchandise" in order to cultivate the "inner plantation, free from outward cumbers," other American Quakers "with the bent of their spirits to this world" were building commercial empires which consumed their time and energy until they lost their sense of obligation to their fellow men. Others, forgetting the lofty aims of Penn's holy experiment and the cross without which there is no crown, became engrossed in a struggle for power so that they forgot Penn's admonition to "strive not, read the fifth of Matthew, the twelfth of Romans [and] . . . see what becomes Christianity even in government."[3] Instead, the political Quakers purchased coveted political power with appropriations of money for the "king's use," knowing full well that this meant military use.

To be sure, an outward fiction of pacifism was maintained as long as it was expedient to do so. When this was no longer expedient, however, and military appropriations were delayed because of disagreement over the method of raising the money, they complained of being rendered "odious . . .

3 Dreer Collection (Hist. Soc. of Pa.), *Letters and Papers of William Penn*, 38.

to the army that is come to protect us." The high point in Quaker antipacifism was reached when the Pennsylvania assembly complained of inability to defend its own estates without protecting those of the proprietors gratis, referring to the proprietors' insistence ·that their estates be exempt from taxation.[4] In the meantime the ships of John Hanbury, London Quaker merchant, functioned well as military transports while Hanbury himself planned military strategy and urged the government to withstand the encroachments of the French for the saving of the British colonial and the Quaker mercantile empires.[5] While many Quakers did remain true to their ancient testimony it is obvious that by 1756 many had reached the point where the complete loss of that testimony could be prevented only by experiencing some kind of awakening for the restoration of the original faith. Samuel Fothergill knew whereof he spoke when he said: "The love of power, the ambition of superiority, the desire of exemption from suffering, strongly operate with many under our name, to continue in stations wherein they sacrifice their testimony, and are a salt which hath lost its savour."[6]

LATER ANABAPTISM AND MATERIALISM

The later history of Anabaptism brings forth similar illustrations of savorless salt. By the end of the nineteenth century it was possible for the government of the Netherlands to enact a new universal military training and service law, omitting all provisions for conscientious objectors, without raising an official protest from the Dutch Mennonites who three centuries earlier had counted their martyrs by the thousands. Apparently economic prosperity played a prominent role here as in the case of the Quakers of London and Philadelphia. At any rate, T. O. Hylkema, a twentieth-century Mennonite Fothergill, says that after the devil failed in his attempt to destroy Dutch Anabaptism by means of persecution he almost succeeded when he changed his tactics and

---

4 *Colonial Records (Minutes of the Provincial Council of Pennsylvania)* 6:628.
5 *Additional Manuscripts* (British Museum) 32853, f. 29; 33029, f. 242.
6 George Crosfield, *Memoirs of Samuel Fothergill* (New York, 1844) 255, 256.

made them rich.[7] A modern student locates the first stage of this spiritual decline in the period following the defeat of Philip II's Armada when the commercial ascendancy of continental Europe shifted from Flanders and Antwerp to Amsterdam and the Netherlands, bringing unprecedented prosperity to the Dutch people.[8] Before they realized what was happening to them, the Dutch Mennonites apparently had accepted the economic pattern of the time with little qualification, if any, and had gone into this new experience with little sense of the implications of the Gospel for the manner in which economic life should express itself.

By the mid-seventeenth century a large share of the whaling business and of the far eastern trade was in their hands; and as their wealth increased their concern for the church and the way of the cross declined. Literature, art, and philosophy came to be accepted as a substitute for the Biblical faith of previous generations, and Sunday services when attended were almost as likely to be featured by a dissertation on Greek philosophy as by a Gospel message on redemption, the way of the cross, and Christian discipleship. Instead of viewing the world as a sub-Christian society in the midst of which the colony of heaven is planted to serve as its conscience for bringing it to Christ, many Dutch Mennonites were assimilated by the pagan disorder whose sub-Christian culture was accepted with little question. By the time of Napoleon military service had been accepted and then it was not long until Mennonites were occupying high posts in the Dutch government, including military posts. A Mennonite deacon at one time even served as minister of the navy. So complete was this cultural assimilation that during World War I the Dutch Mennonites produced but one lone conscientious objector.

Since that time, indeed, Dutch Mennonitism has experienced a notable revival of original Anabaptism. It is significant, moreover, that this revival is accompanied by a serious

7 A statement made in public and in private.
8 Irvin B. Horst, "Some Ideas About the Impact of Economic Prosperity and Cultural Progress on Mennonites" (ms.).

critique of the economic order and that a prominent leader of the Dutch Mennonite peace group recently left her church to join the Society of Brothers in England, a communal group whose economic life is patterned after that of the Hutterian wing of sixteenth-century Anabaptism, and which has recently published a new edition of Peter Rideman's, *Account of Our Religion, Doctrine and Faith,* as a basic book of doctrine. In a recent statement this new convert to Christian community of goods says: "There seems to be a tendency to believe that the following of Christ must needs give material blessing. But is this the way of the cross? The old Anabaptists used to speak about the bitter Christ because of the suffering they had to undergo through discipleship."[9]

Even though one cannot accept the identification of communal ownership of property with the way of the cross in economic relations, the truth of the above statement must nevertheless be recognized, both as to its understanding of sixteenth-century Anabaptism and its critique of twentieth-century Mennonitism. There is no doubt that modern Mennonitism has far too much fallen under the spell of materialism. A few symptomatic illustrations from contemporary Mennonite life give ample evidence of the fact.

(1) Is it not strange (even if not typical) that on one occasion a group of Mennonite Biblicists when asked to cite Scriptures relating to economic matters should have thought first of "be . . . not slothful in business,"[10] and only afterwards of statements in both Old and New Testaments warning against materialism, economic injustice, and the love of money which is said to be the root of all evil?

(2) Is it not incongruous that a Mennonite farmer should object to an article in a Mennonite periodical questioning the ethics of a tax on oleo? He favored the discriminatory tax

---

9 Paula Thijssen, "Community the Outcome of Christian Belief," *The Plough* (Bromdon, Autumn 1954) 2:3:3.

10 Rom. 12:11. It is ironical that the Greek original of this passage should make no reference to "business" whatever. The KJV seems to be the only translation which includes this interpretation. The RSV reads: "Never flag in zeal, be aglow with the Spirit, serve the Lord."

since its effect was to reduce competition with his own economic interests. Can a way-of-the-cross Christian ask that his own interests be favored with special legislation which discriminates against the interests of others? "Look not every man to his own interests but also to the interests of others."

(3) What has happened when sons of the Anabaptist tradition of sobriety, simplicity, and ministry to the needs of others expend $60,000 and more for private residences while most of the people of the world remain ill-clothed, ill-fed, and ill-housed?

(4) What has happened when others of the same tradition accept, apparently without question, the symbols of power and prestige which our age provides and pursue them for their own sake without regard to their social usefulness or the principles of stewardship involved?

The story is told of two members of a certain Mennonite community in an earlier day, one of whom never wore a new suit to church until he had first "worn it at home or on trips to less conspicuous places so that its smartness and newness was worn off a bit. Only after it took on a more modest appearance would he wear it to church." The other man did not use his new buggy until he had first washed it with muddy water to tone down the shine a bit. Both of these men were "faithful churchmen who were bothered by the idea that they would make an undue show of themselves." [10a] It is also reasonable to assume that in these two cases both the suit and the buggy were needed and that they were paid for before reluctantly displaying them in public.

What has happened when in our day many Christians respond to public pressure to follow a course which is almost directly the opposite? (a) The new automobile is purchased regardless of need. (b) Power, style, and size, with the prestige which they symbolize, become the determining criteria for that which is to be purchased. (c) The purchase must be made whether it can be paid for or not, leading to conspicu-

[10a] Esko Loewen, "Hidden reasons for buying cars," *The Canadian Mennonite* (March 21, 1958) 6:12:2.

ous consumption, installment buying, and indebtedness to an extent which "to people from more conservative cultures and nations . . . is no less than shocking."

What has happened when the resulting chronic indebtedness in which many people find themselves leads to financial irresponsibility, laxness in meeting obligations, difficulty with creditors, and a reputation for untrustworthiness? A Christian's word should be "as good as his bond." When the state here described has been reached, however (and there are some cases like it), both the word and the bond will lose their value.

(5) What has happened when Christians in their personal ethics teach and exemplify the simple life and abstinence from the use of tobacco and alcoholic beverages, and at the same time in their economic life engage in the production of wines and tobaccos and the growing of luxury fur-bearing animals?

(6) What has happened when an official Mennonite periodical in a typical year in the midst of the materialistic twentieth century devoted only one half of one per cent of its space to teaching on the stewardship of possessions, and when within this one half of one per cent not a single article specifically mentioned the dangers of wealth and materialism of which the Bible and the Anabaptist fathers have so much to say?[11]

(7) In his baptismal vow the Anabaptist of the sixteenth century frequently promised to give up his material possessions for the use of the brotherhood if need be. "It seems they taught nothing but love, faith, and the cross. . . . They broke bread with each other as a manifestation of unity and love. They helped each other faithfully . . . and . . . called each other brothers."[12] Something has happened, therefore, when a twentieth-century Mennonite at the head of even a small industrial organization finds a gap, threatening to harden

11 M. Gingerich, "Mennonite Attitudes Toward Wealth, Past and Present." *Proceedings of the Conference on Mennonite Educational and Cultural Problems* (Newton, 1953) 9:94.

12 Sebastian Franck, *Chronica, Zeitbuch, und Geschichtbibel* (1531) ccccxlv.

into a gulf, between himself and his workers. Carrying the sixteenth-century spirit of brotherhood over into the twentieth-century industrial world, difficult though it may be, should be regarded as an opportunity and a challenge, not as an impossibility. When a Mennonite employer fails to understand the meaning of a proposal that management and labor co-operatively formulate policies to be followed, and co-operatively resolve the problems which emerge in the area of personnel relations, it is clear that the way of the cross and the Anabaptist vision of brotherhood has become obscured. A young Mennonite who recently emerged from the ranks of labor, through the intermediary stage of foreman, to assume the management of a subsidiary plant of a relatively small industry is disturbed by the counsel of his superiors that he sever social relations with former co-workers who are now his employees. Even though these workers may be members of his own Christian fellowship he is asked not to invite them into his home as guests nor in other ways maintain any form of social intimacy with them. The new manager has reason to be disturbed by this counsel and if the time should come when he bows in acquiescence to it, his usefulness to the cause of Christian personnel relations in industry will have ceased. He will have adopted something other than the way of the cross.

(8) What has happened when twentieth-century Mennonites become conditioned to commercial insurance with its profit features to such an extent that the Anabaptist tradition of mutual aid and "helping each other faithfully" is neglected; or when some in a position to profit personally by commercial insurance programs may even use their influence against the effective operation of brotherhood mutual aid?

(9) The American economy of abundance, in exacting its moral toll, has not excluded those of the Anabaptist tradition from among its victims. Not the least of the problems of the abundant economy, as Reinhold Niebuhr reminds us, is that of self-pride, the temptation to regard this good fortune "as the fruit and proof of our virtues."[13] The average Ameri-

can may have a tendency to attribute American prosperity to superior diligence and energy, perhaps even to superior intelligence, and to the generally superior qualities of freedom and initiative which belong to an American by the simple virtue of being an American. The pious Mennonite, less humanistic in his approach, may give due recognition to divine providence for America's good fortune. Such recognition, however, when spoiled by the assumption that the providential smile is due to a special favor which God has seen fit to bestow upon a "chosen people," can lead to a serious form of pharisaism. During the depression years of the thirties, for example, a Mennonite from the eastern states assumed that the great drought of the western plains obligingly detoured around the Mennonite communities, although working untold havoc in the communities of the Gentiles.

In a period of depression and economic hardship such pious naiveté may serve the useful purpose of stimulating diligence, industry, and thrift, which makes for economic success in spite of difficulties. Under an economy of abundance, however, with wealth continuously on the increase, it can easily lead to an arrogant self-pride which in the end will forget the providence of God and renounce the lordship of Christ without which there can be no Christian discipleship. A Mennonite editor,[14] warning that the wealth of his people is a chief threat to their spirituality and to the survival of their nonconformist witness, cites the following specific temptations which beset them: (a) the temptation to disregard the principle of stewardship; (b) the temptation to accept the ordinary practices of the business world without probing into their ethics; (c) the temptation of luxury spending; (d) the temptation to neglect brotherly sharing; (e) the temptation to inadequate giving; (f) the temptation to disregard and deny the interest and claim of the church in business and financial matters.

13 R. Niebuhr and L. Gordon, *Your Christian Conscience and American Abundance* (New York, 1955) 39.

14 Paul Erb, "Our Increasing Wealth," *Gospel Herald* (May 15, 1956) 49:459.

How pessimistic must one be with respect to the Christ-tian's role in the twentieth-century economic order? Or how optimistic may one be? Is the economic order itself, in this era of the organizational revolution, so hopeless that the way of the cross cannot be followed within it? One earnest disciple has asked the present writer, and I quote him directly: "The cross was to Christ . . . not the acceptance of sacrifice in a general way, but complete, absolute self-giving. Can the cross so understood become a normative principle? . . . Can the principle of the cross . . . be injected as a structural alternative into business affairs and normal human relationships?" Can it; can it indeed? That is the issue which provides the very occasion for this book.

Our Dutch Mennonite friend would seem to answer the question in the negative, finding her solution in the seclusion of a communal society where the management of economic affairs is transferred from the hands of the individual to those of a closely knit religious group. There are others who share her view. The Society of Brothers which began with one small unit in 1920 has since then grown to six units, located in England, Germany, Paraguay, Uruguay, and the United States. Its more than 1,200 members, though drawn from numerous walks of life and from a variety of religious backgrounds, share the common faith that the way of the cross in economic life requires common ownership of property. The new movement is strong in its emphasis on the evils of the economic order and on the inevitable involvement of the individual Christian in those evils so long as he retains his connection with that order. From this point of view the only alternatives would seem to be the communal life on the one hand, or a frank renunciation of the way of the cross on the other. There would seem to be no middle course through the economic jungle of the present world.

It is freely granted that the communal life is one expression of the Christian way. Much as this writer appreciates the sincerity of those who regard it as the only, or even the

best, alternative to a renunciation of the way of love, however, this point of view appears to him too much like the
Niebuhrian doctrine of ambiguity. And he is fearful lest
many of those who become convinced that this is the only
alternative, or who conclude that capitalism in itself is necessarily immoral, will, when the moment of decision is reached,
follow the Niebuhrian and not the communal way.

It would also seem in order seriously to question whether in the long run the communal way and the fulfillment of
the Great Commission can be reconciled. It is obvious, of
course, that the way of the cross must reject many aspects of
the social order. The history of Anabaptism, however, provides illustrations of two divergent ways by which its prophetic witness may be lost. One way is that of accommodation to
the social order, even assimilation, to such a degree that the
life of the kingdom is renounced for the way of the world.
The second way is that of withdrawal from the social order in
such a radical manner for the perfection of the self-contained
exclusive community that the opportunity for making an impact upon society is for all practical purposes lost. Even some
of the intimate cell groups of our time with a concern for the
renewal of the church, wholesome as their emphasis is in
many ways, nevertheless give the impression of expending so
much energy in mutual admonition that little opportunity
remains for making the Great Invitation real to such as might
be waiting to hear it. Too exclusive attention to the social
structure can mean a substitution of form for the Spirit, its
motive force moving on a horizontal plane from mere man to
man. The motive force of the first-century church, however,
and of every dynamic period of its history, moved on a ver-
tical plane, from heaven downward, making the Christian
community a dynamic force which in turn moved out on the
horizontal plane with power into all the world. It was a salt
which was finding its way to that for which it was ordained
to serve. Even a salt with a healthy savor, however, cannot
fulfill its mission if it does not succeed in reaching that which
is to be salted. And if such a condition remains too long, it

will in the end also become a salt which has lost its savor. This would seem to be the hazard which must frankly be faced by communal Christianity in the twentieth century.

Even Niebuhr himself at certain points seems less pessimistic regarding the Christian way in economic life than do some of the more radical current seekers.[15] The problem of justice or equity, which he considers the most important problem of the American economy, he also believes the most easy to solve. Niebuhr says the present century has witnessed a moral achievement in that industrial management has come to recognize justice to the workingman as essential for the health and welfare of the entire economy. The previous century, he feels, would have been quite incapable of anticipating this remarkable development which is now an accomplished fact. In addition to this the economy of abundance is the product of an increased productivity of labor; and the improved balance of economic and social power has achieved a fairer distribution of the national income, so that the living standard of the average American has been raised to a marked degree. The prediction for the future is an even more abundant economy. We are promised power, whether atomic, electric, or solar, almost without cost, "free like the unmetered air."[16] If and when this occurs economic abundance, and presumably a higher degree of equity, will be global in its scope.

ECONOMIC INEQUITIES AND CHRISTIAN RESPONSIBILITY

Without considering for the moment the possible harmful effects of such widespread prosperity on the spiritual life of man, the immediate problem for some time to come will continue to be the inequities in the world economy due to the confinement of abundance to but a small portion of the globe, and the international tension which this condition is bound to perpetuate. For the present America alone has the

15 Cf. Paul Peachey, "The Mennonite Ethical Dilemma," *Gospel Herald* (Nov. 13, 1956) 49:1073, 1074; Niebuhr and Gordon, *op. cit.*, 35.

16 H. R. Luce, "A Speculation About A.D. 1980," *Fortune* (New York, December 1955) 214.

problem of getting rid of its bread, and Trygve Lie reminds us that "in the middle of the twentieth century, most human beings are still hungry most of the time; half the world's people have yet to be taught how to read and write, are constantly ill, and expect to die before the age of thirty-five. Calculations show that the per capita income of almost two thirds of this total is less than a hundred dollars a year; and other evidence proves that most of the world's population cannot afford decent clothing, housing, and recreation, while hundreds of millions still live in bondage and peonage not far removed from slavery." In 1949 when the per capita income in the United States was $1,453, that of western European nations was $473 and of the underdeveloped countries $80 per year. The minimum standard of food consumption per person is considered to be 2,550 calories per day. In the United States, however, the average daily consumption is 3,130 calories, whereas in the underdeveloped countries it is only 2,000 calories resulting in malnutrition which contributes to the incidence of many ills, including malaria, sleeping sickness, and yellow fever.[17]

Maintaining a just relationship between rich and poor neighbors, whether the neighbors are individuals or nations, is never an easy one. No amount of benevolence or philanthropy on the part of the prosperous can take the place of a sound economic program on the part of the poor for the improvement of their own condition. Gifts and various forms of aid are always in order as means of emergency relief; but until the underdeveloped nations have possession of the necessary raw materials, basic resources, technical knowledge and skills, and cheap power, as well as the more intangible resources, a great amount of disparity between them and the so-called advanced nations will continue to exist. This is not always understood by the poor neighbor who is tempted to regard the disparity as proof of the avaricious character of his rich neighbor. Even when the neighbor reaches out his helping hand, be it ever so sincerely, he is likely to be suspected

17 Niebuhr and Gordon, *op. cit.*, 27, 28.

of some ulterior motive. Gratitude is never easy, and when there is the least ground for suspicion of motives ingratitude is easily turned to hatred. For this reason the United States is not loved today by many of the underdeveloped peoples and will continue in that position for some time to come.

It is not that the United States is especially vicious. But neither is she lacking in self-interest. The perpetuation of high tariffs in a day when trade is so essential for the prosperity of every nation will continue to make enemies for us. Despite her faith in democracy and her love for human freedom, her equally great need for oil makes it possible for the United States to play ball with the ruler of Saudi Arabia who lives in fabulous luxury while holding thousands of subjects in abject slavery. These and numerous other illustrations which might be cited help to explain the cynicism, the suspicion, and even the hatred with which many peoples regard the Americans. When in addition to this Americans yield to the temptation to ascribe their good fortune to their own innate virtue and superiority, their pride and arrogance only add fuel to the fire.

Scriptural teaching and the findings of modern science are agreed that there is no basic difference among peoples as to their innate intelligence and capacities; that differences in the cultures and achievements of the nations are due to other factors. The peoples of the underdeveloped nations are fully aware of this fact. It is no easier, however, for the rich and powerful to be humble than it is for the poor and the weak to be grateful. It is therefore necessary for the American people continually to remind themselves that their state of abundance and prosperity is due to a variety of factors, many of which are beyond human contrivance or control. First there was a virgin continent of such size and wealth in natural resources as to make it a natural independent economic unit from the beginning. Then this rich continent was settled by Europeans of an advanced culture who now were able to develop a new civilization, free from traditions which tended to keep other countries in a state of retardation. All of this occurred at a time when technological production and communication were coming into their own, and now the result is mass production and distribution, without obstruction by internal customs barriers, of the necessities and the luxuries of life on a scale never dreamed of by our fathers.

That which can be done to raise the standard of living of the underdeveloped countries is little enough until such time as modern technology and cheap power have had an opportunity to do their work. The least which must be done by the American people, therefore, for the promotion of good relations is to put forth sincere efforts to assist the nations in developing the technology which will enable them to help themselves; to supplement this assistance with capital where necessary; to keep the channels of trade and communication free and open; and to maintain a sense of stewardship and an attitude of humility with respect to their own fortunate situation which comes as an unearned and unmerited gift of nature and providence more than as an achievement by a superior people.

THE DILEMMA OF ABUNDANCE

Ancient Israel was warned to take heed when the land yields its fruit abundantly, when houses are filled with good things, and cities are great and prosperous, lest the God who brought them from bondage to freedom be forgotten. If this warning was needed in the day of Moses it is a thousand times more necessary in America today. Man does not live by bread alone, says Jesus; and James gives a severe warning to those who covet things to consume for their own pleasure.[18] The American economy of abundance and its manner of operation is such, however, that the individual is pressured from every side with temptations to violate every such Scriptural warning and admonition. Conspicuous consumption runs directly counter to the principle of simplicity and sobriety which lies so close to the heart of the Christian ethic. And yet economic

18 Matt. 4:4; Jas. 4 and 5.

production in today's economy is so efficient and the advertising technique so insidious and so insistent that we are continually tempted to buy automobiles for the mere sake of owning a new model which is not needed, or to spend money for furniture, entertainment, gadgets, or what have you, for no better reason than that the culture which surrounds us requires us to do it.

Necessary as these things may be when used with moderation, the Christian committed to the way of the cross knows that at their best they are of secondary importance, never able to provide the deep needs and satisfactions of life, and that at their worst they are destructive to the very end and purpose of man. On the other hand, he also knows that there is no virtue in poverty. What is more, it is the productive economy which has brought a brighter day and a measure of economic justice to the lot of the common man. Going even further it must also be admitted that freedom from depression and economic disaster demands an expanding economy, and that any drastic reduction of the American standard of living would disturb the world economy so as to have a serious effect on other nations. Even though intemperate consumption is not good for the soul, mass consumption is necessary for the maintenance of mass production, and mass production must continue if the injustice due to the imbalance of prosperity among the nations of the world is to be eliminated, and if vast populations are to be provided with even the minimal essentials of life.

This constitutes what John C. Bennett calls the next moral dilemma: "This technological dynamism is here to stay. We cannot basically reject it without denying the goodness of creation since technology is the elaboration of what is given in creation . . . . Yet, there is a dilemma. We are being carried along by a process that is becoming an end in itself and which threatens to overwhelm us."[19] Or as Niebuhr says it: "we are in danger . . . of developing a culture which is

19 J. C. Bennett, "The Next Moral Dilemma," *Christianity and Crisis* (Oct. 17, 1955) 15:129.

enslaved to its productive process, thus reversing the normal relation of production and consumption." It would be foolish indeed "to encourage poverty because poverty is frequently a better discipline of character than is wealth. But in a wealthy culture it is necessary constantly to call attention to the limits of comfort and security in the attainment not only of happiness but of the deepest joys of life."[20] How is this continuous attention to be made effective and how can it be possible for our dilemma to be resolved? This is no doubt one of the most serious questions of our time.

Can the way of the cross be a normative principle in the economic life of the Christian? Can it; can it indeed? Difficult as it may seem this writer can only say that so long as he believes Christian discipleship to have been ordained for this world he must also believe that it was intended for the economic life of this world. If the salt has not lost its savor surely the way of the cross can be found; and Christians led by the Holy Spirit will earnestly seek to find this way and to follow it wherever it may lead. The writer does not claim to have found that way in its fullness, nor to be following it with perfection, for with every other Christian he also is only a sinner saved by grace. Nor is he able to answer every question which can be asked concerning the size which any business should have, the amount of wealth which any person may have in his possession, the precise detail of the relationship which he may or may not have with numerous organizations with which he may be confronted, nor the details of a host of other problems and issues facing the Christian in the economic world. Even to see the issues clearly is not always easy, and to find their solution requires more wisdom than any one Christian can provide. By the grace of God, however, a body of Christians committed to Jesus Christ, to Christian brotherhood and discipleship, by laboring together under the leadership of the Holy Spirit can find the way of the cross.

20 Niebuhr and Gordon, *op. cit.*, 37, 39.

21. THE WAY OF CHRISTIAN BROTHERHOOD

The first requirement for finding the way of the cross and Christian brotherhood is a spiritual one. A heart of humility, and a deep commitment on the part of every soul; a renunciation of self and a giving of oneself completely to Jesus Christ and His way; this is the first essential. With this background a few suggestions would seem to be in order as to some things which Christians can do and which perhaps God can use, if they will let Him, in leading them more fully and completely into the way which they ought to go.

Would it be correct for the Christian to think of his relationship to the organized economic world in somewhat the same way as he regards his relationship to the state? The nonresistant Christian recognizes the state as an agency for the maintenance of justice within the sub-Christian social order. As such he respects it and co-operates with it in so far as such co-operation does not infringe upon the way of the cross. He accepts employment by the state, especially in its welfare services, under such conditions as do not require the violation of his nonresistant principles; but he does not accept such employment or hold such office as would make him responsible for the military or police functions of the state or which would require him otherwise to violate these principles. Would it not be correct for the Christian to regard his relationship with business, labor, and professional organizations in a similar way? As he belongs to Christ and therefore cannot give himself body and soul to the state, so he cannot sell his soul to any social organization of this world.

CHRISTIAN ORGANIZATIONS

If the Christian brotherhood is to live effectively in a world under the spell of the organizational revolution it must

299

have some organization of its own for the promotion of its distinctively Christian purposes and objectives. As an illustration, the historic peace churches of America and peace-minded groups within many of the other churches have their official peace committees and fellowships for education and fellowship within the group, and as a means of prophetic witness to all men concerning the claims of Christ and His lordship over the individual, the church, and the state.

In addition many of these groups have their service organizations as a means of positive witness in a practical way to the cause of peace. The Brethren Service Committee, the American Friends Service Committee, and the Mennonite Central Committee, each have a relief and service program which is world-wide in scope, giving assistance to refugees and other needy persons, bringing a testimony for peace in areas of tension, and extending a helping hand in the name of Christ in numerous ways to many peoples, particularly in underdeveloped portions of the world. So well has this task been performed, and so effective has been its contribution, that the American government has come to recognize it as a suitable service alternative for those whose conscience will not permit them to perform military service. In 1958, for example, a group of unarmed conscientious objectors, operating through an organization known as *Pax,* were engaged in the construction of much-needed civilian housing in war-harassed Algeria, where they had been assigned by the Selective Service System of the United States for service under the administration of the Mennonite Central Committee. This is but one illustration among many which might be cited. In addition to the above, it should also be added that a number of the service organizations and peace fellowships have joined in organizing the National Service Board for Religious Objectors whose task it is to represent the cause of the conscientious objector and his legal rights before the government, thus in many cases helping to make it possible for him to render a type of service in harmony with his faith.

Within American Mennonite circles there has also emerged since World War II a widespread series of local and regional Mennonite Service Organizations concerned primarily with disaster relief and service as in case of tornadoes, floods, or military attack. Sometimes these organizations operate independently, but often in co-operation with the Red Cross or with civilian agencies of the state in such work as coincides with Christian testimony, while firmly saying no to anything connected with war effort or which otherwise does not coincide with the way of the cross. Individuals refrain from membership in the community's civil defense organizations, though ready to co-operate with it indirectly through the MSO in disaster relief, but abstaining from participation in military defense action.

Christian peace groups in Europe have a similar program although it is not as fully developed as in the case of the United States. The British Friends have a service program similar to that of the American Friends Service Committee. The Mennonites of Holland have an official Mennonite Peace Group for fellowship and teaching, and a peace bureau which is concerned with the rights of conscientious objectors in a manner similar to that of the National Service Board for Religious Objectors in the United States. The Dutch Mennonite Peace Group also works in co-operation with Church and Peace, the Dutch section of the Fellowship of Reconciliation. The Dutch and the German Mennonite churches have their respective relief organizations which for many purposes co-ordinate their work with that of the Mennonite Central Committee as well as with that of other private and state organizations when this facilitates their work in harmony with their principles. The International Mennonite Peace Committee serves to co-ordinate the Mennonite peace work of the various European countries. In 1957 steps were taken for the formation of a new co-operative organization for the administration of voluntary service projects to which it was also hoped that conscripted conscientious objectors from various European countries could be assigned for the performance of their alternative service. The new organization, International Christian Service for Peace, also known as *Eirene,* was being organized in the first instance by the Brethren Service Committee, the Mennonite Central Committee, and the International Fellowship of Reconciliation, and it was hoped that various European Mennonite organizations as well as other peace groups would join in the effort. The first service project of the new organization was to be an agricultural reconstruction program in Morocco, and which began actual operations early in 1958.

Altogether the various organizations described above are designed as instruments for doing two things: (1) to find ways and means for the Christian to engage in a ministry of service and of mercy in the name of Christ which his conscience compels him to perform; (2) to discover ways and means whereby the church can more effectively perform its mission as the conscience of the state, pointing it to the way of Christ, and even obtaining its co-operation in the performance of forms of service which accord with the way of the cross. The above illustrates what is meant by the second suggestion for meeting the challenge of the organizational revolution: Christian organizations engaged in a ministry of service in the way of the cross, and serving as a challenge and as a conscience to the great and powerful state.

THE CHRISTIAN AND AGRICULTURAL ORGANIZATIONS

Should not the above description of restricted co-operation with the state, making use of the church's own organizations where these can be a help, serve as a model for the Christian's practical relationship with other areas of the organized social order? In the case of agriculture, it would seem that the Christian farmer should be free to co-operate with the county agent and with organizations specializing in educational and professional services, such as the soil conservation service and the dairy, poultry, and fruit-growing associations. The primary purpose of these organizations is the promotion of scientific agriculture and there is no reason why the Christian farmer should not be in the vanguard of scientific agriculture.

For the Christian, however, the extent and manner of such co-operation must be determined by the motivation which underlies it. More important than scientific agriculture is the question: Scientific agriculture for what? Its motivation can be purely selfish. Even a well-meaning Christian, if not undergirded by a strong sense of mission, can under the spell of materialistically motivated professional associates become as unchristian and as unethical in his outlook as they. A Christian with a strong sense of mission, on the other hand, will use his organizational relationship as a means for promoting the way of the cross. Making full use of his opportunity to bring the challenge of Christian ethics to his associates, the response will frequently be greater than he anticipates; for many of his business and professional associates are also Christians, ready to follow the way of the cross if the leadership is there to show them the way. Instead of regarding their organization merely as a means for the advancement of their own interests they will now, as stewards of God, direct their endeavors to His glory and to the service of their fellow men.

In certain types of agriculture, as in the fruit and dairy industries, marketing is sometimes administered through marketing associations, some of whom have been known to use power tactics such as milk strikes for the compulsory achievement of desired price levels. The Christian farmer who professes to follow the way of the cross will avoid membership in organizations employing these methods and use his influence to keep such methods and the spirit which motivates them out of such organizations as he may be associated with.[1]

Finally, agriculture would seem to provide an opportunity for a strictly Christian organization enabling Christian

1 A number of progressive farmers of the author's acquaintance who are active in the professional and scientific aspects of agricultural organizations have outstanding records of declining to co-operate in policies and practices the ethics of which are questionable, or declining membership in organizations whose policies as a whole are questionable. For a discussion of the Christian's role in a world of organizations see J. C. Wenger, *Separated Unto God* (Scottdale, 1951) Chs. 8, 10-12.

farmers to share their concerns, to sharpen their convictions, and to testify to the government and to organized agriculture generally concerning the way of the cross and its requirements. Such an organization could co-operate in an active way with the Christian service organizations referred to in the previous section in finding the way of peace and love in its own economic relations, and in serving as the conscience of the state and of organized agriculture concerning Christian ethics in agriculture generally. Above all it would co-operate with the same peace, relief, and service organizations in an effort to solve the western problem of abundance and to discharge the responsibility of the west for the needs of the remainder of the world. Such an organization would seek to enlist the services of agricultural missionaries, technicians and helpers who would go into the underdeveloped areas of the world in the name of Christ to help them raise their standard of living as well as to understand the way of the cross in human relations. This would be an agricultural organization with a moral dynamic and a service motive equipping its members for a moral thrust upon the social order and a positive contribution to human welfare, as well as providing a sharpened sense of what is right or wrong in the case of any organization with which they may be involved.

THE CHRISTIAN AND PROFESSIONAL ORGANIZATIONS

Among the professional organizations, as mentioned earlier,[2] the learned societies are concerned almost solely with productive scholarship and the publication of its findings; hence the ethical problem of organized power is absent. The organized service professions such as teaching, medicine, nursing, and social work are similar in character, being primarily concerned with the advancement of science and the dissemination and application of its findings, and with the maintenance of a high level of professional performance.

Members of the service organizations also have their

2 See above, pp. 273-74.

economic concerns, however, and they too can be selfish and materialistic. As a result, power organizations have arisen among them also. While the American Association of University Professors is a pressure group organized from within the profession, the American Federation of Teachers is an illustration of organized labor coming into the professional field employing its usual forms of power weapons, including the strike. In some cases unions have also organized members of the nursing and perhaps of other professions. Then too, as mentioned earlier, it is possible for purely professional organizations to be diverted from their primary objectives to the use of unethical procedures for selfish purposes as was the case of the American Medical Association for a brief period a few years ago.

Since in the professions, as in the case of scientific agriculture, the Christian should be in the vanguard of professional competence, it would seem that he should make use of professional organizations to the extent that they further this interest; that he should avoid the power organizations which operate in this field; and that he should use his influence against the diversion of professional organizations for the purpose of economic and social pressure, declining to co-operate with them in cases where they are so diverted. An illustration of what is meant here is the case of the physicians who at the risk of expulsion from membership declined to pay the American Medical Association's assessment for the support of its unethical fight against co-operative hospital, medical, and health plans.

The professional field also provides excellent opportunities for the operation of special Christian organizations. Organizations of Christian teachers, physicians, nurses, and social workers concentrating on the application of Christian ethics to their profession, including its economic aspects, could do much not only to maintain a high level of ethical performance among themselves, but also to strengthen them for the task of serving as the conscience of the profession as a whole and to make an ethical impact on all organizations operating in the field. As in the case of agriculture the Christian professional associations would also co-operate with Christian peace, relief, and service organizations in their effort to discharge the Christian's social responsibility to a needy world. The Mennonite medical, nurses', and teachers' associations are illustrations of what is meant here, although at present these seem to be primarily fellowship organizations which so far have not realized their possibilities for social action along the lines here suggested.

THE CHRISTIAN AND TRADE ASSOCIATIONS

The principles governing the Christian's relationship with business and trade associations are no different from those having to do with other types of organizations. As mentioned earlier, however, the evils of the organized business world are inherent within the individual firm or corporation itself, more than within the trade association in which the corporation may hold membership. If this is correct it would seem that the most important concern for the businessman should be the internal organization of his own business, its objectives, and its ethical practices, both with respect to his own employees and the general public. As to trade associations themselves, the procedure proposed with respect to professional organizations might well be followed, making use of those connections which serve an educational professional purpose and avoiding those which would make the Christian a party to selfish pressure and lobbying practices and the use of power methods. As an illustration, one industrial firm of the author's acquaintance finds it useful to employ the services of its particular trade association. This company displays its products at the association's annual showing, but it has refrained from membership in the National Association of Manufacturers because its power methods are considered out of line with the Christian ethic. Another business executive of the author's acquaintance was a loyal supporter of his trade association which served a useful purpose professionally, and which generally operated on a high ethical level. One year, however, when the association scheduled a session of its annual meeting on a Sunday this executive was quick to remonstrate, with the result that meetings henceforth were not held on Sunday.

THE CHRISTIAN AND LABOR ORGANIZATIONS

The distinguishing feature of the labor union is its over-balanced and sometimes almost exclusive emphasis on benefits for itself in the form of increased wages, shorter hours, improved working conditions, and other benefits. It is freely recognized that in the past labor has received less than a fair return for its contribution to the economic process, and that this injustice was in need of correction. The correction has been achieved, however, by means of a one-sided emphasis on the rights of labor to be obtained through the exercise of collective power. In addition organized labor has come to be perhaps the strongest power bloc in the American social structure today, a power which is not always exercised in a responsible manner.

Under the medieval guild system the worker was a member of an organization which brought technical training, excellence of craftsmanship, and the welfare of the worker more nearly into balance, and this is true of European workers' organizations even today to a greater degree than is the case in the United States. It is true, of course, that certain American craft unions, as the carpenters and printers, do have a system of apprenticeship which gives the recruit a certain amount of training under union leadership. Technical training in America, however, is provided primarily by engineering and trade schools and under the direction of experienced foremen on the job. In all of this, with some exceptions to be sure, the workers' own organization, the union, plays a negligible part and often none at all.

Well-trained European craftsmen migrating to America sometimes have the disturbing experience upon seeking employment of being confronted by union officials who ignore

the applicant's credentials in the form of certificates of training and experience, while requiring the payment of what
seems to the applicant exorbitant initiation fees as the condition of employment. In some cases, in fact, these officials
themselves do not meet the qualifications of a skilled crafts-
man, since their principal task has to do with organization
for social power rather than with professional excellence. It
is this unbalanced emphasis on collective power without
commensurate responsibility to the employer and the consuming public which constitutes the basic ethical shortcom-
ing of organized labor. An important feature of this situation is the compulsory membership requirement of the union
shop, sometimes reinforced by a compulsory oath of obligation, which invades the worker's basic human right to be free
to join or not to join a union as his conscience may require.
Another essential element in the picture is the use of the
strike as a weapon of coercion which unions, with few exceptions, reserve the right to use.

From this it is obvious that in finding a satisfactory relationship with organized labor the Christian is confronted
with greater difficulty than in the case of many organizations.
This is not because labor is less moral than other occupations and professions. It is rather because of the nature of
the typical labor organization that this is true. Its objectives,
its structure, and its procedures are so limited as to restrict
the individual's freedom to act in harmony with his conscience. In the case of trade associations the individual is free
to join or not to join as he sees fit. Or he may choose to join
a professional type of organization and omit the coercive
type. The same is true of other occupations and professions.
In the case of labor, however, in a union shop situation, the
individual is faced with compulsion to join one organization,
and one alone, even if it should happen to be the most objectionable organization which can be conceived. In this respect
organized labor is less democratic than many organizations
of the American economic and social order.[3]

3 The tendency toward undemocratic procedures in power organizations, and

On the other side of the ledger it can also be said that many labor leaders are ready to give consideration to the Christian whose conscience cannot be reconciled with coercive methods which unions sometimes employ. In the case of Christians who genuinely object to participation in coercion many unions are willing to accept the payment of dues as satisfying its membership requirements, excusing the individual from taking the union obligation or being otherwise active in the organization. In fact, under the provisions of the Taft-Hartley law the union can demand no more than this, even in a situation where a union shop contract is in force.[3a] Various unions have gone farther than this and have signed agreements with the Seventh-Day Adventists, the Mennonite Church, and other Christian groups, excusing their members from union membership and activity. As an alternative the agreement provides that persons so excused will contribute to some benevolent or charitable cause a sum equivalent to the amount of the union dues. There are, of

the social dangers which these involve, does not receive sufficient consideration on the part of those who stress responsibility for the power structure whether of industry or the state. John C. Bennett, for example, says that the nonparticipant in power organizations shuts his eyes to the benefits which he receives from the compromises of others; neglects the larger problems of justice and world order; and passes over the need of unions to improve the status of the worker and to provide the power with which to check the employer's autocracy (*Christian Ethics and Social Policy*, 44, 45).

Concerning this it should be said: (1) That intelligent nonparticipation in the coercive functions of power organizations, whether economic or political, is fully aware of the benefits often achieved by coercive means through improvement of the workers' position, the checking of managerial tyranny, and its contribution to justice in general. (2) That the Christian, however, may never seek benefits, justice, or status through violation of the way of the cross, since the latter is a higher value than the former. When Bennett refers to "the larger problems of justice and world order," he is taking the social order as his frame of reference rather than the kingdom of God. To the Christian, however, the kingdom must take precedence over the social order. For him the values of the kingdom are higher and larger than the problems of justice and world order. Granted the limited benefits of power politics, this writer must nevertheless conclude that they are limited and that those who give priority to justice achieved in this manner are closing their eyes to the way of the cross whose ultimate contribution both to the glory of God and the welfare of man outweighs by far all benefits achieved through the lesser way.

Compulsory membership especially, in any organization, however worthy it may otherwise be, is in itself a form of tyranny which strikes at the roots of the democratic process and all of that for which it stands. On the other hand, the values and achievements of organized labor are so well understood that any union operated with efficiency and integrity need not fear a loss of legitimate power through voluntary membership.

3a Labor Management Relations Act (Taft-Hartley), Sec. 8-a-3.

course, unions which are unwilling to make such concessions and which in strict union shop situations have compelled workers to choose between the forfeiture of their employment and the compromise of their conscience.

It should also be remembered, on the other hand, that even in a day when labor is highly organized there remain many open shop situations in American industry. Furthermore, the public mood in 1958 seemed to demand a more strict regulation of organized labor on the part of the state, looking toward the removal of some of its undesirable features. In 1958 compulsory union membership was illegal in eighteen states, although most of these were not highly industrial states. If legislation of this type should become general, however, the individual Christian would be more free to choose the way which his conscience directs him than is now the case. All of this seems to suggest a possible transition to a new era in which labor may operate on a higher ethical level than has been the case.

If in the future labor organizations should assume more of the technical and professional features which characterize organizations of other occupations and professions, and if the coercive features should be mitigated or eliminated, or if there should be different types of organizations, some including the coercive features and some not so that the individual would have more freedom of choice, the opportunity for the nonresistant Christian to co-operate with organized labor in a constructive way would be greatly increased. In the meantime the present situation serves as a challenge to the Christian industrial worker to find better ways and means of bringing a prophetic witness concerning the way of the cross to the industrial world, and to organized labor in particular.

CHRISTIAN EMPLOYER-EMPLOYEE RELATIONS

If by the admission of labor's own leaders a true application of Christian principles obviates the need for labor organizations operating on the traditional coercive pattern,[4]

4 See above, p. 273.

it would seem that Christian employers and employees should rise to meet this challenge for the blazing of a new trail in industrial relations. For if the way of the cross is to be realized in the modern economic order it must certainly be found in the relations of employers and employees.

While probably no industry has found this way in its fullness, it is certain that some have approached it more nearly than others. The Lincoln electric company[5] is often cited as an industry in which industrial relations are so satisfactory that the employees are not interested in the electrical workers' unions. Nothing is to be gained by affiliating with them. Another illustration is that of the Nunn-Bush shoe company whose story has been told in Henry L. Nunn's, *The Whole Man Goes to Work*. Nunn's basic philosophy is stated in these words: "There is a great difference between a commodity like coal and a human being. The worker has a mind and a will comparable in inherent dignity to those of the employer." Put in this way there are few who would not give verbal assent to the statement, and yet Nunn is correct when he says that "in the mind of the owner or manager who has not thought matters through . . . the worker has about the same relation to the business as coal for power and heat, a necessary but easily obtainable commodity."[6] The sad part of it is that even today there remain too many employers who have not "thought matters through."

As early as 1915 Nunn-Bush helped its employees to organize the Nunn-Bush Co-operative Association, an organization through which the workers would co-operate with management in the discharge and discipline of employees, in the selection of new employees, and in the fixing of wages, hours, and working conditions. By this action the company voluntarily renounced all arbitrary powers customarily exercised by management in a day when organized labor, especially in the shoe industry, was in its infancy. The significant thing

5 Cf. J. F. Lincoln, *Incentive Management: A New Approach to Human Relationships in Industry and Business* (Cleveland, 1951).

6 H. L. Nunn, *The Whole Man Goes to Work: The Life Story of a Businessman* (New York, 1953) 73.

is that this action was taken not because of any pressure from the outside, nor for the purpose of controlling the workers by means of a so-called "company union." It was done because the Nunn-Bush management sincerely believed that the only way in which the intricate human relations of a factory situation can be satisfactorily resolved is through a democratic procedure in which policies are arrived at through mutual agreement between management and duly elected representatives of the workers, after all grievances, problems, and issues have been laid on the table where they can be examined with fairness by all. The association's procedures provided for arbitration if necessary, but seldom was it found to be necessary, because as Mr. Nunn says, "when fear is removed from the human heart, reason enters. A man will not reason when he is out of temper or when his feelings are outraged by threats of arbitrary action. Concessions beget concessions, and trust begets trust."[7]

When the National Recovery Act was passed in 1933 in an effort to revive the ailing American economy, many manufacturers were critical and disinclined to co-operate. Nunn-Bush, however, wired its readiness to sign the emergency code, stating that it was "glad to do it."[8] When the Wagner act was passed in 1935 the form and organization of the Nunn-Bush Co-operative Association were modified to comply with the new law. Although this involved the changing of its name to "The Industrial Union of Master Craftsmen," the character and procedures of the organization remained the same. It did not become, and never had been, a company-dominated union. Neither was it a union organized as a bloc of power to withstand the power of management. It remained a co-operative association for the mutual consideration of the problems of management and labor. When organized labor denounced the association as a "company union" and took steps to unionize the Nunn-Bush workers, management invited the organizers to address the employees in the company's recreation hall.

7 *Ibid.*, 63.
8 *Ibid.*, 94.

They were told that whether they would organize the Nunn-Bush workers or not was a matter for the workers to decide. The organizers were surprised at the open and conciliatory attitude of management, and perhaps even more surprised to find that the body of workers, almost to a man, were not interested in an outside union. The explanation, however, is simple. For twenty years management and workers at Nunn-Bush had learned to trust each other and to formulate their policies, to solve their problems and to resolve their differences by the democratic process of co-operation and mutual agreement. So completely had this spirit permeated the life of the company and its employees that a union organizer found it necessary to report to his international headquarters: "That's no union at Nunn-Bush; that's a religion."[9]

In 1935 Nunn-Bush and the employees' association agreed on a new wage formula which involved an annual wage and 52 checks a year. Investigation had shown that over a nine-year period wages of the workers averaged approximately 20 per cent of net sales. Accepting this as an underlying principle the formula adopted provided that wages should be kept at this ratio. Hereafter, when the total wages paid in a given period dropped below the 20 per cent ratio, the hourly wage rate was raised. When the total rose above the 20 per cent ratio, the rate was lowered. The plan was based on an estimated 48 weeks of work of 40 hours each. This was arrived at by allowing one week for vacation, one week for holidays, and two weeks' loss of work because of sickness or bad business. Instead of paying the worker 48 checks per year, however, at 40 hours each, 52 checks were paid at 37 hours each. As said before, the hourly rate paid for 37 hours per week was always determined by the net sales of the company, total wages being kept at 20 per cent of total net sales.

At Nunn-Bush this system has come to be known as the production sharing plan. It is as if the buyers of shoes divided their payments into two checks, 80 per cent going to management to cover costs of material, manufacturing, sales ex-

9 *Ibid.*, 96.

pense, and earnings of stockholders, and 20 per cent going to labor. No doubt it was the company's frank open-book policy which convinced the workers in the first place that the 20-80 ratio was a fair one; and its long history of co-operative fair dealing which enabled them to trust the company to administer the system to the advantage of labor and management alike.

The management at Nunn-Bush tries to keep its production schedule, and consequently the number of its employees, as regular as possible. All permanent employees come under the production sharing plan and are known as "associates." Temporary and new employees are designed as "employees" and do not come under the production sharing plan. In other words, a certain amount of seniority is required for the worker to come under the program; but when he does come under it he is regarded as a permanent associate. In 1946 it was decided to designate as associates all workers who had been employed as long as two years. The average ratio of associates to employees at Nunn-Bush is 85 to 15, although this is subject to a certain amount of fluctuation.[10]

It is instructive to discover that twenty years before the public heard of Walter Reuther's guaranteed annual wage plan, the Nunn-Bush company had inaugurated the production sharing plan which would seem to be superior to GAW. Nunn-Bush management and workers like their system because it keeps pace automatically with business conditions. Throughout the years Nunn-Bush has always kept in mind three great objectives: (1) the security of the worker; (2) regularity of pay; (3) flexibility of income, in response to inflation and deflation, rising and lowering of prices. So well has the system worked and so great is the confidence which Nunn-Bush and its associates have in each other that since 1936 its board of directors consists of seven directors, two elected by the associates and five by the stockholders.[11]

Henry L. Nunn summarizes the working of the system as follows: "About 85 per cent of Nunn-Bush workers are

10 *Ibid.*, 114, 118.
11 *Ibid.*, 125.

associates, though this percentage fluctuates. Granted normal behavior, associates cannot be laid off. They own their jobs. In times of poor business the work is divided. Each associate does, therefore, have a security that cannot exist where management in times of lessened demand can choose whom it pleases to separate from the factory roll until his services are again required.

"It is possible that prolonged slack demand and few workdays per week would eventually cause reduction in weekly drawings, but the experience of Nunn-Bush causes me to doubt that this is likely ever to be necessary as long as workers pursue the present policy of maintaining sizable reserves.

"Friendly relationships between management and men develop an ever-increasing determination on management's part to strive for constancy of operations. It is easy to reduce operations when no obligation is recognized by management for steady work. All the manager has to do is to put a sign on the factory bulletin board, 'No work next week.' I grant that it is not possible for management, try as hard as it may, to keep production always at an even pace. I do insist, however, that the will to do so is helpful and may bring surprising results.

"Many industries do not lend themselves to the same degree of regularity in production as the shoe industry. Nevertheless, there is the same degree of need by their workers for regularity in pay, and though the nature of the business is such that work is available even as little as half the time, the worker has to eat, be sheltered, and clothed fifty-two weeks a year. It would be much better for management, labor, and society in general for every industry and its personnel to think in terms of annual income and regularity of pay checks, regardless of irregularity of work. I dare say the executives and other salaried people of such companies, cursed with irregularity of demand for their goods, do not earn their pay with the same uniformity of effort as they receive their pay checks.

"What effect does a co-operative attitude on the part of management have upon the attitude of labor? One has only to walk through the Nunn-Bush factory to detect an atmosphere that is as unusual as the system. Workers will be seen busily at their jobs, setting their pace at a rate they can comfortably maintain for the eight hours of the day, yet one that will insure their fulfilling expected quotas and performing a painstaking job. Most of the associates have come to realize that the finer the quality of the work the easier the management can secure a satisfactory price, all of which works to their benefit as well as that of capital. . . .

"Associates will not tolerate poor work on the part of their fellows, any more than they will tolerate individual production of less than the agreed quotas. These workers are in business to make money. Loss of production as well as poor work are their concern as much as they are the concern of capital. Unusual privileges have brought in turn an unusual feeling of responsibility."[12]

Henry L. Nunn says the most important benefit of the Nunn-Bush system is the psychological one. Since workers are partners in production they have a "self-respect and dignity that befits our democratic concept of the inherent rights of man. Suspicion and distrust are removed. There is a new sense of belonging and a pride in 'our' business. No longer is the worker treated as merely a cog in a machine. No longer is he expected to 'live by bread alone.' "[13] The Nunn-Bush example should serve as a challenge to Christian industrialists everywhere. Who among them will rise to the need of the hour and blaze a further new trail, going even beyond the "democratic concept of the inherent rights of man," and frankly basing their enterprise on the way of the cross? Who will be first to develop a modern industry in which the participants constitute a brotherhood of associates each of which seeks the welfare of the group and of the public which it serves to such a degree that it will be universally recognized as something different—as a uniquely Christian enterprise?

12 *Ibid.*, 118-20.
13 *Ibid.*, 197.

Is not this another area in which a distinctly Christian organization could render a useful service? Ought not a group of Christian employers and employees from numerous industries associate themselves for the purpose of exchanging ideas for the promotion of better employer-employee relations? As in the case of the farmers this association also might well work in close co-operation with church-related service organizations and thus enlist their businesses in the larger work of serving the needs of the world.

THE CHRISTIAN AND THE LAW

Another contribution of the industrial and organizational revolutions has been to render more complex the legal aspects of the economic order. Here again the Christian has the responsibility and the opportunity to discover those uses of the law which correspond with the way of the cross and those which do not. Since law exists for the promotion of justice and the protection of human rights, the Christian must stand on the side of law. To be sure, lawmakers can go astray, and when they do so the Christian also has the obligation to prophesy against that which is wrong. But he may never stand in the way of the law's pursuit of its rightful purpose. In the payment of taxes and in the honest reporting of business affairs relating thereto; in faithful compliance with laws designed to protect the health, safety, and welfare of the people; and in cheerful co-operation with the state in the furtherance of these ends there should be no question as to the Christian's obligations. This includes laws for the regulation of working conditions, including such matters as wages, length of the working day, and overtime rates. The Christian's business affairs should be in legal order and legal counsel should be freely employed to make sure that they are so. All of this is using the law as a means for the doing of justice to the brother and the neighbor, while evasion of the law would be to deal with him unjustly.

Since the Christian is included among those for whom justice is promoted he is not out of order when he accepts the state's protection of his own rights. If he strays from the way of the cross, however, he may be tempted to neglect the ministry of reconciliation or even to misuse the protective function of the state for the furtherance of selfish ends. The Christian has an obligation, therefore, to give careful thought as to the use which he may and may not make of the law.

First of all, Christians cannot use the courts for the settlement of disputes among themselves. The New Testament makes it clear that when differences do arise among brethren a means of peaceful settlement within the brotherhood must be found.[14] In the second place it also seems clear that the principle of love and nonresistance forbids the Christian to engage in aggressive litigation directed against any person, be he a Christian or a non-Christian.[14a] The Christian is commanded to beware of covetousness[15] and to love his neighbor as himself, yes even his enemy if there is such. The Christian must exercise a ministry of reconciliation, bearing witness to the way of the cross in order that the neighbor, even one who may have wronged him, may be won for Christ and brought into the kingdom. Aggressive suits at law are in every sense a violation of this mission, for how can a Christian win a man to Christ when he is suing him at law? It is equally clear that the Christian may not evade his responsibilities so as to be the cause for a just legal action to be brought against him. He who willfully evades the payment of his bills, for example, so as to invite legal action against him is even more in the wrong than the aggressor. According to the teaching of Matthew 18 the one falls under the discipline of the church as much as the other.

New Testament precedent, on the other hand, does not forbid an innocent party, when legal action is brought against him, to present his defense in court. When the Apostle Paul was arraigned he did not hesitate to speak out in his own de-

14 I Cor. 6:1-8; Matt. 18:15-22.
14a Matt. 5:38, 39. The Old Testament rule of eye for eye here superseded involved aggressive legal action against an offender, demanding a penalty equal to the injury which he had caused.
15 Luke 12:15.

fense.[16] Obviously, such defense must be an honest statement of the truth, or a forthright statement of one's innocence when such is truly the case, or a plea for mercy in case of guilt before the law. The Christian surely cannot use the legal right of defense as a means of denying his own guilt when such is the case, or as a means of evading the just claims of the law or of a plaintiff against him. On the contrary, if the court finds it necessary to take one's coat, Jesus says, it is better to give one's cloak as well.[17] This is in line with the principle that in the discharge of his obligations the Christian should give full measure and more. In all of this it goes without saying that, in case of a civil claim brought against him, the Christian should make every effort to accomplish a just and peaceful settlement out of court. If he is brought to court the cause for the action ought to lie with the plaintiff and not with the defendant.

In addition to the forms of litigation here assumed there is a "neutral" zone of legal action where the participants are neither aggressive in the sense described above, nor in a position of defense against such aggression. There is the case of the friendly suit where both parties to a real-estate transaction agree to ask the court for a removal of legal obstructions to a clear title. While this procedure may take the legal form of a "suit," it does not involve an action of one party against another in the aggressive or offensive sense. It is rather a means used by both parties to bring their business affairs into proper legal form so as to avoid cause for dispute or misunderstanding later on. There are other types of cases where claims for damages are brought to the court, or to special boards of arbitration or adjustment created for that purpose. The filing of claims for damages when the state uses its right of eminent domain to take one's real estate for the building of a road would be a case in point. This is not a suit in the offensive sense. It is making use of legal procedures for the adjustment of what all parties recognize as a just claim.

16 Acts 24:10-21; 25:10-12.
17 Matt. 5:40.

The presentation of claims against an estate which is in process of settlement, whether for debts owed by the estate, or for the widow's legal share of the estate in the case of an improperly drawn will, would be another illustration. Appearing as a defendant in case of a suit for divorce by a deserting husband and father, and the presentation of claims for support of minor children would seem to be similar in character. In other words, there are certain types of cases such as those involving inheritance, the settlement of estates, and the custody of minor children, as well as claims for damages, where the rights of the various parties are rather clearly defined by law and where the courts or boards of adjustment constitute the machinery for the execution of what the law requires without an aggressive action of one individual against another entering in.

The settlement of automobile accident claims through an insurance adjustment agency is an extra-legal procedure for the peaceful adjustment of claims in this area. Where the operation of the automobile is protected by adequate insurance with a reputable agency which is conscientious in the payment of just claims there should be no occasion for litigation. It is when one or both of these conditions, the adequate insurance and the reputable agency, are lacking that suits of one individual against another find their way to court. In view of the seriousness of the automobile hazard it would seem that the state should require liability insurance which is adequate in amount, while at the same time providing official state adjustment boards to which all insurance agencies and their clients would be required to present their claims for adjustment. Settlement would then be made on an impartial basis, obviating any occasion for aggressive suits at law. Until such provision is made by the state, however, the Christian must exercise great care, first to provide an amount of insurance which is adequate for the payment of such damages as his automobile might inflict; and second to be certain that his insurance is with a reputable company which is conscientious in the payments of its obligations without recourse to litigation or involving the insured in such litigation.

In the Christian's relation to the law, as in all mundane affairs, his first concern is the ministry of reconciliation to which he is called. His material affairs will be ordered in such a way as to demonstrate that he loves the Lord his God with all his heart, and his neighbor as himself. His business, his estate, his will, and all financial affairs will be kept in legal order. He will be informed as to the rightful uses of the law in the neutral area or when on the defensive. In particular, however, he will be concerned that his affairs remain in order as they affect the rights of others, so as not to cause offense and thus invite aggressive action on the part of others. His business procedures, while motivated by Christian love which ever keeps the welfare of his fellow men in the foreground, will also be characterized by prudence so as not to invite covetous fellow men to take advantage of his affairs and thus open the way to trouble, perhaps even tempting the Christian to take aggressive action against an unscrupulous offender. If in spite of all precautions, however, others do take advantage of him, the Christian remembers that the law of love must even in these circumstances govern his every action. He must ever do justice to others, but he may not take aggressive action to compel an offender to do justice to himself.

All of this would seem to point up a need for Christian attorneys qualified to provide the legal counsel which the complexities of the modern economic order require; attorneys who can assist the client to keep his affairs in legal order; attorneys who themselves are walking in the way of the cross, whose services do not include aggressive litigation, and who above all are conscious of a call to assist their fellow Christians in following this way more perfectly.

THE CHRISTIAN AND MUTUAL AID

The reference to insurance in the previous section suggests the need for a discussion of mutual aid at this point.

Obviously, the term "insurance" is a misnomer because nothing which belongs to this transitory world, be it property or life, can be assured. Furthermore, the consistent emphasis of the New Testament on the things of the Spirit which alone can endure, as opposed to material things which must surely pass away, would almost seem to eliminate the word "insurance" from the Christian's vocabulary. Mutual aid, on the contrary, is a Christian term which adequately describes that which can be done in the event of death or loss of property, and which the New Testament definitely requires of the Christian disciple. Life and property cannot be "insured," but when there is loss of goods or property, or when a loved one is taken from a family, Christian friends and neighbors can give spiritual comfort and they can minister to the material needs of those who suffer. When Christians undertake to perform this task in a systematic way so that the need is supplied whenever it occurs within the brotherhood we have a demonstration of mutual aid. Such mutual aid characterized the life of the New Testament church. It also characterized the life of the sixteenth-century Anabaptists, and this same spirit of Christian mutual aid continues among their spiritual descendants today as well as among other Christians who have caught the brotherhood emphasis of the New Testament.

To those who have caught this spirit the emphasis in mutual aid is on the obligation to help the brother who is in need. To be sure, when an individual suffers loss he is not out of place in accepting aid from others or even in hoping to receive it. But the emphasis will be on giving aid, not on receiving it. In an earlier day of a more simple agrarian economy Christian brotherhood groups often used the simple technique of a freewill offering to underwrite the loss of a brother who suffered misfortune, whether the loss of home or an expensive siege of illness. Those who contributed to the offering did so only with the thought of helping the brother; they did not ask: What do we get out of it for ourselves?

The industrial revolution has served to complicate our economy, however, so that even though it is a more abundant economy the dangers and the sources of insecurity inherent within it are also greater than in the case of the earlier economy. One result of this development has been the need for a more systematic and businesslike administration of mutual aid than was required under the earlier rural economy. Thus the industrialization of the social order and its accompanying secularization have produced a vast system of commercial insurance which is purchased and sold like any other commodity in the market place. The operations of the insurance business have become largely impersonal in character and materialistic in spirit, the "buyer" entering the transaction and paying a premium in anticipation of what he might get out of it, with his eye on the most insurance for the least money. The "seller" on the other hand, the salesman at least and often the company which he represents as well, is engaged in a business for economic profit. True, the buyer of insurance receives aid in case of loss but the commercialization of the procedure has offset this advantage with two disadvantages: (1) The benevolent spirit of seeking to help the brother in need has been displaced by a coldly calculating business outlook, sometimes with efforts to contribute less or to obtain more in the transaction than the amount which should fairly be given or received. (2) In actual practice, the ultimate cost of insurance operating on this basis is much greater and the benefits less than in the case of a systematic program of mutual aid operated by a Christian brotherhood in which primary emphasis is placed on providing aid for the brother in need.

Most forms of commercial life insurance combine "protection" (in case of death) with a savings plan. In some policies the buyer is paid a benefit at a specified age unless death occurs before that time. When the buyer pays his premiums on such policies he pays for both protection and savings, but the policies are written in such a way that the buyer or his family receive only one of these two features, although he pays for both. If he dies before the policy matures, his survivors receive the protection money and the insurance company keeps the savings account. If the buyer lives until the policy matures, he receives his accumulated savings, but when he dies at a later date, his survivors do not receive the protection for which he has also paid. If, instead of buying such a policy, the buyer would have purchased a much lower-cost term policy (providing only for protection in case of death at an age when he is most likely to have dependents), and then would have inaugurated a systematic savings plan in a separate operation, his survivors would receive the benefit of the insurance if he died during the time when this is needed, and they would also benefit from the savings accumulated to date. On the other hand, if he lives to a mature age his continuing savings could increase to an amount where the help of continued insurance would not be needed. Everyone who understands the insurance business is fully aware of these facts, and yet most commercial insurance salesmen do not inform their clients of them. Instead, they promote expensive policies which combine savings and insurance because the sale of these policies, so unfair to the buyer, yields the salesman a much higher commission than do those of less expensive term policies which provide protection at the time when it is needed.

It would be unfair at this point not to give due credit to the importance of commercial insurance in the commercial field where it rightfully belongs. Property and other forms of insurance against loss or disaster in the operation of a business or industry, workingmen's compensation as required by the state for the protection of the worker against industrial hazards, group insurance as provided by many industries for their employees, and other types of business and industrial insurance are a necessary protection against loss within the business itself, or against injury or damages suffered by clients, customers, or employees of the business. A business involving thousands or millions of dollars which failed to provide these safeguards against loss and damage would not only be inviting disaster to itself; it would also be derelict in its obligation to hundreds or thousands of people who are in one way or another dependent upon or affected by the business. Insurance on even the family automobile would seem to fall in a similar category since in using the automobile on the hazardous highways one assumes a public responsibility which in case of serious accident most people would be unable to discharge without the compensation which public liability and property damage insurance provide. Granting the place of commercial insurance in the commercial economy, it should be recognized for what it is: a business contract entered into for the effective operation of a commercial enterprise and to guarantee the discharge of one's business responsibilities. It does not take the place of brotherhood mutual aid which in our day is needed as much as it ever was.

Quite apart from the business in which a man may be engaged, he and his wife and children have individual, family, and community needs and obligations which can be met in a really satisfactory manner nowhere except within the Christian community. The church is a fellowship of believers, laborers together with God, for the advancement of His kingdom and for the promotion of each other's welfare both spiritual and material. When there is suffering in the home; when the house and its contents are destroyed; when the mother or the children are ill; when the father is taken in death, or whatever the misfortune, the family stands in need of spiritual consolation and of the material aid of the Christian fellowship. To meet the needs of the family in the Christian community, not something less but something more than insurance is needed. Here is where genuine Christian mutual aid must come in.

In almost every community there are those families which would find it impossible to purchase commercial insurance to meet family needs. As said above, certain forms of commercial insurance run absolutely counter to the spirit of

Christian mutual aid. Even the best and financially soundest commercial policies are often too expensive because of commissions to salesmen and profits to the company; and those who need them most are unable to buy them for financial or physical reasons.

Experience has proved time and again that a brotherhood group operating its own mutual aid plan for the replacement of property destroyed by fire, the payment of expensive hospital and surgical bills, or assistance to the family in case of death, can care for the needs of the brotherhood more effectively as well as more economically than can be done by the best of commercial insurance. Besides this, such a plan helps to preserve and promote the spiritual values of the brotherhood.

An illustration of what is meant here is the organization in 1949 of Mennonite Aid, Incorporated, which by 1958 had grown to a membership of 25,000 and was adding members at the rate of 500 per month. From the beginning this organization provided for hospital, surgical, and burial aid, and in 1958 it was planning for expansion into the area of widows' rehabilitation. As members of the brotherhood came to understand the basis of its operations they began to rediscover the New Testament spirit of mutual aid which they were in danger of losing and to some extent indeed they had lost. When it was understood that in this plan there were no salesmen's commissions, no company profits, and only a small overhead it was clear that this was genuine mutual aid and not a so-called insurance plan. When it was discovered that local congregations were enrolling in the plan, including all members who desired to join regardless of age or condition of health, without a physical examination; and when it was discovered that in some cases the local group paid the assessments of members who were unable to do so themselves, it became clear that this was Christian brotherhood at work. When some brethren enrolled in the plan and paid their assessments regularly, and then did not present their own hospital costs for payment because their financial circumstances did not make it necessary for them to do so, it was clear again that here the emphasis was being placed on helping the brother in need, not on receiving help for oneself. In the face of such experience could any member of this brotherhood think of selling commercial hospital insurance to his brethren?

In order that Christian mutual aid may remain truly that, however, the brotherhood must continually remind itself of the following points: (1) Medical and other costs which the family encounters must be paid, and it should be the purpose of each family wherever possible to pay its own. (2) A mutual aid plan such as that described above is a form of advance payment of these costs, thus relieving the payment of excessive amounts in times of emergency. (3) At the same time it is a means of helping others to meet their needs, even if one never requires the help himself. (4) Mutual aid must never be thought of as a means of getting something for nothing, or for which one does not pay his fair share. (5) To discourage this temptation Mennonite Aid, Inc., declines applications for membership presented for the purpose of receiving payment for immediately anticipated surgery or hospitalization. Such applicants would seem to be concerned first with asking others to help them instead of wishing to help others. This is not the spirit of Christian mutual aid. (6) On the other hand, congregations are invited and encouraged to enroll in MAI as a group, including all members of the congregation regardless of physical condition. When this is done no exclusions or waiting periods are required before individual members of the group may receive assistance. In such cases the congregational group can also arrange to pay the assessments of members unable to do so themselves, or whom for other reasons it may wish to assist in this way. (7) Brethren able to do so should be encouraged to enroll as members of the mutual aid organization for the purpose of assisting others even though they plan never to receive help from the plan even in case of their own hospital and surgical expenses.

It is believed that when mutual aid is carried out with

the spirit and purpose here envisioned it will serve the two-fold purpose of promoting Christian brotherhood within the fellowship group, and of providing a witness and a challenge to society in general.

CHRISTIAN STEWARDSHIP

Finally, he who would make the way of the cross normative in his economic life must maintain a high standard of Christian stewardship. If the American economy of abundance is not to reap within the church itself the bitter fruits of pride, worldly business ethics, luxury spending, and neglect for those who have need, the conscience of every soul must be sensitive to the eternal truth that the things which a man possesses are not his own; that they belong to God who has entrusted them to man for the glory of God and for the welfare of one's fellow men. The conscience so sharpened will be aware of the dilemma inherent within America's abundant economy. It will be aware of the maldistribution of the fruits of the earth among the peoples of the world. It will be pained to live in the midst of luxury when millions of people in the world are hungry every day; and yet it will realize that the technology which has produced this abundance is necessary for the abolition of poverty in other parts of the world. While realizing that abundance is not without its accompanying vices, the Christian with a sensitive social conscience knows that a higher level of abundance is essential for the welfare of many of the people of the world. How then shall this dilemma be resolved?

The first essential, it would seem, is a renewal among us of what E. L. Parsons calls "the sober life." Parsons pleads for an emphasis on the Pauline doctrine that salvation means the renunciation of worldly passions and the living of "sober, upright, and godly lives in this world."[18] He correctly observes that this emphasis on the simple life, in which riches and material wealth count for little, plays a prominent role

18 E. L. Parsons, "Footnote to the Next Dilemma," *Christianity and Crisis* (Jan. 23, 1956) 15:1, 2.

in the ethical teaching of both the Old Testament and the New. And certainly this emphasis was prominent in the life and teaching of the Anabaptists, the Quakers, and the English Puritans. A renewal of this Christian emphasis on simplicity, on the sober, righteous, godly life, is essential for the conquest of luxurious living, of extravagance, of ostentation, materialism, and the religion of success in the midst of which we live, in many cases leading to chronic indebtedness for things which cannot be afforded, with a resulting attitude of irresponsibility for one's financial obligations. Such a renewal and such a conquest, moreover, will provide the atmosphere in which the dilemma of American abundance can find an opportunity for solution.

A second essential would seem to be that every Christian use his earthly occupation, whatever it be, not for the sake of the occupation or for what he may obtain through it, but rather as a means of serving God and the church. The Christian businessman who has found the secret of the sober, upright, and godly life thinks of himself first as a Christian. His business occupies a secondary place as a means of serving his real calling which is the building of the kingdom of God among men. His overriding interest is the church and its work, its mission program at home and abroad, its educational work, and its service program. The support of this great work is the cause for which he lives. Above all, the Gospel which his church proclaims and the way of the cross and the Christian ethic which lie at the heart of that Gospel will determine the manner in which the business is administered, thus giving meaning to everything which the Christian does. These essentials having been met, there would seem to be hope for the solution of the dilemma of abundance and the problem of materialism which characterize the culture in the midst of which we live.

He who has reached this standard will be recognized as a Christian steward, in the best sense of the term. A Christian brotherhood whose members have reached this standard will be noted for its emphasis on stewardship. It will have a program of missions, of church extension, of education, and of service. It will have a philosophy of Christian stewardship and an effective teaching program for its promotion. The brotherhood will have a budget which is carefully planned and adequate for the accomplishment of its task. The members of the brotherhood who are engaged in business will have an important share in the making of this budget; and their various personal budgets will be so planned and so managed as to guarantee the successful operation of the budget of the church.

Food, clothing, shelter, and all that is necessary for man's material welfare belongs to the order of God's creation and is designed to be used for His glory. When misused these elements of the economic order bring dishonor to God and cause much suffering among men. The effective remedy for this state of affairs is to bring the economic life, with all of life, into the way of the cross.

THE WAY OF THE CROSS
IN SOCIAL RELATIONS

22. RACE RELATIONS

It was suggested earlier that nowhere, perhaps, is the Christian in greater danger of losing the way of the cross than in his economic relationships. If this is true it also seems correct to say that perhaps in no area is failure to follow the way of the cross causing more social tension in the mid-twentieth century than in the area of race relations. The prejudice which many so-called Christians feel toward persons of a color or national origin other than their own is usually due to feelings of superiority entirely foreign to the spirit of Jesus Christ the Suffering Servant. This feeling manifests itself in discriminatory practices, frequently causing its victims to develop hatred toward their oppressors. Not only does the resulting tension lead to social antagonism and international ill will. In our time it has dimmed the Christian witness and it has created conditions which challenge the very advance of the Gospel itself. How could it be otherwise, for how can the Gospel advance when those who profess to believe the Gospel deny the spirit and the power thereof?

The Christian faith recognizes only two classes of people, saints and sinners. The only kind of segregation which the Bible condones is that which separates those who are members of the kingdom from those who reject the lordship of Jesus Christ, and this has nothing whatever to do with matters of race, or nationality, or color. Except for this spiritual distinction all men are one. It is really incorrect to speak of races of men, for there is but one human race; and in this, Biblical teaching and scientific observation are agreed. It is Scriptural teaching that God "made of one blood all nations of men."[1] Science has confirmed that all men are of "one blood"; that the various peoples do not differ from each other

1 Acts 17:26 (KJV).

in intellectual capacity; that such physical differences as do exist are only superficial in character, such as stature, color of skin, or texture of hair; and that cultural differences among peoples are due to their respective social environments. Given time, all peoples upon transferring from one social environment to another are capable of modifying their culture and of raising or lowering the level of their intellectual achievement. Thus it is proper to speak of the unity of man in the order of creation which means that "the Christian must regard every man as his brother in the flesh, whom he must love and seek to win to the kingdom of God even as Christ loved and sought those among whom He walked."[2]

Not only are all men one in the order of creation; they are also one in the order of grace; all have been marred by sin and they stand alike in their need of God's redemptive grace. The New Testament presents a beautiful picture of the Good Shepherd whose purpose it is to bring all of His sheep as one flock into the fold. "And I have other sheep, that are not of this fold; I must bring them also, and they will heed my voice. So there shall be one flock, one shepherd."[3] This one flock is the church, His "one body," a new society of men recreated in the image of God, a society in which all human differences count for nought, where there is neither Greek nor Jew, barbarian, Scythian, slave nor free, black nor white.[4]

This unity of the Christian fellowship is not a mere matter of theory. It is a reality which must be realized within the brotherhood on the local as well as on the intercommunity level. The welcoming hand of the church must reach across all social barriers with the call of the Gospel to include all who repent into the fellowship of the church. This is the way of Christian love and nonresistance where the egoisms of nation or race give way to brotherhood and human solidarity. To refuse participation in warfare demands that the Christian likewise rise above attitudes of condescension and prac-

2 *The Way of Christian Love in Race Relations* (Scottdale, 1955) Sec. I-A.
3 John 10:16.
4 Col. 3:11.

tices of discrimination which are a major cause of social conflict as well as international warfare today; that he extend the hand of Christian brotherhood across the barriers of race and color and thus take away the occasion for war.

Christians sometimes do not realize how far removed from the New Testament standards are modern attitudes and practices with respect to race and color. Jesus said: "Men will come from east and west, and from north and south, and sit at table in the kingdom of God."[5] Dare we think of this grand experience as occurring only in heaven? And if Christians cannot sit at table now with their brethren in the faith, how can they hope to do so in the golden future? It is true that Jewish Christians sometimes had difficulty in understanding this great truth as it applied to Gentiles, but the manifestation of God's grace in the conversion of Cornelius taught them that "God shows no partiality"; that "in every nation any one who fears Him and does what is right is acceptable to Him"; that God gave the Holy Spirit to the Gentiles as much as to the Jews; that "He made no distinction between us and them, but cleansed their hearts by faith".[6]

Nowhere in the New Testament do we read of distinctions made on the basis of race or color. The baptism of the Ethiopian occurred as easily as did that of any other person who responded to the Gospel, nor was any question raised about it within the brotherhood. It seems clear that from the time of the Jerusalem conference through the time of the Reformation people of different cultural, national, and racial backgrounds were received into the fellowship of the church. Nowhere in this long period of a millennium and a half does the literature give any indication of a racial basis for admission to the church, or of discrimination and segregation based on race or color.

From whence, then, has come the denial of privileges and the segregation of peoples of different colors in public transportation, in schools, and even in churches, with its

5 Luke 13:29.
6 Acts 10:34, 35; 15:8, 9.

resulting racial tensions as we find it in the United States, in south Africa, and elsewhere in so-called Christian areas of the world? Many advocates of segregation claim to base their case on the Bible itself. A southern governor has even maintained that "God advocates segregation,"[7] and Mr. Malan, the segregationist prime minister of south Africa, is an ordained minister of the Gospel. It was in this same south Africa, in an earlier day, that Mahatma Gandhi, then a young man, on a Sunday morning was denied admission to a Christian church because of his color. At that time Gandhi seems to have had an interest in Christianity. This experience of rejection alone may not have been responsible for the fact that Gandhi never became a Christian, but no doubt it made its contribution. How then has this great departure from the teaching and practice of the ancient and the medieval church come about?

To a large extent discriminatory practices with respect to people of color are the product of modern imperialism, beginning about the time of the discovery of America. The imperial powers considered their conquered peoples, whether black or brown or yellow, to be inferior to themselves and used whatever means seemed necessary to keep them "in their place." In what is now the United States the American Indian was pushed out of his home and hunting ground and was well-nigh exterminated. Beginning in 1619 thousands of Africans were brought to the shores of America as forced laborers, and the institution of slavery was established among us. Two centuries later came the struggle for the abolition of slavery which was achieved only after a civil war followed by an era of reconstruction marked by bitterness and hatred, creating a situation in which the Negro and other people of color in our society have been the unfortunate victims ever since. Since the former slaveholding class could not bear to think of the Negro who had been freed under such humiliating circumstances as its equal, it now resorted to numerous devices to keep him in his place. The result has been the

7 See C. N. Kraus, *Integration: Who's Prejudiced?* (Scottdale, 1958) 11.

denial of privileges; the closing of doors to the best opportunities for employment; assignment to segregated schools and churches; segregated seats and coaches on buses and railway trains; segregated eating places and waiting rooms in railway stations; and other humiliating forms of discrimination, all on the theory that the Negro is an inferior person, who although qualified to be in the company of white people in the capacity of a servant, is not fit to associate with them as an equal.

Out of this situation has grown a vast mythology which speaks of people of color as having an ancestry different from that of the Caucasian, and which is in every way inferior to the latter. Unfortunately, some Christian people have even deepened the confusion by claiming to find Biblical sanction and support for this myth. Thus many Christians find themselves in a position where they deny the basic principles of the Gospel, both in theory and in practice, in a manner never found before in the history of the church.

When the Mennonite Church spoke on this issue officially in 1955[8] it declared its belief that racial prejudice and discrimination, as illustrated in the American pattern of segregation or wherever it may be found, is a sin. Among the reasons given for this belief are the following: "(1) It is a denial of our professed faith that all those who are in Christ are one. . . . (2) It is the perpetuation of a myth long proved false both by Christian faith and modern science. (3) It brands and discredits those discriminated against as undesirable and inferior. (4) It is a violation of the human personality as created by God; a denial of the opportunities and privileges which in the providence of God are meant for all peoples to enjoy. (5) It is a violation of the basic moral law

---

8 This official statement, *The Way of Christian Love in Race Relations,* was adopted by the Mennonite General Conference in August 1955 upon recommendation of its Committee on Economic and Social Relations. The statement in the first instance was the fruit of a conference on race relations held earlier that year. For a full report of the conference see: *Christian Race Relations: Proceedings of the Conference on Christian Community Relations Sponsored by the Committee on Economic and Social Relations of the Mennonite Church and by the Mennonite Community Association* (Goshen, 1955).

which requires a redemptive attitude of love and reconciliation toward all men, and which forbids all falsehood, all feelings of hostility, and all attitudes which lead to strife and ill will among men."

The statement goes on to speak of the consequences of this sin. It has a harmful effect not only upon those directly involved, but also upon the church and upon society as a whole: " (1) It humiliates and frustrates the victim so that it becomes difficult for him to behave as a normal member of society. (2) It scars the soul of the one who practices the sin. (3) It contributes to social tension, to hatred and strife. (4) It is a major cause of present-day international conflict and war. (5) It strengthens the hand of atheistic communism which claims to do away with the very sin which many Christians still defend. (6) It violates the central Christian message of redemption and love and thus discredits before the whole world the Christian Church and the Gospel which it proclaims, and weakens its mission program." The case of Gandhi cited above is the supreme example of this latter point.

The statement includes a confession of the church's own sins in not measuring up to the way of the cross in race relations: We are conscious of the contrast between the message of the Gospel and the conduct of men in their relations with their fellow men. "As Christians we therefore humbly confess our sins. We confess that we have been blind when we should have seen the light; that we have failed to see that mere nonparticipation in violence and bloodshed is not an adequate expression of the doctrine of love to all men; that we have professed a belief in the urgency of the Great Commission without bringing into Christian fellowship our neighbors of 'every kindred, and tongue, and people,' and that we have failed to see that acceptance of the social patterns of segregation and discrimination is a violation of the command to be 'not conformed to this world.' Often we have been silent when others showed race prejudice and practiced discrimination. Too often our behavior has been determined by our selfish considerations of public and social approval more than by our desire to accept the way of the cross. Some of us have accepted the false propaganda of racism and anti-Semitism which has come into our homes in the guise of Christian literature. Too often we have equated our own culture with Christianity without sensing which elements were genuinely Christian and which were merely cultural accretions from a secular society. Many times we have made it difficult for Christians of national origin different from our own to find fellowship among us because our own cultural pride and attitudes of exclusiveness served as obstacles. For these and our many other sins we repent before our fellow men and our God."

The statement then turns to a note of hope, expressing gratitude for many manifestations of the redemptive work of Christ within the brotherhood, and encouraging all to espouse more fully the way of the cross, urging:

" (1) That, as Christians, we cultivate a sense of belonging together on the basis of unity in Christ and discipleship.

" (2) That we recognize that any acceptance of the prevailing customs of discrimination is a violation of the Scriptural principle of nonconformity to the evil of this world.

" (3) That our congregations and mission stations follow the policy of inviting into their fellowship all who receive Christ and follow Him in true discipleship regardless of race or color; that in communities where there are now adjacent segregated congregations, sincere efforts toward intercongregational fellowship be cultivated.

" (4) That institutions and agencies of the church (as schools and colleges, hospitals, and homes for children and the aged, and the various church boards), if they have not yet done so, announce and carry out a policy of admission and service without discrimination on the basis of race, color, or nationality.

" (5) That in work with children, as in the case of summer Bible schools and summer camps, for example, an effort be made to conduct it on an interracial basis wherever there is a natural occasion to do so.

" (6) That we cultivate personal contacts among persons of various racial and other social groups.

" (7) That in our day-by-day social and business activities we become more sensitive to inequalities in practice.

" (8) That we express gratitude for the many manifestations of an awakened social conscience with respect to this question and for the many steps now being taken, especially by our government, to correct the evils of racial intolerance within our society; that in our communities we support efforts to that end which are consistent with Christian principles; and that we give our witness against the evils of prejudice and discrimination wherever they may be found.

" (9) That in all differences of experience, insight, and conviction on this question within the brotherhood, we exercise Christian forbearance, and seek for positive Christian solutions."

As a teaching program for the achievement of these goals the statement proposes: " (1) That we seek to present more clearly the teachings of the Bible, striving particularly to correct misunderstandings as to a supposed Biblical basis for discrimination.

" (2) That we help people to understand that science provides no basis for supposed qualitative differences among races.

" (3) That we deal with the psychological and social factors in race or other prejudice, helping our people to understand what this sin does to men's thought processes and social attitudes.

" (4) That we learn to think of all persons as persons, to meet them as such, and to be natural and at ease in their presence.

" (5) That we teach the necessity of uprooting from our conversation all words, expressions, and stories which lend support to racial prejudice.

" (6) That we call attention to the free interracial association in such countries as Brazil and localities in our own country where good relations have been achieved.

" (7) That on the question of interracial marriage we help our people to understand that the only Scriptural requirement for marriage is that it be "in the Lord"; that there is no valid biological objection to interracial marriage; and that, as in all marriages, the social implications of any proposed union should receive careful consideration."

23. PERSONAL RELATIONS

This book has consistently opposed the unfortunate tendency within Christendom to water down the way of the cross to a mere personal ethic. The major thesis has been that the Christian ethic has to do not only with two-person relationships; that the preferential ethic whether of Augustine, of Luther, or of Niebuhr is unacceptable; and, difficult though it may seem, that the way of the cross is intended for realization within the complex multilateral relationships of the modern social and industrial order.

It is needful, however, to include one chapter to emphasize the fact that the Christian ethic is not social only. It must indeed be a personal ethic before it can be a social ethic. The way of the cross must begin at home. It must hold sway in the intimate relationships of the local Christian brotherhood and in immediate neighborhood affairs. If it does not first reign in the family, in the congregation, and in the intimate community, how can it wage its conquest in the world of business and industry, of the professions and of politics, where the organizational revolution has transformed everything from the simple to the complex?

This observation would seem to be an obvious one. It underlies Niebuhr's oft-repeated dictum that although the individual and the intimate familial group may be able to attain a high standard of unselfishness, and purge out the egoistic elements quite thoroughly, in the complex larger society this cannot be done. The present writer is in agreement with those who object to this supposed inevitable difference between personal and social ethics for the Christian. He must confess, however, to an occasional uneasy feeling lest a Niebuhr or a Bennett, were he thoroughly acquainted with the inner workings and the intimate life of, say the historic peace churches or other brotherhood groups on the congregational and family level, would come to agree that there is little difference between private and public morals—not through convincement of the workability of the high ethic on the multilateral level, but rather through observation of its poor performance on the intimate personal level.

It is a sobering thought for a Christian to realize the possibility of understanding the way of the cross in an intellectual way while missing that way completely in his personal life. The New Testament teaching on nonresistance may be comprehended and fully accepted. Its theological basis may be understood and its social implications may be thought through in a logical manner. The individual may be convinced of the unchristian character of war and assume an unequivocal stand as a conscientious objector. He may even be remarkably successful in avoiding technical involvement and compromise with the unchristian social order. And yet the entire approach can be as legalistic as that of the Pharisees who knew the law of righteousness as to the letter but missed it completely as to the spirit. It is possible to teach love and nonresistance, even to write books expounding the theme, while lacking completely what Paul Erb calls "the nonresistant personality."

Speaking to a Mennonite audience, Erb says he who professes nonresistance and works for peace is in a difficult position. According to the Sermon on the Mount the way-of-the-cross Christian is meek, "but how few of us Christians could be described as meek!" It is possible for an argument for peace to become so heated that peace may not be achieved in the heart. "We probably have the average number of tyrannic parents, of quarreling families, of touchy neighbors, of selfishly arbitrary leaders. The psychiatrist's description of the unloving personality fits many of us. One of our laymen, after many years of observation of the Mennonite scene, said recently, 'We Mennonites are very hard on each other.' "[1]

1 Paul Erb, "The Nonresistant Personality," *Christian Living* (Scottdale, July 1954) 7.

Although this may be an overstatement it probably contains enough truth to give many heirs of the Anabaptist tradition cause for real discomfort. To the extent that it is a true statement, we may ask: Why is it so? While all Christians are human, the way of the cross nevertheless manifests itself in their personality and in their way of life, when they really have it. This was true in the early church; it was true of the early Anabaptists and Quakers; and it is true of Christians who have found the way of the cross today. Even their opponents described the Anabaptists as irreproachable, unassuming, attractive, humble, patient, and meek.[2] If the heirs of this tradition do not correspond to this description today, why do they not? There is probably no one answer to this question. When the salt begins to lose its savor, a variety of factors is usually responsible; with some individuals one factor may be important, and with others another. The following are a few suggestions, however, as to factors which may enter into the situation.

DISTORTED NONCONFORMITY

He who takes the way of the cross must of necessity be a nonconformist to many of the practices of the general social order. It is a deeply rooted, self-giving love which produces the nonconformity in the first instance. It is possible, however, for this deeply rooted source to lose its vitality while the outward nonconformity continues as a tradition. When this occurs the once beautiful conformity to Christ can become an unattractive, even repulsive, nonconformity for its own sake. In its extreme form it assumes that it is always right and everything else wrong. The result is an obsession for being against everybody and everything. Like certain of the disciples the distorted nonconformist may forbid others to speak in the name of Christ, or even wish to call down fire from heaven on others, because "they follow not us."[3] He is

2 See above, p. 158.
3 Luke 9:54; Mark 9:38.

intolerant. He takes a condescending, holier-than-thou attitude toward others. He is tense, unable in a free and relaxed manner to engage in an exchange of views. He cannot, like Jesus, be a friend of sinners that he may save them from their sins. He must, like the Pharisees, be at pains to show others how wrong they are; and to save himself from defilement he must wash his hands if he so much as touches them. This is not the way of the cross. It is arrogant pride.

SOCIAL STRATIFICATION

True brotherhood Christianity leaves no room for aristocracy, whether of power, of prestige, or of possessions. In the colony of heaven the citizens are "members one of another" and "labourers together with God."[4] A distorted nonconformity, however, tends not only to direct the individual and the group against those who are without, against those who "follow not us." It also tends to distort the brotherhood within by segregating persons with presumably superior ability or piety to an elevated position where they cast their eyes downward upon their inferior brethren. Quaker historians tell us that this tendency was especially marked among the eighteenth-century Friends both in England and America. Robert Barclay, the Quaker theologian, disclaimed "any necessity of *Levelling*." Since God has dispensed His creation "diversely, giving to some more, and some less," it was proper that men "may use it accordingly." While all Friends were brethren there were, however, brothers of high degree, "and such as God calls in low degree," who must not envy those "who have greater abundance, knowing that they have received abundance as to the inward man."[5]

It is true, of course, that the New Testament recognizes differences in gifts among brethren which are to be used, each according to the grace given unto him. Paul admonishes each Christian, however, "not to think of himself more highly than

4 Rom. 12:5; I Cor. 3:9 (KJV).
5 Frederick B. Tolles, *Meeting House and Counting House: The Quaker Merchants of Colonial Pennsylvania, 1682-1763* (Chapel Hill, 1948) 111.

he ought to think. . . . For . . . we, though many, are one body in Christ, and individually members one of another. . . . Love one another with brotherly affection; outdo one another in showing honour."[6] Jesus goes even farther when He says the greatest in the kingdom is he who humbles himself as a child, nay "unless you turn and become [humble] like children, you will never enter the kingdom of heaven."[7]

Once Christians have been bitten by the bug of aristocracy, however, they have real difficulty in retaining a child-like humility. Their sin is not that of the intolerant nonconformist-for-nonconformity's-sake, who assumes that he must be against everything and everybody. It is more likely to be that of the benevolent despot, often kindly in manner, generous in distribution of gifts, and even ready to hear the views of others as well as to discuss differences with them. His consciousness of his own superiority, however, together with the shrewdness of his diplomacy, enables him usually to have his own way in all that he does. Even if as an employer he pays labor too small and management too large a proportion of the earnings of his business he can say with Barclay: "Our *Principle* leaves every man to enjoy that peaceably, which either his own industry or his parents have purchased to him."[8] If as an administrator he finds his brethren unable to see the wisdom of a proposed action, thus in effect blocking one road to the achievement of his program, he simply opens another road which leads to the same end. His superior judgment tells him that his goal must be reached, and once having undertaken a course of action the dignity of his position will not permit him to retreat even if his brethren see otherwise. He is like the Quaker whose carriage shed at the meetinghouse was built with an opening at each end. Upon arrival at meeting time he drove his horse and carriage into the shed from one end; and when the meeting was over he drove out at the other end. When questioned about this unusual procedure,

6 Rom. 12:3-10.
7 Matt. 18:3, 4.
8 Tolles, 111.

the old Quaker explained that as a matter of principle he "never liked to back out of anything."[9]

Weighty Friends in the eighteenth-century Quaker meetings, as well as elders and bishops in the Mennonite Church of Europe and America in more recent times, in the administration of their congregations at times have seemed to operate on the same principle of infallibility which would not permit them to back out of anything, not even when they were wrong. This has frequently led to difficulty within the congregation. Individual members have rebelled against what seemed to them an arbitrary rule. Sometimes ministers within the same congregation have taken opposing views on an issue, and whether the question was important or not, none would back out of the position which he had taken. Then if each succeeded in obtaining a following within the congregation the result was a situation filled with factions not unlike that which Paul had to deal with in the church at Corinth. This has been the cause of too many schisms in modern Mennonite history. Such a situation, when it develops within a congregation, tends to negate completely the nonresistant testimony of the church. If brethren cannot find the way of love and the cross in their personal relations within the brotherhood, how can they find it in the business and economic relationships of the world? If they are not at peace among themselves, how can they bring a prophetic witness to the economic and political orders of the modern world?

Peter has prescribed the remedy for the kind of ecclesiastical and pietistic aristocracy which is responsible for situations such as this. In the same epistle in which he points the sheep to the way of the cross, Christ having "suffered for you, leaving you an example, that you should follow in his steps," Peter admonishes the elders to "tend the flock of God that is your charge, . . . not as domineering over those in your charge but being examples to the flock."[10] In the kingdom of

9 Isaac Sharpless, *Quakerism and Politics* (1905) 86-87.
10 I Pet. 2:21; 5:2, 3.

God the sheep and the shepherd are on the same level. If they follow the way of the cross they think of themselves as brethren in the faith, not as high or low, leaders or followers, rulers or subjects.

DISTORTED FAMILY RELATIONSHIPS

As in the case of all social relationships, marriage, the family, and the relation of the sexes in society are established in the order of creation which requires the way of love and the cross if they are to function in accordance with the will of God. The Genesis account gives a picture of man and woman created for co-operative work in loving response to the will of the Creator in whose image they were made. "So God created man in his own image . . . male and female he created them. And God blessed them, and God said to them, 'Be fruitful and multiply, and fill the earth and subdue it' "[11] It is important to note that man *and woman* are created in the image of God; and that *they together* are commanded to multiply and to subdue the earth. In the kingdom of God and in the work of the church, men and women, brethren and sisters, are laborers together with God. In Christ there is "neither Jew nor Greek, . . . neither slave nor free, . . . neither male nor female; for you are all one in Christ."[12]

It is true, of course, that there are certain functional differences, biologically speaking, between male and female; that these differences are reflected in their respective personalities; and that they have certain social implications particularly with respect to the family and the rearing of children. The fact that they are functional differences, however, makes it all the more necessary that in all of life there be a close co-operation between man and woman; for if one of them must work alone, and the function of the other be omitted, life will be so much the poorer. It is obvious that a home without a mother will suffer through the absence of an essential functionary. It should be just as obvious, however,

11 Gen. 1:27, 28.
12 Gal. 3:28.

that a home without a father will suffer likewise. If this is true in the home it is equally true that the church, the school, and the community will suffer to the extent that either the male or the female element of the population fails, for whatever reason, to function as it ought. God has created the human both a social and a sexual being. No one, therefore, can function as a normal human being except as a member of society. Neither can that society function as God intended that it should without the full and free co-operation of both its male and its female constituents.

It should be obvious, therefore, that the functional differences between male and female are not a matter of superiority or inferiority. Nowhere does divine revelation support such a view, although as always the Biblical record is faithful in reporting cases of distorted views on the subject which man had come to accept because of sin, and which were prevalent at the time. One of the results of the fall was the degradation of women to a position of inferiority. Man's function as "head" of the home came to be distorted into a form of tyranny. In many parts of the ancient world a man's wife and children were regarded as his personal property, which he could buy or sell, and over which he had the power of life and death. Even in recent times among certain tribes of people marriageable young women are known to have had a marketable exchange value, such as thirty head of cattle for a prospective bride.

Among the ancient Hebrews the position of women was higher than among the neighboring peoples. The achievement of this goal was one of the purposes for which Abraham was called to found a new nation. Even here, however, the effects of man's sin are still very much in evidence. Despite the fact that monogamy is the order of creation, polygamy is prominent in the Old Testament. Even though it was God's intention that marriage should be a lifelong union of one husband and one wife, the Mosaic code, because of men's "hardness of heart," permitted men in Israel to put away their wives. Jesus makes it clear, however, that "from the beginning it was not so."[13] Just as evil as the divorce itself was the superiority-inferiority concept which permitted the man to put away his wife, while the woman had no right to put away her husband. The husband, the man, was lord of his house. The wife must do his bidding. At times, it would seem, she was not far removed from the property status of the women in neighboring civilizations. This condition was utterly contrary to the order of creation and to the basic teaching of the divine revelation.

The concern of Jesus for women and children, and His tenderness toward them, is outstanding in the New Testament record. He rebuked the disciples when they discouraged mothers from bringing their children to Him. Instead, He blessed the children and said: "to such belongs the kingdom of God."[14] The attention which He gave to the woman of Samaria,[15] the forgiving spirit which He manifested toward the woman accused of adultery,[16] the words of commendation for the woman who anointed His feet,[17] and His healing of the woman who came to Him in faith[18] are manifestations of His spirit and concern. Women played a conspicuous role in the life and work of Jesus. He received a continuous encouragement in His ministry from the house of Mary and Martha.[19] Other women accompanied the Twelve in following His preaching itinerary, and supported His ministry with their means.[20] Among those who followed Jesus to the crucifixion scene these same women are singled out for special mention.[21] Finally, the first of the disciples to learn of His resurrection, and the first to whom He revealed Himself following that event, were women.[22]

Considering the period of history in which the church was founded, the role of women in the work of the early church is remarkable. Women were present in the upper

13 Deut. 24:1; Matt. 19:3-8.
14 Mark 10:13, 14.
15 John 4:7 ff.
16 John 8:3 ff.
17 Luke 7:37 ff.
18 Luke 8:43 ff.
19 Luke 10:38 ff.
20 Luke 8:2, 3.
21 Luke 23:49.
22 Luke 24:22 ff.; John 20:14-18.

room in Jerusalem following the ascension,[23] and apparently participated in the immediate post-ascension work of the church, in the devotion to prayer, in the selection of Matthias, in the receiving of the Holy Spirit with power, and in the sharing of material goods. Reports concerning believers who received baptism or who were persecuted continually include women in their number.[24] Women such as Dorcas and Damaris receive special mention.[25] The church at Philippi had its beginning through the conversion of Lydia.[26] The charter membership of the church at Thessalonica included "not a few . . . leading women."[27]

In the economy of God the prophetic ministry is of major importance; and in both Old and New Testaments women had their part in this ministry. Miriam, Deborah, and Huldah were prophetesses of the Old Testament.[28] Anna was a prophetess in Jerusalem, ministering in the temple and speaking to the people at the time of the presentation of the infant Jesus.[29] Philip the Evangelist had four daughters who were prophetesses,[30] and Paul's teaching in the early part of I Corinthians 11 has to do with the conduct of men and women while praying and prophesying. In writing to the church at Rome Paul commends to them Phoebe, a deaconess, with instruction that she be received and helped "in whatever she may require from you."[31] In this same chapter Paul mentions more than a score of church workers, a considerable number of whom are women. One of them with her husband had "risked . . . [her neck]" for Paul's life, and another had "worked hard among you."[32]

It is true, of course, that certain statements of Paul, if taken alone and out of context, might seem to suggest that women in the early church had nothing to do but to be silent and to receive instruction from their husbands at home. One

23 Acts 1:12 ff.
24 Acts 5:14; 8:3, 12; 9:2.
25 Acts 9:36; 17:34.
26 Acts 16:13 ff.
27 Acts 17:4.
28 Ex. 15:20; Judg. 4:4; II Kings 22:14.
29 Luke 2:36.
30 Acts 21:9.
31 Rom. 16:1, 2.
32 Rom. 16:3, 6.

of these statements, however, is directed at a disorderly situation in the Corinthian church where many women, as well as men, were using the gift of speech for unholy purposes.[33] The other is in the pastoral epistle where Paul is speaking of the office of bishop.[34] Apparently Paul means to say that the office of bishop is to be held by a man; and that women, as well as men, are to be orderly in the work and worship of the church, "for God is not a God of confusion but of peace."[35] In a church where there were deaconesses and prophetesses, however, it is hardly conceivable that women had no share in the administration and teaching work of the church. The tenor of the New Testament as a whole is opposed to this idea.

Properly understood, Paul was giving practical advice for a difficult church situation in an age when women generally had no rights. Within the young Christian church women discovered that they too had a place of responsibility; and no doubt some of them were tempted to misuse their newly found freedom, perhaps even to use wrong methods to achieve their rights in opposition to some men whose thinking had not been sufficiently emancipated from the authoritarian ways of the pagan society about them. This was one cause for the disorderly situation which needed correction in the church at Corinth.

The situation with respect to women was not too different from that with respect to slavery. The institution of slavery was well established in the ancient world, and it was not long until both slaves and masters found their way into the church. Obviously, one of the fruits of the Gospel would necessarily be the eventual abolition of this institution among Christian people. The tenor of the New Testament points consistently in that direction. And yet, as a matter of practical advice, in order to avoid social upheaval and to discourage unchristian methods for the obtaining of freedom, Paul

33 I Cor. 14:34-36.
34 I Tim. 2:12.
35 I Cor. 14:33.

admonishes slaves to be obedient to their masters. Actually, however, his advice to masters, as when he admonished Philemon to receive Onesimus "no longer as a slave but . . . as a beloved brother,"[36] was bound in course of time to do away with the institution of slavery among Christians, which it did. Paul's teaching is an appeal to both masters and slaves to follow the way of the cross. When slaves find that way they serve their masters with a heart of love. When masters find that way they love their slaves as brethren, which in turn leads them to grant the freedom which is the right of the Christian brother. The way of the cross leads to the abolition of slavery through mutual forbearance, and love, and the doing of justice; not by means of self-assertion and the demand for justice.

Paul's advice concerning the place of women in certain situations must be seen in a similar light. The order of creation and the teaching of Scripture require the co-operative labor of men and women in the kingdom of God. The world of the first century militated against this ideal to such an extent that it is really astonishing how large a share women did have in the work of the early church, a share which was destined to increase as time went on, as the Gospel had opportunity to change the hearts of men and to ameliorate the lot of women. The part which Christianity has had in elevating the position of women in our society is often not appreciated until we discover how radical has been the improvement of their lot in countries like India and Japan since the coming of Christianity in recent times.

It is not only the power of the Gospel, however, which brings changes among men. The social order itself is constantly changing; and as it does so it brings new situations with which the Gospel must cope. Since the beginning of the industrial revolution this change has brought a more rapid shift in the economic and social role of women than many Christian people were prepared to accept. When in the mid-nineteenth century it became clear that our society

36 Philem. 16.

13

was still dominated by males, many of whom seemed no farther advanced in their basic thinking than were those of the
church at Corinth, militant women in their determination to
obtain justice and the rights and goals which the new day required, resorted to ways and means for the achievement of
their ends which were also as much out of line as were the
actions of some women at Corinth. Neither the antiquated
ideas of some men, nor the militant actions of some women
during the past century and a half are in harmony with the
New Testament standard of co-operative work as between
male and female.

Referring to Lynn, Massachusetts, Benjamin Mudge has
said: "In all my school days, which ended in 1801, I never saw
but three females in public schools, and they were there only
in the afternoons to learn to write."[37] A story with an authentic ring, whether genuine or apocryphal, tells of a New England town council about 1825 permitting the teaching of
geography in its school with the proviso that girls be excluded, lest they become gadabouts. When the first colleges for
women were opened in the 1830's there were presidents of
men's colleges who argued seriously that the tender brains of
women could not endure the strain of academic discipline.
The first women to enter medical school did so only in the
face of tremendous opposition. When certain local antislavery societies in America appointed women delegates to the
World's Anti-Slavery Convention in London in 1840, the
credentials of these women were rejected because they were
held by women.[38]

It is not surprising that some women responded to this
attitude by going to the opposite extreme. Some were determined to demonstrate that women could and should equal if
not outdo men in every trade or profession which had hitherto been considered a man's calling. Others rejected the calling of motherhood and homemaking as beneath the dignity

---

37 Quoted in Thomas Woody, *A History of Women's Education in the United
States* (New York, 1929) 1:146.
38 Cf. A.M. Schlesinger, *New Viewpoints in American History* (New York,
1922) 137, 138.

of an intelligent woman. For more than a century higher education has suffered from the effects of these extreme views and only now is a more balanced view being generally accepted, a view which gives adequate recognition to the co-operative roles of men and women in every phase of society's work, whether the home, the church, the school, or the market place.

The most important aspect of this question is the relationship of husband and wife and parents and children in the immediate family itself. What happens here in the long run determines the shape of society in general. If husbands and wives and parents and children discover the way of the cross in their mutual relationships, the prospect for the future life of the church and community is good. If there is dictatorship, tyranny, and selfishness, disobedience, rebellion, and general lack of co-operation, the prospect is not good.

It would seem that a people like those of the Anabaptist tradition, in whose history the way of the cross has played such a conspicuous role, should be most successful in this respect. In other words, Mennonite life should be especially noted for its happy homes and harmonious family life. It seems doubtful, however, whether twentieth-century Mennonitism can claim great distinction in this respect. At a recent conference for the discussion of family problems, when a leader remarked that, while Mennonite life has been relatively free from divorce, it can hardly be said that the happiness of its homes has been exceptional, no one questioned the statement. When the theatrical world produces a twentieth-century play, *Papa Is All*,[39] to portray an outmoded type of patriarchal tyranny, and puts it in a Mennonite setting, it should give cause for reflection. The production is obviously unfair, grossly false in its interpretation. But why should it have occurred to the author to malign the Mennonite name in this way? Is it simply to be dismissed as another illustration of the evil which a hostile world always speaks against the Christian disciple? The fact that it is a wartime production,

39 P. Greene, *Papa Is All* (New York, 1942).

with an anti-nonresistant undertone very much in evidence, would give some support to this view. Or can it be explained as a case of an uninformed author seeking for sensational effect regardless of truth or consequences? Whatever the explanation, Mennonites searching their own souls might well ask themselves whether a record of family life on the highest level, so overwhelming as to make it a major characteristic in the mind of all who know them, might not have prevented so great a misunderstanding, or have helped even an unsympathetic author to avoid an absurdity so great as the one in question.

It should be obvious, however, that the way of the cross in family relationships is a primary requisite if the children of that home are to find the way of the cross in the larger areas of human relationships. If love and nonresistance are not practiced in the home, even though it may be taught in theory, how can the children be expected to know the meaning of nonresistance as it relates to military service and other social questions? A recent study of 149 Mennonite families by J. Howard Kauffman shows that the acceptance by the children of the values and principles cherished by the Mennonite Church is dependent, (1) upon the degree to which the parents themselves accept these values and principles, and (2) upon the quality of the parent-child relationships within the family.[40]

Kauffman classifies the families studied into two general categories, the "traditional" and the "emergent" type. The traditional type is represented by the family where the role of the husband is definitely dominant. He makes all the decisions. He seldom helps with work in the house. He bosses his wife. The wife and children have no share in the management of the family's finances; they have money for use only when he doles it out to them. He always drives the car. The wife seldom has any function outside the home. The husband seldom demonstrates outwardly his affection for his wife

40 J. H. Kauffman, "Tradition and Change in Mennonite Family Life," *Proceedings of the Conference on Mennonite Educational and Cultural Problems* (North Newton, 1957) 11:127.

and children. The emergent type is represented by the family in which the husband and wife share authority. He does not boss his wife. He frequently helps with the housework. The wife and children share in the decision-making process, including the management of family finances. The wife as well as the husband drives the car, and at least occasionally performs certain functions outside the home. Affection between husband and wife and parents and children is openly demonstrated.

While there are exceptions to all rules, the rule is that husband-wife and parent-child relationships are better in the emergent than in the traditional family type. There are situations, of course, where the father is a *benevolent* despot, and where family relationships on the whole seem harmonious enough. In an earlier day this may frequently have been the case. In the twentieth century, however, in most cases it does not work that way. A democratic society, become so through the influence of Christianity itself, demands the practice of Christian democracy in the home where character is formed and where children are prepared for life in the larger society. Where this is lacking, in most cases the result will be needless tension at best and hopeless chaos at worst, with children rejecting first their parents and then the values and principles which the parents cherish most. Kauffman's study of Mennonite families shows that both husband-wife and parent-children relations are better in families where responsibility is shared than in those where everything is controlled by a single hand. "The four families with lowest child-parent relations scores are in the husband-definitely-dominant category."[41]

Most important of all, is the finding that in families such as these the children are most likely to reject the values and principles cherished by the parents. By way of summary Kauffman says: "It is concluded that the quality of the child-parent relationship is a significant element in the transmission of cultural values from one generation to the next. It is

41 *Ibid.,* 11:125.

concluded also that the poor showing of the children in some traditional families on the value-acceptance test is, in part at least, a reflection of poor child-parent relations in these families. Examples of the compulsive rejection of Mennonite values by the children of some authoritarian patriarchal fathers are perhaps known to all students of this problem. . . . In unconsciously rejecting his parent, the child also unknowingly rejects the value system which his parents represent."[42] What a tragedy, then, for the principle of love and nonresistance and the way of the cross to be cherished theoretically in a family where parent-child relations are such as to encourage their rejection by the children.

Finally, it should be stated that Kauffman's limited study does suggest that the happiness of Mennonite families, despite their failures, may be higher than that of the average American urban family. Using scoring and rating devices very similar to those employed by E. W. Burgess in his study of 526 urban couples, which showed 21.5 percent of these couples to be unhappily married,[42a] Kauffman found approximately 10 percent of his 149 Mennonite couples to be unhappily married. Both the Burgess and the Kauffman studies are too limited for the drawing of final conclusions. In so far as they are valid, however, one may conclude tentatively that Mennonite families are less unhappy than the average American urban family, but not as happy as they ought to be. The way of the cross is being realized in part, but more progress needs to be made before it is realized in full.

Lest this discussion be mistaken for an encouragement of the opposite extreme, let it be said at once that the ideal family here envisioned is not a family characterized by disciplinary anemia. The co-operative-Christian-democratic family is not one in which the mother is concerned with "major" interests outside the home, while the "minor" task of bringing up the children is turned over to a baby sitter of sub-

42 *Ibid.*, 11:127, 128.
42a Cf. E. W. Burgess and L. S. Cottrell, Jr., *Predicting Success or Failure in Marriage* (New York, 1939) Ch. 3.

normal intelligence. Nor is it a matriarchate where husband and children are the victims of domination by wife and mother, the latter situation, if anything, being even more unfortunate than that of a male despotism. The ideal here envisioned is that of a family where the worth and dignity of every member is recognized, and where every member shares, each according to his age and capacity to understand, in the common tasks of the family and in the formulation of its policies. In such a family husbands love their wives as their own bodies, and wives reciprocate with reverence and cooperation. Parents love their children, not provoking them to anger, but bringing them up in the discipline and instruction of the Lord. Such discipline in the home will be of the same firm but gentle character as that in the church as described in Matthew 18, where faults are frankly discussed between person and person, and even before the entire council if need be, but where forgiveness is always extended, even unto seventy times seven. Such discipline is not punitive in character. It is a form of mutual burden bearing where children learn to reverence their elders because of their love, their wisdom, and the diligence with which they lead their children in finding the way in life which enables them to minister to the welfare of others and which brings to their own souls the deepest satisfactions which life can provide.

This writer has long had a feeling that the Quakers have done better in this respect than most Christian groups, at least in the place which women have held in their society. It may be that their English democratic origin has dealt more kindly with them in this respect than has the more authoritarian Germanic background of the Mennonites. The consistent manner in which they have carried through their objection to undemocratic and unscriptural titles has also been a help in this matter. Among them John Smith is just that; not Mr. Smith, nor Dr. Smith, nor Bishop Smith, nor the Reverend Mr. Smith, nor any other stratifying title. Likewise his wife is Mary Smith; not Mrs. Smith, nor Mrs. John

Smith. Mennonites have been reasonably consistent in speaking of Brother John Smith, but this attempt at Christian democracy breaks down in the case of the wife. Under secular influence she becomes Mrs. John Smith. More pious Mennonites bent on preserving the forms of brotherhood (and sisterhood), while nevertheless requiring the wife to lose her identity, have made her Sister John Smith. Certainly husband and wife are one, but this does not mean that the husband is the one. The two are laborers together in the marriage relationship. Each deserves the dignity of a personal name and all that is implied by it.

This does not mean that the woman should aspire to be a man, any more than the man should aspire to be a woman. There are functional differences between the two, and if the woman assumes the man's functions her own will not be performed. Woman's task is to perform the queenly function of the home, the church, and the community. As queen of the home she looks to her husband to lead out in the rougher work of general administration while she leads in the exercise of tender love and intuitive understanding, in providing the aesthetic touch, in deep meditation on the meaning of faith and life, and in setting the tone of quiet, worshipful dignity which is the crowning glory of the home. In such a home, maintained through the loving and faithful co-operation of husband and wife, there is an atmosphere where children can be nurtured in the fear of God and in the way of the cross.

The queenly function, however, with its attendant fruits must be extended beyond the home.[43] In an earlier day, in the simple agrarian economy when both husband and wife were confined more closely to the home base than is the case today, it occurred to no one that women did not work. Was there not an old saying to the effect that woman's work is

---

43 For helpful discussions on this theme see Carl Kreider, "Potentialities of Women for Christian Service" (ms.) (An address at the dedication of High Park Residence for Women and the Arts Building of Goshen College, Oct. 18, 1957); Elaine Sommers Rich, "Woman's Place in the World," *Gospel Herald* (Jan. 14, 1958) 51:30, 31; Paul M. Miller, "Woman's Role as the Glory of the Race," *ibid.*, 51: 25, 26, 43.

never done? Unfortunately, when the scene of economic production was shifted from the farm to the more distant office or shop this materialistic age began to think of work only as something located away from home, while the home itself was a place where nothing very significant was happening. Women who did not marry found their career in the office, or schoolroom, or shop. Those who married discovered that earlier marriages, better health, and greater longevity gave them years of time for other significant work after their children had been raised, especially when labor saving devices had reduced to a minimum the amount of time required for the performance of household mechanics. The advance of women's education during the past century and a half has opened for them business and professional opportunities of which their mothers never dreamed. To this should be added the fact that many widows, and even wives with husbands, find it necessary to "work" for a livelihood. Their mothers and grandmothers also worked for a livelihood. The difference is that the livelihood was formerly earned on the home estate whereas today it is done in the schoolroom, the office, or the shop. In many cases this has resulted in a certain amount of confusion with harmful effects on both men and women, as well as on their children and on society in general. (1) In some cases the shift to work outside the home has caused women to become mere imitators of men, to the neglect of the queenly function. (2) When the queenly function is gone the home is no longer a home. (3) This is followed by failure of husband and wife to co-operate in the management of the home. (4) The final result is parental and juvenile delinquency with all of its attendant evils and its deleterious effects upon society. Under such conditions the way of the cross in family relations does not prevail.

As a remedy for this two things are essential. First, it must be understood that it is impossible to make as sharp a distinction between man's work and woman's work as it was once supposed. It is true that more women than men are good teachers of kindergarten children and that more men than women have an aptitude for higher mathematics. We have also come to think of nursing as a woman's profession and medicine and surgery as a profession for men. And yet there are numerous individual cases where the aptitudes, training, and qualifications of men and women are the exact reverse of the commonly accepted pattern, and when this is the case should it not be accepted? If a woman is endowed with a scientific mind capable of unveiling the laws of physics should she be denied the opportunity of exercising her gifts? And if a man has the aptitude for being a good nurse why should he not follow this calling?

Second, we must learn that men and women need to co-operate in every area of life, so as to insure the operation of both masculine and feminine functions in each area. It is not that the teaching of children is a feminine function and the practice of medicine a masculine function. It is rather that the teaching of children is a profession in which both masculine and feminine functions need to operate together; and the healing arts and sciences likewise require the co-operation of both the masculine and the feminine functions. The same is true of every work which belongs to the human society, whether it be in the home, in the church, or in the community. Once this point is kept clear it should be possible to find a way out of the present confusion. Women should then be able to move freely in doing the work of their profession, whatever that is, and with it perform their real function, the queenly, feminine function without the benefit of which no work is well done. And once this point is kept clear the man should be able to resume his part of the co-operative role in the home, in school, in church, and in community, making full use of his masculine contribution without which also no work is well done.

Progress in the education of women has opened almost every profession to them. Men who are in positions of administrative responsibility, if they are wise—and Scriptural, will make full use of women among them who are qualified by gifts, training, and leisure time, to do a given necessary work even if heretofore only men have done it. Women have found their way into business and industry. It is taken for granted that they are needed in the schoolroom. Nursing and various forms of social work employ the services of women in large numbers. In 1950, 23 per cent of college teachers in America were women. In 1957, 29 per cent of the teaching staff in five four-year Mennonite colleges consisted of women. This would seem to indicate that as far as higher education is concerned the Mennonites were abreast, even a little ahead, of the nation as a whole in utilizing the services of women. On the foreign mission field for more than a half century Mennonite women have worked singly or as part of a team of husband and wife and they have been recognized by the church as having status equal to that of their masculine colaborers. A similar role for women is gradually being achieved in the far-flung voluntary service and social work program of the church. Publication work is making increasing use of the services of women. Increasingly women with leisure time, especially those whose children are grown, find opportunities for service as part-time workers in church and community, serving in institutions, in lay groups, on committees, and in a variety of ways. This is as it should be and will do much to bring about that kind of masculine-feminine co-operation so necessary for the proper functioning of our society, whether in home, in school, in church, or in community.

Not recognized as it should be, however, is the potential for the service of women on policy-making boards and committees in the administration of the church. If women have their voice in choosing a minister or in other decision-making processes in the local congregation, is there any reason why a few of them, especially in cases of special qualification by virtue of gift or training, ought not serve on church-wide committees and boards, or as conference delegates? It would seem that, next to the home, here is where the queenly func-

tion which only woman can perform is needed more than anywhere else. While the male members of boards and committees exercise their logical minds as they deal with budgets and
a hundred administrative problems, would not the entire
process be greatly facilitated by the tender love and intuitive
understanding, the aesthetic touch, the meditative depth, and
the quiet worshipful dignity of the queenly feminine presence which is the glory of every social situation, whether the
home, the school, the church, or the community? And how
certain can men be that in many cases the minds of women
are not as logical as their own? Given a harmonious way-of-
the-cross relationship between man and woman, husband and
wife, the foundation has been laid for this way to be realized
in all of life.

PROVINCIALISM

Immediately after telling the church at Philippi that
they were a colony of heaven,[44] with all that this meant, Paul
found it necessary to entreat two sisters in the colony, Euodia
and Syntyche, "to agree in the Lord."[45] Here were two saints,
who had "labored side by side . . . in the gospel" with Paul
and other fellow workers "whose names are in the book of
life."[46] What is more, they were feminine members of his
Gospel team, possessors of the worshipful dignity and queenly presence mentioned above as so essential for the work of
the kingdom. And yet it was necessary for Paul to reprimand
them because of petty provincialism in their attitudes one to
the other. It is obvious that citizens of the kingdom, even
those who walk in the way of the cross, are still human. They
were so in Paul's day; and they are so in our day as well.

It is even possible that the heirs of the Anabaptist tradition have more than their share of temptations like those of
Euodia and Syntyche. If they can become victims of a distorted nonconformity or of distorted views on family rela-

44 Phil. 3:20.
45 Phil. 4:2.
46 Phil. 4:3.

tionships, they can also develop a distorted view of life which manifests itself in small community pettiness. The sixteenth-century Anabaptists were missionaries of the first order. The world was their field of labor, and they had little time for local pettiness. Conrad Grebel and his associates in 1525 did not think first of separation from the Zurich church. They were aggressive advocates of the New Testament order as they understood it, and only after the Zwinglian authorities denied them fellowship did the Anabaptists begin to think of themselves as a separate group. After several generations of persecution had produced an era of quietism, however, many of those who did not make their peace with the world settled down in exclusive enclaves where they developed a feeling of inferiority common to isolated rural people. When this occurred their sense of mission was gone, and too often their highest aim seemed to be separation for separation's sake. Often they were not well educated. Their limited religious and cultural interests made it difficult for them to distinguish between great and small issues. The narrow outlook caused them to be petty in spirit, devoting too much time and energy to quarreling about little things when they should have been diligently promoting the greater work of the kingdom.

The way of the cross does not make it impossible for differences of opinion to emerge within the colony of heaven. Nor is it desirable that it should do so. It provides a perspective, however, whereby these differences can be channeled into constructive work for the advancement of the kingdom rather than having them deteriorate into mere petty dissension. Paul and Barnabas had their disagreement with respect to the ministry of John Mark. The problem was solved, however, when Paul took Silas in one direction and Barnabas took John Mark in another.[47] As a result there were two missionary journeys instead of one and the final outcome was the advancement of the kingdom.

When a similar difference arises between leaders of an

47 Acts 15:36-41.

ingrown enclave which has lost its missionary vision, however, there is no way whereby this energy can be harnessed for constructive purposes. All that remains is for the parties to the disagreement to compete for support within the brotherhood. The result is a festering sore which bears its fruit in the form of gossip, ill will, factions, and schisms. The later history of the heirs of the Anabaptist tradition has too many illustrations of situations such as this. Differences have emerged which were assumed to be based on fundamental principles, but which have proved to be little more than personality conflicts and petty loyalties like those which marred the Corinthian church. In spite of all the difficulties recounted in the first epistle, however, Paul was able to devote his second Corinthian letter to a more pleasant theme, recounting the triumphs of the Gospel mission where Christians were known as "the aroma of Christ," spreading "the fragrance of the knowledge of him everywhere."[48] Too many petty loyalties in later history, however, have had a different sequel. Too often the aroma of Christ has been exchanged for an offensive odor which has driven brethren farther apart, created permanent divisions, and rendered the Christian community uninviting to those who should have been drawn to it.

THE REMEDY

Happily, there is a remedy for the numerous forces which militate against the way of the cross in human relations. That way was found in the Corinthian church and it can, it must, be found today. (1) A first essential is for the church to recover its positive mission of reconciliation. He who is fully conscious of having been entrusted with Christ's ministry of reconciliation, "God making his appeal through us,"[49] can find no time for trivia which make for petty factions in the church. (2) A second essential is aggressive action as the conscience of society. The way-of-the-cross Christian does not detach himself from his fellow men. He pursues them,

48 II Cor. 2:14, 15.
49 II Cor. 5:18, 20.

he challenges, he prods them to forsake the bad for the good, and the good for the best. The only nonconformity which he knows is that elevated conformity to Christ, which small and petty spirits find themselves unable to reach.

(3) A third essential is a perspective of the mission of the church which is "full of meaning on the world map." As Littell says, the first Anabaptists declared the earth to be the Lord's and "that they were forerunners of a time to come, in which the Lord would establish His people and His Law throughout the earth."[50] Such a view leaves no room for a mere "enclave perspective"; petty trivia must give way to the great things of the kingdom. As J. D. Graber says: "To be conscious of standing within a stream that moves forward to a glorious consummation by the mighty power of God alone, of such faith and conviction are ever born the flaming evangels and the singing martyrs."[51] Men with such a sure note of triumph on their hearts and lips will have little difficulty in understanding what Paul means when he says: "Agree in the Lord. . . . Let all men know your forbearance. . . . Have no anxiety . . . . Finally, . . . whatever is true, whatever is honourable, whatever is just, whatever is pure, whatever is lovely, whatever is gracious, if there is any excellence, if there is anything worthy of praise, think about these things."[52]

(4) This perspective should enable the Christian to meet the requirement of a fourth essential, which is the ability to take life seriously with a calm assurance, with a buoyant hope, and even with a sense of humor. The Christian who is conscious that the future is in God's hand is in earnest, and he will work hard. Having performed his duty, however, he knows how to relax and to smile, for the future depends on God, not on himself, and his relaxing smile will draw men to the kingdom whereas the anxious tension of the distorted nonconformist will but drive them away.

(5) A fifth essential for him who would follow the way

50 F. H. Littell, *The Anabaptist View of the Church*, 94.
51 Guy F. Hershberger (ed.), *The Recovery of the Anabaptist Vision* (Scottdale, 1957) 156.
52 Phil. 4:2-8.

of the cross is a study of the science of human relations. Much of what we have been speaking in this chapter is a matter of knowing how to get along with people; and much of this can be learned by him who has an earnest desire to do so. The desire must be genuine, of course, and a conversion to the way of the cross will do more than anything to make it so. Even after this goal has been reached, however, there remains much to be learned through self-analysis, self-discipline, and hard work. It is possible to improve the ease with which one makes friends. One can learn to accept himself as he is, to overcome his own mistakes, and to refrain from blaming others for them. The acceptance of criticism can be cultivated. One can learn to win with moderation and to lose gracefully; to face fear realistically and with poise; to carry on calmly even when upset; and to make decisions with quiet readiness to accept the consequences. The bossy or the jealous personality can become aware of itself and do something about it. The harsh tone of voice can be softened. The tense can learn to relax. And he who would have friends can learn to make himself friendly. Other persons who have the art of getting along with people can help us. There are many books which are helpful.[53] If necessary, a Christian psychiatrist should be consulted to help us to know ourselves better and to find our way in the art of human relations. A study of the principles of human relations and an earnest effort at their application can bring rich rewards.

(6) A sixth essential is the cultivation of a heart of love. No matter how serious the wrong or how grievous the offense of another, the Christian must approach him, not with a look of scorn but with tears, not with arrogance but with a heart of compassion. He must cultivate the nonresistant personality.[54] The nonresistant personality knows how to apologize and to ask forgiveness; it is able to yield and to forbear; it is not boastful. The heart of love does not take selfish advan-

---

53 A helpful inexpensive little book is H. E. Bullis and Cordelia W. Kelly, *Human Relations in Action* (New York, 1954).

54 Paul Erb, "The Nonresistant Personality," *loc. cit.*, 7, 41.

tage; it knows no jealousy; and it is more concerned with giving than with receiving justice. The nonresistant personality goes the second mile; it is not arrogant or resentful; it covers the fault of others with a cloak of charity; it "contends for the truth without being contentious."

(7) A seventh essential for the Christian is always to bear in mind that he is a member of the body of Christ. "For by one Spirit we were all baptized into one body . . . . The body does not consist of one member but of many. . . . The eye cannot say to the hand, 'I have no need of you,' nor again the head to the feet, 'I have no need of you.' . . . If one member suffers, all suffer together; if one member is honoured, all rejoice together."[55]

Each member of the body may rightfully desire to exercise his own particular gift and seek to do the same. More important than this, however, is that each learn to appreciate the gifts of his fellow members and to understand the more excellent way of love and forbearance to all.

"If I speak in the tongues of men and of angels, but have not love, I am a noisy gong or a clanging cymbal. And if I have prophetic powers, and understand all mysteries and all knowledge, and if I have all faith, so as to remove mountains, but have not love, I am nothing. If I give away all I have, and if I deliver my body to be burned, but have not love, I gain nothing.

"Love is patient and kind; love is not jealous or boastful; it is not arrogant or rude. Love does not insist on its own way; it is not irritable or resentful; it does not rejoice at wrong, but rejoices in the right. Love bears all things, believes all things, hopes all things, endures all things.

"Love never ends; as for prophecy, it will pass away; as for tongues, they will cease; as for knowledge, it will pass away. For our knowledge is imperfect and our prophecy is imperfect; but when the perfect comes, the imperfect will pass away. When I was a child, I spoke like a child, I thought

55 I Cor. 12:13-26.

like a child, I reasoned like a child; when I became a man, I gave up childish ways. For now we see in a mirror dimly, but then face to face. Now I know in part; then I shall understand fully, even as I have been fully understood. So faith, hope, love abide, these three; but the greatest of these is love."[56]

56 I Cor. 13.

CONSUMMATION

24. THE KINGDOM OF OUR LORD

The theme of this book begins with theological foundations. It must likewise find its goal in a theological consummation. It begins with the divine order and the human disorder. It continues with the way of the cross as God's own program for the redemption of man. It must close with the triumph of our Lord and the final restoration of the order of God. While more or less aware of man's disorder, Christendom's understanding of the human problem has varied greatly from age to age, and all too often the way of the cross has been but dimly seen. The *Corpus Christianum*, whether the Roman or the Protestant variety, has been inclined to identify the kingdom of God and the social order to such a degree that from time to time the line of distinction between the divine Christ and human culture has been well-nigh imperceptible.

The social gospel was inclined to deify man who it was supposed would shortly achieve a heavenly kingdom of his own creation. Since Christian Action has donned the mantle the emphasis is on social responsibility and a resignation to the lesser evils of the social order, with a vague possibility of something better "beyond history." John C. Bennett, while granting that "there are no conclusive intellectual arguments against" the idea of an eschatological kingdom of God's own creation, and while recognizing that this generation "cannot go on much longer with the assumption that the question is not important," nevertheless is inclined to prefer the eschatology of the previous generation. "The worth of life does not depend" on the kingdom beyond history; "only the final security of life and it may be that it is our fate to experience worth without such assurance of final security. . . . If we are wise we will not be too dependent upon it, but make the most

of the other elements in our eschatology which do not go so
far beyond the evidence."[1]

At the other extreme is dispensationalism, with major
emphasis on the future kingdom in which citizenship is guaranteed by the doctrine of eternal security. For the present the
high ethic of the New Testament is ignored, however, since
this belongs to the future age where it can "be more easily
obeyed" than now. The important thing for the present age
is faith. Discipleship is deferred to the "kingdom age" where
it will be less difficult.[2]

The man-made kingdom without a cross has proved to
be a mirage. Social responsibility which exchanges the way of
the cross for the lesser evil is not too sure of a kingdom at all.
Others who proclaim the kingdom most earnestly would likewise by-pass the way of the cross. Surely an adequate conception of the Christian faith must include a commitment to
the way of the cross as well as a New Testament view of the
kingdom, with the two in a functional relationship to each
other, a requirement which is fulfilled by neither of the three
positions above.

FAITH AND HISTORY

In order to bring the way of the cross and the kingdom
into proper perspective it is necessary to grasp the essential
nature of Christianity as faith and history. Christianity is not
primarily a system of thought or even a set of ethical principles, although these are included. Christianity is faith in a
Person who acts in history. Divine revelation is a history of
the mighty works of God which were manifest first in the creation, then in the redemptive work of Christ, and which the
New Testament tells us will continue until their consummation in the age which is to come. " 'I am the Alpha and the
Omega,' says the Lord God, who is and who was and who is
to come, the Almighty."[3]

---

1 John C. Bennett, *Social Salvation* (New York, 1935) 178, 179.
2 See L. S. Chafer, *Dispensationalism* (Dallas, 1951) 34, 35, 44, 45, 50, 85, 96.
3 Rev. 1:8.

The religions of the Graeco-Roman world had a very different concept of God and the world and man. God is not a person, but rather an immanent universal soul, an "atmosphere," which exists above time and space. The eternal world, the universe, has no past or future. It is rather a state, the sphere of the universal soul. It does not proceed from a beginning toward a goal. It remains at rest while it vivifies the world. Eternity is the eternal now. Time likewise is a state, the sphere of the soul of man, identical with the order of this world. It is the form which the soul creates for itself when it desires to reproduce eternal ideas as living and creative activities. This world order, all of nature including man, is involved not in a progressive movement from beginning to end, but in a repetitive cyclical movement which leads nowhere. As the seasons go their round from winter through spring to summer, autumn, and winter again; as the circular movement of the stars, ever in motion but always retiring to the point from whence they came; so the soul upon its descent from the world soul enters the body, is born, matures and dies, then perhaps repeats the cycle in another form, until the succession of cycles completes its own great cycle, and losing its identity the soul is again absorbed by the universal soul where it comes to rest in the eternal now which has no past or future.

What was true of the individual soul was also true of the race. As Brunner says: "The thought . . . that humanity as a whole is implicated in a continuous movement of progress and amelioration, that . . . history in its totality is moving toward a goal which is more worth while, . . . is a thought which was . . . foreign to the men of classical antiquity."[4] Toynbee rightly says that such a view takes the significance out of history, "and, indeed, out of the universe itself"; that from this point of view it is difficult for the historian to believe "that his own here and now," or that of any other man "ever had, or will ever have, any special importance."[5] No wonder that

---

4 Emil Brunner, *Eternal Hope* (London, 1954) 15.
5 Arnold Toynbee, *An Historian's Approach to Religion* (New York, 1956) 10.

Marcus Aurelius Antonius, his rational soul having ranged "over the whole cosmos and the surrounding void . . . and . . . the periodic new birth of the universe," reached the conclusion "that there will be nothing new to be seen by those who come after us, and that, by the same token, those who have gone before us have not seen anything, either, that is beyond *our* ken. In this sense it would be true to say that any man of forty who is endowed with moderate intelligence has seen—in the light of the uniformity of nature—the entire past and future."[6] If this view is correct, then Homer was justified in his gloomy outlook for the future when he said: "Speak not comfortably to me of death. . . . Rather would I live upon the soil as the hireling of another, with a landless man who had no great livelihood, than bear sway among all the dead that are no more."[7]

How different is the God, the world, and man, the past, the present, and the future of Christian revelation! Here we are confronted with a divine personality, the Almighty One, who knows, and who feels, and who wills, and who acts. Here is the all-knowing one, the creator of the universe, the Alpha and the Omega, who moves on the stage of history performing His mighty works among men from the beginning to the consummation. For God is the God of history, and it is His mighty works for the redemption of man that constitute the stuff of history as He ever continues to make "all things new."[8] Christianity sees history as a straight and continuous line in which the historical and personal element is carried from the divine creation in the beginning to its logical conclusion in the divine goal "at the end of days." "This cosmic extension of the historical line," says Cullman, makes it clear that in its essence all Christian theology is Biblical history. "On a straight line of an ordinary process in time God here reveals himself, and from that line he controls not only the whole of history, but also what happens in nature!"[9]

6 Quoted in *ibid.*, 10, 11.
7 A. H. Strong, *The Great Poets and Their Theology* (1897) 56.
8 Rev. 21:5.
9 Oscar Cullman, *Christ and Time* (Philadelphia, 1950) 23.

The central point in God's time line is Jesus Christ, His advent, His death, and His resurrection. Our very system of reckoning time begins at this mid-point. We speak of B.C., the time before Christ, and of A.D., the time after Christ. For it was in the incarnation that God Himself broke into human history, literally coming down to earth and revealing Himself to man in person. So full of meaning is history for the Christian, and so significant for the affairs of men are the purposes and the mighty acts of God, that Cullman even refers to the life and work of the Incarnate Christ as D-day, for it was here that the decisive battle with Satan was won. Time on this side of the mid-point is the end time; for the back of sin has been broken and the church now awaits the dawning of V-day when Christ will reign triumphant and supreme; when behold, He makes all things new. "From this mid-point all history is to be understood and judged."[10]

It is well at this point to remind ourselves that the time line of which we speak is God's line, not man's. Only God can "make all things new." As Brunner says: "God alone can truly revolutionize, he who is the Creator and Redeemer."[11] Looking at history strewn with wreckage due to a "deep-seated and pervasive sinfulness, corrupting the life of mankind," the World Council of Churches in 1954 declared that "Christians must reject all doctrines of automatic progress. . . . Man's hope is not in any process or achievement of history. It is in God . . . the Lord of history."[12] The optimism born of modern rationalism tends to overlook the fact that while there is progress in good, progress in evil continues at the same time. Increase in knowledge and the improvement of technology do not necessarily represent a moral advance. In fact, as Brunner reminds us, they provide a twofold temptation in the opposite direction. The first temptation is to misuse power for man's own destruction, the reality of which in 1958 few would be prepared to deny. The second tempta-

10 *Ibid.*, 19.
11 Brunner, 61.
12 World Council of Churches, *Christ, the Hope of the World* (Geneva, 1954) 24.

tion is even more dangerous, "that of intoxication by power, of the mad sense of independence, of self-deification." Thus the culmination of mere human progress tends to demand emancipation from moral law, an "unfettering of the egoistic will," and a domination over men's minds, by organizing their conversion "to the required collectivist-technocratic-totalitarian mode of thought and surrender of judgment. . . . It becomes clear that here lies its real enemy" and that thus "the man of progress becomes antichrist and the struggle against Christ develops into a life and death struggle."[13]

Dark as this picture may seem, however, it provides no ground for despair. If the Christian is not a rationalistic optimist, neither is he a pessimist. The World Council statement which rejects all doctrines of automatic progress also rejects the "doctrine of fated decline."[14] Since God is the Lord of history the triumph of truth and righteousness is certain. For assuredly, Christ is the hope of the world. "The promised Deliverer has come. The powers of the coming kingdom are already at work. . . . God in Jesus Christ has entered into the tangled web of earthly history and met and mastered evil in all its forms. By His life, death, and resurrection He became for us both sin's Victim and at the same time sin's Victor. . . . His coming fulfilled the hope of earlier times—and transformed it. He brought to men a new birth into a new life, a new community and a new hope. . . . This fellowship in the Spirit is but the foretaste, the earnest, of the inheritance laid up for us. . . . The kingdom which is now real moves with God's power and faithfulness towards its full realization in the manifestation of God's glory throughout all creation. The King reigns; therefore He will reign until He has put all enemies under His feet. . . . Those who are now sons of God will receive the fullness of their inheritance as joint heirs with Christ. There will be a new heaven and a new earth. We shall all be changed. The dead will be raised incorruptible, receiving a body of heavenly glory. . . . The Holy City will

---

13 Brunner, 78, 79.
14 World Council of Churches, *ibid.*, 24.

appear. . . . God's people will enter into the sabbath rest, and all created things will be reconciled in the perfect communion of God with His people."[15]

Bennett is correct when he says that this vision of the consummation of history "staggers the imagination of many," and that "it is not a part of the working capital of large numbers of the most devoted Christians of our time."[16] A careful reading of the New Testament, however, should underline the centrality of the lordship of Christ in the faith and life of the early Christians. Indeed it was their devoted commitment to this lordship, perhaps more than any single factor, which accounts for the power of the New Testament church. As Ray Petry has shown, social thought and achievement as well as evangelism in the history of the Christian Church have been largely barren to the extent that the lordship of Christ and the "inner vitality of eschatology" have been lost.[17]

In the New Testament the time line includes the entire gamut of God's mighty works from the beginning to the consummation of history, with the incarnation not only occupying the mid-point, but with Jesus Christ playing the central role in the entire drama of creation, redemption, and restoration until in a final triumphant order of truth, love, and righteousness in the new heavens and the new earth He reigns supreme. The first chapter of Hebrews says God in these last days "has spoken to us by a Son, whom he appointed the heir of all things, through whom also he created the world. He reflects the glory of God and bears the very stamp of his nature, upholding the universe by his word of power."[18] John's well-known prologue says: "In the beginning was the Word . . . ; all things were made through him . . . . And the Word became flesh and dwelt among us, full of grace and truth."[19] Paul's letter to the Colossians proclaims Christ in whom "all things were created, in heaven and on earth, visible and

15 *Ibid.*, 8, 11, 12.
16 *Social Salvation*, 179.
17 Ray Petry, *Christian Eschatology and Social Thought* (New York, 1956) 16
18 Heb. 1:2, 3.
19 John 1:1, 3, 14.

invisible, whether thrones or dominions or principalities or
authorities . . . ." Through Him God has "delivered us from
the dominion of darkness and transferred us to the kingdom
of his beloved Son, in whom we have redemption . . . . He is
before all things, and in him all things hold together."[20] The
majestic second chapter of the epistle to the Philippians says
of Christ that, "though he was in the form of God," He "emptied himself, taking the form of a servant . . . and became
obedient unto death . . . . Therefore God has highly exalted
him and bestowed on him the name which is above every
name, that at the name of Jesus every knee should bow, in
heaven and on earth and under the earth, and every tongue
confess that Jesus Christ is Lord to the glory of God the
Father."[21] These majestic words, says the Revelation of John,
are words of "grace . . . and peace from him who is and who
was and who is to come . . . from Jesus Christ . . . the first-
born of the dead, and the ruler of kings on earth. To him
who loves us and has freed us from our sins . . . and made us
a kingdom . . . to him be glory and dominion for ever and
ever. Amen. . . . 'I am the Alpha and the Omega,' says the
Lord God, who is and who was and who is to come, the
Almighty."[22]

In these words we have a graphic picture of the kingdom
of God for which Israel had hoped, which Jesus and His disciples proclaimed as now at hand, and of which it is said there
will be no end.[23] It is this version of the kingdom which gives
meaning to history. It is not a man-made kingdom. It is a
kingdom which Christ Himself has established. Those who
through Christ are reconciled unto God, and by this act are
translated into the kingdom through the renewing of their
minds, are commissioned to pray with the Master, "Thy kingdom come, thy will be done, on earth as it is in heaven."[24]
The kingdom has come. It is here now. Those who have
been reconciled unto God are its citizens. They constitute

20 Col. 1:13, 14, 16, 17.   23 Matt. 10:7; Luke 1:33.
21 Phil. 2:6-11.   24 Matt. 6:10.
22 Rev. 1:4-6, 8.

the colony of heaven in the midst of a world which has not yet acknowledged the sovereignty of the King.

The kingdom has come, but only in part. It is yet to come in all its fullness when the Lord shall have put all His enemies under His feet. Once the mid-point of history had been reached and the kingdom established, the end time had arrived; not the end, but the *end time*. It is a time of twilight, of lights and of shadows. It is a time of tension for the Christian, for the spirit of Antichrist is ever present seeking to thwart the kingdom and all its work. The end time is also a time of suffering, but the disciple is admonished to receive this discipline with patience: "For to this you have been called, because Christ also suffered for you, leaving you an example, that you should follow in his steps."[25] The kingdom which now is, is no utopia. Neither is it a kingdom in defeat. "Blessed are those who are persecuted for righteousness' sake, for theirs is the kingdom of heaven. . . . Rejoice and be glad, for your reward is great in heaven, for so men persecuted the prophets who were before you."[26] The end time is a time to "endure hardness, as a good soldier of Jesus Christ."[27] Most of all it is a day of hope: "For the grace of God has appeared . . . training us to renounce irreligion and worldly passions, and to live sober, upright, and godly lives in this world, awaiting our blessed hope, the appearing of the glory of our great God and Saviour Jesus Christ,"[28] at whose coming he who endures will be made a pillar in the temple of God and he shall never go out of it.[29]

The kingdom which now is, is the earnest, the guarantee of that which is to come. It was at the mid-point that the decisive battle of world history was won. The incarnate Christ who came as the representative of sinful men, who lived the cross life in complete reconciliation with God, and who suffered death on the cross, in His resurrection achieved the victory over sin and death. It was a moral victory which

25 I Pet. 2:20, 21.
26 Matt. 5:10-12.
27 II Tim. 2:3 (KJV).

28 Titus 2:11-13.
29 Rev. 3:12.

has entered into the spiritual history of the race. The Christian disciple who enters into this experience does so with confidence that the victory of Christ is the guarantee of the final victory over death at the consummation of history. "For as in Adam all die, so also in Christ shall all be made alive. . . . Christ the first fruits, then at his coming those who belong to Christ."[30] Since "the last enemy to be destroyed is death," the Christian looks forward with confident assurance to this the absolute and final victory over sin and death: "Then comes the end, when he delivers the kingdom to God the Father after destroying every rule and every authority and power. For he must reign until he has put all his enemies under his feet. The last enemy to be destroyed is death."[31]

DISCIPLESHIP

Girded by this confident assurance the Christian disciple enters into the redemptive experience with Christ, following His steps, conscious of the fact that as an ambassador of Christ, God now makes His appeal through him.[32] Being a member of the colony of heaven, the Christian recognizes that his manner of life in this the end time must bear the image of his heavenly citizenship. The way of love and the cross must control both his personal and his social ethic. How else can men know that he is a disciple? How else can God make His appeal through him? "By this all men will know that you are my disciples, if you have love for one another."[33]

The colony of heaven is a gathered community whose citizens follow the way of the cross. The gathered community, however, is planted in the midst of history in a world of sin. Therefore they who follow the steps of Christ with inward confidence and assurance are outwardly nevertheless in a continuous state of tension. When scarcely one half of the population in a so-called Christian nation is even nominally Christian it cannot be otherwise; for in many places, as John Bright reminds us, the church "crouches behind iron curtains

30 I Cor. 15:22, 23.   32 II Cor. 5:20.
31 I Cor. 15:24-26.   33 John 13:35.

a martyr church, having made the full circle to the catacombs in which she was born."[34] We do not like this tension; and alas too many succumb to the temptation of eliminating it by attempting to be both the church and the world at the same time.

As Bright again reminds us, however: "God help the church that so blends into society that there is no longer any difference! Such a church will produce no quality of behavior other than that which society in general produces. . . . It will make itself a tool of society whose main business it is to protect and to dignify with divine support the best interests of its constituents. And that is stark tragedy! The end of it is a poverty-stricken church which utters no Word . . . , summons to no destiny. . . . And such a church . . . has failed to be the church."[35] Despite all of their idealism, the great weakness of the social gospel and of its Christian Action successor has been their futile attempt to make the Christian ethic effective within just such a blend of church and society, of Christ and culture. The effort is futile and ends in frustration for the simple reason, as Bright says, that "a non-Christian world will not put into practice the ethics of Christ and cannot, for all our chiding, be made to do so. . . . To realize the ethics of the kingdom it is first necessary that men submit to the rule of that kingdom."[36]

CHRIST AND CULTURE

This does not mean, however, that everything in our culture is to be rejected. Culture is that which man and society have produced for their use, for their enjoyment, for the expression of their ideals and aspirations, for the performance of their obligations, and even for the worship of God Himself. Without culture, indeed, it is impossible to live in this world. When man builds a house or finds a means of feeding his body he has produced a culture which he needs must use.

---

34 John Bright, *The Kingdom of God* (New York, 1953) 252.
35 *Ibid.*, 263.
36 *Ibid.*, 222.

His language, his literature, his art, and his music give expression to his ideals and aspirations. His code of ethics and his worship are a response to the divine command and its author, be that response one of acceptance or rejection.

Culture as such, the manipulation of nature for the use of man, is neither good nor evil. Culture, as such, is therefore not incompatible with Christian discipleship. As Paul Mininger has said, the conflict "is not between culture and 'no culture,' but between the good and the evil within culture, or between the good and evil uses of culture."[37] It is precisely this, however, which makes the question of Christ and culture what H. Richard Niebuhr calls "the enduring problem."[38] Some aspects of culture the way-of-the-cross Christian will accept, using them even in co-operation with his non-Christian neighbors. Other aspects of culture he will reject. "I pray not that thou shouldest take them out of the world," said Jesus to the Father, referring to the disciples, "but that thou shouldest keep them from the evil."[39] But to live in a world whose culture is a mixture of good and evil, to appropriate the one and to reject the other, and to follow a course which is consistently prophetic in its judgment upon culture is not easy. This is precisely the mission, however, to which the Christian has been called.

When Christ summons the disciples to their task He also provides the means for performing it. "For the word of the cross is folly to those who are perishing, but to us who are being saved it is the power of God."[40] He who enters into the redemptive work of Christ has the power and the authority of the risen Lord behind him. He has a new dynamic giving him a sense of direction for bringing the culture of this world under the judgment of God and into the service of Christ. His is a prophetic mission bringing the mind of Christ to bear on culture, to use it "for the expression, communication,

37 Paul Mininger, "Culture for Service," *Mennonite Quarterly Review* (January 1955) 29:8.
38 H. Richard Niebuhr, *Christ and Culture* (New York, 1951) 1.
39 John 17:15 (KJV).
40 I Cor. 1:18.

and extension of the Gospel of Christ," yes, even for the creation of culture to the praise and glory of God.[41] This is not to suggest that the disciple of Christ attains perfection in this age. The citizens of the colony of heaven, though saints, are nevertheless human; and being planted in the midst of a sinful world order they will reveal many imperfections. Paul himself was frank to admit that he had not arrived nor was he yet perfect, but he was bold to say that "forgetting what lies behind and straining forward to what lies ahead, I press on toward the goal for the prize of the upward call of God in Christ Jesus."[42]

Pressing toward the goal requires a continuing evaluation of every aspect of culture with which the Christian may be confronted. The scale of values arrived at will not always measure up to the New Testament standard. Some choices will be regarded as good and yet not the best. Richard Niebuhr illustrates the point by citing the case of Tertullian who regarded virginity as better than marriage; marriage to a believer better than to an unbeliever; and one marriage better than two.[43] There are many areas of life in which choices such as these must be made and in many cases a considerable range of choices is conceivable as within the realm of the colony of heaven, taking into consideration the enlightenment of the individual, as always must be done. The ethical problems described earlier which confront the Christian in the modern economic world are real dilemmas for the Christian today. In making his choices mistakes will be made and inconsistencies will be apparent. But the Christian who is earnestly pressing toward the goal will never be satisfied with his achievement, and ever and anon he will find himself at a point where he must say: Thus far and no farther. The Christian may never upon viewing the evil of this world throw up his hands in despair. Never may he conclude that all is evil; that the best which can be done is to choose the lesser evil.

41 Cf. Mininger, *op. cit.,* 12, 13.
42 Phil. 3:12-14.
43 Niebuhr, *Christ and Culture,* 74.

14

Jesus Christ who walked the way of the cross overcame the power of sin and death in His resurrection, and the risen Lord bids us follow in His steps. "Have this mind among yourselves, which you have in Christ Jesus," were Paul's words of admonition to the Philippians, "that you may be blameless and innocent, children of God without blemish in the midst of a crooked and perverse generation, among whom you shine as lights in the world."[44]

THE WAY OF THE CROSS

Jesus promised, however, that they who follow in His steps as loyal citizens of the kingdom in this crooked and perverse generation must be prepared to endure hardship and persecution. "He who does not take his cross and follow me is not worthy of me."[45] And "a servant is not greater than his master. If they persecuted me, they will persecute you."[46] The way of the cross is intended for precisely such situations as this. "Bless those who persecute you," says Paul; "bless and do not curse them."[47] Persecution has been the experience of Christians in many periods of church history, in the first century and the third, in the sixteenth, the seventeeth, and the twentieth, and there is every reason to believe that it will continue to be so. But if so, Jesus in the Great Commission assured His disciples that He would be with them, yes with them even in persecution, unto the end of the age.[48] The epistle to the Hebrews describes the sufferings of saints in all ages and then bids the reader to reflect on the suffering of Christ "who endured from sinners such hostility against himself, so that you may not grow weary or faint-hearted."[49]

This view of history and of the kingdom is prominent in Anabaptist theology. Discipleship and the making of disciples, persecution and suffering, and the ultimate triumph of righteousness and truth are ever recurring themes in their literature. Conrad Grebel's well-known statement comes to

44 Phil. 2:5, 15.
45 Matt. 10:38.
46 John 15:20.

47 Rom. 12:14.
48 Matt. 28:20.
49 Heb. 12:3.

mind: "Go forward with the Word and establish a Christian Church with the help of Christ and His rule, as we find it instituted in Matthew 18. . . . True Christian believers . . . must be baptized in anguish and affliction, tribulation, persecution, suffering, and death; they . . . must reach the fatherland of eternal rest, not by killing their bodily, but by mortifying their spiritual enemies."[50] Balthasar Hubmaier summed up this basic idea in his motto, *Die Wahrheit ist untödlich*.[51] In other words, the earthly life of the Christian may be taken from him, but *Truth can never die*. As the cross life and the cross death of Christ were followed by His triumphant resurrection, so the Christian taking his place as a disciple of Christ will in the end find his sufferings replaced by a triumphant end when his Redeemer and Lord brings history to its final consummation. For the time being suffering may even increase, since Satan who failed in his conflict with Jesus Christ now turns upon his disciples with a vengeance. It is the last act in the apocalyptic drama where the city of God and the city of Satan are engaged in the final struggle.

In this struggle the Christian cannot "escape into a religion of pietism."[52] He is a soldier of the cross fighting the good fight of faith. "Dear brethren, be comforted in the Lord and bear your tribulation calmly as pious knights of Christ," says Menno Simons, "that you may please Him who has called you and chosen you as soldiers. . . . Fight the fight courageously and your king will look with favor upon you. But if ye become fearful, if ye throw down your weapons and your swords and forsake the battle, ye shall receive no crown; for Christ says: He that endureth to the end shall be saved."[53] This is no carnal warfare, however. It is a spiritual warfare fought with spiritual weapons. The way of the cross is the way of love and nonresistance, and it is because the defense-

---

50 Letter of Grebel to Thomas Müntzer, Sept. 5, 1524, in H. S. Bender, *Conrad Grebel* (Goshen, 1950) 284, 285.
51 See Ethelbert Stauffer, "The Anabaptist Theology of Martyrdom," *Mennonite Quarterly Review* (July 1945) 19:184.
52 *Ibid.*, 19:203.
53 *The Complete Writings of Menno Simons*, 617.

less Christians have consistently followed this way that the
forces of Antichrist have opposed them. The opponents justify their tyranny and carnal warfare by referring to the Old
Testament wars, "but they do not reflect," says Menno, "that
Moses and his successors have served their day with their iron
sword, and that Christ has now given us a new commandment
and has girded us with another sword."[54]

Girded with this spirit of love and forgiveness, confident
that the powers of this world are under the control of the
Lord of the universe, Menno quotes the words of Jesus:
"Blessed are ye, when men shall revile you, and persecute you
. . . . Rejoice, and be exceeding glad: for great is your reward
in heaven."[55] Again he says: "For even though in His first appearance He was sacrificed as an innocent lamb, and opened
not His mouth, nevertheless the time will come when He will
appear as a triumphant prince and a victorious King to bring
judgment."[56] With the psalmist he admonishes the reader:
"Fret not thyself because of evildoers, neither be thou envi-
ous against the workers of iniquity. For they shall soon be cut
down like the grass, and wither as the green herb."[57]

There is keen awareness here of the judgment of God
upon sin and evil. True to the spirit of nonresistance, however, the Anabaptist hope for the consummation of history
bears no note of vengeance. As Ethelbert Stauffer says, they
"do not look for satisfaction of a primitive urge for vengeance, nor for fulfillment of a moral demand. They look
rather for an answer to the problem of theodicy. Not for the
sake of the martyrs but for His own sake God must disclose
His power and His justice, must prove that He, God, has the
last word in history, namely, the word which gives to all history its meaning and without which there could be no serious
appreciation of that history. This is the deepest motive of
the apocalypse of martyrdom as of all apocalyptic writing at
large: the extremities of history can find their answer only in

54 *Ibid.*, 603.
55 Matt. 5:11, 12 (KJV).
56 *Complete Writings*, 622.
57 *Ibid.*, 618, quoting Psalm 37:1, 2.

a last redeeming event of history itself."[58] Thus Menno was able to say that though the cross of the saints seems harsh and grievous it is in reality a cause for rejoicing. "O soldiers of God, prepare yourselves and fear not! . . . Him that overcometh will God make a pillar in His temple. . . . Joy and exultation will never forsake you, for your king . . . and redeemer, Christ Jesus, will remain with you forever."[59]

THE STATE

Playing a significant role in the present age, and often responsible for the suffering of the saints, has been the state. Under the providence of God the state has its place for the maintenance of order in the present world. As such it merits the honor and respect of the Christian, even though its mode of operation is "outside the perfection of Christ." When it moves beyond its sphere, however, exceeding the authority which divine providence has accorded it, demanding the ultimate allegiance of its subjects, and imposing on them its own religion or system of values, the state becomes a demonic power in this world.[60] What the demonic state does not know is that in this age the state as well as the church is subject to the lordship of Christ, for He is Lord of all. "In him all things were created . . . whether thrones or dominions or principalities or authorities";[61] "who has gone into heaven and is at the right hand of God, with angels, authorities, and powers subject to him."[62] So conscious was the New Testament church of this fact, Cullman reminds us, that the earliest confession of faith was embodied in the simple, terse formula, *Kyrios Christos* (Christ is Lord).[63] Paul underlines the importance of this confession when he says, "if you confess with your lips that Jesus is Lord and believe in your heart

58 Ethelbert Stauffer, *op. cit.*, 19:203.
59 *Complete Writings*, 621, 622.
60 Cf. H. Butterfield, *Christianity, Diplomacy and War* (New York, n.d., 1953?) and review by J. H. Yoder in *Mennonite Quarterly Review* (July 1954) 230-32.
61 Col. 1:16.
62 I Pet. 3:22.
63 Oscar Cullman, *The Earliest Christian Confessions* (London, 1949). See also Cullman, *Christ and Time*, 152, 153.

that God raised him from the dead, you will be saved."[64] In the classic statement of Philippians 2 Paul declares God to have exalted Christ "and bestowed on him the name which is above every name, that at the name of Jesus every knee should bow, in heaven and on earth and under the earth, and every tongue *confess that Jesus Christ is Lord,* to the glory of God the Father."[65]

In the kingdom which now is, between the mid-point and the consummation of history, the lordship of Christ is a twofold one. First, Christ is Lord of the church. The saints who make up the body of Christ are aware of His lordship, they confess Him as Lord, they are obedient to His command, and they walk in the way of Christian discipleship. Secondly, Christ is Lord of the world which lies beyond the body of Christ. Included in this outside world are principalities and powers, referred to repeatedly in the New Testament, and the state which is their executive agent. The powers and the state are given a place in the divine order for the maintenance of order during this age, and are therefore under the lordship of Christ, although they are unaware of the fact. The rulers of this age, says Paul, do not understand this, "for if they had, they would not have crucified the Lord of glory."[66] This relationship of the two realms under the lordship of Christ gives to the church a responsibility for the world which Cullman states as follows: "The rest of the visible and invisible world is also ruled by Christ, but for the time being does not know it. It can stand *unconsciously* under the lordship of Christ, since it is indeed subjected to Him. But the church has to proclaim to all the world that all stand under the same lordship, whether they belong to the church or not. Because the church alone knows of this *Kyrios Christos,* it must preach this lordship to those who, without knowing it, are also subject to it and fulfill the function assigned to them."[67]

A study of Romans 13:1-7 in relation to the New Testa-

64 Rom. 10:9.
65 Phil. 2:9-11 (italics added).
66 I Cor. 2:6-8.
67 Cullman, *Christ and Time,* 188.

ment teaching concerning principalities and powers gives further light on the Christian's relation to the state as previously discussed,[68] as well as to the ultimate end of the state. If Cullman's interpretation is correct, the authorities of Romans 13 and the rulers of I Corinthians 2:8 are identical with the principalities and powers of Romans 8:38, which are unable "to separate us from the love of God in Christ Jesus our Lord," and of which the Roman state was at the time the visible earthly expression. The statement in I Corinthians 2:8 says the rulers do not understand the lordship of Christ, nevertheless Romans 13:1 commands the Christian to be subject to these same rulers. Romans 13:1 says the authorities have been instituted by God, and yet I Corinthians 6:1-7 bids Christians not to use the state's courts for the settlement of their own disputes. Among the reasons for this prohibition is the fact that the saints will judge the world and angels, or principalities. In other words, the state belongs to God's order for this world, but it operates outside the perfection of Christ whose lordship the church acknowledges. Finally, while Romans 13:1-7 recognizes the state as authorized by God to operate in the present world order, within the limits which the lordship of Christ has prescribed, Revelation 13 describes the same Roman state as a beast, speaking blasphemies and making war for the persecution of the saints. This is a description of what always occurs when the state which knows not the lordship of Christ goes beyond its rightful sphere of operation.

The state is not ordained or instituted by God in the sense that the church is established by Him. The state is an expression of the wrath of God operating through the laws of human nature for the correction of evil within the fallen human order. Since the whole universe is subject to His word of power, the state too is under the lordship of Christ, although its relationship to Him is not the same as that of the church, the body of Christ.[69] In this connection it is in

---

68 See above, chs. 10-13.
69 See above, pp. 20-21.

order to call attention again to the location of Romans 13:1-7, in the midst of a passage teaching love, nonresistance, and the way of the cross. The passage begins in chapter 12 where Paul says: "Repay no one evil for evil . . . never avenge yourselves, but leave it to the wrath of God . . . overcome evil with good."[70] Then comes the discussion of the state, after which Paul reverts to the original theme of love. The passage in its entirety would seem to teach that while the Christian is obliged to renounce all vengeance and follow wholly the way of love and the cross, he must nevertheless also recognize the place of the state under the lordship of Christ for the maintenance of order in a sub-Christian society.

We would do well to take seriously the reminder of Cullman that the state is not an ultimate institution and that it is destined to "vanish when this age does; the Christian believer will always place over against the state a final question mark and will remain watchful and critical, because he knows that behind it stand powers which do indeed have their place in the divine order determined by the victory of Christ, but which nevertheless for the time being still have a certain possibility of permitting their demonic strivings for independence to flare up into apparent power."[71]

The final limits of the state and the powers were set by Christ Himself when He was raised from the dead and made to sit in the heavenly places, "far above all rule and authority and power and dominion."[72] In His victory over death "He disarmed the principalities and powers and made a public example of them, triumphing over them in him."[73] However, since this is but the penultimate victory, the guarantee of that which is to come, the conflict continues to the end of the age, "against the principalities, against the powers, against the world rulers of this present darkness, against the spiritual hosts of wickedness in the heavenly places."[74] Then at the

70 Rom. 12:17-21.
71 Cullman, *Christ and Time*, 199, 200.
72 Eph. 1:20, 21.
73 Col. 2:15.
74 Eph. 6:12.

close of the age comes the ultimate victory, the consummation, when the risen Lord in a final triumphant act "delivers the kingdom to God the Father after destroying every rule and every authority and power."[75]

LIVING IN HOPE

If the risen Christ is Lord of the universe, if in Him all things hold together, then even in this end time there is more than conflict and tension. There is confident hope. Indeed, the Christian disciple, fighting the good fight of faith, is so filled with rejoicing for the hope which is in him that little time remains for bemoaning such suffering as may be for the time. "For I reckon," says Paul, "that the sufferings of this present time are not worthy to be compared with the glory which shall be revealed in us."[76] Indeed, the glory which is to be is revealed even now. Not the least feature of the glorious hope is the inner sense of satisfaction experienced by him who as he presses toward the ultimate goal is conscious that he is making his contribution to the realization of the kingdom now. He who possesses this hope has within himself the only motive power for true progress in this age.

First of all, a sound eschatology provides the necessary motive for a high personal ethic which is the basis for all moral progress. He who belongs to the kingdom and looks for its consummation, submits to its rule now. "What manner of persons ought ye to be in all holy living and godliness, looking for and earnestly desiring the coming of the day of God?" asks Peter. The answer is obvious: "Seeing that ye look for these things, give diligence that ye may be found in peace, without spot and blameless in his sight."[77] Christian eschatology and Christian ethics belong together. In Paul's first epistle to the Corinthians there are two classic chapters, the thirteenth on Christian love, and the fifteenth on the resurrection and the parousia. There is good reason for the

---

75 I Cor. 15:24.
76 Rom. 8:18 (KJV).
77 II Pet. 3:11, 12, 14 (ASV).

proximity of these two themes, for as J. E. Fison says, the love
portrayed in the former chapter is inconceivable in this age
except through the power of the risen Christ; and the resurrection theme "is just a display of intellectual fireworks about
the future without its present basis in I Corinthians 13."[78]
The Christian ethic is a divine ethic, not man-made, but
belonging to the Lord of life and the eternal world. He
whose life and hope are in the eternal world will have a prophetic message for this age. He who is comfortably adjusted
to the present age has no prophetic message regarding the
future. Christian ethics and Christian eschatology belong
together.

Secondly, social progress is dependent upon an adequate
eschatology. The temporal imperfect social order can be
transformed only to the extent that it draws its power from
the eternal and perfect order. The agency for the transmission of the divine power is the body of Christ, the colony of
heaven. Ray Petry puts it thus: "The church is two societies
in one. It derives from the perfect society of heaven the pattern and the divine energies for judging, redeeming, and—to
a limited degree during history—for transforming the society
of earth. The church . . . becomes the servant of the eternal
kingdom in the temporal order."[79] Before there can be true
social progress the secular orientation in which the word
"social" is commonly placed must be exchanged for an eternal
orientation capable of producing a kingdom society, a society
whose author and finisher is God and not man.

Secular parochialism always finds it difficult to see this
point. Its perspective is limited to the problems which can be
immediately seen so that it fails to perceive the larger issues
which are at stake. When the Graeco-Roman world charged
the early Christians with social irresponsibility as they sought
first the kingdom of God and its righteousness, Origen replied
that "men of God are assuredly the salt of the earth; they
preserve the order of the world; and society is held together

78 J. E. Fison, *The Christian Hope* (New York, 1954) 126.
79 Ray Petry, *Christian Eschatology and Social Thought* (New York, 1956) 373.

as long as the salt is uncorrupted."[80] Chrysostom says that when Christians pray, "Thy will be done in earth, as it is in heaven," and act upon their own prayer, they are laboring to "make the earth a heaven." With real justification Petry asks: "What stronger impulsion for social action can be found than this which Chrysostom so patently derives from the power-giving society of the kingdom."[81]

In reviewing the course of history to evaluate the comparative social worth of eschatological Christianity and the terrestrially oriented Roman culture Arthur E. Holt comes to the conclusion that the church fathers were right: "The more one thinks about the early Christian communities and the Roman Empire, the more one is convinced that the only piece of permanent social building was that carried on by the Christian community in the face of the Roman Empire."[82] As mentioned earlier,[83] even Walter Rauschenbusch with an eschatology based on human development which has no final consummation, because "its consummations are always the basis of further development," found it necessary to admit that the principles of the Sermon on the Mount have had a tragic fate when accepted only as social ideals to be realized by a social order which is anthropocentric and this-worldly in its orientation. "Only those church bodies which have been in opposition to organized society," he says, "and have looked for a better city with its foundations in heaven have taken the Sermon on the Mount seriously."[84]

Ernst Troeltsch, at the close of his monumental two-volume survey of *The Social Teaching of the Christian Churches*, comes to the same conclusion, that the highest ethical power in the social world can be achieved only as it proceeds from the source of ethical power, the kingdom of our Lord whose consummation lies in the future. Says Troeltsch:

80 *Ante-Nicene Fathers* (Roberts and Donaldson, eds., New York, 1925) 4:666 (*Origen vs. Celsus*, 8:70).
81 Petry, 103.
82 A. E. Holt, *Christian Roots of Democracy in America* (New York, 1941) 129.
83 See above, pp. 95, 96.
84 Walter Rauschenbusch, *A Theology for the Social Gospel* (New York, 1918) 133-38.

"The Christian Ethos gives to all social life and aspiration a goal which lies far beyond all the relativities of this earthly life, compared with which, indeed, everything else represents merely approximate values. The idea of the future kingdom of God, which is nothing less than faith in the final realization of the Absolute (in whatever way we may conceive this realization), does not, as shortsighted opponents imagine, render this world and life in this world meaningless and empty; on the contrary, it stimulates human energies, making the soul strong through its various stages of experience in the certainty of an ultimate, absolute meaning and aim for human labour. Thus it raises the soul above the world without denying the world. . . . The life beyond this world is, in very deed, the inspiration of the life that now is."[85]

Thirdly, the certainty of ultimate reality gives meaning to the redemptive history which is the heart of the New Testament message, which is central to the Christian faith, and which is the source of ethics and true social progress. Indeed, since by the resurrection of Christ the victory is assured, the Christian has the sense of participation in a winning cause to such a degree that the primary emphasis is not on eschatological expectation of the future, but on participation in the victorious conquest.

The Christian realizes first that he is caught up in the stream of redemptive history; that this stream has been made effective for his personal redemption in Christ. Once this has occurred he becomes a colaborer with God, an ambassador for Christ, God through him making His appeal to men that they may be reconciled to God and thus also enter the stream of redemptive history as it moves forward to flood tide. This is the light in which Paul thought of his own ministry. "We know that the whole creation has been groaning in travail together until now; and not only the creation, but we ourselves, who have the first fruits of the Spirit, groan inwardly as we wait for adoption as sons, the redemption of our

85 Ernst Troeltsch, *The Social Teaching of the Christian Churches* (London, 1931) 2:1005, 1006.

bodies."[86] "But how are men to call upon him in whom they have not believed?" he asks. "And how are they to believe in him of whom they have never heard? And how are they to hear without a preacher? And how can men preach unless they are sent?"[87] It needs to be emphasized, says Cullman, "that the apostolic consciousness of Paul is founded in redemptive history." What is true of Paul, moreover, is true of every Christian. Not only the apostle and his office, "but even the most modest service in the church of Christ belongs in the redemptive history."[88]

It is from this redemptive stream that Christian ethics flows. Since it is a holy stream of which the Christian is a part, his ethics are of the same holy substance as the stream itself. The question is no longer, What should or can I do in the light of my present circumstances? The question is rather, What does the holy stream of redemptive history require of the present circumstance? As Cullman says, this sets the moral law of the Decalogue "in the light of the imminent kingdom of God, that is, sets it in the situation in which one must be radically obedient to the divine will at every moment."[89] Merely to refrain from destroying the body of one's fellow man no longer satisfies the requirement of the sixth commandment. What is now required is the way of love and the cross, following the steps of the Suffering Servant who for our sake emptied Himself in complete self-giving service. The way of the cross is eschatologically oriented. He who follows in this way finds himself so absorbed in the discharge of his ultimate responsibility to the kingdom of God that he cannot be too much disturbed by ideas of responsibility for a social order based on lesser foundations. "The abiding characteristic of true Christian thought is that it is not co-ordinated with the present society as the true center of reference. Because of this, alone, kingdom-destined men can give the present its true, socializing impact. . . . To be truly productive, the pres-

---

86 Rom. 8:22, 23.
87 Rom. 10:14, 15.
88 Cullman, *Christ and Time*, 224.
89 *Ibid.*, 226.

ent social order must respond to, and be broken into, by the future and eternal one."[90]

Roland H. Bainton says of the sixteenth-century Anabaptists that "they took their stand in the light of eternity regardless of what might or might not happen in history. They did not fall into the error of those who treat the way of the cross as if it were a weapon, a political strategy by which to put over a program. . . . The cross is not a strategy. It is a witness before God, no matter whether there may or may not be any historical consequences."[91] Concerning the ultimate consequences for the kingdom of God, however, they had no doubt. For the time being, indeed, the results seemed tragic enough. In the long run, however, it seems clear that Anabaptism is another illustration of ethical power released by an eschatologically oriented movement proceeding from the stream of redemptive history. Rufus M. Jones says: "Judged by the principles which were put into play by the men who bore this reproachful nickname, it must be pronounced one of the most momentous and significant undertakings in man's eventful religious struggle after the truth. It gathered up the gains of earlier movements, and it is the spiritual soil out of which all nonconformist sects have sprung, and it is the first plain announcement in modern history of a programme for a new type of Christian society which the modern world, especially in America and England, has been slowly realizing—an absolutely free and independent religious society, and a state in which every man counts as a man, and has his share in shaping both church and state."[92]

In the fourth place, the lordship of Christ and the reality of the ultimate kingdom have always been a potent missionary force in the history of the church. Throughout the New Testament the central theme in the preaching of the apostles and evangelists was the lordship of the risen Christ and the good news of His kingdom. Jesus went from village to vil-

90 Petry, *op. cit.*, 67, 68.
91 Guy F. Hershberger (ed.), *The Recovery of the Anabaptist Vision* (Scottdale, 1957) 325.
92 R. M. Jones, *Studies in Mystical Religion* (London, 1909) 369.

lage, "preaching the gospel of the kingdom."[93] The Twelve likewise were sent on their missionary journeys to preach, saying, "The kingdom of heaven is at hand."[94] The thirteenth chapter of Matthew alone has eight "parables of the kingdom," including that of the wheat and the tares portraying the ultimate elimination of sin and evil and the triumph of the righteous who "will shine like the sun in the kingdom of their Father." The entire Sermon on the Mount is a description of the character of the kingdom and its citizens. Peter's great sermon at Pentecost proclaimed the risen Christ who is the Lord.[95] Following the persecution associated with the stoning of Stephen the Christians were scattered, going from place to place proclaiming Christ and His kingdom.[96] In practically all of the New Testament epistles the theme of the risen Christ and His lordship holds a central place, whether the book of Hebrews which speaks of Him as "upholding the universe by his word of power"[97]; or Paul writing to the Colossians of Him who "is the head of all rule and authority"[98]; or to the Corinthians of this mortal nature which "must put on immortality," for which "thanks be to God, who gives us the victory through our Lord Jesus Christ." Assurance of the victory, says Paul, is good reason to "be steadfast, immovable, always abounding in the work of the Lord, knowing that in the Lord your labor is not in vain."[99]

Latourette, in interpreting the meaning of the growth of Christianity, says: "Christians have found a special power which came in a peculiar way after the resurrection of Jesus and which has continued to come, and through which they have been convinced that they are in immediate fellowship with Jesus Himself and with the God who is at once the Creator, the Dominant Power in the universe, and the one whom through Jesus they have learned to call Father. Through nineteen centuries Christians have shared in an experience

93 Matt. 9:35.
94 Matt. 10:7.
95 Acts 2.
96 Acts 8.

97 Heb. 1:3.
98 Col. 2:10.
99 I Cor. 15:54-58.

which they have felt they could best describe as being with a Presence which they have associated with the historic Jesus seen in the pages of the New Testament and with the eternal God. Of their honesty in reporting that enduring and repeated experience there can be no doubt. Nor can there be doubt that through that experience they themselves have been transformed. Through it they have been lifted out of moral defeat and impotence into victory and from despair to triumphant hope. Through it they have found power to go through suffering, disappointment, and the loss of loved ones, of health, and of worldly goods, and to face physical death, not only unafraid but also with a quiet confidence and joy. Through it strength has come to them to battle, singlehandedly or with a small company of kindred spirits, against enthroned wrong and agelong evils, and yet to do so in humility, without vindictiveness, and in love. . . . The Christian need not despair. . . . Trusting . . . that the God seen in Jesus is dominant in the universe, he believes that ultimately, in some fashion which man cannot yet envision, He will be victorious over the forces of disorder and evil."[100]

It is probably correct to say that throughout the history of the church the vitality of the Christian missionary witness has varied more or less in direct proportion to the confidence and the vigor with which the lordship of Christ and the hope of His kingdom have been proclaimed. J. D. Graber has said: "The nerve of missionary endeavor is cut when we cease to believe in a new world to come, when we lose our sense of destiny, our sense of being directly in God's stream of history pressing forward to fulfillment in the coming of His kingdom."[101] It was this sense of destiny which enabled the Anabaptists, in the face of violent persecution, to stand out as the missionary pioneers of the Protestant era. As said earlier[102] their theology of martyrdom was a theology of triumph and

---

100 K. S. Latourette, *Anno Domini: Jesus, History, and God* (New York, 1940) 236-40.

101 Hershberger, *op. cit.,* 155.

102 See above, ch. 9; p. 386 ff.

aggressive evangelism. The time of suffering would not be long. In the end the followers of Christ would reign with Him. Armed with this triumphant faith they went forth to proclaim the Gospel throughout all the land. Every member among them, whether man or woman, was regarded as a missionary. Applicants for baptism were instructed in their obligation as carriers of the Gospel.[103]

Michael Sattler in his letter of 1527 urged the congregation at Horb to "pray that reapers may be constrained into the harvest; for the time of threshing is at hand."[104] Menno Simons in his writings repeatedly speaks of being constrained by the love of Christ and the hope of His coming to give his life and all that he has in order that the Gospel may be preached to those who know it not. "We desire with ardent hearts even at the cost of life and blood that the holy Gospel of Jesus Christ and His apostles, which only is the true doctrine and will remain so until Jesus Christ comes again upon the clouds, may be taught and preached through all the world as the Lord Jesus Christ commanded His disciples as a last word to them while He was on earth.[105]

"This is my only joy and heart's desire: to extend the kingdom of God, reveal the truth, reprove sin, teach righteousness, feed hungry souls with the Word of the Lord, lead the straying sheep into the right path, and gain many souls to the Lord through His Spirit, power, and grace. . . .[106]

"Therefore, we preach, as much as is possible, both by day and by night, in houses and in fields, in forests and wastes, hither and yon, at home or abroad, in prisons and in dungeons, in water and in fire, on the scaffold and on the wheel, before lords and princes, through mouth and pen, with possessions and blood, with life and death. We have done this these many years, and we are not ashamed of the Gospel of the glory of Christ."[107]

103 John Horsch, *The Hutterian Brethren* (Goshen, 1931) 29, footnote 36.
104 Orley Swartzentruber, "The Piety and Theology of the Anabaptist Martyrs in van Braght's *Martyrs' Mirror*," *Mennonite Quarterly Review* (January 1954) 28:21.
105 *Complete Writings*, 303.
106 *Ibid.*, 189.   107 *Ibid.*, 633.

CONSUMMATION

In the New Testament the creative work of God, the redemptive work of Christ, and all the mighty works of Father, Son, and Holy Spirit are seen as moving toward their consummation at the end of the age when all things are made new[108] and when those who respond to the Gospel and its redemptive work "will come from east and west, and from north and south, and sit at table in the kingdom of God."[109] The consummation coincides with the parousia, the coming of Christ for the completion of His work when the last enemy is destroyed[110] and "the kingdom of the world has become the kingdom of our Lord and of his Christ, and he shall reign for ever and ever."[111]

Although this view of history has always been an integral part of Christian theology, it has, since the Renaissance and the rise of modern science, lost much of its meaning for large sections of Christendom. With theology replaced by science as the unifying factor in modern thought, Christian people have been so affected by the new intellectual climate that even many who do not reject the eternal verities completely nevertheless allow them little more than a symbolic meaning, thus rendering them ineffective as a part of their working faith. Even many Christians, whose faith in the redeeming work of Christ at history's mid-point, His incarnation, death, and resurrection remains unshaken, have been influenced by naturalistic views of the kingdom of God to such a degree that they give little thought to Christ as the finisher of the work which He has begun. If God has broken into history once in the incarnation, what cause is there for hesitation at the thought of a second intervention in the parousia and the consummation of the age? Bennett has answered our question when he says "there are no conclusive intellectual arguments against" the view, although "it goes beyond the evidence." That is, while it cannot be ruled out theologically, nevertheless since it is a matter of faith, the reality of which has not

108 Rev. 21:5.
109 Luke 13:29.
110 I Cor. 15:26.
111 Rev. 11:15.

been demonstrated by empirical science, it will be wiser not to be "too dependent upon it."[112]

To this view of the divine breaking into history for the final destruction of evil and the making of all things new, however, there would seem to be only two alternatives. The first alternative is to believe that the forces of evil will never be vanquished; that man will continue in sin, perhaps using his intellectual powers for the manipulation of nature toward evil ends until he at last destroys himself and human history comes to an end at the hands of man himself. This view would seem to mean that in the cosmic conflict between good and evil, God Himself will eventually go down in defeat. To hold such a view would seem no better than not to believe in God at all. Would not atheism itself be more noble than belief in a God who is no God? The first alternative, that of a God whose cause is lost, can be dismissed by the Christian without further consideration.

The remaining alternative to New Testament eschatology is the view that by a process of slow but gradual and progressive development "the forces emanating from Jesus will lift mankind to successively higher levels"[113] until the kingdom of God is realized in ever-increasing fullness. The best form of this view would hold that increasingly, even if ever so slowly, men by the process of conversion, renouncing sin, and accepting the saving grace of God through Christ, will be brought into the kingdom until eventually all men acknowledge the lordship of Christ and the kingdoms of this world will have become the kingdom of God. If progress seems slow it should be remembered that, "measured by sidereal and even by geologic time, Jesus has been at work for only a few moments. It may be that we are only at the beginning of His effect on the planet and that in the course of the next few tens of thousands of years and by much the same process of advance as in the past He will fully prevail."[114]

112 Bennett, *Social Salvation*, 179.
113 Latourette, *Anno Domini*, 239.
114 *Ibid.*, 239.

Since this, the best form of the second alternative, gives recognition to the place of conversion and God's saving grace it cannot be ruled out as basically unchristian although the idea that all men will eventually be reconciled to Christ would seem to coincide neither with the testimony of human history, nor with the New Testament revelation which speaks of the continued conflict between good and evil to the end of the age.

The worst form of the second alternative to New Testament eschatology would assume a naturalistic, humanistic progress by a similar process of gradual development until eventually social salvation is achieved. If this end product were to be called the kingdom of God the justification would seem to be that it consists of more stately mansions built by a philotheistic soul who out of his beneficence has seen fit to invite a kindly but not too necessary God to share its benefits. It hardly needs to be argued that this view is not Christianity at all.

However inviting the various eschatologies of human progress may have seemed a generation or two ago, it is clear that today they have lost much of their appeal. Instead of lauding scientific achievement as leading men along the path of unending progress, numerous prophets in this age of the hydrogen bomb and intercontinental ballistic missiles are deploring its capacity to destroy not only man and his civilization, but the earth as well. To a degree at least the second alternative to New Testament eschatology has given way to the first; the prophets of inevitable progress have given way to the prophets of inevitable doom. The latter prophets' view of history has been described as follows by Roger L. Shinn: "After a long period of cosmic evolution, of which we know almost nothing, and a shorter period of biological evolution, of which we know somewhat more, there appeared the being, perhaps misnamed, *homo sapiens*. After some millennia of an existence now described as primitive, men began to build societies which, because of their achievements in control of nature and social organization, are called civilizations. Numerous efforts had varying degrees of success, but none lasted very long on the time scale of history. Later ages may hope for better and more enduring achievements of their own. But whatever the probabilities of fairly long-range success, presumably history is destined to a final doom. Whether with a whimper or with a bang history may be expected to run out; the planet, perhaps the universe, will know human life and history no more."[115]

Karl Jaspers, using the language of the scientist rather than that of the philosopher, gives us an equally discouraging picture: "Technology . . . increases the peril beyond all measure, to the point at which we contemplate the possibility of pulverizing the globe in space. . . . With the atom bomb, a piece of solar substance has been brought to the earth. The same thing happens to it on the surface of the earth which has hitherto happened only in the sun. . . . It is uncertain beyond what dividing-line the explosion will lay hold on further elements and terrestrial matter as a whole, like a conflagration. The whole globe would explode, whether intentionally or unintentionally. Then our solar system would be temporarily lit up, a *nova* would have appeared in space."[116]

So persistent is modern man's anthropocentric thinking, however, that whether all seems to be going well in the world as a generation or two ago, or whether the world is doomed as now seems more likely, man must receive the credit in either case, for there is not much that God can do about it. Petry says the contemporary literature of despair seems to assume "that God Himself has no other choice than to terminate man's collective pilgrimage on earth with the very instruments of destruction that science has wrested from unwilling nature. Presumably, and all too presumptuously, we are asked to grant the superiority of man's will to total annihilation, at

115 Roger L. Shinn, *Christianity and the Problem of History* (New York, 1953) 11, 12. In the original this paragraph appears in italics.
116 Karl Jaspers, *The Origin and Goal of History* (New Haven, 1953) 209.

his own chosen place and time, over God's possibly vetoing purpose."[117]

The nuclear age may be a turning point in history, but does not Toynbee overstate the case when he calls it "a turning point in man's destiny"?[118] There is a difference. Henry N. Wieman goes even farther and says: "The bomb that fell on Hiroshima cut history in two like a knife. Before and after are two different worlds. That cut is more abrupt, decisive, and revolutionary than the cut made by the star over Bethlehem."[119] Well might Shinn ask: "Who is right—Paul or Wieman?"[120] Where, indeed, is the mid-point in human history to be found, in nuclear physics or in Jesus Christ; in the doings of the Kremlin and the Pentagon or in the deeds of Him who walked in Galilee, was crucified and rose again? In commenting on the reaction to the Russian sputniks, Paul Erb says: "Hysteria struck the American people. The new moons have deprived us of our sanity. This is the new lunacy. . . . Responsible senators talk about securing control of the outer spaces (There's an awful lot of it out there, Senator!). It is suggested that we spend billions .digging shelters in which to survive. Dorothy Thompson wisely asks who would want to survive a thermonuclear deluge. . . There is a classical proverb, that whom the gods would destroy they first make mad. . . . In the midst of a propaganda-provoked hysteria, Christians should pray and strive that they might not lose their senses."[121]

It would help us to keep our senses if we would ponder the words of the writer to the Hebrews: "In these last days he has spoken to us by a Son, whom he appointed the heir of all things, through whom also he created the world. He reflects the glory of God and bears the very stamp of his nature, up-

---

117 Petry, *op. cit.,* 14.
118 "A Turning Point in Man's Destiny," *New York Times Magazine* (Dec. 26, 1954) 5.
119 H. N. Wieman, *The Source of Human Good* (Chicago, 1946) 37.
120 Shinn, *op, cit.,* 13.
121 Paul Erb, "The New Lunacy," *Gospel Herald* (Scottdale, Jan. 21, 1958) 51:51.

holding the universe by his word of power."[122] Man's misdeeds and his hysteria can indeed do a great amount of harm. But it is the God of history, and not the doings of evil men, that determines the destiny of the world and the end of history. As God's breaking into history in the incarnation did not depend on human ingenuity (although man was involved), so His breaking through in the parousia and the consummation of the age will also be the mighty work of God and not the doings of man, although man again will be involved; indeed every knee shall bow and every tongue confess that Jesus Christ is Lord, to the glory of God the Father.

Jaspers' description of the terrible scientific possibilities for this planet quoted above sounds much like Peter's words about the heavens passing away with a loud noise and the elements dissolving with fire.[123] We need to be cautious and humble in our statements about the future concerning which we know so little. Surely, as the mighty works of the God of history are always related to the doings of man it is not impossible that the destructive powers of modern man will in some way be related to the end of the age. It would be altogether untrue to New Testament revelation, however, to assume that the consummation of the age of which it speaks will be merely the result of human manipulation of the forces of nature. The end of the age of which the New Testament speaks is God's doing. He is the Alpha and the Omega, the first and the last, the beginning and the end, who is and who was and who is to come. This is not a time for hysteria concerning the human control of outer space. There is too much of it. This is a time for humility before God, a time for seeking the mind of Christ, a time for walking the way of the cross, following His steps with confidence that if we suffer with Him we shall also reign with Him in His kingdom which has no end.[124]

122 Heb. 1:2, 3.
123 II Pet. 3:10.
124 II Tim. 2:12; Luke 1:33.

Paul Erb in his little book, *The Alpha and the Omega*,[125] has summarized the New Testament teaching concerning the need and purpose of the parousia in eight points. (1) Christ must come to complete His work. The outcome of the conflict between good and evil was determined at the mid-point of history, the incarnation, the cross, and the resurrection. That which was determined at the mid-point, however, is yet to be finished. He who is the Son of God, the Maker of the universe, must bring His work to a final and climactic culmination, for He is the beginning and the end.

(2) A second feature of the eschatological consummation must be the spiritual maturity of the saints. "For now we see in a mirror dimly, but then face to face. Now I know in part; then I shall understand fully, even as I have been fully understood."[126] The life of the Christian disciple in this age is, to be sure, a life of power and joyful service in the kingdom. And yet it is only a partial, a provisional realization of the ultimate spiritual reality which is to come. That which we now have is "the guarantee of our inheritance until we acquire possession of it, to the praise of his glory."[127]

(3) At the consummation the kingdom will be perfected. The kingdom is here now, but in limited form. The Christian community is not heaven, but a colony of heaven; an eschatological community in a world of tension, which at the end of the age becomes the kingdom of God in all its fullness and in glorious perfection. Division of loyalties as between Christ and Antichrist will have come to an end. At the name of Jesus every knee shall bow, and every tongue confess that Jesus is Lord to the glory of God the Father.

(4) A fourth feature of the consummation is the defeat of death. In the New Testament death is described as the "last enemy."[128] Death is not a friend, a liberator of the soul from the prison of the body. This is the pagan concept of

---

125 Paul Erb, *The Alpha and the Omega* (Scottdale, 1955).
126 I Cor. 13:12.
127 Eph. 1:14.
128 I Cor. 15:26.

immortality which thinks of the soul and body as being in antithesis to each other, the soul longing for separation and deliverance. The New Testament calls death the wages of sin.[129] Jesus Himself shrank from it in Gethsemane and in His triumph defeated the enemy in the resurrection. As Christ was raised from the dead, so shall we be raised. "If in this life only we have hope in Christ, we are of all men most miserable."[130] His triumph over death is the Christian's guarantee of the same experience, a glorious redemption of the whole person, to be forever with the Lord. "Then shall come to pass the saying that is written: Death is swallowed up in victory? O death, where is thy victory? O death, where is thy sting?"[131]

(5) Accompanying the conquest of death will be the defeat of the enemies of God. Satan will be finally defeated. The Antichrist will be overcome and Christ will reign supreme "Then comes the end, when he delivers the kingdom to God the Father after destroying every rule and every authority and power. For he must reign until he has put all his enemies under his feet."[132]

(6) The consummation includes the last judgment when the tares are separated from the wheat. Even as the kingdom has come in part in the present age, so has judgment come in part. Much of chaos remains, however, and all disorder must be changed into the order of God. "Just as the resurrection puts an end to death," says Brunner, "so judgment terminates the state of confusion and obscurity, of inconclusiveness. Judgment spells ultimate decision, and thus ultimate discrimination. . . . For the obscurity of the provisional stage, the condition in which the lordship of Christ and that of Antichrist coexist is intolerable."[133]

(7) The consummation means the final triumph of the church. The church is no longer a pilgrim church, filled with imperfections and divisions, sufferings and persecutions, lan-

---

129 Rom. 5:12; 6:23.
130 I Cor. 15:19 (KJV).
131 I Cor. 15:54, 55.

132 I Cor. 15:24, 25.
133 Brunner, *Eternal Hope*, 175, 176.

guishing in prisons and catacombs and behind iron curtains. The fellowship of saints, the body of Christ, is now complete; the colony of heaven has become a full-grown kingdom. The way of the cross has reached its goal at the gate of triumph. That which began in obscurity and with seeming insignificance has drawn men from east and west and from north and south to sit at table in the kingdom of God. The oft-despised body of Christ has emerged in triumph to reign with Him forever and ever. The way of love which many rejected as the way of weakness has proved to be the power which moves the world, and which reigns supreme. They who ran with patience the race which was set before them have joined the author and the finisher of their faith at the right hand of God.

(8) Finally, the consummation of the age brings to a completion God's purposes for the earth. He who is the Alpha, the Creator, is also the Omega, the Finisher. The work of redemption established and assured at the mid-point must be continued to the end. The goal toward which history has been moving must be reached. The mark of disorder, confusion, and sin must be removed. The relativities, the ambiguities, and the incongruities of the social order must be resolved. Social salvation there must be, and it will come at last; not by naturalistic and humanistic programs of reform; but "as the regenerative process comes to maturity eschatologically."[134] "According to his promise," says Peter, "we wait for new heavens and a new earth in which righteousness dwells."[135] In the Revelation John sees the promise fulfilled as the first heaven and the first earth had passed away and he who sat upon the throne said: "Behold, I make all things new."[136]

Admittedly, when we speak of the consummation of the age and the fulfillment of history we speak as they who see in a mirror dimly and who know in part. Indeed the part which

---

134 Paul Peachey, "Toward an Understanding of the Decline of the West," *Concern* (Scottdale, June 1954) 1:37.
135 II Pet. 3:13.
136 Rev. 21:1, 5.

we know is exceedingly small. Here we have to do with that which is beyond the powers of human reason and empirical science to reveal. Here we have to do only with that which God has seen fit to reveal. The New Testament references to the end of time and the consummation of the age, to the new heavens and the new earth, are filled with figurative and symbolic language the mysteries of which are beyond the powers of our finite minds to comprehend. This, however, is as it ought to be. For if the glory which is to be were revealed to us in all its fullness at this time, where would be the joyous experience of the new revelation when the goal has been reached? Deep though the mystery may be, this is clear that according to the teaching of the New Testament, God is the God of history, the Creator and Redeemer, who is and who was and who is to come. In these last days, in the mid-point of history, He has spoken to us by His Son through whom also He created the world. He is before all things and in Him all things hold together. Though He was God He emptied Himself and was found in human form. Though He was tempted in all points like as we are, yet He was without sin. Nevertheless He was obedient to death, even the death of the cross, after which God has highly exalted Him.

Therefore, having been reconciled to God through Christ who has given unto us the ministry of reconciliation, let us have this mind among ourselves which we have in Christ Jesus, following His steps in the way of the cross, blameless and innocent, children of God without blemish in the midst of a crooked and perverse generation, among whom we shine as lights in the world. Let us run with perseverance the race that is set before us looking unto Jesus the pioneer and perfecter of our faith, who has disarmed principalities and powers, and triumphed over them, has brought all things to their consummation and made all things new, whence He shall reign forever and ever. I am the Alpha and the Omega, says the Lord God, who is and who was and who is to come, the Almighty.

INDEX

Abbott, Lyman, 82

Abrams, Ray H., 69n, 133n

Abundance, economic, 245f, 296f

Accommodation, 200f, 292f

Acres of Diamonds, 79, 239

Adam, 25

Adams, Charles Francis, 236

Adams, James Luther, 15n

Admonishing Request to the Magistracy, 190

Agricultural Adjustment Administration, 260

Agricultural organizations, 259-68, 302-4; business and educational aspects, 266f; and the Christian, 302f; and the general welfare, 264f; and legislation, 260f; lobbying, 262f; specialized, 267f

Agriculture, mechanized, 244f

Alpha and the Omega, The, 408

Althaus, Paul, 68, 68n

Ambrose, 60, 66-68, 98

American Association of University Professors, 274, 305

American Chemical Society, 274

American Council of Churches, 133, 135

American creed, 5

American Economic Foundation, 139

American · economic policy and foreign relations, 265f, 295f

American Federation of Labor, 274

American Federation of Teachers, 274, 305

American Friends Service Committee, 300, 301

American Medical Association, 275-78, 305

Amsterdam Assembly of the World Council, on war, 119

Anabaptism, 155f; and the economic order, 220; and the Great Commission, 163; and the social order, 155; and the state, 165f; approximates New Testament Christianity, 199

Anabaptist brotherhood emphasis, 223f; ethical significance of, 398; theology of martyrdom, 161f; view of the church, 159; view of Sermon on the Mount, 193; vision, recovery of, 201f

Anabaptists, as awakeners, 164; and community of goods, 221f; as restorers, 158; as viewed by contemporaries, 158

Antonius, Marcus Aurelius, 376

Apostles of Discord, 135

Aquinas, 66

Aristotle, ethics of, 61

Asceticism, 34

Asceticism, worldly, 74

Assemblies of God, 140

Associations, Trade, 254f

413